Unsexing Gender, Engendering Activism: Readings in Gender Studies

Revised Printing

Edited By

Danielle M. DeMuth
Julia M. Mason
Ayana K. Weekley
Kathleen Underwood
Grand Valley State University

Kendall Hunt
publishing company

Kendall Hunt
publishing company

www.kendallhunt.com
Send all inquiries to:
4050 Westmark Drive
Dubuque, IA 52004-1840

Copyright © 2009, 2015 by Grand Valley State Women and Gender Studies Program

ISBN 978-1-5249-9541-6

Published in the United States of America

BRIEF CONTENTS

CONTENTS

ACKNOWLEDGMENTS

Teaching and learning, at its best, is a collaborative process. It is our hope that this text reflects the best of our collective knowledge of both content and pedagogy gathered through teaching Women, Gender and Sexuality Studies. It helps to refine our feminist pedagogy individually and together.

The editors are deeply grateful for all the support, encouragement and critical feedback provided by colleagues. Our colleagues and partners in pedagogy and justice work on campus from the Women's Center, including Brittany Dernberger, JoAnn Wassenar and Jessica Jennrich, have contributed ideas and feedback in this process. Mary O'Kelly, the women and gender studies librarian and head of instructional services at GVSU, has been an ongoing partner in pedagogy with regard to information literacy. Several of the assignments included in this edition have been refined in collaboration with her feedback and support over several semesters. Erica Kubik, women and gender studies adjunct faculty, also contributed an exercise to this edition to help us round out the variety of assignments and topics included.

Women and gender studies alum also contributed to the making of this book: Brittany Dernberger, Devin Lagasse and Danielle Meirow each contributed exercises for the book based on their experiences and knowledge from their women and gender studies majors. Julia Blok's keen editorial eye was valuable in the early development of the second edition.

Women and gender studies students—Mikayla Benbow, Anthony Clemons, Chelsea Covyeau, Kanyn Doan, Challie Frostick, Mackenzie Kibbe, Jepkoech Kottutt and Jasmine Ward—provided valuable feedback on the questions and exercises developed for this edition as well as suggestions for the development of additional activities to support their peers learning.

Finally, we would like to thank the women and gender studies professional support staff, Sally Vissers. As we all know, the work we do is often supported and made to appear seamless by those who go unseen and not thanked enough.

Thank you to all the contributors who made this endeavor a success. We are deeply grateful.

FOREWORD

It has been five years since the first edition of *Unsexing Gender, Engendering Activism: Readings in Gender Studies* presented students at Grand Valley State University (GVSU) a set of interdisciplinary readings that would provide them the means to describe and analyze how gender stereotypes develop and their importance in shaping everyday decisions. The readings drew on a wide range of authors, including novelists, journalists, sociologists, psychologists, and historians. More than 2500 students at GVSU have benefited from these readings that lay a firm foundation for continued study in women, gender, and sexuality, regardless of undergraduate major.

Women, gender, and sexuality is a rapidly growing scholarly discipline and this second edition reflects that growth. The editors have added four new readings. More important, they have designed guides for each reading and several assignments that encourage students to apply what they read to contemporary society.

Like the first edition, this volume lays a firm foundation for understanding *gender*, with articles and essays that explore how we define and talk and write about gender. The editors have provided a thematic table of contents with clusters of readings that examine gender in social institutions like schools, the workplace, and the family, and focus on the ways in which gender has an impact on bodies. The final section develops an understanding of activism and its significance for ending the inequality that embedded in our culture. Coming to grips with these important topics ground you in the major concepts in the field of women and gender studies and will permit you to rethink your own individual and social environments.

This second edition of *Unsexing Gender, Engendering Activism* continues the collaborative approach that characterizes feminist teaching. Dr. Danielle DeMuth and Dr. Julia Mason have each studied and taught about women and gender for more than a decade. While they bring unique interests to their teaching—DeMuth's graduate work was in English, Mason's in American Culture Studies—they share a commitment to providing students a common foundation for understanding and analyzing *gender* that will serve for future study. That collaborative approach has been central to the revision: two new scholar/teachers have joined the faculty and both have played central roles in the work of revision. Dr. Ayana Weekley and Dr. Debjani Chakravarty both have PhDs in feminist studies. Each brings many years of teaching to this project, both at GVSU and elsewhere. Undergraduate majors in Women and Gender Studies have also been collaborators on this edition, especially in vetting the reading guides and the subsequent assignments. As always, decisions about what to include in this Reader have been shaped by the hundreds of students with whom the editors have shared classrooms over many semesters.

I hope that you will seriously engage with the materials in *Unsexing Gender, Engendering Activism: Readings in Gender Studies*. If you do, you will gain significant new knowledge, strengthen your analytical skills, and gain a more nuanced understanding of the world you inhabit.

Kathleen Underwood
Professor Emeritas, History and Women, Gender,
and Sexuality Studies
Grand Valley State University

PREFACE

The first courses in Women's Studies appeared at colleges in the United States in the 1960s. These courses were taught throughout the university curriculum and were aimed at looking specifically at the experience of women in literature, history and the social sciences. Initially these courses corrected a gap in their respective disciplines; for example, history curricula lacked women's history, while English classes lacked literature by women. The voices and experience of women were missing throughout the curriculum. By 1970, when it became clear that the various classes about women throughout the curriculum formed a more cohesive study, the first program in Women's Studies was founded at San Diego State University. The interdisciplinary study of women grew from one program in 1970 to 276 Women's Studies programs in 1977 and by 1989 that number had nearly doubled to 525.[1] In 2007, the National Women's Studies Association (NWSA), reported 650 diverse women and gender studies programs in community colleges, four-year colleges, and universities nationwide.[2]

The field has grown in important ways. Men's Studies emerged as a field in the 1980s. While some might suggest that the entire university curriculum outside of Women's Studies departments was already "men's studies," research in most fields was androcentric, generalizing from men to the rest of humanity, and little research was being done on the specific experience of masculinity. Some programs maintained an emphasis on "Women's Studies," whereas other programs expanded their emphasis to "Gender Studies" in order to emphasize femininity and masculinity in relationship to each other—as concepts that rely on each other for meaning. "Gender Studies," rooted in the study of women and feminism, necessarily includes Lesbian, Gay, Bisexual, Transgender Studies and Queer Studies (LGBTQ) and queer theory, thus more programs are expanding their focus to include Sexuality Studies.

THEMES IN THE READINGS

While it is relatively easy to locate an excellent text that introduces the field of Women's Studies, finding a text that represents the study of gender across the disciplines is much more difficult. This collection includes work by fiction writers and poets, journalists, essayists and activists as well as articles from academics in Women and Gender Studies, Anthropology, Biology, Communication Studies, Cultural Studies, English, Education, Psychology, Social Work and Sociology.

This text emerged from our desire to bring foundational concepts, questions, and methods in the interdisciplinary field of Gender Studies together with a focus on activism. We chose the title *Unsexing Gender, Engendering Activism* to highlight four important aspects of the field of Gender Studies: the study of gender as a pervasive social construct; "nature vs. nurture" debates on gendered traits and differences; the intersection of gender with other social and cultural identities (such as class, race, age, ethnicity, nationality and sexuality); and an emphasis on activism meant to show what you can *do* with this emergent research and information.

---

[1] Reynolds, Michael, ShobhaShagle and LekhaVenkataraman. "A National Census of Women's and Gender Studies Programs in U.S. Institutions of Higher Education." Chicago, IL: National Opinion Research Center. December 26, 2007, 3.
[2] Ibid, 3.

We have selected 28 readings that highlight foundational questions in the field of Gender Studies. These readings represent foundational question and theories in studying gender and suggest the new directions in the field. The second edition of *Unsexing Gender, Engendering Activism* is a collaborative effort of the faculty in Women and Gender Studies at Grand Valley State University. Some of the readings collected here are read each semester by tens of thousands of students across the U.S. in classes similar to this one. In addition to some foundational feminist essays, such as Peggy McIntosh's essay "Unpacking the Invisible Knapsack," Adrienne Rich's "Claiming an Education" and Audre Lorde's "Uses of the Erotic," this collection includes readings gathered from academic journals publishing cutting-edge research in feminism and gender studies, such as *Signs: Journal of Women in Culture and Society, Gender and Society, Social Work* and *Race, Sex & Class: an Interdisciplinary* as well as *the Gay and Lesbian Review Worldwide, Ms. Magazine, Women's Health.*

Research is beginning to show a much more complicated relationship than the simple opposition "nature vs. nurture" might suggest. Initially, many argued that women's behaviors, achievements and desires were both driven and constrained by biology. Early gender theorists challenged those ideas and instead argued that *women were made, not born.* To put it more simply, female and male behavior was not determined by biology but was instead shaped by culture. Rather than assume that male/masculine and female/feminine are natural, essential and biologically determined, gender theorists assert that we live in a "sex-gender system"—a system that divides labor differently and grants gendered meanings to the relatively meaningless biological categories of "male" and "female," and ascribes to these categories differing values, behaviors and desires. More recently, some theorists have challenged the idea that sex and gender are connected—suggesting instead that the cultural categories of gender are not linked to the biological categories of sex. Rather than the simple analogy, "male is to masculine as female is to feminine," new gendered categories have emerged—such as "female masculinity." Readings in anthropology, sociology, and psychology further challenge biological explanations of gender by suggesting that what we often assume to be gendered behavior is neither natural nor universal. Instead, different cultures sometimes exhibit gender relationships very different than what we might assume to be stereotypical behaviors. Readings in sociology suggest that gender is one category used, in combination with race, class, ethnicity, sexual orientation, able-bodiedness and national citizenship, to maintain social inequalities.

Readings in the themes of *Bodies and Genders* and the *Social Construction of Gender* and *Masculinity* tackle these debates and foreground new research. These readings also emphasize the ways in which our experience of our bodies is shaped by the culture and politics of gender, race, class, ethnicity, and sexuality. Topics include: body image, sex education, uses of pleasure and the erotic, and historical perspectives on changing standards of beauty. The theme of *Masculinity* also addresses the specific experience of masculinity in this system. The construction of masculinity as it relates to heterosexuality, sexual assault and consent, privilege and power and social justice work are essential to the study of gender.

Gender is much more complicated than the simple and rather stereotypical ideas of femininity and masculinity that most people envision. The readings in *Privilege, Identities and Intersectionalities, Homophobia, Sexualities* and *LGBTQ Studies* unpack the ways that gender, race, sexuality, dis/ability and class shape social location and are designed to help each reader examine her/his own position, which is the first step in examining the role of gender in shaping our lives, institutions, and interactions, and also the first step in working toward social change.

Readings in the theme of *Education* and *Families and Relationships* explore the two most significant cultural institutions that play a part in socializing us to race, gender, and class expectations throughout our lifespan. These readings offer explanations of how these institutions work and examples of activism meant to improve these institutions. The sections also highlight alternatives—including gay families and radical heterosexuality.

Gender and Public Policy, *Gendered Violence* and *Sexual Assault and Sexual Consent* focus on issues of public policy, sex education, welfare and welfare reform, ending gender-based violence. These readings raise questions related to social change and highlight campus-based initiatives to end sexual assault, including men's efforts to educate other men. Readings in *Feminisms and Social Movements* weave together the history, lived experiences, and activism that has created more than 150 years of feminist and social justice activism in the United States.

Accompanying each of the 28 readings is a set of questions aimed at helping students grapple with the content. These questions are also aimed at applying the ideas from the readings beyond the classroom. Additionally, this book provides you with exercises as tools and examples for observing, analyzing, researching, participating, engaging, transforming as you learn about the study of gender and the field of gender studies.

CLAIMING AN EDUCATION

What do you have a right to expect from your professor or instructor, your program of study, and your university? First and foremost to be taken seriously. To be challenged, to be treated fairly, to be heard. Crucial to each student's success in this class is what Adrienne Rich calls "claiming an education." *Claiming* rather than "receiving" an education requires a contract between you (the student) and your professor or instructor, your program of study, and the university itself. In order to hold up your end of this contract, you must take yourselves seriously, come prepared, and take advantage of the opportunities offered by this class. This book and our classrooms are designed to offer diverse perspectives in order to support you in developing a critical stance and informed opinion on foundational ideas and current trends in Gender Studies. Students say that courses in Gender Studies are challenging, exciting, and transformative.

Danielle M. DeMuth
Associate Professor
Women, Gender and Sexuality Studies
Grand Valley State University
Allendale, MI

NEW TO THIS EDITION

In this edition, we have supplemented the essays with reflection questions and exercises we have found most useful in teaching the content and supporting students' in their learning process. The included essays have been revised to reflect the content we find most important to the field today, topics we believe students most need to know about the world they live in (e.g., gender and politics, biologically based gender claims, the intersection of gender with other pertinent social identities such as class and race), and, of course, student interests.

Every essay now includes a set of thought provoking discussion questions to consider before and after reading. The questions range from a focus on knowledge garnered from the essay and providing a quick assessment on reading comprehension skills to more advanced synthesis, analysis, and application questions. Additionally, each essay includes a list of relevant key terms to assist students in developing stronger reading comprehension, note-taking and study skills.

Finally, included in the second edition of *Unsexing Gender* is a collection of activities designed to support the application of course content to gendered topics and settings outside of the classroom. The exercises include activities such as observing gender in a public location, civic engagement assignments designed to encourage students to learn more about their campus and community, researching gender and politics, analyzing gendered discourses in television or on the web, and researching future employment opportunities and pay inequity. These exercises are longer assignments that can be used with various pairings of readings and are designed to support both students learning and instructors' assessment.

We have included an alphabetized and thematic table of contents for both the readings and the exercises in the second edition. We hope that this will make the book more user-friendly for both students and instructors. For students, we hope that the groupings of texts topically along with the suggestions for further reading will support you in guiding your education and making it easier for you to locate additional information on topics of interest. For instructors, we hope that these editions will better support you with course preparation and more easily organizing the pairing of course readings and assignments.

A NOTE TO STUDENTS USING THIS BOOK

Most importantly, this book is designed with you in mind. As you prepare to use this book, be attentive to how the structure is designed to support the development of excellent study skills.

1. Before reading an essay, always read the pre-reading questions. The questions are designed to assist you in recalling what you may already know about a subject and prepare you to think critically about the content you are about to read.
2. Read the list of key terms and concepts before you read the essay. Some of the terms may be familiar to you, some may not. They will be addressed in the essay and you should make note of the ways they are being used. List the terms in your notes and define them as you read. After reading, if there are any terms that are still unclear do some additional research so that your notes are complete. Concepts such as *gender*, *sexism*, and *feminism*, for example, show up in multiple readings. Each time you encounter these terms, your definitions of them and your understanding of their significance will grow.

3. After reading the essay, answer the reading questions provided at the end. If there are questions you cannot fully answer return to the essay and re-read sections that will provide more clarity.

4. Return to the pre-reading questions. How would you answer those questions now that you have learned more about the topic?

5. Finally, see the "If you want to read more about…" section at the beginning of each essay to find themes and other essays related to the topic for further reading that may be of interest to you.

Have a great Semester!

Ayana K. Weekley
Associate Professor, Women, Gender and Sexuality Studies
Grand Valley State University

ALPHABETICAL LIST OF AUTHORS AND ESSAYS

THEMATIC LIST OF AUTHORS AND ESSAYS

BODIES AND GENDERS

Adair, Vivyan C. "Branded with Infamy: Inscriptions of Poverty and Class in the United States"

Gould, Lois. "X: A Fabulous Child's Story"

Helliwell, Christine. "'It's Only a Penis': Rape, Feminism and Difference"

Lorde, Audre. "Uses of the Erotic: The Erotic as Power"

Serano, Julia. "Boygasms and Girlgasms: A Frank Discussion about Hormones and Gender Differences" from *Whipping Girl: A Transsexual Woman on Sexism and the Scapegoating of Femininity*

EDUCATION

Block, Stephanie. "Sex(less) Education: The Politics of Abstinence-only Programs in the United States"

Rich, Adrienne. "Claiming an Education"

Sandler, Bernice R. "The Chilly Climate: Subtle Ways in Which Women Are Often Treated Differently at Work and in Classrooms"

FEMINISM AND SOCIAL MOVEMENTS

Collins, Patricia Hill. "Toward a New Vision: Race, Class, and Gender as Categories of Analysis and Connection"

Feinberg, Leslie. "We Are All Works in Progress" from *Trans Liberation: Beyond Pink or Blue*

Frye, Marilyn. "Oppression"

Helliwell, Christine. "'It's Only a Penis': Rape, Feminism and Difference"

hooks, bell. "Feminism a Movement to End Sexist Oppression" from *Feminist Theory: From Margin to Center*

Katz, Jackson. "More Than a Few Good Men" from *The Macho Paradox*

Pharr, Suzanne. "Homophobia: a Weapon of Sexism" from *Homophobia a Weapon of Sexism*

Rich, Adrienne. "Claiming an Education"

Stanton, Elizabeth Cady. "The Declaration of Sentiments"

MASCULINITY

Abrams, Andrew. "Asking for Consent Is Sexy"

Gilbert, Elizabeth. "My Life as a Man"

Johnson, Allan G. "Privilege, Power, Difference, and Us"

Katz, Jackson. "More Than a Few Good Men" from *The Macho Paradox*

Pascoe, CJ "Dude You're A Fag": Adolescent Masculinity and the Fag Discourse

PRIVILEGE, IDENTITIES, AND INTERSECTIONALITIES

Adair, Vivyan C. "Branded with Infamy: Inscriptions of Poverty and Class in the United States"

Collins, Patricia Hill. "Toward a New Vision: Race, Class, and Gender as Categories of Analysis and Connection"

Feinberg, Leslie. "We Are All Works in Progress" from *Trans Liberation: Beyond Pink or Blue*

Frye, Marilyn "Oppression"

hooks, bell. From *Feminism is For Everybody*

Johnson, Allan G. "Privilege, Power, Difference, and Us"

McIntosh, Peggy. "White Privilege: Unpacking the Invisible Knapsack"

Rich, Adrienne. "Compulsory Heterosexuality"

Sandler, Bernice R. "The Chilly Climate: Subtle Ways in Which Women Are Often Treated Differently at Work and in Classrooms"

SEXUAL ASSAULT AND SEXUAL CONSENT

Abrams, Andrew. "Asking for Consent Is Sexy"

Helliwell, Christine. "'It's Only a Penis': Rape, Feminism and Difference"

Pfister, Bonnie. "Swept Awake! Negotiating Passion on Campus"

SEXUALITIES

Block, Stephanie. "Sex(less) Education: The Politics of Abstinence-only Programs in the United States"

Fairyington, Stephanie. "Bisexuality and the Case Against Dualism"

Lorde, Audre. "Uses of the Erotic: The Erotic as Power"

Rich, Adrienne. "Compulsory Heterosexuality"

Serano, Julia. "Boygasms and Girlgasms: A Frank Discussion about Hormones and Gender Differences" from *Whipping Girl: A Transsexual Woman on Sexism and the Scapegoating of Femininity*

xxii   UNSEXING GENDER, ENGENDERING ACTIVISM: READINGS IN GENDER STUDIES

SOCIAL CONSTRUCTION OF GENDER

Fairyington, Stephanie. "Bisexuality and the Case Against Dualism"

Feinberg, Leslie. "We Are All Works in Progress" from *Trans Liberation: Beyond Pink or Blue*

Gilbert, Elizabeth. "My Life as a Man"

Gould, Lois. "X: A Fabulous Child's Story"

Helliwell, Christine. "'It's Only a Penis': Rape, Feminism and Difference"

Lorde, Audre. "Uses of the Erotic: The Erotic as Power"

Pascoe, CJ "'Dude You're A Fag': Adolescent Masculinity and the Fag Discourse"

Rich, Adrienne. "Compulsory Heterosexuality"

Serano, Julia. "Boygasms and Girlgasms: A Frank Discussion about Hormones and Gender Differences" from *Whipping Girl: A Transsexual Woman on Sexism and the Scapegoating of Femininity*

ABOUT THE EDITORS

Unsexing Gender is a collaboration of the Women, Gender and Sexuality Studies faculty who teach at Grand Valley State University who, after years of searching for a reader for the Introduction to Gender Studies course, determined to develop their own.

Danielle M. DeMuth is Associate Professor in Women, Gender and Sexuality Studies. In addition to Introduction to Gender Studies she teaches courses on global feminism, Arab and Arab-American Feminism, feminist theory, and lesbian, gay and queer literature. Her research interests include lesbian and queer literature and feminism in the Arab world. DeMuth started teaching Introduction to Gender Studies in 1997 while working on her PhD in English at the University of Toledo. She is grateful to more than fifteen years of students in Women and Gender Studies who have claimed their education and continue to inspire her as they apply their knowledge and activism in the world.

Julia M. Mason is Associate Professor of Women, Gender and Sexuality Studies. She regularly teaches Introduction to Gender Studies as well as courses on gender and popular culture and women, health and environment. She earned her doctorate in American Culture Studies, with graduate certificates in Women's Studies and Ethnic Studies, from Bowling Green State University. Mason's research centers on representations of women in popular culture in mainstream magazines and contemporary television. She is committed to fostering a deeper understanding of relevant connections as a means to create and sustain positive social change in the classroom, at our university, and in the community.

Ayana K. Weekley is Associate Professor of Women, Gender and Sexuality Studies at Grand Valley State University. In addition to Introduction to Gender Studies, she teaches courses on feminist theory, including black feminist theory. Her research interests include representations of race, gender and the HIV/AIDS epidemic, AIDS activism, black feminisms, and the scholarship of teaching and learning. Weekley earned her PhD in Feminist Studies at the University of Minnesota. She is committed to supporting students in their educational journeys find the same passion she found through critical inquiry in Women and Gender Studies.

Kathleen Underwood retired in 2015 as chair of the Women, Gender, and Sexualities Department and associate professor of History at Grand Valley State University. Under her leadership, the Women and Gender Studies Program grew to a full department. Underwood received her PhD in History at UCLA (1982). In 1998, she joined the History faculty at Grand Valley and became director of the Women and Gender Studies program in 2002. Since retirement, Underwood has devoted much of her time to social justice activism centered on immigration and undocumented residents and in 2018 was arrested in the Senate Office building in support of DACA.

Asking for Consent is Sexy

Andrew Abrams

Andrew Abrams earned a BA degree in Anthropology from Antioch College. His essay about his involvement in creating the Antioch Sexual Offense Policy was published in Just Sex: Students Rewrite the Rules on Sex, Violence, Activism, and Equality *(2000) edited by Jodi Gold and Susan Villari.*

PRE-READING QUESTIONS

1. How do you indicate sexual consent? How do you know that your partner is giving consent?
2. How would you describe the sexual climate on your campus? What kinds of programs are available on campus to educate peers and/or discuss sexuality? Do parties or social gatherings on your campus encourage sexual objectification? (e.g., "pimps and hoes" parties)

KEY TERMS

sexual consent
sexual offense policy (SOP)
Womyn of Antioch

SEE THE THEMATIC TABLE OF CONTENTS, IF YOU WANT TO READ MORE ESSAYS ABOUT:

Gender and Public Policy
Gendered Violence
Masculinity
Sexual Assault and Sexual Consent

Asking for Consent is Sexy

Andrew Abrams

In June 1992—the spring term of my junior year—the board at Antioch College passed an amendment to the school's sexual offense policy: a new clause about sexual consent. Basically, the consent clause says that if two people are going to have sex, then whoever initiates the sex needs to ask the other person if it's okay and the other person needs to say yes or no. That way, you'll know that you're not raping or sexually harassing someone; it's not enough to assume that you can tell nonverbally. Ideally, the policy kicks in when you first begin to touch.

Everyone outside the college always wants to know if I follow the policy step by step. They think that it's crazy because they've never tried it.

It makes sense. On TV and in the mass media, all you ever see is people who know each other for five minutes, look in each other's eyes, and then get it on. But the fact is that sex is just better when you talk.

Before the consent policy, I was infatuated with an artist named Leah. She lived downstairs in the dorm and was friends with my roommate. We started hanging out together in the second quarter. I sat down in her room one night and said, "I just want you to know—you probably know this already—but I am attracted to you." She didn't say a word. She wouldn't look at me, wouldn't respond to what I said. Somehow during my second year we became friends. She was very uncomfortable with sex, and so we would lie in bed and I'd ask her: "Is it all right if I kiss you?" "Can I put my hand on your stomach?" The progression was very slow. I asked her permission basically every step of the way. It seems like a lot of work, but it's sexy to ask permission to kiss a woman, and it's exciting to hear her say yes.

People say that Antioch is topsy-turvy: The men are beaten down and the women are on top. But I'm not submissive, I don't feel beaten down, and I've never felt like my life at Antioch was controlled by the agenda of women. The policy isn't asking me to do anything that I don't think I should be doing anyway.

The fall term of my second year was the quarter from hell. A student had died in a van accident, and in a community this small, when one person dies, it's traumatic. The next quarter a woman died of a brain aneurysm during a meeting in front of fifty people, and a friend of mine was killed in a car accident. There were also two student rapes reported on campus. That fall was easily the worst quarter I had as a student at Antioch.

Antioch has a tradition of holding community meetings to discuss campus issues. Around this time a new group, the Womyn of Antioch, showed up at one unannounced. About seventy-five people were there, sitting in a lecture-class auditorium. The Womyn walked in dressed in black, filing down the stairs to the front of the room. They had pieces of tape with the word "RAPED" written on them, and every three minutes they would put one on another woman's back. They explained that every three minutes a woman is raped, and they demanded a policy to deal with sexual offenses on campus. Soon after that they drafted a sexual offense policy and brought it to the administrative council at a hearing packed with student supporters. It became official in 1991. The thing to remember is that the SOP was brought about by students, and that a majority of students still support it.

At the cafeteria, in my friends' rooms, the question I kept on hearing from men was, "What if someone is unfairly accused?" Lots of men see it as a threat even to this day. But why would someone lie about being raped? I can't imagine that anyone would put themselves through all the emotional stress of the hearing process just to attack someone. Basically, you have nothing to worry about as long as you ask.

I think it's important to ask and to be asked in sexual situations, in order to feel comfortable with the person you are with, and to deal with issues about safer sex. Asking a woman if you can kiss her makes it easier to ask whether she has had high-risk partners, to talk about what being safe means to each other. It seems crazy to risk your life just because you're not comfortable talking about condoms. Also, men tend to be more assertive in sexual situations, and I think that the policy balances that out.

I never stayed in one relationship for a long time: That isn't unusual at Antioch. But after a series of sexual experiences—some of them very good ones—I started looking at that as a real problem. About a year ago a woman invited me back to her room. We were fooling around, and at what you might call the height of passion I realized this wasn't what I wanted. I said, "I'm sorry, this isn't comfortable for me." As a man, I'd been brought up to believe that I should be capable, ready, willing all of the time. But the policy made me realize that I had sexual choices—that it was okay sometimes to say, "Time out."

I've been in a relationship with a woman now for close to five months. I met Lorien playing volleyball: She's tall and she's a good athlete. We took Human Sexuality together, but we stayed friends for a year before we started going out. The first time Lorien and I kissed, we talked about the idea of becoming physically intimate for an hour beforehand. Finally she said, "So are we going to kiss or what?" I said, "I think you should kiss me." So she kissed my hand. Then I kissed her hand. She kissed my cheek and I kissed hers. . . .

That doesn't mean that every time we kiss each other we have a ten-minute discussion. You don't always stop when you're falling asleep together to ask, "May I kiss you good night?" But if we're having sex, we talk about what we want and what feels good. I don't like rough sex and I hate hickeys; I like to be touched softly. But nobody's going to know that automatically. If you don't talk, then all you've got is guesswork. Go home and try it, see what happens. I bet you'll end up thanking me.

Asking for Consent is Sexy

Andrew Abrams

1. How would you describe Abram's experience at Antioch with the Antioch Sexual Office Policy?

2. What questions would you ask the students who developed the Antioch Policy?

3. What changes would you suggest to the Antioch Policy?

4. In your own words, write an explanation of sexual consent for a friend or a first year student on campus.

Now, try to convey this idea in 140 characters. You know, make it tweet-able.

"Branded with Infamy: Inscriptions of Poverty and Class in the United States"

Vivyan C. Adair

Vivyan Adair is professor of Women's Studies at Hamilton College. She earned her PhD in English from the University of Washington. Her research and teaching centers around feminist theory, critical literary theory, and public policy. She formerly held the Elihu Root Peace Fund Chair (2004–2009). This essay appeared in Signs: Journal of Women in Culture and Society (2002).

PRE-READING QUESTIONS

1. What do the words *branded* and *infamy* bring to mind?
2. What are the different socioeconomic classes in the United States? What are the defining characteristics of each?
3. What do you know about welfare? Who benefits from welfare? List the welfare programs provided by the government.

KEY TERMS

Aid to Families with Dependent Children (AFDC)
bodily/social inscription
class
feminist theories of class production
Foucault, Michel
hegemonic
ideology
material deprivation
Personal Responsibility and Work Opportunity Reconciliation Act (PRWORA)
poverty
socialization
socioeconomic class
stratification
welfare policy
welfare reform
welfare-to-work
welfare queen

SEE THE THEMATIC TABLE OF CONTENTS, IF YOU WANT TO READ MORE ESSAYS ABOUT:

Bodies and Genders
Gender and Public Policy
Privilege, Identities and Intersectionalities

Branded with Infamy: Inscriptions of Poverty and Class in the United States

Vivyan C. Adair

My kids and I been chopped up and spit out just like when I was a kid. My rotten teeth, my kids' twisted feet. My son's dull skin and blank stare. My oldest girl's stooped posture and the way she can't look no one in the eye no more. This all says we got nothing and we deserve what we got. On the street good families look at us and see right away what they'd be if they don't follow the rules. They're scared too, real scared.

— Welfare recipient and activist, Olympia, Washington, 1998

I begin with the words of a poor, white, single mother of three. Although officially she has only a tenth-grade education, she expertly reads and articulates a complex theory of power, bodily inscription, and socialization that arose directly from the material conditions of her own life. She sees what many far more "educated" scholars and citizens fail to recognize: that the bodies of poor women and children are produced and positioned as texts that facilitate the mandates of a didactic, profoundly brutal and mean-spirited political regime. The clarity and power of this woman's vision challenges feminists to consider and critique our commitment both to textualizing displays of heavy-handed social inscription and to detextualizing them, working to put an end to these bodily experiences of pain, humiliation, and suffering.

Traditionally, Marxist and Weberian perspectives have been employed as lenses through which to examine and understand the material and bodily "injuries of class."[1] Yet feminists have clearly critiqued these theories for their failure to address the processes through which class is produced on the gendered and raced bodies of its subjects in ways that assure for the perpetuation of systems of stratification and domination.[2] Over the past decade or so, a host of inspired feminist welfare scholars and activists has addressed and examined the relationship between state

[*Signs: Journal of Women in Culture and Society* 2001, vol. 27, no. 2]

[1]Richard Sennett and Jonathan Cobb realized that thinking of class in terms of systems obscured the human costs of being constructed within a hierarchical class system. In *The Hidden Injuries of Class*—exploring themes found only among their "working-men"—they began to consider the degree to which "social legitimacy in Americans has its origins in public calculations of social value" (1972, 296). Yet Sennett and Cobb failed to examine directly the processes through which class is produced on the gendered and raced bodies of its subjects.

[2]For a more complete analysis of the limits of Marxian and Weberian theory for feminists attempting to understand the workings of class, see Crompton and Mann 1986.

power and the lives of poor women and children.[3] As important and insightful as these exposés are, with few exceptions, they do not get at the closed circuit that fuses together systems of power, the material conditions of poverty, and the bodily experiences that allow for the perpetuation—and indeed for the justification—of these systems. They fail to consider what the speaker of my opening passage recognized so astutely: that systems of power produce and patrol poverty through the reproduction of both social and bodily markers.

This essay is dedicated to poor women around the world who struggle together against oppression and injustice. With thanks to Margaret Gentry, Nancy Sorkin Rabinowitz, Sandra Dahlberg, and the reviewers and editors at *Signs*. And as always, for my mother and my daughter.

What is inadequate, then, even in many feminist theories of class production, is an analysis of this nexus of the textual and the corporeal. Here Michel Foucault's ([1977] 1984a) argument about the inscriptions of bodies is a powerful mechanism for understanding the material and physical conditions and bodily costs of poverty across racial difference and for interrogating the connection between power's expression as text, as body, and as site of resistance.[4]

In *Foucault and Feminism: Power, Gender, and the Self*, Lois McNay reminds us that "to a greater extent than any other post-structuralist thinker, feminists have drawn on Foucault's work" even though "[they] are also acutely aware of its critical limitations" (1993, 2–3). Particularly useful for feminists has been Foucault's theory that the body is written on and through discourse as the product of historically specific power relations. Feminists have used this notion of social inscription to explain a range of bodily operations from cosmetic surgery (Morgan 1991; Brush 1998), prostitution (Bell 1994), and anorexia nervosa (Bordo 1993; Hopwood 1995) to motherhood (Smart 1992; Chandler 1999), race (Stoler 1995; Ford-Smith 1996), and cultural imperialism (Desmond 1991). As these analyses illustrate, Foucault allows us to consider and critique the body as it is invested with meaning and inserted into regimes of truth via the operations of power and knowledge. On the other hand, feminist scholars have neglected to consider the ways in which other dimensions of social difference, such as class, are inscribed upon the body in manners as fundamental as those of sexuality, gender, and race.[5]

Foucault clarifies and expands on this process of bodily/social inscription in his early work. In "Nietzsche, Genealogy, History," he positions the physical body as virtual text, accounting for the fact that "the body is the inscribed surface of events that are traced by language and dissolved by ideas" ([1977] 1984b, 83). Foucault's powerful scholarship points toward a body that is given form through semiotic systems and written on by discourse. For Foucault, the body and text are inseparable. In his logic, power constructs and holds bodies, which Foucault variously describes as "foundations where language leaves its traces" ([1977] 1984b, 176) and "the writing pad[s] of the sovereign and the law" ([1977] 1984b, 177).

---

[3]Mimi Abramovitz (1989, 2000), Randy Albelda (1997), Teresa Amott (1993), Frances Fox Piven and Richard Cloward (1993), Linda Gordon (1995), Wahneema Lubiano (1992), and Gwendolyn Mink (1996, 1998) have begun to unravel the historical, economic, rhetorical, and social markings of class embedded in welfare policy and poverty, while Ann Withorn and Rochelle Lefkowitz (1986), Diane Dujon and Ann Withorn (1996), Donna Langston (1998), Kathryn Edin and Laura Lein (1997), Bonnie Thornton Dill and Bruce Williams (1992), Theresa Funiciello (1998), and Ruth Sidel (1998) have worked directly with poor women and their children to critique the material implications of those policies.

[4]Racism, classism, sexism, and heterosexism collide in the rhetoric of welfare bashing. Clearly, poor women and children of color are multiply marked in this discourse and punished in their lived lives. Their bodies are also positioned to represent the alleged pathology of an entire culture of poor women and children. Yet it is also true, as my survey results illustrate, that across racial difference the bodies of poor unmarried women and their children are marked and made to bear meaning as signs of danger and pathology, as they are publicly both punished and disciplined.

[5]Notably, Donna Langston has recognized that class markers determine "the way we talk, think, act, move," look, and are valued or devalued in our culture (1998, 127). Langston adds, "we experience class at every level of our lives," so that even if our status changes, our class marking "does not float out in the rinse water" (128).

In *Discipline and Punish*, Foucault sets out to depict the genealogy of torture and discipline as it reflects a public display of power on the body of subjects in the seventeenth and eighteenth centuries. In graphic detail Foucault begins his book with the description of a criminal being tortured and then drawn and quartered in a public square. The crowds of good parents and their growing children watch and learn. The public spectacle works as a patrolling image, socializing and controlling bodies within the body politic. Eighteenth-century torture "must mark the victim: it is intended, either by the scar it leaves on the body or by the spectacle that accompanies it, to brand the victim with infamy. It traces around or rather on the very body of the condemned man signs that can not be effaced" ([1977] 1984a, 179). For Foucault, public exhibitions of punishment served as a socializing process, writing culture's codes and values on the minds and bodies of its subjects. In the process punishment discursively deconstructed and rearranged bodies.

But Foucault's point in *Discipline and Punish* is precisely that public exhibition and inscription have been replaced in contemporary society by a much more effective process of socialization and self-inscription. According to Foucault, today discipline has replaced torture as the privileged punishment, but the body continues to be written on. Discipline produces "subjected and practiced bodies, 'docile bodies'" (1984a, 182). We become subjects not of the sovereign but of ideology, disciplining and inscribing our own bodies/minds in the process of becoming stable and singular subjects. Power's hold on bodies is in both cases maintained through language systems. The body continues to be the site and operation of ideology, as subject and representation, body and text.

Indeed, while we are all marked discursively by ideology in Foucault's paradigm, in the United States today poor women and children of all races are multiply marked with signs of both discipline and punishment that cannot be erased or effaced.[6] They are systematically produced through both twentieth-century forces of socialization and discipline and eighteenth-century exhibitions of public mutilation. In addition to coming into being as disciplined and docile bodies, poor single welfare mothers and their children are physically inscribed, punished, and displayed as the dangerous and pathological other. It is important to note, when considering the contemporary inscription of poverty as moral pathology etched onto the bodies of profoundly poor women and children, that these are more than metaphoric and self-patrolling marks of discipline. Rather, on myriad levels—sexual, social, material, and physical—poor women and their children, like the "deviants" publicly punished in Foucault's scenes of torture, are marked, mutilated, and made to bear and transmit signs in a public spectacle that brands the victim with infamy.

TEXT OF THE BODY, BODY OF THE TEXT: THE (NOT SO) HIDDEN INJURIES OF CLASS

Recycled images of poor, welfare women permeate and shape our national consciousness.[7] Yet—as is so often the case—these images and narratives tell us more about the culture that spawned and embraced them than they do about the object of the culture's obsession. Simple, stable, and often widely skewed cover stories tell us what is "wrong" with some people, what is normative, and what is pathological; by telling us who "bad" poor women are, we reaffirm and reevaluate who

---

[6]bell hooks has said that in the language of welfare "poor whites have been erased, while poor blacks have been demonized" (1999). This is surely true at the level of discourse and at the systemic level, and yet I would argue that at the level of the body poor white women and children—like poor women and children of color—are both erased and demonized, as the scripts of those devaluations are written on their very bodies.

[7]Throughout this essay I use the terms *welfare recipient* and *poor working women* interchangeably because as the recent Urban Institute study made clear, today these populations are, in fact, one and the same (Loprest 1999).

we, as a nation and as a people—of allegedly good, middle-class, white, able-bodied, independent, male citizens—are. At their foundations, stories of the welfare mother intersect with, draw from, reify, and reproduce myriad mythic American narratives associated with a constellation of beliefs about capitalism, male authority, the "nature" of humans, and the sphere of individual freedom, opportunity, and responsibility. These narratives purport to write the story of poor women in an arena in which only their bodies have been positioned to "speak."[8] They promise to tell the story of who poor women are in ways that allow Americans to maintain a belief in both an economic system based on exploitation and an ideology that claims that we are all beyond exploitation.

These productions orchestrate the story of poverty as one of moral and intellectual lack and of chaos, pathology, promiscuity, illogic, and sloth, juxtaposed always against the order, progress, and decency of "deserving" citizens. Trying to stabilize and make sense of unpalatably complex issues of poverty and oppression and attempting to obscure hegemonic stakes in representation, these narratives reduce and collapse the lives and experiences of poor women to deceptively simplistic dramas, which are then offered for public consumption. The terms of these dramas are palatable because they are presented as simple oppositions of good and bad, right and wrong, independent and dependent, deserving and undeserving. Yet as a generationally poor woman I know that poverty is neither this simple nor this singular. Poverty is rather the product of complex systems of power that at many levels are indelibly written on poor women and children in feedback loops that compound and complicate politically expedient readings and writings of our bodies.

I am, and will probably always be, marked as a poor woman. I was raised by a poor, single, white mother who had to struggle to keep her four children fed, sheltered, and clothed by working at what seemed like an endless stream of minimum-wage, exhausting, and demeaning jobs. As a child poverty was written onto and into my being at the level of private and public thought and body. At an early age my body bore witness to and emitted signs of the painful devaluation carved into my flesh; that same devaluation became integral to my being in the world. I came into being as a disciplined body/mind while at the same time I was taught to read my abject body as the site of my own punishment and erasure. In this excess of meaning the space between private body and public sign was collapsed.

For many poor children this double exposure results in debilitating—albeit politically useful—shame and lack. As Carolyn Kay Steedman reminds us in *Landscape for a Good Woman* (1987), the mental life of poor children flows from material deprivation. Steedman speaks of the "relentless laying down of guilt" she experienced as a poor child living in a world where identity was shaped through envy and unfulfilled desire and where her own body "told me stories of the terrible unfairness of things, of the subterranean culture of longing for that which one can never have" (1987, 8). For Steedman, public devaluation and punishment "demonstrated to us all the hierarchies of our illegality, the impropriety of our existence, our marginality within the social system" (9). Even as an adult she recalls, "The baggage will never lighten for me or my sister. We were born, and had no choice in the matter; but we were social burdens, expensive, unworthy, never grateful enough. There was nothing we could do to pay back the debt of our existence" (19).

Indeed, poor children are often marked with bodily signs that cannot be forgotten or erased. Their bodies are physically inscribed as "other" and then read as pathological, dangerous, and

---

[8] In recent years an increasingly lucrative industry has sprung up around making meaning of the presence of the poor in America. Politicians, welfare historians, social scientists, policy analysts, and all stripe of academician produce and jealously guard their newfound turf as they vie for a larger market share of this meaning-making economy. In the shadow of this frenzied and profitable proliferation of representation exists a profound crisis in the lives of poor women and children whose bodies continue to be the site and operation of ideology, as they are written and read as dangerous and then erased and rendered mute in venues of authority and power.

undeserving. What I recall most vividly about being a child in a profoundly poor family was that we were constantly hurt and ill, and, because we could not afford medical care, small illnesses and accidents spiraled into more dangerous illnesses and complications that became both a part of who we were and written proof that we were of no value in the world.

In spite of my mother's heroic efforts, at an early age my brothers and sister and I were stooped, bore scars that never healed properly, and limped with feet mangled by ill-fitting, used Salvation Army shoes. When my sister's forehead was split open by a door slammed in frustration, my mother "pasted" the angry wound together on her own, leaving a mark of our inability to afford medical attention, of our lack, on her very forehead. When I suffered from a concussion, my mother simply put borrowed ice on my head and tried to keep me awake for a night. And when throughout elementary school we were sent to the office for mandatory and very public yearly checkups, the school nurse sucked air through her teeth as she donned surgical gloves to check only the hair of poor children for lice.

We were read as unworthy, laughable, and often dangerous. Our schoolmates laughed at our "ugly shoes," our crooked and ill-serviced teeth, and the way we "stank," as teachers excoriated us for our inability to concentrate in school, our "refusal" to come to class prepared with proper school supplies, and our unethical behavior when we tried to take more than our allocated share of "free lunch."[9] Whenever backpacks or library books came up missing, we were publicly interrogated and sent home to "think about" our offenses, often accompanied by notes that reminded my mother that as a poor single parent she should be working twice as hard to make up for the discipline that allegedly walked out the door with my father. When we sat glued to our seats, afraid to stand in front of the class in ragged and ill-fitting hand-me-downs, we were held up as examples of unprepared and uncooperative children. And when our grades reflected our otherness, they were used to justify even more elaborate punishment that exacerbated the effects of our growing anomie.

Friends who were poor as children, and respondents to a survey I conducted in 1998, tell similar stories of the branding they received at the hands of teachers, administrators, and peers.[10] An African-American woman raised in Yesler Terrace, a public housing complex in Seattle, Washington, writes:

> Poor was all over our faces. My glasses were taped and too weak. My big brother had missing teeth. My mom was dull and ashy. It was like a story of how poor we were that anyone could see. My sister Evie's lip was bit by a dog and we just had dime store stuff to put on it. Her lip was a big scar. Then she never smiled and no one smiled at her cause she never smiled. Kids call[ed] her "Scarface." Teachers never smiled at her. The principal put her in detention all the time because she was mean and bad (they said).[11]

And a white woman in the Utica, New York, area remembers:

> We lived in dilapidated and unsafe housing that had fleas no matter how clean my mom tried to be. We had bites all over us. Living in our car between evictions was even worse—then we didn't have a bathroom so I got kidney problems that I never had doctor's help for. When my teachers wouldn't let me go to the bathroom every hour or so I would wet my pants in class. You can imagine what the kids did to me about that. And the teachers would refuse to let me go to the bathroom because they said I was willful.[12]

---

[9] As recently as 1993, in my daughter's public elementary school cafeteria, "free lunchers" (poor children who could not otherwise afford to eat lunch, including my daughter) were reminded with a large and colorful sign to "line up last."

[10] The goal of my survey was to measure the impact of the 1996 welfare reform legislation on the lives of profoundly poor women and children in the United States. Early in 1998 I sent fifty questionnaires and narrative surveys to four groups of poor women on the West and the East coasts; thirty-nine were returned to me. I followed these surveys with forty-five-minute interviews with twenty of the surveyed women.

[11] Unpublished survey, June 1998, Seattle, Washington.

[12] Unpublished survey, December 1998, Utica, New York.

Material deprivation is publicly written on the bodies of poor children in the world. In the United States poor families experience violent crime, hunger, lack of medical and dental care, utility shut-offs, the effects of living in unsafe housing and/or of being homeless, chronic illness, and insufficient winter clothing (Edin and Lein 1997, 224–31). According to Jody Raphael of the Taylor Institute, poor women and their children are also at five times the risk of experiencing domestic violence (2000).

As children, our disheveled and broken bodies were produced and read as signs of our inferiority and undeservedness. As adults our mutilated bodies are read as signs of inner chaos, immaturity, and indecency as we are punished and then read as proof of the need for further discipline and punishment. When my already bad teeth started to rot and I was out of my head with pain, my choices as an adult welfare recipient were either to let my teeth fall out or to have them pulled out. In either case the culture would then read me as a "toothless illiterate," as a fearful joke. In order to pay my rent and to put shoes on my daughter's feet I sold blood at two or three different clinics on a monthly basis until I became so anemic that they refused to buy it from me. A neighbor of mine went back to the man who continued to beat her and her scarred children after being denied welfare benefits when she realized that she could not adequately feed, clothe, and house her family on her own minimum-wage income. My good friend sold her ovum to a fertility clinic in a painful and potentially damaging process. Other friends exposed themselves to all manner of danger and disease by selling their bodies for sex in order to feed and clothe their babies.

Poverty becomes a vicious cycle that is written on our bodies and intimately connected with our value in the world. Our children need healthy food so that we can continue working; yet working at minimum-wage jobs, we have no money for wholesome food and very little time to care for our families. So our children get sick, we lose our jobs to take care of them, we fall deeper and deeper into debt before our next unbearable job, and then we really cannot afford medical care. Starting that next minimum-wage job with unpaid bills and ill children puts us further and further behind so that we are even less able to afford good food, adequate child care, health care, or emotional healing. The food banks we gratefully drag our exhausted children to on the weekends hand out bags of rancid candy bars, hot dogs that have passed their expiration dates, stale broken pasta, and occasionally a bag of wrinkled apples. We are either fat or skinny, and we seem always irreparably ill. Our emaciated or bloated bodies are then read as a sign of lack of discipline and as proof that we have failed to care as we should.[13]

Exhaustion also marks the bodies of poor women in indelible script. Rest becomes a privilege we simply cannot afford. After working full shifts each day, poor mothers trying to support themselves at minimum-wage jobs continue to work to a point of exhaustion that is inscribed on their faces, their bodies, their posture, and their diminishing sense of self and value in the world. My former neighbor recently recalled:

> I had to take connecting buses to bring and pick up my daughters at childcare after working on my feet all day. As soon as we arrived at home, we would head out again by bus to do laundry. Pick up groceries. Try to get to the food bank. Beg the electric company to not turn off our lights and heat again. Find free winter clothing. Sell my blood. I would be home at nine or ten o'clock at night. I was loaded down with one baby asleep and one crying. Carrying lots of heavy bags and ready to drop on my feet. I had bags under my eyes and no shampoo to wash my hair so I used soap. Anyway I had to stay up to wash diapers in the sink. Otherwise they wouldn't be dry when I left the house in the dark with my girls. In the morning I start all over again.[14]

---

[13] Adolescent psychologist Maria Root claims that a beautiful or "fit" body becomes equated with "purity, discipline—basically with goodness" (DeClaire 1993, 36).

[14] Unpublished survey, June 1998, Seattle, Washington.

This bruised and lifeless body, hauling sniffling babies and bags of dirty laundry on the bus, was then read as a sign that she was a bad mother and a threat that needed to be disciplined and made to work even harder for her own good. Those who need the respite less go away for weekends, take drives in the woods, take their kids to the beach. Poor women without education are pushed into minimum-wage jobs and have no money, no car, no time, no energy, and little support, as their bodies are made to display marks of their material deprivation as a socializing and patrolling force.

Ultimately, we come to recognize that our bodies are not our own, that they are rather public property. State-mandated blood tests, interrogation of the most private aspects of our lives, the public humiliation of having to beg officials for food and medicine, and the loss of all right to privacy, teach us that our bodies are only useful as lessons, warnings, and signs of degradation that everyone loves to hate. In "From Welfare to Academe: Welfare Reform as College-Educated Welfare Mothers Know It," Sandy Smith-Madsen describes the erosion of her privacy as a poor welfare mother:

> I was investigated. I was spied upon. A welfare investigator c[a]me into my home and after thoughtful deliberation granted me permission to keep my belongings. Like the witch hunts of old, if a neighbor reports you as a welfare queen, the guardians of the state's compelling interest come into your home and interrogate you. While they do not have the right to set your body ablaze on the public square, they can forever devastate heart and soul by snatching away children. Just like a police officer, they may use whatever they happen to see against you, including sexual orientation. Full-fledged citizens have the right to deny an officer entry into their home unless they possess a search warrant; welfare mothers fork over citizenship rights for the price of a welfare check. In Tennessee, constitutional rights go for a cash value of $185 per month for a family of three. (in press, 185)

Welfare reform policy is designed to publicly expose, humiliate, punish, and display "deviant" welfare mothers. "Workfare" and "Learnfare"—two alleged successes of welfare reform—require that landlords, teachers, and employers be made explicitly aware of the second-class status of these very public bodies. In Ohio, the Department of Human Services uses tax dollars to pay for advertisements on the side of Cleveland's RTA buses that show a "Welfare Queen" behind bars with a logo that proclaims "Crime does not pay. Welfare fraud is a crime" (Robinson 1999). In Michigan a pilot program mandating drug tests for all welfare recipients began on October 1, 1999. Recipients who refuse the test will lose their benefits immediately (Simon 1999). In Buffalo, New York, a county executive proudly announced that his county would begin intensive investigation of all parents who refuse minimum-wage jobs that are offered to them by the state. He warned: "We have many ways of investigating and exposing these errant parents who choose to exploit their children in this way" (Anderson 1999). In Eugene, recipients who cannot afford to feed their children adequately on their food stamp allocations are advised through fliers issued by a contractor for Oregon's welfare agency to "check the dump and the residential and business dumpsters" in order to save money (Women's Enews, 2001b). In April 2001, Jason Turner, New York City's welfare commissioner, told a congressional subcommittee that "workplace safety and the Fair Labor Standards Act should not apply to welfare recipients who, in fact, should face tougher sanctions in order to make them work" (Women's Enews, 2001a). And welfare reform legislation enacted in 1996 as the Personal Responsibility and Work Opportunities Reconciliation Act (PRWORA) requires that poor mothers work full-time, earning minimum-wage salaries with which they cannot support their children. Since these women are often denied medical, dental, and child-care benefits and are unable to provide their families with adequate food, heat, or clothing, through this legislation the state mandates child neglect and abuse. The crowds of good parents and their growing children watch and learn.

READING AND REWRITING THE BODY OF THE TEXT

The bodies of poor women and children, scarred and mutilated by state-mandated material deprivation and public exhibition, work as spectacles, as patrolling images socializing and controlling bodies within the body politic. That "body politic" is represented in Foucault's work as the other half of the discipline and punishment circuit of socialization. It is here that material elements and techniques "serve as weapons, relays, communication routes and supports for the power and knowledge relations that invest human bodies and subjugate them, turning them into objects of knowledge" ([1977] 1984a, 28). Again Foucault writes of the body and the text: text is in and of the body, body is in and of the text, in ways in which signifier and signified, metaphor and referent never replace each other but simply trace and chase each other. In this cycle of power a template of meaning is produced through which only specific, politically viable readings of the bodies of poor welfare recipients and their children are possible.

Spectacular cover stories of the "Welfare Queen" play and replay in the national mind's eye, becoming a prescriptive lens through which the American public as a whole reads the individual dramas of the bodies of poor women and their place and value in the world. These dramas produce "normative" citizens as independent, stable, rational, ordered, and free. In this dichotomous, hierarchical frame the poor welfare mother is juxtaposed against a logic of "normative" subjectivity as the embodiment of dependency, disorder, disarray, and otherness. Her broken and scarred body becomes proof of her inner pathology and chaos, suggesting the need for further punishment and discipline.

In contemporary narratives welfare women are imagined to be dangerous because they refuse to sacrifice their desires and fail to participate in legally sanctioned heterosexual relationships; theirs is read, as a result, as a selfish, "unnatural," and immature sexuality. In this script, the bodies of poor women are viewed as being dangerously beyond the control of men and are as a result construed as the bearers of perverse desire. In this androcentric equation fathers become the sole bearers of order and of law, defending poor women and children against their own unchecked sexuality and lawlessness.

For Republican Senator John Ashcroft writing in the *St. Louis Dispatch*, the inner city is the site of "rampant illegitimacy" and a "space devoid of discipline" where all values are askew. For Ashcroft, what is insidious is not material poverty but an entitlement system that has allowed "out-of-control" poor women to rupture traditional patriarchal authority, valuation, and boundaries (1995, A23). Impoverished communities then become a site of chaos because without fathers they allegedly lack any organizing or patrolling principle. George Gilder agrees with Ashcroft when he writes in the conservative *American Spectator* that "the key problem of the welfare culture is not unemployed women and poor children. It is the women's skewed and traumatic relationships with men. In a reversal of the pattern of civilized societies, the women have the income and the ties to government authority and support. This balance of power virtually prohibits marriage, which is everywhere based on the provider role of men, counterbalancing the sexual and domestic superiority of women" (1995, B6). For Gilder, the imprimatur of welfare women's sordid bodies unacceptably shifts the focus of the narrative from a male presence to a feminized absence.

When welfare mothers are positioned as sexually chaotic, irrational, and unstable, their figures are temporarily immobilized and made to yield meaning as a space that must be brought under control and transformed through public displays of punishment. Poor single mothers and children who have been abandoned, have fled physical, sexual, and/or psychological abuse, or have in general refused to capitulate to male control within the home are mythologized as dangerous, pathological, out of control, and selfishly unable—or unwilling—to sacrifice their "naturally" unnatural desires. They are understood and punished as a danger to a culture resting on a foundation of inviolate male authority and absolute privilege in both public and private spheres.

William Raspberry frames poor women as selfish and immature, when in "Ms. Smith Goes after Washington," he claims, "Unfortunately AFDC [Aid to Families with Dependent Children] is paid to an unaccountable, accidental and unprepared parent who has chosen her head of household status as a personal form of satisfaction, while lacking the simple life skills and maturity to achieve love and job fulfillment from any other source. I submit that all of our other social ills—crime, drugs, violence, failing schools are a direct result of the degradation of parenthood by emotionally immature recipients" (1995, A19). Raspberry goes on to assert that, like poor children, poor mothers must be made visible reminders to the rest of the culture of the "poor choices" they have made. He claims that rather than "coddling" her, we have a responsibility to "shame her" and to use her failure to teach other young women that it is "morally wrong for unmarried women to bear children," as we "cast single motherhood as a selfish and immature act" (1995, A19).

Continuous, multiple, and often seamless, public inscription, punishing policy, and lives of unbearable material lack leave poor women and their children scarred, exhausted, and confused. As a result their bodies are imagined as an embodiment of decay and cultural dis-ease that threatens the health and progress of our nation. Readings that position poor women's bodies and presences in the world as illegal posit an inherent connection between control, autonomy, progress, and social value. In valuing science, history, and allegedly masculine logic, progress is imagined as linear and teleological. This narrative of movement celebrates an active move from a feminizedstagnant, chaotic, abject, and darkworld to a state of masculinist autonomy, progress, discipline, and order. What the protagonist leaves behind in this foundational American myth is stasis and putrefaction.[15] As a result the narrative sets up a series of dichotomous images juxtaposing our national obsession with movement and progress against our abhorrence for, and fear of, poor women who are constructed as static and stagnant.

In a 1995 *USA Today* article entitled "America at Risk: Can We Survive without Moral Values?" for example, the inner city is portrayed as a *"dark"* realm of *"decay* rooted in the *loss* of values, the *death* of work ethics, and the *deterioration* of families and communities." Allegedly, here "all morality has *rotted* due to a *breakdown* in discipline." This space of disorder and disease is marked with tropes of race and gender. It is also associated with the imagery of "communities of women *without* male leadership, cultural values and initiative" (1995, C3; emphasis added). In George Will's *Newsweek* editorial he proclaims that *"illogical* feminist and racial *anger* coupled with *misplaced* American emotion may be a part or a cause of the *irresponsible* behavior *rampant* in poor neighborhoods." Will continues, proclaiming that here "mothers *lack* control over their children and have *selfishly* taught them to embrace a *pathological* ethos that values *self-need* and *self-expression* over self-control" (1995, 88; emphasis added).

Poor women and children's bodies, publicly scarred and mutilated by material deprivation, are read as expressions of an essential lack of discipline and order. In response to this perception, journalist Ronald Brownstein of the *Los Angeles Times* proposed that the *"Republican Contract with*

---

[15]In "Rhetoric of (Female) Savagery: Welfare Reform in the United States and Aotearoa/New Zealand" (2000), Catherine Kingfisher notes that "the discourse of welfare reform in Aotearoa/New Zealand and the United States is pervaded by a symbolic association of the 'undeserving' poor, most notably poor single mothers, with savagery. The savage is commonly constructed as wild, uncivilized, uncontrollable, and living in a 'natural' state that lies outside, or historically occurred prior to, civilization" (2).

America" will "*restore* America to its path, *enforcing* social *order* and common *standards* of behavior, and replacing *stagnation* and *decay* with *movement* and *forward* thinking *energy*" (1995, A1; emphasis added). In these rhetorical fields poverty is metonymically linked to a lack of progress that would allegedly otherwise order, stabilize, and restore the culture. What emerges from these diatribes is the positioning of patriarchal, racist, capitalist, hierarchical, and heterosexist "order" and movement against the alleged stagnation and decay of the body of the "Welfare Queen."

Race is clearly written on the body of the poor single mother. The welfare mother, imagined as young, never married, and black (contrary to statistical evidence) is positioned as dangerous and in need of punishment because she "naturally" emasculates her own men, refuses to service white men, and passes on—rather than appropriate codes of subservience and submission—a disruptive culture of resistance, survival, and "misplaced" pride to her children (Collins 2000).[16] In stark contrast, widowed women with social security and divorced women with child support and alimony are imagined as white, legal and propertied mothers whose value rests on their abilities to stay in their homes, care for their own children, and impart traditional cultural mores to their offspring, all for the betterment of the dominant culture. In this narrative welfare mothers have only an "outlaw" culture to impart. Here the welfare mother is read as both the product and the producer of a culture of disease and disorder. These narratives imagine poor women as a powerful contagion capable of infecting, perhaps even lying in wait to infect, their own children as raced, gendered, and classed agents of their "diseased" nature. In contemporary discourses of poverty racial tropes position poor women's bodies as dangerous sites of "naturalized chaos" and as potentially valuable economic commodities who refuse their "proper" roles.

Gary MacDougal in "The Missing Half of the Welfare Debate" furthers this image by referring to the "crab effect of poverty" through which mothers and friends of individuals striving to break free of economic dependency allegedly "pull them back down." MacDougal affirms—again despite statistical evidence to the contrary—that the mothers of welfare recipients are most often themselves "generational welfare freeloaders lacking traditional values and family ties who can not, and will not, teach their children right from wrong." "These women," he asserts, "would be better off doing any kind of labor regardless of how little it pays, just to get them out of the house, to break their cycles of degeneracy" (1995, A16).

In this plenitude of images of evil mothers, the poor welfare mother threatens not just her own children but all children. The Welfare Queen is made to signify moral aberration and economic drain; her figure becomes even more impacted once responsibility for the destruction of the "American Way of Life" is attributed to her. Ronald Brownstein reads her "spider web of dependency" as a "crisis of character development that leads to a morally bankrupt American ideology" (1995, A6).

These representations position welfare mothers' bodies as sites of destruction and as catalysts for a culture of depravity and disobedience; in the process they produce a reading of the writing on the body of the poor woman that calls for further punishment and discipline. In New York City, "Workfare" programs force *lazy* poor women to take a job—"any job"—including working for the city wearing orange surplus prison uniforms picking up garbage on the highway and in parks for about $1.10 per hour (Dreier 1999). "Bridefare" programs in Wisconsin give added benefits to *licentious* welfare women who marry a man—"any man"—and publish a celebration of their "reform" in local newspapers (Dresang 1996). "Tidyfare" programs across

---

[16]In the two years directly preceding the passage of the PRWORA, as a part of sweeping welfare reform, in the United States the largest percentage of people on welfare were white (39 percent), and fewer than 10 percent were teen mothers (U.S. Department of Health and Human Services 1994).

the nation allow state workers to enter and inspect the homes of poor *slovenly* women so that they can monetarily sanction families whose homes are not deemed to be appropriately tidied.[17] "Learnfare" programs in many states publicly expose and fine *undisciplined* mothers who for any reason have children who do not (or cannot) attend school on a regular basis (Muir 1993). All of these welfare reform programs are designed to expose and publicly punish the *misfits* whose bodies are read as proof of their refusal or inability to capitulate to androcentric, capitalist, racist, and heterosexist values and mores.

RESISTING THE TEXT: ON THE LIMITS OF DISCURSIVE CRITIQUE AND THE POWER OF POOR WOMEN'S COMMUNAL RESISTANCE

Despite the rhetoric and policy that mark and mutilate our bodies, poor women survive. Hundreds of thousands of us are somehow good parents despite the systems that are designed to prohibit us from being so. We live on the unlivable and teach our children love, strength, and grace. We network, solve irresolvable dilemmas, and support each other and our families. If we somehow manage to find a decent pair of shoes, or save our food stamps to buy our children a birthday cake, we are accused of being cheats or living too high. If our children suffer, it is read as proof of our inferiority and bad mothering; if they succeed, we are suspect for being too pushy, for taking more than our share of free services, or for having too much free time to devote to them. Yet, as former welfare recipient Janet Diamond says in the introduction to *For Crying Out Loud:* "In spite of public censure, welfare mothers graduate from school, get decent jobs, watch their children achieve, make good lives for themselves. Welfare mothers continue to be my inspiration, not because they survive, but because they dare to dream. Because when you are a welfare recipient, laughter is an act of rebellion" (Dujon and Withorn 1996, 1).

Foucault's later work acknowledges this potential for rebellion inherent in the operation of power. Indeed, in *Power/Knowledge: Selected Interviews and Other Writings* (1980), he positions discourse as an amalgam of material power and nonmaterial knowledge that fosters just such resistance. As Lois McNay points out, for Foucault power is a productive and positive force rather than a purely negative, repressive entity. McNay notes that, for Foucault, "in relation to the body power does not simply repress its unruly forces, rather it incites, instills and produces effects in the body" (1993, 38). She adds: "Resistance arises at the points where power relations are at their most rigid and intense. For Foucault, repression and resistance are not ontologically distinct, rather repression produces its own resistance: 'there are no relations of power without resistance; the latter are all the more real and effective because they are formed right at the point where relations of power are exercised'" (39).

Because power is diffuse, heterogeneous, and contradictory, poor women struggle against the marks of their degradation. Resistance swells in the gaps and interstices of productions of the self. For Foucault, "discourse transmits and produces power; it reinforces it, but also undermines and exposes it, renders it fragile and makes it possible to thwart it" (1978, 101). Yet here we also recognize what McNay refers to as the "critical limitations" of Foucault and of poststructuralism in general. For although bodily inscriptions of poverty are clearly textual, they are

---

[17]"Tidyfare" programs additionally required that caseworkers inventory the belongings of Aid to Families with Dependent Children (AFDC; welfare) recipients so that they could require them to "sell-down" their assets. In my own case, in 1994 a section eight inspector from the U.S. Department of Housing and Urban Development came into my home, counted my daughter's books, checked them against his list to see that as a nine-year-old she was entitled to have only twelve books, calculated what he perceived to be the value of the excess books, and then had my welfare check reduced by that amount in the following month.

also quite physical, immediate, and pressing, devastating the lives of poor women and children in the United States today. Discursive critique is at its most powerful only when it allows us to understand and challenges us to fight together to change the material conditions and bodily humiliations that scar poor women and children in order to keep us all in check.

Poor women rebel by organizing for physical and emotional respite and eventually for political power. My own resistance was born in the space between self-loathing and my love of and respect for poor women who were fighting together against oppression. In the throes of political activism (at first I was dragged blindly into such actions, ironically, in a protest that required, according to the organizer, just so many poor women's bodies) I became caught up in the contradiction between my body's meaning as a despised public sign and our shared sense of communal power, knowledge, authority, and beauty. Learning about labor movements, fighting for rent control, demanding fair treatment at the welfare office, sharing the costs, burdens, and joys of raising children, forming food cooperatives, working with other poor women to go to college, and organizing for political change became addictive and life-affirming acts of resistance. Through shared activism we became increasingly aware of our individual bodies as sites of contestation and of our collective body as a site of resistance and as a source of power.[18]

Noemy Vides, in "Together We Are Getting Freedom," reminds us that "by talking and writing about learned shame together, [poor women] pursue their own liberation" (Vides and Steinitz 1996, 305). Vides adds that it is through this process that she learned to challenge the dominant explanations that decreed her value in the world, "provoking an awareness that the labels—ignorant peasant, abandoned woman, broken-English speaker, welfare cheat—have nothing to do with who one really is, but serve to keep women subjugated and divided. [This communal process] gives women tools to understand the uses of power; it emboldens us to move beyond the imposed shame that silences, to speak out and join together in a common liberatory struggle" (1996, 305).

In struggling together we contest the marks of our bodily inscription, disrupt the use of our bodies as public sign, change the conditions of our lives, and survive.[19] In the process we come to understand that the shaping of our bodies is not coterminous with our beings or abilities as a whole.[20] Contestation and the deployment of new truths cannot erase the marks of our poverty, but the process does transform the ways in which we are able to interrogate and critique our bodies and the systems that have branded them with infamy. As a result these signs are rendered fragile, unstable, and ultimately malleable.

Department of Women's Studies

Hamilton College

---

[18]Communal affiliation among poor women is discouraged, indeed in many cases prohibited, by those with power over our lives. Welfare offices, for example, are designed to prevent poor women from talking together; uncomfortable plastic chairs are secured to the ground in arrangements that make it difficult to communicate, silence is maintained in waiting rooms, case workers are rotated so that they do not become too "attached" to their clients, and, reinforced by "Welfare Fraud" signs covering industrially painted walls, we are daily reminded not to trust anyone with the details of our lives for fear of further exposure and punishment. And so, like most poor women, I had remained isolated, ashamed, and convinced that I was alone in, and responsible for, my suffering.

[19]In the process poor and working poor women begin to see clearly that when we are divided we lose and that when we capitulate to the pressure to engage in the blaming game—where the "have-nots" are pitted against the "have-nothings"—power is allowed to replicate itself, and we remain fragmented, broken, and silenced.

[20]Many questions remain to be addressed. As feminist scholars, it is crucial to consider at what point public punishment forecloses the possibility of resistance, to explore the histories and epistemologies of power and resistance, to appreciate and work to improve the material lives of poor women and children, to make real the connections between our understanding of poor women as subjects and our commitment to them as sisters, and to critique our own exclusionary politics that have allowed us to neglect and to silence this population of women, both in and out of the academy.

REFERENCES

Abramovitz, Mimi. 1988. *Regulating the Lives of Women: Social Welfare Policy from Colonial Times to the Present*. Boston: South End.

——. 2000. *Under Attack, Fighting Back: Women and Welfare in the United States*. New York: Monthly Review.

Albelda, Randy. 1997. *Glass Ceilings and Bottomless Pits: Women's Work, Women's Poverty*. Boston: South End.

Amott, Teresa. 1993. *Caught in the Crisis: Women and the U.S. Economy Today*. New York: Monthly Review.

Anderson, Dale. 1999. "County to Investigate Some Welfare Recipients." *Buffalo News*, August 18, B5.

Ashcroft, John. 1995. "Illegitimacy Rampant." *St. Louis Dispatch*, July 2, A23.

Bell, Shannon. 1994. *Reading, Writing, and Rewriting the Prostitute Body*. Bloomington: Indiana University Press.

Bordo, Susan. 1993. *Unbearable Weight: Feminism, Western Culture, and the Body*. Berkeley: University of California Press.

Brownstein, Ronald. 1995. "Latest Welfare Reform Plan Reflects Liberals' Priorities." *Los Angeles Times*, January 24, A6.

Brush, Pippa. 1998. "Metaphors of Inscription: Discipline, Plasticity and the Rhetoric of Choice." *Feminist Review*, no. 58 (Spring): 22–43.

Chandler, Mielle. 1999. "Queering Maternity." *Journal of the Association for Research on Mothering* 1(2):21–32.

Collins, Patricia Hill. 2000. *Black Feminist Thought: Knowledge, Consciousness, and the Politics of Empowerment*. New York: Routledge.

Crompton, Rosemary, and Michael Mann, eds. 1986. *Gender and Stratification*. New York: Polity.

DeClaire, Joan. 1993. "Body by Barbie." *View*, October, 36–43.

Desmond, Jane. 1991. "Dancing Out the Difference: Cultural Imperialism and Ruth St. Denis's 'Radha' of 1906." *Signs: Journal of Women in Culture and Society* 17(1):28–49.

Dill, Bonnie Thornton, and Bruce Williams. 1992. "Race, Gender and Poverty in the Rural South: African American Single Mothers." In *Rural Poverty in America*, ed. Cynthia M. Duncan, 97–109. New York: Auburn House.

Dreier, Peter. 1999. "Treat Welfare Recipients Like Workers." *Los Angeles Times*, August 29, M6.

Dresang, Joel. 1996. "Bridefare Designer, Reform Beneficiary Have Role in Governor's Address." *Milwaukee Journal Sentinel*, August 14, 9.

Dujon, Diane, and Ann Withorn. 1996. *For Crying Out Loud: Women's Poverty in the United States*. Boston: South End.

Edin, Kathryn, and Laura Lein. 1997. *Making Ends Meet: How Single Mothers Survive Welfare and Low-Wage Work*. New York: Russell Sage.

Ford-Smith, Honor. 1995. "Making White Ladies: Race, Gender and the Production of Identity in Late Colonial Jamaica." *Resources for Feminist Research* 23(4):55–67.

Foucault, Michel. 1978. *The History of Sexuality: An Introduction*. Trans. Robert Hurley. New York: Pantheon.

——. 1980. *Power/Knowledge: Selected Interviews and Other Writings, 1972–1977*. Ed. Collin Gordon. New York: Pantheon.

——. (1977) 1984a. *Discipline and Punish*. In *The Foucault Reader*, ed. Paul Rabinow, 170–256. New York: Pantheon.

——. (1977) 1984b. "Nietzsche, Genealogy, History." In *The Foucault Reader*, ed. Paul Rabinow, 76–99. New York: Pantheon.

Funiciello, Theresa. 1998. "The Brutality of Bureaucracy." In *Race, Class, and Gender: An Anthology*, ed. Margaret L. Andersen and Patricia Hill Collins, 377–81. Belmont, Calif.: Wadsworth.

Gilder, George. 1995. "Welfare Fraud Today." *American Spectator*, September 5, B6.

Gordon, Linda. 1995. *Pitied but Not Entitled: Single Mothers and the History of Welfare, 1890–1935*. New York: Belknap.

hooks, bell. 1999. "Thinking about Race, Class, Gender and Ethics." Presentation at Hamilton College, April 12, Clinton, New York.

Hopwood, Catherine. 1995. "My Discourse/My-self: Therapy as Possibility (For Women Who Eat Compulsively)." *Feminist Review*, no. 49 (Spring): 66–82.

Kingfisher, Catherine. 2000. "Rhetoric of Female Savagery: Welfare Reform in the United States and Aotearoa/New Zealand." *NWSA Journal*, no. 1 (Spring): 1–20.

Langston, Donna. 1998. "Tired of Playing Monopoly?" In *Race, Class, and Gender: An Anthology*, ed. Margaret L. Andersen and Patricia Hill Collins, 126–36. Belmont, Calif.: Wadsworth.

Loprest, Pamela. 1999. "Families Who Left Welfare: Who Are They and How Are They Doing?" Urban Institute, Washington, D.C., August, B1.

Lubiano, Wahneema. 1992. "Black Ladies, Welfare Queens, and State Minstrels: Ideological War by Narrative Means." In *Race-ing Justice, En-gendering Power: Essays on Anita Hill, Clarence Thomas, and the Construction of Social Reality*, ed. Toni Morrison, 323–63. New York: Pantheon.

MacDougal, Gary. 1995. "The Missing Half of the Welfare Debate." *Wall Street Journal*, September 6, A16.

McNay, Lois. 1993. *Foucault and Feminism: Power, Gender, and the Self*. Boston: Northeastern University Press.

Mink, Gwendolyn. 1996. *The Wages of Motherhood: Inequality in the Welfare State, 1917–1942*. Ithaca, N.Y.: Cornell University Press.

——. 1998. *Welfare's End*. Ithaca, N.Y.: Cornell University Press.

Morgan, Kathryn. 1991. "Women and the Knife: Cosmetic Surgery and the Colonization of Women's Bodies." *Hypatia* 6(3):25–53.

Muir, Kate. 1993. "Runaway Fathers at Welfare's Final Frontier." *New York Times*, July 19, A2.

Piven, Frances Fox, and Richard Cloward. 1993. *Regulating the Poor: The Functions of Public Welfare*. New York: Vintage.

Raphael, Jody. 2000. "Saving Bernice: Women, Welfare and Domestic Violence." Presentation at Hamilton College, May 23, Clinton, New York.

Raspberry, William. 1995. "Ms. Smith Goes after Washington." *Washington Post*, February 1, A19.

Robinson, Valerie. 1999. "State's Ad Attacks the Poor." *Plain Dealer*, November 2, B8.

Sennett, Richard, and Jonathan Cobb. 1972. *The Hidden Injuries of Class*. New York: Vintage.

Sidel, Ruth. 1998. *Keeping Women and Children Last: America's War on the Poor*. New York: Penguin.

Simon, Stephanie. 1999. "Unlikely Support for Drug Tests on Welfare Applicants." *Los Angeles Times*, December 18, A1.

Smart, Carol. 1992. *Regulating Womanhood: Historical Essays on Marriage, Motherhood and Sexuality*. New York: Routledge.

Smith-Madsen, Sandy. In press. "From Welfare to Academe: Welfare Reform as College-Educated Welfare Mothers Know It." In *Against All Odds: Women, Poverty and the Promise of*

Education in America, ed. Vivyan Adair and Sandra Dahlberg, 160–86. Philadelphia: Temple University Press.

Steedman, Carolyn Kay. 1987. *Landscape for a Good Woman: A Story of Two Lives*. New Brunswick, N.J.: Rutgers University Press.

Stoler, Ann Laura. 1995. *Race and the Education of Desire: Foucault's History of Sexuality and the Colonial Order of Things*. Durham, N.C.: Duke University Press.

USA Today. 1995. *"America at Risk: Can We Survive without Moral Values?"* USA Today, October 10, C3.

U.S. Department of Health and Human Services. 1994. "An Overview of Entitlement Programs." Washington, D.C.: U.S. Government Printing Office.

Vides, Noemy, and Victoria Steinitz. 1996. "Together We Are Getting Freedom." In Dujon and Withorn 1996, 295–306.

Will, George. 1995. "The Welfare Crisis Is Better Described as a Crisis of Character Development." *Newsweek*, December 12, 88.

Withorn, Ann, and Rochelle Lefkowitz. 1986. *For Crying Out Loud: Women and Poverty in the United States*. New York: Pilgrim Press.

Women's Enews. 2001a. "Civil Rights Bad for Welfare Moms." Mailing list, available on-line at http://www.womensenews.org, May 4.

——. 2001b. "Oregon to Women on Welfare: Dumpster Dive." Mailing list, available on-line at http://www.womensenews.org, May 5.

"Branded with Infamy"

Vivyan C. Adair

1. Consider the opening quote and other first person narratives in the article. What are the physical manifestations of poverty?

2. What are some of the stereotypes of poverty that circulate in the media?

3. How is poverty inscribed on the body?

4. What is the relationship between power and the body? How do poor women's bodies become "public property"? How do women resist this domination?

5. Notice how Adair connects poverty, sexuality and motherhood. What are the characteristics of a "good mother"? How do those differ by socioeconomic class?

6. Find a copy of the Personal Responsibility and Work Opportunity Reconciliation Act (PRWORA) of 1996 online and read Section 101 (http://www.gpo.gov/fdsys/pkg/PLAW-104publ193/html/PLAW-104publ193.htm). Evaluate it as a welfare policy using the information and insights gained from this article. How do the dominant ideas about women, poverty, motherhood, etc. get created and/or reinforced in this public policy? (Use a separate sheet).

Sex(less) Education
The Politics of Abstinence-only Programs in the United States

Stephanie Block

Stephanie Block was a Student Fulbright Scholar in Chile when she developed this article from a report she prepared when she earlier worked as an intern with the Latin American and Caribbean Demographic Center (CELADE), affiliated with the United Nations Population Fund. CELADE developed the first population survey in Latin America and has served as a leader in researching population issues for over 50 years. The article appeared in Women's Health Journal of the Latin American and Caribbean Women's Health Network in 2005.

PRE-READING QUESTIONS

1. Think about your personal experiences with sex-education curricula at your schools. What stands out?
2. Is sex education in schools important? For whom? Why?

KEY TERMS

abstinence
abstinence-only sex education
Adolescent Family Life Act (ADFL)
Advocates for Youth
Center for Disease Control (CDC)
censorship
Christian Right
comprehensive sex education
contraceptive
The Education of Shelby Knox
Just Say No!
HIV/AIDS
Maternal and Child Health (MCH) Bureau

National Education Association (NEA)
Personal Responsibility and Work Opportunity Reconciliation Act (PRWORA)
Section 510(b) of the Social Security Act
Sexuality Information and Education Council of the United States (SIECUS)
sexually transmitted infections (STIs)
Special Projects of Regional and National Significance-Community Based Abstinence Education (SPRANS-CBAE)
Waxman, Henry A.

SEE THE THEMATIC TABLE OF CONTENTS, IF YOU WANT TO READ MORE ESSAYS ABOUT:

Gender and Public Policy
Sexualities

Sex(less) Education
The Politics of Abstinence-only Programs in the United States

Stephanie Block

INTRODUCTION

The United States has the highest rate of teen pregnancy and sexually transmitted infections (STIs) in the industrialized world. Each year, one out of three teenage girls becomes pregnant.[1] Although teen pregnancy rates have dropped from 61.8 births per 1,000 in 1991 to 41.7 births per 1,000 in 2003, pregnancy rates in the U.S. still are declining at slower rates than those in other developed nations.[2]

These sobering statistics are the basis of an ongoing battle: the fight for abstinence-only versus comprehensive sex education. Although proponents of both types of sex education aim to reduce teenage pregnancy and STIs, their approaches vary greatly. Abstinence-only advocates believe that sex before marriage is immoral and harmful; they promote abstinence as the sole option to help young people avoid STIs and teen pregnancy, mentioning condoms and contraceptives only in terms of their failure rates.[3] Abstinence advocates feel that "Americans are not suffering from a lack of knowledge about sex but an absence of values."[4]

In contrast, proponents of comprehensive sex education and abstinence-plus-education promote abstinence as a good method for avoiding pregnancy and STIs but also teach students the benefits of condoms and different contraceptive methods.

Although comprehensive sex education programs have greater recorded success in delaying the age of sexual initiation and in reducing teenage pregnancy, abstinence-only programs have gained increasing political support and federal funding over the past twenty years. This article explores the roots of the abstinence-only movement and its newfound popularity.

A BRIEF HISTORY OF SEX EDUCATION IN THE U.S.

According to a poll by the Alan Guttmacher Institute, 75 percent of parents in the U.S. want their children to receive a variety of information on subjects including contraception and condom

---

[1] International Planned Parenthood Federation, "Country Profiles: The United States," http://www.ippfnet.ippf.org/pub/IPPF_Regions/IPPF_CountryProfile.asp.

[2] Albert R. Hunt, "Beware the Moral Cops," *The Wall Street Journal*, December 2, 2004.

[3] Planned Parenthood of New York City, "Issues and Trends in Reproductive Health: Federal Sex Education Policy," http://www.ppnyc.org/facts/facts/federal_policy.html.

[4] Concerned Women for America, "Abstinence: Why Sex is Worth the Wait," September 2002, http://www.cwfa.org/articledisplay.asp?id=1195&department=CWA&categoryid=family.

use, STIs, sexual orientation and safer sex practices.[5] Given the choice, only one to five percent of parents remove their children from comprehensive sex education programs. Nevertheless, abstinence-only programs continue to gain federal support, despite the absence of evidence proving their effectiveness.

The issue of sex education first arose in the United States in 1912 when the National Education Association called for teacher-training programs on sexuality education. The issue resurfaced in 1940 when the U.S. Public Health Service strongly advocated sexuality education in the schools, calling it an "urgent need." By 1953, the American School Health Association launched a nationwide program in "family life education." Two years later, the American Medical Association and the National Education Association worked together to publish pamphlets for schools commonly referred to as "the sex education series."[6]

By the 1960s, all leading public health organizations were calling for sex education in America's schools, and by the 1970s, sex education's most vocal opponents had united: the political and the Christian Right. Alarmed by growing sexual promiscuity and the breakdown of what is considered 'traditional' values, the Christian Crusade, an early expression of right-wing Christianity, aimed to bar sex education from schools, calling it "smut" and "raw sex." The John Birch Society, political allies of the Christian Right, called the effort to teach sexuality "a filthy Communist plot," and Phyllis Schlafly, the leader of the far-right Eagle Forum, argued that sex education increased sexual activity among teens.[7]

The war over sexual education had begun, and for many years, social conservatives lost. Evidence showing that sex education programs delay sexual activity and decrease teen pregnancy helped such initiatives gain widespread support. By 1983, sexuality education was being taught within the context of more comprehensive family life education programs. Courses emphasizing not only reproduction but also the importance of self-esteem, responsibility and decision making spread across the nation.

However, the arrival of the HIV/AIDS epidemic in the 1980s forever changed the sex education debate. In 1986, U.S. Surgeon General C. Everett Koop issued a report calling for comprehensive HIV/AIDS and sexuality education in public schools beginning as early as the third grade. "There is now no doubt that we need sex education in schools . . . The need is critical, and the price of neglect is high," he said. Even social conservatives could no longer deny the need to educate U.S. teens. Accordingly, the Christian Right changed its strategy from denouncing "sex ed" altogether to advocating *abstinence-only education*.[8]

The Christian Right—an umbrella group of conservative Christians that unites behind shared causes—includes evangelicals, Pentecostals and other conservative Protestants and conservative Roman Catholics. The focus of their campaign—the "values clarification movement"—can be defined broadly as defending "traditional Christian values such as the authority of the Bible in all

> Abstinence-only advocates believe that sex before marriage is immoral and harmful; they promote abstinence as the sole option to help young people avoid STIs and teen pregnancy, mentioning condoms and contraceptives only in terms of their failure rates.

---

[5]Planned Parenthood Federation of America, "Abstinence Only 'Sex' Education," http://www.plannedparenthood.org/pp2/portal/files/portal/medicalinfo/teensexualhealth/factabstinence-education.xml.
[6]Priscilla Pardini, "The History of Sexuality Education." *Rethinking Schools Online* (Summer 1998), http://www.rethinkingschools.org/archive/12_04/sexhisto.shtml.
[7]Ibid.
[8]Priscilla Pardini, "Abstinence-Only Education Continues to Flourish," *Rethinking Schools Online* (Summer 1998), http://www.rethinkingschools.org/archive/12_04/sexhisto1.shtml.

areas of life."[9] This position includes banning or heavily restricting abortion; banning stem cell research with human embryos; fighting the gay-rights movement; supporting the presence of Christianity in the public sphere (i.e., prayer in schools and the teaching of creationism); ending government funding restrictions against religious charities and schools; opposing U.S. court decisions on the separation of Church and State; and censoring books, music, television programs and films that they view as "indecent."[10]

Through grassroots organizing the Christian Right has become a powerful political force and an important base of support for the Republican Party.[11] According to a study in the Washington magazine *Campaigns and Elections*, Christian conservatives now exercise either "strong" or "moderate" influence in 44 Republican state committees, as compared with 31 committees in 1994. Their control is "weak" only in six states, all in the north-east of the country. Ralph Reed, the Christian Coalition leader until 1997, now runs the Georgia Republican party.[12] Before the 2004, presidential elections, Reverend Jerry Falwell, one of the Christian Coalition's principal leaders, stated that "the Republican Party does not have the head count to elect a president without the support of religious conservatives." Evangelical Christians are now by far the largest constituency within the Republican Party, Falwell continued, and "if the candidate running for president is not pro-life, pro-family . . . [he's] not going to win."[13]

In fact, a Republican did win: President George W. Bush, an evangelical Christian, fully committed to his socially conservative constituency. Since 2000, Bush has appointed at least five abstinence-only proponents to key government posts, including Dr. Joe McIlhaney to the Advisory Committee of the Center for Disease Control (CDC). In the 1990s, the Texas Commission of Health questioned McIlhaney's accountability, finding that his presentations on STIs were misleading. Bush also has pressured the CDC into supporting an abstinence-only stance even though every public agency responsible for disseminating health and sexuality education information recommends comprehensive education. In 2002, a list of sexuality education "Programs that Work" disappeared from the CDC's website because they were not abstinence-only.[14] Increasingly, public health organizations that support comprehensive sex education have become subject to government harassment—both SIECUS and Advocates for Youth have been audited with unusual frequency over the past years.[15]

Alarmed by the government's growing financial support for untested abstinence-only programs, Democratic Representative Henry A. Waxman ordered a minority staff report entitled *The Content of Federally Funded Abstinence-Only Education Programs* in December 2004. The report found that abstinence-only programs contained false information about the effectiveness of contraceptives and the risks of abortion; that they blurred religion and science and included scientific errors; and that they treated stereotypes about girls and boys as scientific fact.[16] Worse still, abstinence programs

---

[9]Grant Walker, "The Christian Right" (Duke University Divinity School National Humanities Center), http://www.nhc.rtp.nc.us/tserve/twenty/tkeyinfo/chr_rght.htm.

[10]Wikipedia, "The Christian Right," http://en.wikipedia.org/wiki/Christian_right.

[11]Planned Parenthood Federation of America, op. cit.

[12]"A Conservative President Has More Problems with One Section of his Party's Right-Wing Base Than You May Think," *The Economist*, May 2003, http://www.economist.com/world/na/printerfriendly.cfm?story_ID=1781279.

[13]Scott Shepard, "Falwell Says Evangelical Christians Now in Control of Republican Party," *Cox News Service*, September 2004, http://www.signonsandiego.com/uniontrib/20040925/news_1n25christ.html.

[14]Kate Petre, "The Sexual Miseducation of the American Teen," *Los Angeles City Beat*, January 2005, http://www.lacitybeat.com/article.php?id=1541&IssueNum=84.

[15]Ibid.

[16]Henry A. Waxman, *The Content of Federally Funded Abstinence-Only Education Programs* (United States House of Representatives Committee on Government Reform—Minority Staff Special Investigations Division, December 2004), http://www.democrats.reform.house.gov.

ignored the reality that more than 80 percent of all people in the U.S. have intercourse before marriage and that more than half of all U.S. adolescents are sexually active by the age of 18.[17]

There is no evidence that young people who participate in abstinence-only programs delay sexual intercourse longer than others. However, when they do become sexually active, adolescents who have received abstinence-only education often fail to use condoms or other contraceptives. In fact, 88 percent of students who pledged virginity in middle and high school still engage in premarital sex. Students who break this pledge are less likely to use contraception at first intercourse, and they have similar rates of STIs as non-pledgers. Meanwhile, students in comprehensive sexuality education courses do not engage in sexual activity more often or earlier, but they do use contraception and practice safer sex more consistently once they are sexually active.[18]

FEDERAL SUPPORT FOR ABSTINENCE-ONLY EDUCATION

Since the 1960s, social conservatives have united with the Republican Party to push an abstinence-only agenda. By steadily increasing federal funding, Republicans aim to implement abstinence-only education on a national scale. Both health organizations and policy-makers opposed to abstinence-only education are working together to overcome growing government support for abstinence-only education, but the future of sexuality education in the U.S. is uncertain. It seems that as long as the Christian Right continues to wield great influence over the Republican policy, federal funding for abstinence-only education will flow.

A Republican government first invested in abstinence-only education in 1981, when the U.S. Office of Population Affairs began administering the Adolescent Family Life Act (AFLA), known as the "Chastity Act." Designed to promote "self-discipline and other prudent approaches to the problem of adolescent premarital sexual relations," it allocated US$11 million in grants to public and nonprofit organizations promoting chastity and providing care to pregnant adolescents and teen parents.

Soon after the initiation of the program, the national debate over the legality of abstinence-only programs began. Because AFLA often promoted specific religious values, the American Civil Liberties Union filed suit in 1983, charging that AFLA violated the separation of Church and State.[19] In 1985, a U.S. district judge found AFLA unconstitutional, but on appeal in 1988, the U.S. Supreme Court reversed the decision and remanded the case to a lower court. In 1993, an out-of-court settlement stipulated that AFLA could continue functioning so long as its sexuality education programs: 1) did not include religious references; 2) were medically accurate; 3) respected the "principle of self-determination" regarding contraceptive referral for teenagers; and 4) did not allow grantees to use church premises for their programs or to give presentations in parochial schools during school hours. Within these limitations, AFLA continues to finance abstinence-only education. In 2000, it disbursed US$19 million in federal funds.[20]

> Nevertheless, abstinence-only programs continue to gain federal support, despite the absence of evidence proving their effectiveness.

Fifteen years later in 1996, a new abstinence-only program was passed surreptitiously as part of welfare reform. During the final version of the Welfare Reform Act, when only small corrections and technical revisions normally are made, conservative members of Congress quietly

[17]Petre, op. cit.
[18]Planned Parenthood Federation of America, op. cit.
[19]Advocates For Youth, "Abstinence-Only-Until-Marriage Programs: History of Government Funding," http://www.advocatesfromyouth.org/rrr/history.htm.
[20]Ibid.

inserted a provision for abstinence-only education into the sweeping bill. The authors of the provision aimed to "put Congress on the side of social tradition—never mind that some observers now think the tradition outdated—that sex should be confined to married couples. That both the practices and standards in many communities across the country clash with the standard required by the law is precisely the point."[21]

Never openly discussed by the public nor in Congress, Section 510(b) of the Social Security Act was approved as part of the expansive Personal Responsibility and Work Opportunity Reconciliation Act (PRWORA) and signed into law by President Clinton. The provision guaranteed US$50 million in annual funding for abstinence-only education grants to the states over five years (1998–2002) although funding has been extended every year since the date of expiration. Funds under this program are awarded through the Maternal and Child Health (MCH) Bureau and allocated to states based on a federal formula related to the number of low-income children in each state. States must contribute three dollars for every four dollars of federal money.[22]

For the purposes of the legislation, the term "abstinence education" means an educational or motivational program that:

"Just Say No!"

EXAMPLES OF ABSTINENCE-ONLY EDUCATION IN THE UNITED STATES

- **Public funds go to religious institutions for anti-sexuality education.** In Montana, the Catholic diocese of Helena received US$14,000 from the state's Department of Health & Human Services for classes in the "Assets for Abstinence." In Louisiana, a network of pastors is bringing the abstinence-only message to religious congregations with public funds, and the Governor's Program on Abstinence appointed regional coordinators and other staff members from such religious organizations as the Baptist Collegiate Ministries, Rapides Station Community Ministries, Diocese of Lafayette, Revolution Ministries, Caring to Love Ministries, All Saints Crusade Foundation, Concerned Christian Women of Livingston, Catholic Charities, Christian Counseling Center and Community Christian Concern.

- **Public schools host "chastity" events.** In California, Pennsylvania, Alabama and many other states, schools regularly host chastity pledges and rallies on school premises during school hours. During these rituals, students often pledge "to God" that they will remain abstinent until they marry.

- **Textbooks are censored.** The Texas State Board of Education approved the purchase of new health textbooks that exclusively promote abstinence. As Texas is the second largest buyer of textbooks in the United States, it is likely that these same books will appear in classrooms throughout the nation. The school board in Franklin County, North Carolina, ordered three chapters literally sliced out of a ninth-grade health textbook because the material did not adhere to state law mandating abstinence-only education. The chapters covered AIDS and other sexually transmitted infections, marriage and partnering, and contraception. In Lynchburg, Virginia, school board members refused to approve a high school science textbook unless an illustration of a vagina was covered or cut out.

---

[21]SIECUS, Sexuality Information and Education Council of the United States, "Exclusive Purpose: Abstinence-Only Proponents Create Federal Entitlement in Welfare Reform," *SIECUS Report* 24: 4. Available online at http://www.siecus.org/policy/sreport/srep0001.html.
[22]Ibid., 2.

- **Crucial health programs are canceled.** A petition from 28 parents resulted in the cancellation of a highly regarded, comprehensive AIDS-prevention presentation for high-school students in the Syracuse, New York, area given by the local AIDS Task Force. In Illinois, critics blasted a U.S. Centers for Disease Control and Prevention program called "Reducing the Risk," because they claim it was inconsistent with an abstinence-only message.
- **Sexuality education teachers are disciplined for doing their jobs.** In Belton, Missouri, a seventh-grade health teacher was suspended when a parent complained that she had discussed "inappropriate" sexual matters in class. The teacher had answered a student's query about oral sex. In Orlando, Florida, a teacher was suspended when he showed a student-made videotape called *Condom Man and his K-Y Commandos* about preventing AIDS transmission.
- **Teachers are threatened with lawsuits; student journalists intimidated.** In Granite Bay, California, an article in the student paper prompted charges that a sexuality education teacher engaged in "sexual misconduct" and threats of a lawsuit against the teacher and the paper's faculty adviser. The article took the position that newly mandated abstinence-only education was doing nothing to stop either sexual activity or widespread sexual ignorance among students. In Santa Clarita, California, a high-school principal censored from the student paper an article entitled "Sex: Raw and Uncensored." The article was actually about the benefits of abstinence and methods of safer sex.
- **Students suffer from ignorance.** Comprehensive, medically accurate sexuality education is becoming the exception rather than the rule. As a result, more students lack basic information. In Granite Bay, one student asked where his cervix was, and another inquired if she could become pregnant from oral sex. Students in New York City protested that the increased focus on abstinence-only has curtailed access to education about HIV/AIDS. The Colorado Council of Black Nurses decided to return $16,000 in abstinence-only funding because the program "was just too restrictive. It did not teach responsible sexual behavior."

*From the website of the Planned Parenthood Federation of America, http://www.plannedparenthood.org

A. has the exclusive purpose of teaching the social, physiological and health gains to be realized by abstaining from sexual activity;

B. teaches abstinence from sexual activity outside marriage as the expected standard for all school-age children;

C. teaches that abstinence from sexual activity is the only certain way to avoid out-of-wedlock pregnancy, sexually transmitted diseases and other associated health problems;

D. teaches that a mutually faithful, monogamous relationship in the context of marriage is the expected standard of human sexual activity;

E. teaches that sexual activity outside of the context of marriage is likely to have harmful psychological and physical effects;

F. teaches that bearing children out-of-wedlock is likely to have harmful consequences for the child, the child's parents and society;

G. teaches young people how to reject sexual advances and how alcohol and drug use increases vulnerability to sexual advances; and

H. teaches the importance of attaining self-sufficiency before engaging in sexual activity.[23]

[23]Cynthia Dailard, "Abstinence Promotion and Teen Family Planning: The Misguided Drive for Equal Funding," *The Guttmacher Report on Public Policy* 5:1 (February 2002): 2, http://www.guttmacher.org/pubs/tgr/05/1/gr050101.html.

While grant recipients of Section 510(b) are not required to emphasize equally all eight points listed above, the information they provide cannot be inconsistent with any of them. Because the first element requires that programs have the "exclusive purpose" of promoting abstinence outside of marriage, programs may not in any way advocate contraceptive use or discuss contraceptive methods except to emphasize their failure rates.[24]

> There is no evidence that young people who participate in abstinence-only programs delay sexual intercourse longer than others. However, when they do become sexually active, adolescents who have received abstinence-only education often fail to use condoms or other contraceptives.

Nevertheless, it is up to each state to decide whether to implement abstinence education in the way that the federal government intends it to be used. States may either administer the programs themselves directly, or they can award grants to nonprofit, private, faith-based or public organizations. While some states narrowly interpret the definition of abstinence-only education, others have been more flexible, circumventing an exclusive focus on abstinence education by funding programs that include tutoring, career counseling and community service.[25]

Displeased by individual states' loose interpretation of abstinence education, Congress passed new—and far more restrictive—legislation under President Bush in 2000. The Special Programs of Regional and National Significance-Community Based Abstinence Education grants (SPRANS-CBAE) are awarded directly by the federal government to community-based organizations that teach abstinence only to youth, completely avoiding state intervention.[26] Programs awarded SPRANS funds must adhere to a far stricter definition of abstinence education. While programs receiving Section 510(b) funds only must be *consistent* with the eight-point definition of abstinence-only education, SPRANS recipients must be *responsive* to them, directly addressing each of the points.

Since its inception, SPRANS has become the largest and fastest growing source of abstinence-only education. The program awards two types of grants: one-year planning grants that range from US$50,000 to 75,000 and three-year implementation grants that range from US$250,000 to 1 million.[27] In its first year of funding (Fiscal Year 2001), SPRANS received US$20 million for grants to 33 organizations. A year later, the amount doubled to US$40 million. By 2004, the program had over 100 grantees and a budget of US$75 million. The current funding for SPRANS is US$104 million, a 30% increase since last year, although President Bush originally asked for US$186 million for the program.[28]

There is no sign that support for abstinence-only education will taper off any time soon; federal funding for abstinence education in FY 2005 reached US$167 million—more than twice its original funding in 1996 but far less than the US$270 million proposed by President Bush. Although there is no proof that abstinence education has any effect on reducing rates of teenage pregnancy or sexually transmitted infections, abstinence-only programs continue to obtain federal funding.[29]

---

[24]Ibid.
[25]Planned Parenthood of New York City, op. cit.
[26]Ibid.
[27]Chris Collins, Priya Alagiri and Todd Summers, *Abstinence Only vs. Comprehensive Sex Education* (Policy Monograph Series, San Francisco: AIDS Policy Research Center & Center for AIDS Prevention Studies, 2002) 6.
[28]Waxman, op. cit., 2.
[29]Ibid.

The Education of Shelby Knox

In "The Education of Shelby Knox," a new film by Marion Lipschutz and Rose Rosenblatt, 15-year-old Knox pledges to abstain from sexual relations until marriage. She celebrates her decision with her parents, pastor and peers in a ceremony at her Baptist church in Lubbock, Texas. But Knox's life takes an unexpected turn when she discovers that the rates of teen pregnancy and sexually transmitted diseases in her county are among the highest in the state.

Convinced that her high school's abstinence-only policy is keeping teens in the dark, Knox becomes an advocate for comprehensive sex education. The filmmakers follow Knox as she persuades her city-sponsored youth group to take up the cause and as she weathers the resulting media storm with aplomb.

In heart-to-hearth talks with her evangelical pastor, Knox struggles to convey that she has not abandoned her faith. Rather, she has embraces the Christian values of compassion and respect for difference. But the film's moist poignant moments are Knox's searching discussions with her parents who gently point out the ramifications of her decisions but never withdraw their support, even when they disagree.

*From: Elizabeth Coleman, "Unlikely Advocate," Ford Foundation Report, Spring/Summer 2005. For more information, visit http// www.pbs.org/pov/pov2005/shelbyknox.

CONCLUSION

The debate over sexuality education represents democracy at work with all of its virtues and flaws. Abstinence-only education is not popular among the majority of Americans. No scientific evidence has shown its effectiveness; if anything, abstinence education is probably harmful, causing a decrease in condom and contraceptive use once teens do initiate sexual activity. Nevertheless, because it is a pet cause of an important Republican Party constituency, it enjoys widespread political support. The only way to win the war of abstinence versus comprehensive sex education is through politics. Those who oppose abstinence-only education must make their voices as loud and as demanding as the voices of those of who support it.

Sex(less) Education
The Politics of Abstinence-only Programs in the United States

Stephanie Block

1. What are the different forms of sex education? How are they distinct?

2. What are the different ways the federal government is involved in sex education?

3. How is the notion of "democracy" related to differing views on sex education?

4. What does the politics surrounding sex-education teach us about gender and sexuality norms prevalent in society?

5. Create a set of talking points for a school board meeting to inform them and persuade them to adopt your ideal sex education curriculum.

Toward a New Vision
Race, Class, and Gender as Categories of Analysis and Connection

Patricia Hill Collins

Patricia Hill Collins is a distinguished University Professor of Sociology at the University of Maryland. She earned her PhD at Brandeis University. Her research examines the intersections of race, gender, class, sexuality and nation in several books including Black Feminist Thought: Knowledge, Consciousness, and the Politics of Empowerment *(1990) and* Black Sexual Politics: African Americans, Gender, and the New Racism *(2004). This piece was delivered as the keynote address at the Workshop on Integrating Race and Gender into the College Curriculum at Memphis State University in 1989 and appeared in* Race, Sex & Class: an Interdisciplinary Journal *(1993).*

PRE-READING QUESTIONS

1. What do you thinkthe relationship is between race, class and gender?
2. Read the opening quote by Audre Lorde. What is your interpretation?

KEY TERMS

coalitions around common causes
cumulative effect of oppression
dichotomous thinking
empathy
individual dimension of oppression
institutionof patriarchy
institutional dimension of oppression
interlocking structures of oppression
oppression
power
privilege
social change
symbolic dimension of oppression

SEE THE THEMATIC TABLE OF CONTENTS, IF YOU WANT TO READ MORE ESSAYS ABOUT:

Feminism and Social Movements
Privilege, Identities and Intersectionalities

Toward a New Vision
Race, Class, and Gender as Categories of Analysis and Connection

Patricia Hill Collins

The true focus of revolutionary change is never merely the oppressive situations which we seek to escape, but that piece of the oppressor which is planted deep within each of us.

—AUDRE LORDE, *Sister Outsider,* 123

Audre Lorde's statement raises a troublesome issue for scholars and activists working for social change. While many of us have little difficulty assessing our own victimization within some major system of oppression, whether it be by race, social class, religion, sexual orientation, ethnicity, age or gender, we typically fail to see how our thoughts and actions uphold someone else's subordination. Thus, white feminists routinely point with confidence to their oppression as women but resist seeing how much their white skin privileges them. African-Americans who possess eloquent analyses of racism often persist in viewing poor White women as symbols of white power. The radical left fares little better. "If only people of color and women could see their true class interests," they argue, "class solidarity would eliminate racism and sexism." In essence, each group identifies the type of oppression with which it feels most comfortable as being fundamental and classifies all other types as being of lesser importance.

Oppression is full of such contradictions. Errors in political judgment that we make concerning how we teach our courses, what we tell our children, and which organizations are worthy of our time, talents and financial support flow smoothly from errors in theoretical analysis about the nature of oppression and activism. Once we realize that there are few pure victims or oppressors, and that each one of us derives varying amounts of penalty and privilege from the multiple systems of oppression that frame our lives, then we will be in a position to see the need for new ways of thought and action.

To get at that "piece of the oppressor which is planted deep within each of us," we need at least two things. First, we need new visions of what oppression is, new categories of analysis that are inclusive of race, class, and gender as distinctive yet interlocking structures of oppression. Adhering to a stance of comparing and ranking oppressions—the proverbial, "I'm more oppressed than you"—locks us all into a dangerous dance of competing for attention, resources, and theoretical supremacy. Instead, I suggest that we examine our different experiences within the more fundamental relationship of domination and subordination. To focus on the particular arrangements that race or class or gender takes in our time and place without seeing these structures as sometimes parallel and sometimes interlocking dimensions of the more fundamental relationship of domination and subordination may temporarily ease our consciences. But while such thinking may lead to short-term social reforms, it is simply inadequate for the task of bringing about long-term social transformation.

While race, class and gender as categories of analysis are essential in helping us understand the structural bases of domination and subordination, new ways of thinking that are not accompanied by new ways of acting offer incomplete prospects for change. To get at that "piece of the oppressor which is planted deep within each of us," we also need to change our daily behavior. Currently, we are all enmeshed in a complex web of problematic relationships that grant our mirror images full human subjectivity while stereotyping and objectifying those most different than ourselves. We often assume that the people we work with, teach, send our children to school with, and sit next to . . . will act and feel in prescribed ways because they belong to given race, social class or gender categories. [These judgments by category relationships that transcend the legitimate differences created by race, class and gender as categories of analysis.] We require new categories of connection, new visions of what our relationships with one another can be. . . .

[This discussion] addresses this need for new patterns of thought and action. I focus on two basic questions. First, how can we reconceptualize race, class and gender as categories of analysis? Second, how can we transcend the barriers created by our experiences with race, class and gender oppression in order to build the types of coalitions essential for social exchange? To address these questions I contend that we must acquire both new theories of how race, class and gender have shaped the experiences not just of women of color, but of all groups. Moreover, we must see the connections between the categories of analysis and the personal issues in our everyday lives, particularly our scholarship, our teaching and our relationships with our colleagues and students. As Audre Lorde points out, change starts with self, and relationships that we have with those around us must always be the primary site for social change.

HOW CAN WE RECONCEPTUALIZE RACE, CLASS AND GENDER AS CATEGORIES OF ANALYSIS?

To me, we must shift our discourse away from additive analyses of oppression (Spelman, 1982; Collins, 1989). Such approaches are typically based on two key premises. First, they depend on either/or, dichotomous thinking. Persons, things and ideas are conceptualized in terms of their opposites. For example, Black/White, man/woman, thought/feeling, and fact/opinion are defined in oppositional terms. Thought and feeling are not seen as two different and interconnected ways of approaching truth that can coexist in scholarship and teaching. Instead, feeling is defined as antithetical to reason, as its opposite. In spite of the fact that we all have "both/and" identities (I am both a college professor and a mother—I don't stop being a mother when I drop my child off at school, or forget everything I learned while scrubbing the toilet), we persist in trying to classify each other in either/or categories. I live each day as an African-American woman—a race/gender specific experience. And I am not alone. Everyone has a race/gender/class specific identity. Either/or, dichotomous thinking is especially troublesome when applied to theories of oppression because every individual must be classified as being either oppressed or not oppressed. The both/and position of simultaneously being oppressed and oppressor becomes conceptually impossible.

A second premise of additive analyses of oppression is that these dichotomous differences must be ranked. One side of the dichotomy is typically labeled dominant and the other subordinate. Thus, Whites rule Blacks, men are deemed superior to women, and reason is seen as being preferable to emotion. Applying this premise to discussions of oppression leads to the assumption that oppression can be quantified, and that some groups are oppressed more than others. I am frequently asked, "Which has been most oppressive to you, your status as a Black person or your status as a woman?" What I am really being asked to do is divide myself into little boxes and rank my various statuses. If I experience oppression as a both/and phenomenon, why should I analyze it any differently?

Additive analyses of oppression rest squarely on the twin pillars of either/or thinking and the necessity to quantify and rank all relationships in order to know where one stands. Such approaches typically see African-American women as being more oppressed than everyone else because the majority of Black women experience the negative effects of race, class and gender oppression simultaneously. In essence, if you add together separate oppressions, you are left with a grand oppression greater than the sum of its parts.

I am not denying that specific groups experience oppression more harshly than others—lynching is certainly objectively worse than being held up as a sex object. But we must be careful not to confuse this issue of the saliency of one type of oppression in people's lives with a theoretical stance positing the interlocking nature of oppression. Race, class and gender may all structure a situation but may not be equally visible and/or important in people's self-definitions. In certain contexts, such as the antebellum American South and contemporary South America, racial oppression is more visibly salient, while in other contexts, such as Haiti, El Salvador and Nicaragua, social class oppression may be more apparent. For middle-class White women, gender may assume experiential primacy unavailable to poor Hispanic women struggling with the ongoing issues of low-paid jobs and the frustrations of the welfare bureaucracy. This recognition that one category may have salience over another for a given time and place does not minimize the theoretical importance of assuming that race, class and gender as categories of analysis structure all relationships.

In order to move toward new visions of what oppression is, I think that we need to ask new questions. How are relationships of domination and subordination structured and maintained in the American political economy? How do race, class and gender function as parallel and interlocking systems that shape this basic relationship of domination and subordination? Questions such as these promise to move us away from futile theoretical struggles concerned with ranking oppressions and towards analyses that assume race, class and gender are all present in any given setting, even if one appears more visible and salient than the others. Our task becomes redefined as one of reconceptualizing oppression by uncovering the connections among race, class and gender as categories of analysis.

I. The Institutional Dimension of Oppression

Sandra Harding's contention that gender oppression is structured along three main dimensions—the institutional, the symbolic and the individual—offers a useful model for a more comprehensive analysis encompassing race, class and gender oppression (Harding 1986). Systemic relationships of domination and subordination structured through social institutions such as schools, businesses, hospitals, the workplace and government agencies represent the institutional dimension of oppression. Racism, sexism, and elitism all have concrete institutional locations. Even though the workings of the institutional dimension of oppression are often obscured with ideologies claiming equality of opportunity, in actuality, race, class and gender place Asian-American women, Native American men, White men, African-American women and other groups in distinct institutional niches with varying degrees of penalty and privilege.

Even though I realize that many . . . would not share this assumption, let us assume that the institutions of American society discriminate, whether by design or by accident. While many of us are familiar with how race, gender and class operate separately to structure inequality, I want to focus on how these three systems interlock in structuring the institutional dimension of oppression. To get at the interlocking nature of race, class and gender, I want you to think about the antebellum plantation as a guiding metaphor for a variety of American social institutions. Even though slavery is typically analyzed as a racist institution, and occasionally as a class institution, I suggest that slavery was a race, class, gender specific institution. Removing any one piece from our analysis diminishes our understanding of the true nature of relations of domination and subordination under slavery.

Slavery was a profoundly patriarchal institution. It rested on the dual tenets of White male authority and White male property, a joining of the political and the economic within the institution of the family. Heterosexism was assumed and all Whites were expected to marry. Control over affluent White women's sexuality remained key to slavery's survival because property was to be passed on to the legitimate heirs of the slave owner. Ensuring affluent White women's virginity and chastity was deeply intertwined with maintenance of property relations.

Under slavery, we see varying levels of institutional protection given to affluent White women, working class and poor White women and enslaved African women. Poor White women enjoyed few of the protections held out to their upper class sisters. Moreover, the devalued status of Black women was key in keeping all White women in their assigned places. Controlling Black women's fertility was also key to the continuation of slavery, for children born to slave mothers themselves were slaves.

African-American women shared the devalued status of chattel with their husbands, fathers and sons. Racism stripped Blacks as a group of legal rights, education and control over their own persons. African-Americans could be whipped, branded, sold, or killed, not because they were poor, or because they were women, but because they were Black. Racism ensured that Blacks would continue to serve Whites and suffer economic exploitation at the hands of all Whites.

So we have a very interesting chain of command on the plantation—the affluent White master as the reigning patriarch, his White wife helpmate to serve him, help him manage his property and bring up his heirs, his faithful servants whose production and reproduction were tied to the requirements of the capitalist political economy and largely propertyless, working class White men and women watching from afar. In essence, the foundations for the contemporary roles of elite White women, poor Black women, working class White men and a series of other groups can be seen in stark relief in this fundamental American social institution. While Blacks experienced the most harsh treatment under slavery, and thus made slavery clearly visible as a racist institution, race, class and gender interlocked in structuring slavery's systemic organization of domination and subordination.

Even today, the plantation remains a compelling metaphor for institutional oppression. Certainly the actual conditions of oppression are not as severe now as they were then. To argue, as some do, that things have not changed all that much denigrates the achievements of those who struggled for social change before us. But the basic relationships among Black men, Black women, elite White women, elite White men, working class White men and working class White women as groups remain essentially intact.

A brief analysis of key American social institutions most controlled by elite White men should convince us of the interlocking nature of race, class and gender in structuring the institutional dimension of oppression. For example, if you are from an American college or university, is your campus a modern plantation? Who controls your university's political economy? Are elite White men overrepresented among the upper administrators and trustees controlling your university's finances and policies? Are elite White men being joined by growing numbers of elite White women helpmates? What kinds of people are in your classrooms grooming the next generation who will occupy these and other decision-making positions? Who are the support staff that produce the mass mailings, order the supplies, fix the leaky pipes? Do African-Americans, Hispanics or other people of color form the majority of the invisible workers who feed you, wash your dishes, and clean up your offices and libraries after everyone else has gone home?

If your college is anything like mine, you know the answers to these questions. You may be affiliated with an institution that has Hispanic women as vice-presidents for finance, or substantial numbers of Black men among the faculty. If so, you are fortunate. Much more typical are colleges where a modified version of the plantation as a metaphor for the institutional dimension of oppression survives.

2. The Symbolic Dimension of Oppression

Widespread, societally sanctioned ideologies used to justify relations of domination and subordination comprise the symbolic dimension of oppression. Central to this process is the use of stereotypical or controlling images of diverse race, class and gender groups. In order to assess the power of this dimension of oppression, I want you to make a list, either on paper or in your head, of "masculine" and "feminine" characteristics. If your list is anything like that compiled by most people, it reflects some variation of the following:

Masculine	Feminine
aggressive	passive
leader	follower
rational	emotional
strong	weak
intellectual	physical

Not only does this list reflect either/or dichotomous thinking and the need to rank both sides of the dichotomy, but ask yourself exactly which men and women you had in mind when compiling these characteristics. This list applies almost exclusively to middle class White men and women. The allegedly "masculine" qualities that you probably listed are only acceptable when exhibited by elite White men, or when used by Black and Hispanic men against each other or against women of color. Aggressive Black and Hispanic men are seen as dangerous, not powerful, and are often penalized when they exhibit any of the allegedly "masculine" characteristics. Working class and poor White men fare slightly better and are also denied the allegedly "masculine" symbols of leadership, intellectual competence, and human rationality. Women of color and working class and poor White women are also not represented on this list, for they have never had the luxury of being "ladies." What appear to be universal categories representing all men and women instead are unmasked as being applicable to only a small group.

It is important to see how the symbolic images applied to different race, class and gender groups interact in maintaining systems of domination and subordination. If I were to ask you to repeat the same assignment, only this time, by making separate lists for Black men, Black women, Hispanic women and Hispanic men, I suspect that your gender symbolism would be quite different. In comparing all of the lists, you might begin to see the interdependence of symbols applied to all groups. For example, the elevated images of White womanhood need devalued images of Black womanhood in order to maintain credibility.

While the above exercise reveals the interlocking nature of race, class and gender in structuring the symbolic dimension of oppression, part of its importance lies in demonstrating how race, class and gender pervade a wide range of what appears to be universal language. Attending to diversity in our scholarship, in our teaching, and in our daily lives provides a new angle of vision on interpretations of reality thought to be natural, normal and "true." Moreover, viewing images of masculinity and femininity as universal gender symbolism, rather than as symbolic images that are race, class and gender specific, renders the experiences of people of color and of nonprivileged White women and men invisible. One way to dehumanize an individual or group is to deny the reality of their experiences. So when we refuse to deal with race or class because they do not appear to be directly relevant to gender, we are actually becoming part of someone else's problem.

Assuming that everyone is affected differently by the same interlocking set of symbolic images allows us to move forward toward new analyses. Women of color and White women have different relations to White male authority and this difference explains the distinct gender symbolism applied to both groups. Black women encounter controlling images such as the mammy, the matriarch, the mule and the whore, that encourage others to reject us as fully human people. Ironically, the negative nature of these images simultaneously encourages us to reject them. In contrast, White women are offered seductive images, those that promise to reward them for supporting the status quo. And yet seductive images can be equally controlling. Consider, for example, the views of Nancy White, a 73-year-old Black woman, concerning images of rejection and seduction:

> My mother used to say that the black woman is the white man's mule and the white woman is his dog. Now, she said that to say this: we do the heavy work and get beat whether we do it well or not. But the white woman is closer to the master and he pats them on the head and lets them sleep in the house, but he ain't gon' treat neither one like he was dealing with a person. (Gwaltney, 148)

Both sets of images stimulate particular political stances. By broadening the analysis beyond the confines of race, we can see the varying levels of rejection and seduction available to each of us due to our race, class and gender identity. Each of us lives with an allotted portion of institutional privilege and penalty, and with varying levels of rejection and seduction inherent in the symbolic images applied to us. This is the context in which we make our choices. Taken together, the institutional and symbolic dimensions of oppression create a structural backdrop against which all of us live our lives.

3. The Individual Dimension of Oppression

Whether we benefit or not, we all live within institutions that reproduce race, class and gender oppression. Even if we never have any contact with members of other race, class and gender groups, we all encounter images of these groups and are exposed to the symbolic meanings attached to those images. On this dimension of oppression, our individual biographies vary tremendously. As a result of our institutional and symbolic statuses, all of our choices become political acts.

Each of us must come to terms with the multiple ways in which race, class and gender as categories of analysis frame our individual biographies. I have lived my entire life as an African-American woman from a working class family and this basic fact has had a profound impact on my personal biography. Imagine how different your life might be if you had been born Black, or White, or poor, or of a different race/class/gender group than the one with which you are most familiar. The institutional treatment you would have received and the symbolic meanings attached to your very existence might differ dramatically from that you now consider to be natural, normal and part of everyday life. You might be the same, but your personal biography might have been quite different.

I believe that each of us carries around the cumulative effect of our lives within multiple structures of oppression. If you want to see how much you have been affected by this whole thing, I ask you one simple question—who are your close friends? Who are the people with whom you can share your hopes, dreams, vulnerabilities, fears and victories? Do they look like you? If they are all the same, circumstance may be the cause. For the first seven years of my life I saw only low income Black people. My friends from those years reflected the composition of my community. But now that I am an adult, can the defense of circumstance explain the patterns of people that I trust as my friends and colleagues? When given other alternatives, if my friends and colleagues reflect the homogeneity of one race, class and gender group, then these categories of analysis have indeed become barriers to connection.

I am not suggesting that people are doomed to follow the paths laid out for them by race, class and gender as categories of analysis. While these three structures certainly frame my opportunity structure, I as an individual always have the choice of accepting things as they are, or trying to change them. As Nikki Giovanni points out, "we've got to live in the real world. If we don't like the world we're living in, change it. And if we can't change it, we change ourselves. We can do something" (Tate 1983, 68). While a piece of the oppressor may be planted deep within each of us, we each have the choice of accepting that piece or challenging it as part of the "true focus of revolutionary change."

HOW CAN WE TRANSCEND THE BARRIERS CREATED BY OUR EXPERIENCES WITH RACE, CLASS AND GENDER OPPRESSION IN ORDER TO BUILD THE TYPES OF COALITIONS ESSENTIAL FOR SOCIAL CHANGE?

Reconceptualizing oppression and seeing the barriers created by race, class and gender as interlocking categories of analysis is a vital first step. But we must transcend these barriers by moving toward race, class and gender as categories of connection, by building relationships and coalitions that will bring about social change. What are some of the issues involved in doing this?

1. Differences in Power and Privilege

First, we must recognize that our differing experiences with oppression create problems in the relationships among us. Each of us lives within a system that vests us with varying levels of power and privilege. These differences in power, whether structured along axes of race, class, gender, age or sexual orientation, frame our relationships. African-American writer June Jordan describes her discomfort on a Caribbean vacation with Olive, the Black womanwho cleaned her room:

> . . . even though both "Olive" and "I" live inside a conflict neither one of us created, and even though both of us therefore hurt inside that conflict, I may be one of the monsters she needs to eliminate from her universe and, in a sense, she may be one of the monsters in mine (1985, 47).

Differences in power constrain our ability to connect with one another even when we think we are engaged in dialogue across differences. Let me give you an example. One year, the students in my course "Sociology of the Black Community" got into a heated discussion about the reasons for the upsurge of racial incidents on college campuses. Black students complained vehemently about the apathy and resistance they felt most White students expressed about examining their own racism. Mark, a White male student, found their comments particularly unsettling. After claiming that all the Black people he had ever known had expressed no such beliefs to him, he questioned how representative the viewpoints of his fellow students actually were. When pushed further, Mark revealed that he had participated in conversations over the years with the Black domestic worker employed by his family. Since she had never expressed such strong feelings about White racism, Mark was genuinely shocked by class discussions. Ask yourselves whether that domestic worker was in a position to speak freely. Would it have been wise for her to do so in a situation where the power between the two parties was so unequal?

In extreme cases, members of privileged groups can erase the very presence of the less privileged. When I first moved to Cincinnati, my family and I went on a picnic at a local park. Picnicking next to us was a family of White Appalachians. When I went to push my daughter on the swings, several of the children came over. They had missing, yellowed and broken teeth, they wore old clothing and their poverty was evident. I was shocked. Growing up in a large eastern city, I had never seen such awful poverty among Whites. The segregated neighborhoods in which I grew up made White poverty all but invisible. More importantly, the privileges attached to my newly acquired social class position allowed me to ignore and minimize the poverty among Whites that I did encounter. My reactions to those children made me realize how confining phrases such as "well, at least they're not Black," had become for me. In learning to grant human subjectivity to the Black victims of poverty, I had simultaneously learned to demand White victims of poverty. By applying categories of race to the objective conditions confronting me, I was quantifying and ranking oppressions and missing the very real suffering which, in fact, is the real issue.

One common pattern of relationships across differences in power is one that I label "voyeurism." From the perspective of the privileged, the lives of people of color, of the poor, and of women are interesting for their entertainment value. The privileged become voyeurs, passive onlookers who do not relate to the less powerful, but who are interested in seeing how the "different" live. Over the years, I have heard numerous African-American students complain about professors who never call on them except when a so-called Black issue is being discussed. The students' interest in discussing race or qualifications for doing so appear unimportant to the professor's efforts to use Black students' experiences as stories to make the material come alive for the White student audience. Asking Black students to perform on cue and provide a Black experience for their White classmates can be seen as voyeurism at its worst.

Members of subordinate groups do not willingly participate in such exchanges but often do so because members of dominant groups control the institutional and symbolic apparatuses of oppression. Racial/ethnic groups, women, and the poor have never had the luxury of being voyeurs of the lives of the privileged. Our ability to survive in hostile settings has hinged on our ability to learn intricate details about the behavior and world view of the powerful and adjust our behavior accordingly. I need only point to the difference in perception of those men and women in abusive relationships. Where men can view their girlfriends and wives as sex objects, helpmates and a collection of stereotypes categories of voyeurism—women must be attuned to every nuance of their partners' behavior. Are women "naturally" better in relating to people with more power than themselves, or have circumstances mandated that men and women develop different skills?. . .

Coming from a tradition where most relationships across difference are squarely rooted in relations of domination and subordination, we have much less experience relating to people as different but equal. The classroom is potentially one powerful and safe space where dialogues among individuals of unequal power relationships can occur. The relationship between Mark, the student in my class, and the domestic worker is typical of a whole series of relationships that people have when they relate across differences in power and privilege. The relationship among Mark and his classmates represents the power of the classroom to minimize those differences so that people of different levels of power can use race, class and gender as categories of analysis in order to generate meaningful dialogues. In this case, the classroom equalized racial differences so that Black students who normally felt silenced spoke out. White students like Mark, generally unaware of how they had been privileged by their whiteness, lost that privilege in the classroom and thus became open to genuine dialogue. . .

2. Coalitions around Common Causes

A second issue in building relationships and coalitions essential for social change concerns knowing the real reasons for coalition. Just what brings people together? One powerful catalyst fostering group solidarity is the presence of a common enemy. African-American, Hispanic, Asian-American, and women's studies all share the common intellectual heritage of challenging what passes for certified knowledge in the academy. But politically expedient relationships and coalitions like these are fragile because, as June Jordan points out:

> It occurs to me that much organizational grief could be avoided if people understood that partnership in misery does not necessarily provide for partnership for change. When we get the monsters off our backs all of us may want to run in very different directions (1985, 47).

Sharing a common cause assists individuals and groups in maintaining relationships that transcend their differences. Building effective coalitions involves struggling to hear one another and developing empathy for each other's points of view. The coalitions that I have been involved in that lasted and that worked have been those where commitment to a specific issue mandated collaboration as the best strategy for addressing the issue at hand.

Several years ago, masters degree in hand, I chose to teach in an innercity parochial school in danger of closing. The money was awful, the conditions were poor, but the need was great. In my job, I had to work with a range of individuals who, on the surface, had very little in common. We had White nuns, Black middle class graduate students, Blacks from the "community," some of whom had been incarcerated and/or were affiliated with a range of federal anti-poverty programs. Parents formed another part of this community, Harvard faculty another, and a few well-meaning White liberals from Colorado were sprinkled in for good measure.

As you might imagine, tension was high. Initially, our differences seemed insurmountable. But as time passed, we found a common bond that we each brought to the school. In spite of profound differences in our personal biographies, differences that in other settings would have hampered our ability to relate to one another, we found that we were all deeply committed to the education of Black children. By learning to value each other's commitment and by recognizing that we each had different skills that were essential to actualizing that commitment, we built an effective coalition around a common cause. Our school was successful, and the children we taught benefited from the diversity we offered them.

. . . None of us alone has a comprehensive vision of how race, class and gender operate as categories of analysis or how they might be used as categories of connection. Our personal biographies offer us partial views. Few of us can manage to study race, class and gender simultaneously. Instead, we each know more about some dimensions of this larger story and less about others . . . Just as the members of the school had special skills to offer to the task of building the school, we have areas of specialization and expertise, whether scholarly, theoretical, pedagogical or within areas of race, class or gender. We do not all have to do the same thing in the same way. Instead, we must support each other's efforts, realizing that they are all part of the larger enterprise of bringing about social change.

3. Building Empathy

A third issue involved in building the types of relationships and coalitions essential for social change concerns the issue of individual accountability. Race, class and gender oppression form the structural backdrop against which we frame our relationship—these are the forces that encourage us to substitute voyeurism . . . for fully human relationships. But while we may not have created this situation, we are each responsible for making individual, personal choices concerning which elements of race, class and gender oppression we will accept and which we will work to change.

One essential component of this accountability involves developing empathy for the experiences of individuals and groups different than ourselves. Empathy begins with taking an interest in the facts of other people's lives, both as individuals and as groups. If you care about me, you should want to know not only the details of my personal biography but a sense of how race, class and gender as categories of analysis created the institutional and symbolic backdrop for my personal biography. How can you hope to assess my character without knowing the details of the circumstances I face?

Moreover, by taking a theoretical stance that we have all been affected by race, class and gender as categories of analysis that have structured our treatment, we open up possibilities for using those same constructs as categories of connection in building empathy. For example, I have a good White woman friend with whom I share common interests and beliefs. But we know that our racial differences have provided us with different experiences. So we talk about them. We do not assume that because I am Black, race has only affected me and not her or that because I am a Black woman, race neutralizes the effect of gender in my life while accenting it in hers. We take those same categories of analysis that have created cleavages in our lives, in this case, categories of race and gender, and use them as categories of connection in building empathy for each other's experiences.

Finding common causes and building empathy is difficult, no matter which side of privilege we inhabit. Building empathy from the dominant side of privilege is difficult, simply because individuals from privileged backgrounds are not encouraged to do so. For example, in order for those of you who are White to develop empathy for the experiences of people of color, you must grapple with how your white skin has privileged you. This is difficult to do, because it not only entails the intellectual process of seeing how whiteness is elevated in institutions and symbols, but it also involves the often painful process of seeing how your whiteness has shaped your personal biography. Intellectual stances against the institutional and symbolic dimensions of racism are generally easier to maintain than sustained self-reflection about how racism has shaped all of our individual biographies. Were and are your fathers, uncles, and grandfathers really more capable than mine, or can their accomplishments be explained in part by the racism members of my family experienced? Did your mothers stand silently by and watch all this happen? More importantly, how have they passed on the benefits of their whiteness to you?

These are difficult questions, and I have tremendous respect for my colleagues and students who are trying to answer them. Since there is no compelling reason to examine the source and meaning of one's own privilege, I know that those who do so have freely chosen this stance. They are making conscious efforts to root out the piece of the oppressor planted within them. To me, they are entitled to the support of people of color in their efforts. Men who declare themselves feminists, members of the middle class who ally themselves with anti-poverty struggles, heterosexuals who support gays and lesbians, are all trying to grow, and their efforts place them far ahead of the majority who never think of engaging in such important struggles.

Building empathy from the subordinate side of privilege is also difficult, but for different reasons. Members of subordinate groups are understandably reluctant to abandon a basic mistrust of members of powerful groups because this basic mistrust has traditionall been central to their survival. As a Black woman, it would be foolish for me to assume that White women, or Black men, or White men or any other group with a history of exploiting African-American women have my best interests at heart. These groups enjoy varying amounts of privilege over me and therefore I must carefully watch them and be prepared for a relation of domination and subordination.

Like the privileged, members of subordinate groups must also work toward replacing judgments by category with new ways of thinking and acting. Refusing to do so stifles prospects for effective coalition and social change. Let me use another example from my own experiences. When I was an undergraduate, I had little time or patience for the theorizing of the privileged. My initial years at a private, elite institution were difficult, not because the coursework was challenging (it was, but that wasn't what distracted me) or because I had to work while my classmates lived of family allowances (I was used to work). The adjustment was difficult because I was surrounded by so many people who took their privilege for granted. Most of them felt entitled to their wealth. That astounded me.

I remember one incident watching a White woman down the hall in my dormitory try to pick out which sweater to wear. The sweaters were piled up on her bed in all the colors of the rainbow, sweater after sweater. She asked my advice in a way that let me know that choosing a sweater was on of the most important decisions she had to make on a daily basis. Standing kneedeep in her sweaters, I realized how different our lives were. She did not have to worry about maintaining a solid academic average so that she could receive financial aid. Because she was in the majority, she was not treated as a representative of her race. She did not have to consider how her classroom comments or basic existence on campus contributed to the treatment her group would receive. Her allowance protected her from having to work, so she ws free to spend her time studying, partying, or in her case, worrying about which sweater to wear.

The degree of inequality in our lives and her unquestioned sense of entitlement concerning that inequality offended me. For a while, I categorized all affluent White women as being superficial, arrogant, overly concerned with material possessions, and part of my problem. But had I continued to classify people in this way, I would have missed out on making some very good friends whose discomfort with their inherited or acquired social class privileges pushed them to examine their position.

Since I opened with the words of Audre Lorde, it seems appropiate to close with another of her ideas. . . .

> Each of us called upon to take a stand. So in these days ahead, as we examie ourselves and each other, our works, our fears, our differences, our sisterhood and survivals, I urge you to tackle what is most difficult for us all, self-scrutiny of our complacencies, the idea that since each of us believes she is one the side of right, she need not examine her position (1985).

I urge you to examine your position.

REFERENCES

Acker, Joan. 1994a. The Gender Regime of Swedish Banks. *Scandinavian Journal of Management* 10, no. 2: 117–30.

Acker, Joan, and Donald Van Houston. 1974. Differential Recruitment and Control: The Sex Structuring of Organizations. *Administrative Science Quarterly* 19 (June, 1974): 152–63.

Amott, Teresa, and Julie Matthaei. 1996. *Race, Gender, and Work: A Multi-cultural Economic History of Women in the United States.* Revised edition. Boston: South End Press.

Beneria, Lourdes. 1999. Globalization, Gender and the Davos Man. *Feminist Economics* 5, no.3:61–83.

Bremner, Robert H. 1956. *From the Depths: The Discovery of Poverty in the United States.* New York: New York University Press.

Brodkin, Karen. 1998. Race, Class, and Gender: The Metaorganization of American Capitalism. *Transformine Anthropology* 7, no. 2: 46–57.

Brown, Michael K., Martin Carnoy, Elliott Currie, Troy Duster, David B. Oppenheimer, Marjorie M. Shultz, and David Wellman. 2003. *White-Washing Race: The Myth of a ColorBlind Society.* Berkeley: University of California Press.

Burris, Beverly H. 1996. Technocracy, Patriarchy and Management. In *Men as Managers, Managers as Men*, ed. David L. Collinson and Jeff Hcarn. London: Sage.

Cockburn, Cynthia. 1983. *Brothers* London: Pluto Press.

———. 1991. *In the Way of Women: Men's Resistance to Sex Equality in Organization.* Ithaca, N.Y.: ILR Press.

Cohn, Samuel. *1985. The Process of Occupational Sex-Typing: The Femininization of Clerical Labor in Great Britain*, Philadelphia: Temple University Press.

Collins, Patricia Hill. 2000. *Black Feminist Thought*, second edition, New York and London: Routledge.

Collinson, David L., and Jeff Hearn. 1996. Breaking the Silence: On Men, Masculinities and Managements. In *Men as Managers, Managers as Men*, ed. David L. Collinson and Jeff Hearns. London: Sage.

Connell, R. W. 2000. *The Men and the Boys.* Berkeley: University of California Press.

———. 1995. *Masculinities*, Berkeley: University of California Press.

———. 1987. *Gender & Power*, Stanford, Calif.: Stanford University Press.

Figart, Deborah M., Ellen Mutarl, and Marilyn Power. 2002. *Living Wages, Equal Wages*. London and New York: Routledge.

Foner, Philip S. 1947. *History of the Labor Movement in the United States*. New York: International Publishers.

Frankel, Linda. 1984. Southern Textile Women: Generations of Survival and Struggle. In *My Troubles Are Going to Have Trouble with Me*, ed. Karen Brodkin Sacks and Dorothy Remy. New Brunswick, N.J.: Rulgers University Press.

Glenn, Evelyn Nakano. 2002. *Unequal Freedom: How Race and Gender Shaped American Citizenship and Labor*. Cambridge: Harvard University Press.

Goldin, Claudia. 1990. *Understanding the Gender Gap: An Economic History of American Women*. New York and Oxford: Oxford University Press.

Gutman, Herbert G. 1976. *Work, Culture Society in Industrializing America*. New York: Alfred A. Knopf.

Hartmann, Heidi. 1976. Capitalism, Patriarchy, and Job Segregation by Sex. *Sigus* 1, no. 3, part 2: 137–69.

Hearn, Jeff. 1996. Is Masculinity Dead? A Critique of the Concept of Masculinity/Masculinities. In *Understanding Masculinities: Social Relations and Cultural Arenas*, ed. M. Mac an Ghaill. Buckingham: Oxford University Press.

———. 2004. From Hegomonic Masculinity to the Hegemony of Men. *Feminist Theory* 5, no. 1: 49–72.

Hearn, Jeff, and Wendy Parkin. 2001. *Gender, Sexuality and Violence in Organizations*. London: Sage.

Janiewski, Dolores. 1996. Southern Honour, Southern Dishonour: Managerial Ideology and the Construction of Gender, Race, and Class Relations in Southern Industry. In *Feminism & History*, ed. Joan Wallach Scott. Oxford: Oxford University Press.

Kanter, Rosabeth Moss. 1977. *Men and Women of the Corporation*. New York: Basic Books.

Keister, Lisa. 2000. *Wealth in America: Trends in Wealth Inequality*. Cambridge: Cambridge University Press.

Kessler-Harris, Alice. 1982. *Out to Work: A History of Wage-Earning Women in the United States*, New York: Oxford University Press.

Kilbourne, Barbara, Paula England, and Kurt Beron 1994. Effects of Individual, Occupational, and Industrial Characteristics on Earnings: Intersections of Race and Gender. *Social Forces* 72: 1149–76.

McDowell, Linda. 1997. A Tale of Two Cities? Embedded Organizations and Embodied Workers in the City of London. In *Geographies of Economies*, ed. Roger Lee and Jane Willis, 118–29. London: Arnold.

Middleton, Chris. 1983. Patriarchal Exploitation and the Rise of English Capitalism. In *Gender, Class and Work*, ed. Eva Gamarnikow, David H. J. Morgan, June Purvis, and Daphne E. Taylorson. London: Heinemann.

Milton, David. 1982. *The Politics of U.S. Labor: From the Great Depression to the New Deal*. New York: Monthly Review Press.

Omi, Michael, and Howard Winant. 1994. *Racial Formation in the United States*. New York: Routledge.

Padavic, Irene, and Barbara Reskin. 2002. *Women and Men at Work*, second edition. Thousand Oaks, Calif.: Pine Forge Press.

Perrow, Charles. 2002. *Organizing America*. Princeton and Oxford: Princeton University Press.

Read, Rosslyn. 1996. Entrepreneurialism and Paternalism in Australian Management: A Gender Critique of the "Self-Made" Man. In *Men as Managers, Managers as Men*, ed. David L. Collinson and Jeff Hearn. London: Sage.

Reskin, Barbara F., Debra B. McBrier, and Julie A. Kmec. 1999. The Determinants and Consequences of Workplace Sex and Race Composition. *Annual Review of Sociology* vol. 25: 335–61.

Royster, Deirdre A. 2003. *Race and the Invisible Hand: How White Networks Exclude Black Men from Blue-Collar Jobs*. Berkeley: University of California Press.

Seidler, Victor J. 1989. *Rediscovering Masculinity: Renson, Language, and Sexuality*. London and New York: Routledge.

Taylor, Paul F. 1992. Bloody Harlan: The United Mine Workers in Harlan County, Kentucky, 1931–1941. Lanham, Md.: University Press of America.

Wacjman, Judy. 1998. *Managing Like a Man*. Cambridge: Polity Press.

Williams, Eric. 1944. *Capitalism and Slavery*. Chapel Hill: University of North Carolina Press.

Name _____   Date _____

Course & section: _____   Instructor _____

Toward a New Vision
Race, Class, and Gender as Categories of Analysis and Connection

Patricia Hill Collins

1. How is racism connected to sexism?

2. What was the old model for understanding oppression? What is Collins' "new vision"?

3. What are the different dimensions of oppression? Why is it important to examine multiple structures of oppression? Give examples of the different dimensions and structures.

4. According to Patricia Hill Collins, how can we go beyond our individual and intersectional identities that separate us, to build coalitions for social change? Do you agree with her approach? How can this approach impact organizations or social movements you belong to?

5. Collins suggests that in order to transcend the barriers created by race, class and gender oppression that we must build relationships and coalitions around common causes. Think about causes on your campus around which a coalition might be built; common causes might include bias incidents, eating disorders, homophobic bullying, hunger and food security, sex education sexual assault, etc.

Which cause would you like to focus on?

Find your university's list of student organizations and choose two organizations on campus that could form a coalition around the cause you have chosen. Which two organizations do you think could build a coalition around this cause?

Now write a letter to that group inviting them to form a coalition. Why should they collaborate? Consider Collins's suggestions for *how* we must build relationships that transcend race, class and gender oppression. Recommend steps for building relationships based on Collins' new vision. (Use a separate sheet.)

Bisexuality and the Case Against Dualism

Stephanie Fairyington

Stephanie Fairyington *is founder and co-editor of* Slant *and a journalist who has contributed essays on gender, sexuality and bisexuality for publications including* the Advocate, OUT *and the* Gay and Lesbian Review Worldwide, *in which this essay was first published in 2005.*

PRE-READING QUESTIONS

1. What is sexuality and how is it connected to gender?
2. What do you know about bisexuality?

KEY TERMS

Beemyn, Genny (Brett)
bisexuality
dualistic paradigm of sexuality
Freud, Sigmund
intersexual
Kinsey, Alfred C.
Kinsey Scale
Klein Sexual Orientation Grid
LeVay, Simon
Rust, Paula
Stekel, Wilhelm
Ulrichs, Karl

SEE THE THEMATIC TABLE OF CONTENTS, IF YOU WANT TO READ MORE ESSAYS ABOUT:

LGBTQ Studies
Sexualities
Social Construction of Gender

Bisexuality and the Case Against Dualism

Stephanie Fairyington

It was seeing the movie Kinsey that triggered a heated discussion about bisexuality between me and my girlfriend Meg, whom I had "accused" of being bisexual in light of her history of dating men several years earlier. She vehemently denied that this earlier life made her bisexual, giving rise to that age-old discussion of just what makes a person "bi": Does it involve love or is it only about sex? Do serial partners of both sexes count, or do they have to be simultaneous? Are fantasies about sexual relations with both men and women sufficient, or does one have to act on both impulses? All the theories and stereotypes also came out in the course of our discussion: that bisexuals are sex fiends who'll sleep with anything that moves; that they're unable to commit to a sexual identity; that bisexuality doesn't really exist but serves as a hedge for semicloseted gay men and sexually adventuresome straight women. That last one reminded us of an old joke: "Bisexual men and bisexual women have one thing in common. They'll both be having sex with men five years from now."

Why is it so hard for us to wrap our minds around bisexuality? Our cultural struggle to conceptualize bisexuality stems in part from the freighted history of the term. When it first appeared in a dictionary in 1824, "bisexual" referred to people possessing the characteristics of both sexes, now referred to as "intersexuals" (or, popularly, as "hermaphrodites"). In the mid-1860's, Karl Heinrich Ulrich postulated that men who have same-sex desires have female souls trapped inside male bodies. Subsequent sex researchers argued that people who desire their own sex have an inverted gender identity. From this sort of logic it was deduced that bisexuals are "psycho-sexual hermaphrodites."

Freud upended the conversation on bisexuality beginning in the early 20th century when he used the term in the modern sense and hypothesized that all people are initially bisexual before a fixed, usually hetero-, sexual identity takes hold. Basing his theories upon contemporary ideas, later discredited, as to the biological bisexuality of the fetus, Freud hypothesized that everyone had a primary and innate bisexual disposition with respect to sex-object choice. But instead of arguing that bisexuality might be a normal manifestation of this inherent predisposition, Freud went on to spin an account of normal human development whereby same-sex desires are repressed or sublimated and heterosexual ones allowed to arise, relegating homosexuality and bisexuality to exceptional states that develop as the result of a series of psychological malfunctions.

Interestingly, one of Freud's associates, Wilhelm Stekel, challenged Freud's hypothesis while using his terminology, pointing out that if bisexuality is the original state and the creation of homosexuality and heterosexuality relies on sublimation and repression, then logically the latter two sexual orientations are the troubled psychosexual states, not bisexuality. Not surprisingly, this theory didn't gain much traction at the time.

A dualistic paradigm of sexuality stayed firmly in place until the groundbreaking and binary-breaking work of Alfred C. Kinsey and his team. What would come to be known as the "Kinsey Scale" posited that sexual orientations form a continuum from 0 to 6, with 0 representing a totally heterosexual person and 6 a totally homosexual one, with many degrees of bisexuality in between. Despite some flaws in Kinsey's research methods, such as the use of snowball sampling, his work exposed a radical disjunction between the sexual mores of post-war America and the reality of people's sex lives. Perhaps most astonishing was his finding that 46 percent of the male population had engaged in both hetero- and homosexual activities in their adult (i.e., sexually mature) lives.

The Kinsey Scale's assault on the hetero-homo divide was nothing short of breathtaking for its time, exposing the complexity of human sexuality while hinting subversively that the heterosexual you know may not be as hetero as you think. As a practical matter, the wall between gay and straight didn't exactly come tumbling down in the wake of Kinsey's research, which did, however, pave the way for more sophisticated models for measuring sexuality, such as Fritz Klein's Sexual Orientation Grid (KSOG), introduced in his 1978 classic, The Bisexual Option.

Klein's grid dramatically improved upon Kinsey's scale, combining five discrete dimensions: sexual attraction, behavior, fantasies, emotional preference, and social preference (lifestyle and self-identification). Assessing a person's past and present behavior along with ideal sexual situations, the KSOG rates desire on a seven-point scale similar to Kinsey's but with simple verbal descriptors (1 = other sex only, 2 = other sex mostly, 3 = other sex somewhat more, 4 = both sexes, 5 = same sex somewhat more, 6 = same sex mostly, 7 = same sex only). Despite these long strides forward, the hetero-homo dichotomy has proved a hard nut to crack. From Kinsey's time to the present, sex research almost always aggregates bisexual and homosexual activities or identities into one category, thereby erasing the concept of bisexuality altogether. (For example, Simon LeVay's famous study of male brains, which found a difference between the brains of gay and straight men, clumped bisexuals with gay men.)

While there are respectable studies that offer reliable statistics on the prevalence of bisexuality, the details about this group are often missing. As researcher Paula C. Rust has observed, only "by triangulating the many studies that have been done to date can we achieve an overall picture of sexuality in the United States. Taken together, these studies provide us with a rough estimate of the prevalence of bisexual behaviors, feelings, and identities in the United States." Keeping Rust's caveat in mind, it is staggering to note that every study I've reviewed reflects a greater amount of bisexual than exclusively homosexual activity and desire, yet popular wisdom has it that there are far fewer bisexuals than homosexuals. Starting with Kinsey's astronomically high estimate—that 46 percent of adult males registering as bi, which is now considered overblown—subsequent research has produced more modest findings but repeatedly confirms that the proportion of people with a bisexual orientation—able to relate to both sexes sexually and emotionally—is greater than the proportion of exclusive homosexuals.

Despite these findings, barriers to the study of bisexuality remain in place, and it is thus an under-researched phenomenon. Let me focus on some of these barriers and consider possible remedies.

The first hurdle is the lack of a clear definition for the term. Who is bisexual? Is a male hustler who markets himself to men by night, but maintains exclusively romantic relations with women by day, bisexual? Are men who engage in same-sex relations in prison but resume exclusive heterosexuality upon release to be classified as "bi"? What about my girlfriend Meg, who had fulfilling romantic relationships with men up until six years ago but now dates only women? What if you have same-and-opposite sex sexual fantasies and desires but never act on half of them? These disparate cases, all of them quite prevalent in the real world, raise the question whether we can even speak of "bisexuality" as a single phenomenon.

A second problem is that many people who are bisexual in a behavioral sense do not self-identify as bi. There are myriad reasons why this may be the case. For one, bisexuals experience disapproval not only from the dominant society but from the gay and lesbian community, as well. Many gay people are reluctant to date someone who's bi because they feel there's an ever-present temptation hovering over every bisexual in a same-sex relationship to "go straight." Because heterosexuality and homosexuality create the fence that bisexuality is forced to sit on, bisexuals have a harder time finding a grounded community to come out to. Brett Beemyn, coauthor of *Bisexuality in the Lives of Men* (2000), argues that in coming out, "bisexuals rarely can count on finding places where they will be embraced by others like themselves. With only a few exceptions, we don't have bisexual-specific bars, community centers, political organizations, softball teams, and circuit parties."

Because many people refuse to self-identify as bisexual for whatever reason, it might make sense to drop the identity categories altogether and go back to Kinsey's purely behavioral approach whereby research subjects are asked about their activities and fantasies but not about the labels they use. Brett Beemyn endorses this approach: "Most studies are formulated using standard sexual orientation labels: lesbian, gay, bisexual, and heterosexual. To develop a better understanding of human sexuality, researchers need to ask about sexual attraction and behavior, rather than how people label their sexuality." Loraine Hutchins espouses a similar view, arguing that in terms of researching bisexuality "it's much better to talk about exactly what kind of sex and what kind of relationship, as those involved define it, exists." But Rust, arguably the foremost expert on bisexuality, argues for the continued use of the term so longs as its meaning is clearly defined in a given research context.

Once the definition of the term is nailed down, assuming that's possible, the next obstacle is finding a representative sample. Rust, author of the compendious *Bisexuality in the United States* (Columbia, 1999), describes the difficulty of finding such a sample. "A lot of research is done by convenience samples. For instance, if I go to a gay coffee house and 25 percent of the people are bi, I can't use data extracted from that population in any other context or draw any conclusions from such a sample about the general population." Another essay in Rust's compilation, "Behavior Patterns and Sexual Identity of Bisexual Males," explains that "like virtually all available data on human sexuality, studies have relied on nonprobability 'convenience' samples, including patients of STD clinics, members of accessible organizations, persons who frequent public places for sexual contact, and volunteer respondents to magazine and other publicly-announced surveys," skewing the data in unknown ways. Research on the Internet is another way of obtaining a sample of the general population, but here the problem is one of self-selection. What's more, observes Rust: "People present personas other than their own. Though it's easy to get a large quantity of data on the Internet, it's not representative of the larger population." Some avenues to obtaining more representative samples are electoral registers, postcode files, and telephone numbers; however, these forms of random sampling under-represent certain groups whose lifestyles and behaviors differ from the general population.

Yet another barrier to researching bisexuality has been the sheer lack of funding for this endeavor. Psychologist Lisa Diamond explains: "I know only a few serious scientists who are looking at bisexuality specifically. Major sex research centers are under attack and underfunded."

Loraine Hutchins emphasized that only by sheer persistence have most been able to pursue sex research over many years with no funding, citing her friend and colleague Ron Fox for his tenacious commitment to the topic. (Fox is the editor of a recent collection of works studying bisexuality through the lens of psychology and sociology entitled *Current Research on Bisexuality*. *Haworth*, 2004). Hutchins echoes Diamond's point, bemoaning the lack of sponsorship: "No one has done the kind of comprehensive survey that Kinsey did; no one will fund it. We live in such an uptight climate." These are indeed conservative times. In 2003, Rep. Patrick Toomey (R-Pa.) proposed to de-fund four NIH grants for research on human sexuality; it didn't pass, but only by a meager two votes. Soon thereafter, the National Institute of Mental Health, which had funded Boston University's Sexuality and Research Treatment Program for twenty years, withdrew its funds, shutting down the operation completely. In recent years, many sex researchers have been forced to seek sponsorship from pharmaceutical companies, constraining the type of research they can pursue. The questions have been reduced to the mechanical, rather than the psychological aspects of sex—a mere clip of the bigger picture.

But the biggest problem researchers have in conceptualizing bisexuality has to do with the unfortunate fact that, in Rust's words, "Westerners think in neat, discrete categories." We are not accustomed to thinking in the space between any two polarized extremes. Martin Weinberg, co-author of Dual Attraction (Oxford University Press, 1994), a study of members of the San Francisco Bisexual Center during the pre-antiretroviral AIDS crisis, has encountered the same problem, concluding that: "People have a difficult time thinking analytically or in anything but the most simplistic (binary) way." Almost every bisexual activist and scholar I spoke with expressed the same viewpoint: "The dichotomy thing, which we also often call binary thinking or either/or thinking, has been our nemesis forever," gripes Hutchins.

Bisexuality erodes the border between homo- and heterosexuality, but it's a boundary that our society is heavily invested in maintaining. Doubtless the reason bisexuality is not adequately researched or understood is because it poses a threat to straight people, first and foremost, who feel secure behind an impenetrable wall of heterosexuality. This is bisexuality's subversive power. The promise of increased research on bisexuality is that just getting people to recognize its prevalence could help chip away at the hetero-versus-homo monolith and facilitate a dissolution of oppressive, traditional notions of what it means to be a man and a woman.

On an even broader scale, the lesson that bisexuality bares is a good one for the 21st century. We live in a world whose reality is more complicated than the simplified binaries of our language and understanding. Learning to reason in the middle of two polarized extremes might dissolve the us-them dichotomy that has spurred an ideological and political civil war in this country. Bisexuality as the synthesis, the middle ground between seemingly irreconcilable differences, is a form of thinking that has boundless possibilities for social progress—but first we have to acknowledge its existence and its prevalence in society.

Bisexuality and the Case Against Dualism

Stephanie Fairyington

1. How has bisexuality been framed as a psychological malfunction?

2. Search on the web for the Kinsey Scale, Klein Sexual Orientation Grid and the Storms Scale. Compare them. What is the Kinsey Scale? According to Fairyington how does the Klein Sexual Orientation Grid improve upon it? Which of these do you think is most useful in explaining sexual orientation? Why?

3. One of the barriers to studying and understanding bisexuality is that of definition. What are the drawbacks and benefits of defining bisexuality based on behavior? Based on self-identification?

4. What are some examples of binary thinking or dualisms besides the gender dualism? What are the pitfalls of binary thinking? How might we overcome them?

5. Create your own visual representation of a model of sexuality that improves upon previous ones.

We Are All Works in Progress
from *Trans Liberation: Beyond Pink or Blue*

Leslie Feinberg

Leslie Feinberg was a revolutionary communist, journalist and transgender, peace, labor, socialist and anti-racist activist. Ze has written two novels. Feinberg passed away in 2014. Stone Butch Blues *(1993), hir first novel, received the Lambda Literary Award as well as the American Library Association Award for Gay and Lesbian Literature. Hir other books include* Drag King Dreams *(2006),* Transgender Warriors: Making History from Joan of Arc to Rupaul(s) *(1997). This essay comes from* Trans Liberation: Beyond Pink or Blue *(1998), a compiled volume of hir speeches.*

PRE-READING QUESTIONS

1. Read the biography at the beginning of the essay. What do you notice? Why might it be important?
2. How are transgender topics covered in mainstream media?

KEY TERMS

bigotry
coalition
gender
gender expression
gender-neutral pronouns
gender transgression
intersex/intersexual
oppression
sex
social construct
transliberation
transgender
transsexual
women's liberation movement

SEE THE THEMATIC TABLE OF CONTENTS, IF YOU WANT TO READ MORE ESSAYS ABOUT:

Feminism and Social Movements
LGBTQ Studies
Privilege, Identities and Intersectionalities
Social Construction of Gender

We are all Works in Progress
from *Trans Liberation: Beyond Pink or Blue*

Leslie Feinberg

The sight of pink-blue gender-coded infant outfits may grate on your nerves. Or you may be a woman or a man who feels at home in those categories. Trans liberation defends you both.

Each person should have the right to *choose* between pink or blue tinted gender categories, as well as all the other hues of the palette. At this moment in time, that right is denied to us. But together, we could make it a reality.

And that's what this book is all about.

I am a human being who would rather not be addressed as Ms. or Mr., ma'am or sir. I prefer to use gender-neutral pronouns like *sie* (pronounced like "see") and *hir* (pronounced like *"here"*) to describe myself. I am a person who faces almost insurmountable difficulty when instructed to check off an "F" or an "M" box on identification papers.

I'm not at odds with the fact that I was born female-bodied. Nor do I identify as an intermediate sex. I simply do not fit the prevalent Western concepts of what a woman or a man "should" look like. And that reality has dramatically directed the course of my life.

I'll give you a graphic example. From December 1995 to December 1996, I was dying of endocarditis-a bacterial infection that lodges and proliferates in the valves of the heart. A simple blood culture would have immediately exposed the root cause of my raging fevers. Eight weeks of round-the-clock intravenous antibiotic drips would have eradicated every last seedling of bacterium in the canals of my heart. Yet I experienced such hatred from some health practitioners that I very nearly died.

I remember late one night in December my lover and I arrived at a hospital emergency room during a snowstorm. My fever was 104 degrees and rising. My blood pressure was pounding dangerously high. The staff immediately hooked me up to monitors and worked to bring down my fever. The doctor in charge began physically examining me. When he determined that my anatomy was female, he flashed me a mean-spirited smirk. While keeping his eyes fixed on me, he approached one of the nurses, seated at a desk, and began rubbing her neck and shoulders. He talked to her about sex for a few minutes. After his pointed demonstration of "normal sexuality," he told me to get dressed and then he stormed out of the room. Still delirious, I struggled to put on my clothes and make sense of what was happening.

The doctor returned after I was dressed. He ordered me to leave the hospital and never return. I refused. I told him I wouldn't leave until he could tell me why my fever was so high. He said, "You have a fever because you are a very troubled person."

This doctor's prejudices, directed at me during a moment of catastrophic illness, could have killed me. The death certificate would have read: Endocarditis. By all rights it should have read: Bigotry.

As my partner and I sat bundled up in a cold car outside the emergency room, still reverberating from the doctor's hatred, I thought about how many people have been turned away from medical care when they were desperately ill-some because an apartheid "whites only" sign hung over the emergency room entrance, or some because their visible Kaposi's sarcoma lesions kept personnel far from their beds. I remembered how a blemish that wouldn't heal drove my mother to visit her doctor repeatedly during the 1950s. I recalled the doctor finally wrote a prescription for Valium because he decided she was a hysterical woman. When my mother finally got to specialists, they told her the cancer had already reached her brain.

Bigotry exacts its toll in flesh and blood. And left unchecked and unchallenged, prejudices create a poisonous climate for us all. Each of us has a stake in the demand that every human being has a right to a job, to shelter, to health care, to dignity, to respect.

I am very grateful to have this chance to open up a conversation with you about why it is so vital to also defend the right of individuals to express and define their sex and gender, and to control their own bodies. For me, it's a life-and-death question. But I also believe that this discussion will have great meaning for you. All your life you've heard such dogma about what it means to be a "real" woman or a "real" man. And chances are you've choked on some of it. You've balked at the idea that being a woman means having to be thin as a rail, emotionally nurturing, and an airhead when it comes to balancing her checkbook. You know in your guts that being a man has nothing to do with rippling muscles, innate courage, or knowing how to handle a chain saw. These are really caricatures. Yet these images have been drilled into us through popular culture and education over the years. And subtler, equally insidious messages lurk in the interstices of these grosser concepts. These ideas of what a "real" woman or man should be straightjacket the freedom of individual self-expression. These gender messages play on and on in a continuous loop in our brains, like commercials that can't be muted.

But in my lifetime I've also seen social upheavals challenge this sex and gender doctrine. As a child who grew up during the McCarthyite, Father-Knows-Best 1950s, and who came of age during the second wave of women's liberation in the United States, I've seen transformations in the ways people think and talk about what it means to be a woman or a man.

Today the gains of the 1970s women's liberation movement are under siege by right-wing propagandists. But many today who are too young to remember what life was like before the women's movement need to know that this was a tremendously progressive development that won significant economic and social reforms. And this struggle by women and their allies swung human consciousness forward like a pendulum.

The movement replaced the common usage of vulgar and diminutive words to describe females with the word *woman* and infused that word with strength and pride. Women, many of them formerly isolated, were drawn together into consciousness-raising groups. Their discussions-about the root of women's oppression and how to eradicate it-resonated far beyond the rooms in which they took place. The women's liberation movement sparked a mass conversation about the systematic degradation, violence, and discrimination that women faced in this society. And this consciousness raising changed many of the ways women and men thought about themselves and their relation to each other. In retrospect, however, we must not forget that these widespread discussions were not just organized to *talk* about oppression. They were a giant dialogue about how to take action to fight institutionalized anti-woman attitudes, rape and battering, the illegality of abortion, employment and education discrimination, and other ways women were socially and economically devalued.

This was a big step forward for humanity. And even the period of political reaction that followed has not been able to overturn all the gains made by that important social movement.

Now another movement is sweeping onto the stage of history: Trans liberation. We are again raising questions about the societal treatment of people based on their sex and gender expression. This discussion will make new contributions to human consciousness. And trans communities, like the women's movement, are carrying out these mass conversations with the goal of creating a movement capable of fighting for justice-of righting the wrongs.

We are a movement of masculine females and feminine males, cross-dressers, transsexual men and women, intersexuals born on the anatomical sweep between female and male, gender-blenders, many other sex and gender-variant people, and our significant others. All told, we expand understanding of how many ways there are to be a human being.

Our lives are proof that sex and gender are much more complex than a delivery room doctor's glance at genitals can determine, more variegated than pink or blue birth caps. We are oppressed for not fitting those narrow social norms. We are fighting back.

Our struggle will also help expose some of the harmful myths about what it means to be a woman or a man that have compartmentalized and distorted your life, as well as mine. Trans liberation has meaning for you-no matter how you define or express your sex or your gender.

If you are a trans person, you face horrendous social punishments-from institutionalization to gang rape, from beatings to denial of child visitation. This oppression is faced, in varying degrees, by all who march under the banner of trans liberation. This brutalization and degradation strips us of what we could achieve with our individual lifetimes.

And if you do not identify as transgender or transsexual or intersexual, your life is diminished by our oppression as well. Your own choices as a man or a woman are sharply curtailed. Your individual journey to express yourself is shunted into one of two deeply carved ruts, and the social baggage you are handed is already packed.

So the defense of each individual's right to control their own body, and to explore the path of self-expression, enhances your own freedom to discover more about yourself and your potentialities. This movement will give you more room to breathe-to be yourself. To discover on a deeper level what it means to be your self.

Together, I believe we can forge a coalition that can fight on behalf of your oppression as well as mine. Together, we can raise each other's grievances and win the kind of significant change we all long for. But the foundation of unity is understanding. So let me begin by telling you a little bit about myself.

I am a human being who unnerves some people. As they look at me, they see a kaleidoscope of characteristics they associate with both males and females. I appear to be a tangled knot of gender contradictions. So they feverishly press the question on me: woman or man? Those are the only two words most people have as tools to shape their question.

"Which sex are you?" I understand their question. It sounds so simple. And I'd like to offer them a simple resolution. But merely answering woman or man will not bring relief to the questioner. As long as people try to bring me into focus using only those two lenses, I will always appear to be an enigma.

The truth is I'm no mystery. I'm a female who is more masculine than those prominently portrayed in mass culture. Millions of females and millions of males in this country do not fit the cramped compartments of gender that we have been taught are "natural" and "normal." For many of us, the words *woman* or *man, ma'am* or *sir, she* or he-in and of themselves-do not total up the sum of our identities or of our oppressions. Speaking for myself, my life only comes into focus when the word *transgender* is added to the equation.

Simply answering whether I was born female or male will not solve the conundrum. Before I can even begin to respond to the question of my own birth sex, I feel it's important to challenge the assumption that the answer is always as simple as either-or. I believe we need to take a critical look at the assumption that is built into the seemingly innocent question: "What a beautiful baby-is it a boy or a girl?"

The human anatomical spectrum can't be understood, let alone appreciated, as long as female or male are considered to be all that exists. "Is it a boy or a girl?" Those are the only two categories allowed on birth certificates.

But this either-or leaves no room for intersexual people, born between the poles of female and male. Human anatomy continues to burst the confines of the contemporary concept that nature delivers all babies on two unrelated conveyor belts. So are the birth certificates changed to reflect human anatomy? No, the U.S. medical establishment hormonally molds and shapes and surgically hacks away at the exquisite complexities of intersexual infants until they neatly fit one category or the other.

A surgeon decides whether a clitoris is "too large" or a penis is "too small." That's a highly subjective decision for anyone to make about another person's body. Especially when the person making the arbitrary decision is scrubbed up for surgery! And what is the criterion for a penis being "too small"? Too small for successful heterosexual intercourse. Intersexual infants are already being tailored for their sexuality, as well as their sex. The infants have no say over what happens to their bodies. Clearly the struggle against genital mutilation must begin here, within the borders of the United States.

But the question asked of all new parents: "Is it a boy or a girl?" is not such a simple question when transsexuality is taken into account, either. Legions of out-and-proud transsexual men and women demonstrate that individuals have a deep, developed, and valid sense of their own sex that does not always correspond to the cursory decision made by a delivery-room obstetrician. Nor is transsexuality a recent phenomenon. People have undergone social sex reassignment and surgical and hormonal sex changes throughout the breadth of oral and recorded human history.

Having offered this view of the complexities and limitations of birth classification, I have no hesitancy in saying I was born female. But that answer doesn't clear up the confusion that drives some people to ask me "Are you a man or a woman?" The problem is that they are trying to understand my gender expression by determining my sex-and therein lies the rub! Just as most of us grew up with only the concepts of *woman* and *man*, the terms *feminine* and *masculine* are the only two tools most people have to talk about the complexities of gender expression.

That pink-blue dogma assumes that biology steers our social destiny. We have been taught that being born female or male will determine how we will dress and walk, whether we will prefer our hair shortly cropped or long and flowing, whether we will be emotionally nurturing or repressed. According to this way of thinking, masculine females are trying to look "like men," and feminine males are trying to act "like women."

But those of us who transgress those gender assumptions also shatter their inflexibility.

So why do I sometimes describe myself as a masculine female? Isn't each of those concepts very limiting? Yes. But placing the two words together is incendiary, exploding the belief that gender expression is linked to birth sex like horse and carriage. It is the social contradiction missing from Dick-and-Jane textbook education.

I actually chafe at describing myself as masculine. For one thing, masculinity is such an expansive territory, encompassing boundaries of nationality, race, and class. Most importantly, individuals blaze their own trails across this landscape.

And it's hard for me to label the intricate matrix of my gender as simply masculine. To me, branding individual self-expression as simply feminine or masculine is like asking poets: Do you write in English or Spanish? The question leaves out the possibilities that the poetry is woven in Cantonese or Ladino, Swahili or Arabic. The question deals only with the system of language that the poet has been taught. It ignores the words each writer hauls up, hand over hand, from a common well. The music words make when finding themselves next to each other for the first time. The silences echoing in the space between ideas. The powerful winds of passion and belief that move the poet to write.

That is why I do not hold the view that gender is simply a social construct-one of two languages that we learn by rote from early age. To me, gender is the poetry each of us makes out of the language we are taught. When I walk through the anthology of the world, I see individuals express their gender in exquisitely complex and ever-changing ways, despite the laws of pentameter.

So how can gender expression be mandated by edict and enforced by law? Isn't that like trying to handcuff a pool of mercury? It's true that human self-expression is diverse and is often expressed in ambiguous or contradictory ways. And what degree of gender expression is considered "acceptable" can depend on your social situation, your race and nationality, your class, and whether you live in an urban or rural environment.

But no one can deny that rigid gender education begins early on in life-from pink and blue color-coding of infant outfits to gender-labeling toys and games. And those who overstep these arbitrary borders are punished. Severely. When the steel handcuffs tighten, it is human bones that crack. No one knows how many trans lives have been lost to police brutality and street-corner bashing. The lives of trans people are so depreciated in this society that many murders go unreported. And those of us who have survived are deeply scarred by daily run-ins with hate, discrimination, and violence.

Trans people are still literally social outlaws. And that's why I am willing at times, publicly, to reduce the totality of my self-expression to descriptions like masculine female, butch, bulldagger, drag king, cross-dresser. These terms describe outlaw status. And I hold my head up proudly in that police lineup. The word *outlaw* is not hyperbolic. I have been locked up in jail by cops because I was wearing a suit and tie. Was my clothing really a crime? Is it a "man's" suit if I am wearing it? At what point-from field to rack-is fiber assigned a sex?

The reality of why I was arrested was as cold as the cell's cement floor: I am considered a masculine female. That's a *gender* violation. My feminine drag queen sisters were in nearby cells, busted for wearing "women's" clothing. The cells that we were thrown into had the same design of bars and concrete. But when we-gay drag kings and drag queens-were thrown into them, the cops referred to the cells as bull's tanks and queen's tanks. The cells were named after our crimes: gender transgression. Actual statutes against cross-dressing and cross-gendered behavior still exist in written laws today. But even where the laws are not written down, police, judges, and prison guards are empowered to carry out merciless punishment for sex and gender "difference."

I believe we need to sharpen our view of how repression by the police, courts, and prisons, as well as all forms of racism and bigotry, operates as gears in the machinery of the economic and social system that governs our lives. As all those who have the least to lose from changing this system get together and examine these social questions, we can separate the wheat of truths from the chaff of old lies. Historic tasks are revealed that beckon us to take a stand and to take action.

That moment is now. And so this conversation with you takes place with the momentum of struggle behind it.

What will it take to put a halt to "legal" and extralegal violence against trans people? How can we strike the unjust and absurd laws mandating dress and behavior for females and males from the books? How can we weed out all the forms of trans-phobic and gender-phobic discrimination?

Where does the struggle for sex and gender liberation fit in relation to other movements for economic and social equality? How can we reach a point where we appreciate each other's differences, not just tolerate them? How can we tear down the electrified barbed wire that has been placed between us to keep us separated, fearful and pitted against each other? How can we forge a movement that can bring about profound and lasting change-a movement capable of transforming society?

These questions can only be answered when we begin to organize together, ready to struggle on each other's behalf. Understanding each other will compel us as honest, caring people to fight each other's oppression as though it was our own.

This book is one of my contributions to this societal discussion. Many of the chapters are adaptations of talks I gave in the spring of 1997, as I set out on the rocky road to recover my health. In the weeks after the last intravenous tubes were removed from my arms and chest, I emerged from illness like a resistance fighter climbing up from a sewer into the sunlight. I faced a calendar filled with opportunities to speak with people at universities, conferences, and rallies. That particular spring was a precious gift I could not take for granted. I'd fought so hard to live.

I remember the enormous physical effort it took to lug my suitcase off a conveyorbelt, to walk long distances through crowded airports. But I also remember amazing conversations I had with many wonderful individuals. I found people were ready to talk about sex and gender liberation in every part of the United States I visited-from Manhattan to Tallahassee, from Birmingham to Denver. I was moved by the emotional and enthusiastic responses I received from audiences in Berlin, Leipzig, Koln, and Hamburg, Germany.

Some of those speeches are included in this book. I've prefaced them with a description of the circumstances, audiences, and surroundings, so that you can feel yourself a part of it. I've also included the voices of other trans people-each of whom I deeply respect. These trans people have different identities, experiences, and viewpoints from mine, so you can hear the wider conversation that is now underway.

The poet Rainer Maria Rilke wrote, "Be conversant with transformation." This book is my voice in this conversation. I look forward to hearing yours.

Name _____   Date _____

Course & section: _____   Instructor _____

We Are All Works in Progress
from *Trans Liberation: Beyond Pink or Blue*

Leslie Feinberg

1. What does Feinberg mean by transliberation? Outline the goals and benefits. In your own words, write an explanation of transliberation for a friend or a first-year student on campus.

   Now try to convey this idea in 140 characters. You know, make it tweet-able.

2. What have been the goals of feminist movements? Successes? Setbacks? What is the relationship between transliberation and feminist movements?

3. Explain Feinberg's position on the nature versus nurture debate.

4. Do you think there has been progress in transliberation that impacts your life? Provide examples. How would you answer Feinberg's question "How can we forge a movement that can bring about lasting change for transforming society?"

5. Go to Campus Pride Index (http://www.campusprideindex.org/) and look up your campus' rating and evaluation. What is your campus' score? What is your campus' ranking? Do you agree with the assessment? Why or why not? In what areas does your campus need to improve? What could your campus do to improve this rating?

"Oppression"

Marilyn Frye

Marilyn Frye was a university distinguished professor of philosophy and feminist theory before retirement from Michigan State University. She is the author of two books of feminist theory *The Willful Virgin* (1992) and *The Politics of Reality* (1989) from which this essay is excerpted.

PRE-READING QUESTIONS

1. Think about the word *oppression*. What is the root of the word? Try to define it.
2. What is the difference between being miserable or frustrated and being oppressed?

KEY TERMS

oppression

SEE THE THEMATIC TABLE OF CONTENTS, IF YOU WANT TO READ MORE ESSAYS ABOUT:

Feminism and Social Movements
Privilege, Identities, and Intersectionalities
Social Construction of Gender

Oppression

Marilyn Frye

It is a fundamental claim of feminism that women are oppressed. The word "oppression" is a strong word. It repels and attracts. It is dangerous and dangerously fashionable and endangered. It is much misused, and sometimes not innocently.

The statement that women are oppressed is frequently met with the claim that men are oppressed too. We hear that oppressing is oppressive to those who oppress as well as to those they oppress. Some men cite as evidence of their oppression their much-advertised inability to cry. It is tough, we are told, to be masculine. When the stresses and frustrations of being a man are cited as evidence that oppressors are oppressed by their oppressing, the word "oppression" is being stretched to meaninglessness; it is treated as though its scope includes any and all human experience of limitation or suffering, no matter the cause, degree, or consequence. Once such usage has been put over on us, then if ever we deny that any person or group is oppressed, we seem to imply that we think they never suffer and have no feelings. We are accused of insensitivity; even of bigotry. For women, such accusation is particularly intimidating, since sensitivity is one of the few virtues that has been assigned to us. If we are found insensitive, we may fear we have no redeeming traits at all and perhaps are not real women. Thus are we silenced before we begin: the name of our situation drained of meaning and our guilt mechanisms tripped.

But this is nonsense. Human beings can be miserable without being oppressed, and it is perfectly consistent to deny that a person or group is oppressed without denying that they have feelings or that they suffer.

We need to think clearly about oppression, and there is much that mitigates against this. I do not want to undertake to prove that women are oppressed (or that men are not), but I want to make clear what is being said when we say it. We need this word, this concept, and we need it to be sharp and sure.

I

The root of the word "oppression" is the element "press." *The press of the crowd; pressed into military service; to press a pair of pants; printing press; press the button.* Presses are used to mold things or flatten them or reduce them in bulk, sometimes to reduce them by squeezing out the gasses or liquids in them. Something pressed is something caught between or among forces and barriers which are so related to each other that jointly they restrain, restrict, or prevent the thing's motion or mobility. Mold. Immobilize. Reduce.

The mundane experience of the oppressed provides another clue. One of the most characteristic and ubiquitous features of the world as experienced by oppressed people is the double bind—situations in which options are reduced to a very few, and all of them expose one to penalty, censure, or deprivation. For example, it is often a requirement upon oppressed people that we smile and be cheerful. If we comply, we signal our docility and our acquiescence in our situation. We need not, then, be taken note of. We acquiesce in being made invisible, in our occupying no space. We participate in our own erasure. On the other hand, anything but the sunniest countenance exposes us to being perceived as mean, bitter, angry, or dangerous. This means, at the least, that we may be found "difficult" or unpleasant to work with, which is enough to cost one one's livelihood; at worst, being seen as mean, bitter, angry or dangerous has been known to result in rape, arrest, beating, and murder. One can only choose to risk one's preferred form and rate of annihilation.

Another example: It is common in the United States that women, especially younger women, are in a bind where neither sexual activity nor sexual inactivity is all right. If she is heterosexually active, a woman is open to censure and punishment for being loose, unprincipled, or a whore. The "punishment" comes in the form of criticism, snide and embarrassing remarks, being treated as an easy lay by men, scorn from her more restrained female friends. She may have to lie and hide her behavior from her parents. She must juggle the risks of unwanted pregnancy and dangerous contraceptives. On the other hand, if she refrains from heterosexual activity, she is fairly constantly harassed by men who try to persuade her into it and pressure her to "relax" and "let her hair down"; she is threatened with labels like "frigid," "uptight," "man-hater," "bitch," and "cocktease." The same parents who would be disapproving of her sexual activity may be worried by her inactivity because it suggests she is not or will not be popular, or is not sexually normal. She may be charged with lesbianism. If a woman is raped, then if she has been heterosexually active she is subject to the presumption that she liked it (since her activity is presumed to show that she likes sex), and if she has not been heterosexually active, she is subject to the presumption that she liked it (since she is supposedly "repressed and frustrated"). Both heterosexual activity and heterosexual nonactivity are likely to be taken as proof that you wanted to be raped, and hence, of course, weren't *really* raped at all. You can't win. You are caught in a bind, caught between systematically related pressures.

Women are caught like this, too, by networks of forces and barriers that expose one to penalty, loss, or contempt whether one works outside the home or not, is on welfare or not, bears children or not, raises children or not, marries or not, stays married or not, is heterosexual, lesbian, both, or neither. Economic necessity; confinement to racial and/or sexual job ghettos; sexual harassment; sex discrimination; pressures of competing expectations and judgments about *women, wives,* and *mothers* (in the society at large, in racial and ethnic subcultures and in one's own mind); dependence (full or partial) on husbands, parents, or the state; commitment to political ideas; loyalties to racial or ethnic or other "minority" groups; the demands of self-respect and responsibilities to others. Each of these factors exists in complex tension with every other, penalizing or prohibiting all of the apparently available options. And nipping at one's heels, always, is the endless pack of little things. If one dresses one way, one is subject to the assumption that one is advertising one's sexual availability; if one dresses another way, one appears to "not care about oneself" or to be "unfeminine." If one uses "strong language," one invites categorization as a whore or slut; if one does not, one invites categorization as a "lady"—one too delicately constituted to cope with robust speech or the realities to which it presumably refers.

The experience of oppressed people is that the living of one's life is confined and shaped by forces and barriers which are not accidental or occasional and hence avoidable, but are systematically related to each other in such a way as to catch one between and among them and restrict or penalize motion in any direction. It is the experience of being caged in: All avenues, in every direction, are blocked or booby trapped.

Cages. Consider a birdcage. If you look very closely at just one wire in the cage, you cannot see the other wires. If your conception of what is before you is determined by this myopic focus, you could look at that one wire, up and down the length of it, and be unable to see why a bird would not just fly around the wire any time it wanted to go somewhere. Furthermore, even if, one day at a time, you myopically inspected each wire, you still could not see why a bird would have trouble going past the wires to get anywhere. There is no physical property of any one wire, *nothing* that the closest scrutiny could discover, that will reveal how a bird could be inhibited or harmed by it except in the most accidental way. It is only when you step back, stop looking at the wires one by one, microscopically, and take a macroscopic view of the whole cage, that you can see why the bird does not go anywhere; and then you will see it in a moment. It will require no great subtlety of mental powers. It is perfectly *obvious* that the bird is surrounded by a network of systematically related barriers, no one of which would be the least hindrance to its flight, but which, by their relations to each other, are as confining as the solid walls of a dungeon.

It is now possible to grasp one of the reasons why oppression can be hard to see and recognize: one can study the elements of an oppressive structure with great care and some good will without seeing the structure as a whole, and hence without seeing or being able to understand that one is looking at a cage and that there are people there who are caged, whose motion and mobility are restricted, whose lives are shaped and reduced.

The arresting of vision at a microscopic level yields such common confusion as that about the male door-opening ritual. This ritual, which is remarkably widespread across classes and races, puzzles many people, some of whom do and some of whom do not find it offensive. Look at the scene of the two people approaching a door. The male steps slightly ahead and opens the door. The male holds the door open while the female glides through. Then the male goes through. The door closes after them. "Now how," one innocently asks, "can those crazy women's libbers say that is oppressive? The guy *removed* a barrier to the lady's smooth and unruffled progress." But each repetition of this ritual has a place in a pattern, in fact in several patterns. One has to shift the level of one's perception in order to see the whole picture.

The door-opening pretends to be a helpful service, but the helpfulness is false. This can be seen by noting that it will be done whether or not it makes any practical sense. Infirm men and men burdened with packages will open doors for able-bodied women who are free of physical burdens. Men will impose themselves awkwardly and jostle everyone in order to get to the door first. The act is not determined by convenience or grace. Furthermore, these very numerous acts of unneeded or even noisome "help" occur in counter-point to a pattern of men not being helpful in many practical ways in which women might welcome help. What *women* experience is a world in which gallant princes charming commonly make a fuss about being helpful and providing small services when help and services are of little or no use, but in which there are rarely ingenious and adroit princes at hand when substantial assistance is really wanted either in mundane affairs or in situations of threat, assault, or terror. There is no help with the (his) laundry; no help typing a report at 4:00 A.M.; no help in mediating disputes among relatives or children. There is nothing but advice that women should stay indoors after dark, be chaperoned by a man, or when it comes down to it, "lie back and enjoy it."

The gallant gestures have no practical meaning. Their meaning is symbolic. The door-opening and similar services provided are services which really are needed by people who are for one reason or another incapacitated—unwell, burdened with parcels, etc. So the message is that women are incapable. The detachment of the acts from the concrete realities of what women need and do not need is a vehicle for the message that women's actual needs and interests are unimportant or irrelevant. Finally, these gestures imitate the behavior of servants toward masters and thus mock women, who are in most respects the servants and caretakers of men. The message of the false helpfulness of male gallantry is female dependence, the invisibility or insignificance of women, and contempt for women.

One cannot see the meanings of these rituals if one's focus is riveted upon the individual event in all its particularity, including the particularity of the individual man's present conscious intentions and motives and the individual woman's conscious perception of the event in the moment. It seems sometimes that people take a deliberately myopic view and fill their eyes with things seen microscopically in order not to see macroscopically. At any rate, whether it is deliberate or not, people can and do fail to see the oppression of women because they fail to see macroscopically and hence fail to see the various elements of the situation as systematically related in larger schemes.

As the cageness of the bird cage is a macroscopic phenomenon, the oppressiveness of the situations in which women live our various and different lives is a macroscopic phenomenon. Neither can be *seen* from a microscopic perspective. But when you look macroscopically you can see it—a network of forces and barriers which are systematically related and which conspire to the immobilization, reduction, and molding of women and the lives we live . . .

III

It seems to be the human condition that in one degree or another we all suffer frustration and limitation, all encounter unwelcome barriers, and all are damaged and hurt in various ways. Since we are a social species, almost all of our behavior and activities are structured by more than individual inclination and the conditions of the planet and its atmosphere. No human is free of social structures, nor (perhaps) would happiness consist in such freedom. Structure consists of boundaries, limits, and barriers; in a structured whole, some motions and changes are possible, and others are not. If one is looking for an excuse to dilute the word "oppression," one can use the fact of social structure as an excuse and say that everyone is oppressed. But if one would rather get clear about what oppression is and is not, one needs to sort out the sufferings, harms, and limitations and figure out which are elements of oppression and which are not.

From what I have already said here, it is clear that if one wants to determine whether a particular suffering, harm, or limitation is part of someone's being oppressed, one has to look at it *in context* in order to tell whether it is an element in an oppressive structure: one has to see if it is part of an enclosing structure of forces and barriers which tends to the immobilization and reduction of a group or category of people. One has to look at how the barrier or force fits with others and to whose benefit or detriment it works. As soon as one looks at examples, it becomes obvious that not everything which frustrates or limits a person is oppressive, and not every harm or damage is due to or contributes to oppression.

If a rich white playboy who lives off income from his investments in South African diamond mines should break a leg in a skiing accident at Aspen and wait in pain in a blizzard for hours before he is rescued, we may assume that in that period he suffers. But the suffering comes to an end; his leg is repaired by the best surgeon money can buy and he is soon recuperating in a lavish suite, sipping Chivas Regal. Nothing in this picture suggests a structure of barriers and forces. He is a member of several oppressor groups and does not suddenly become oppressed because he is injured and in pain. Even if the accident was caused by someone's malicious negligence, and hence someone can be blamed for it and morally faulted, that person still has not been an agent of oppression.

Consider also the restriction of having to drive one's vehicle on a certain side of the road. There is no doubt that this restriction is almost unbearably frustrating at times, when one's lane is not moving and the other lane is clear. There are surely times, even, when abiding by this regulation would have harmful consequences. But the restriction is obviously wholesome for most of us most of the time. The restraint is imposed for our benefit, and does benefit us; its operation tends to encourage our *continued* motion, not to immobilize us. The limits imposed by traffic regulations are limits most of us would cheerfully impose on ourselves given that we knew others would follow them too. They are part of a structure which shapes our behavior, not to our reduction and immobilization, but rather to the protection of our continued ability to move and act as we will.

Another example: The boundaries of a racial ghetto in an American city serve to some extent to keep white people from going in, as well as to keep ghetto dwellers from going out. A particular white citizen may be frustrated or feel deprived because s/he cannot stroll around there and enjoy the "exotic" aura of a "foreign" culture, or shop for bargains in the ghetto swap shops. In fact, the existence of the ghetto, of racial segregation, does deprive the white person of knowledge and harm her/his character by nurturing unwarranted feelings of superiority. But this does not make the white person in this situation a member of an oppressed race or a person oppressed because of her/his race. One must look at the barrier. It limits the activities and the access of those on both sides of it (though to different degrees). But it is a product of the intention, planning, and action of whites for the benefit of whites, to secure and maintain privileges that are available to whites generally, as members of the dominant and privileged group. Though the existence of the barrier has some bad consequences for whites, the barrier does not exist in systematic relationship with other barriers and forces forming a structure oppressive to whites; quite the contrary. It is part of a structure which oppresses the ghetto dwellers and thereby (and by white intention) protects and furthers white interests as dominant white culture understands them. This barrier is not oppressive to whites, even though it is a barrier to whites.

Barriers have different meanings to those on opposite sides of them, even though they are barriers to both. The physical walls of a prison no more dissolve to let an outsider in than to let an insider out, but for the insider they are confining and limiting while to the outsider they may mean protection from what s/he takes to be threats posed by insiders—freedom from harm or anxiety. A set of social and economic barriers and forces separating two groups may be felt, even painfully, by members of both groups and yet may mean confinement to one and liberty and enlargement of opportunity to the other.

The service sector of the wives/mommas/ assistants/girls is almost exclusively a woman-only sector; its boundaries not only enclose women but to a very great extent keep men out. Some men sometimes encounter this barrier and experience it as a restriction on their movements, their activities, their control or their choices of "life-style." Thinking they might like the simple nurturant life (which they may imagine to be quite free of stress, alienation, and hard work), and feeling deprived since it seems closed to them, they thereupon announce the discovery that they are oppressed, too, by "sex roles." But that barrier is erected and maintained by men, for the benefit of men. It consists of cultural and economic forces and pressures in a culture and economy controlled by men in which, at every economic level and in all racial and ethnic subcultures, economy, tradition—and even ideologies of liberation—work to keep at least local culture and economy in male control.[1*]

The boundary that sets apart women's sphere is maintained and promoted by men generally for the benefit of men generally, and men generally do benefit from this existence, even the man who bumps into it and complains of the inconvenience. That barrier is protecting his classification and status as a male, as superior, as having a right to sexual access to a female or females. It protects a kind of citizenship which is superior to that of females of his class and race, his access to a wider range of better paying and higher status work, and his right to prefer unemployment to the degradation of doing lower status or "women's" work.

If a person's life or activity is affected by some force or barrier that person encounters, one may not conclude that the person is oppressed simply because the person encounters that barrier or force; nor simply because the encounter is unpleasant, frustrating, or painful to that person at that time; nor simply because the existence of the barrier or force, or the processes which maintain or apply it, serve to deprive that person of something of value. One must look at the barrier or force and answer certain questions about it. Who constructs and maintains it? Whose interests are served by its existence? Is it part of a structure which tends to confine, reduce, and immobilize some group? Is the individual a member of the confined group? Various forces, barriers, and limitations a person may encounter or live with may be part of an oppressive structure or not, and if they are, that person may be on either the oppressed or the oppressor side of it. One cannot tell which by how loudly or how little the person complains.

IV

Many of the restrictions and limitations we live with are more or less internalized and self-monitored and are part of our adaptations to the requirements and expectations imposed by the needs and tastes and tyrannies of others. I have in mind such things as women's cramped postures and attenuated strides and men's restraint of emotional self-expression (except for anger). Who gets what out of the practice of those disciplines, and who imposes what penalties for improper relaxations of them? What are the rewards of this self-discipline?

Can men cry? Yes, in the company of women. If a man cannot cry, it is in the company of men that he cannot cry. It is men, not women, who require this restraint and men not only require it, they reward it. The man who maintains a steely or tough or laid-back demeanor (all are forms which suggest invulnerability) marks himself as a member of the male community and is esteemed by other men. Consequently, the maintenance of that demeanor contributes to the man's self-esteem. It is felt as good, and he can feel good about himself. The way this restriction fits into the structures of men's lives is as one of the socially required behaviors which, if carried off, contribute to their acceptance and respect by significant others and to their own self-esteem. It is to their benefit to practice this discipline.

Consider, by comparison, the discipline of women's cramped physical postures and attenuated stride. This discipline can be relaxed in the company of women; it generally is at its most

---

[1*]Of course this is complicated by race and class. Machismo and "Black manhood" politics seem to help keep Latin or Black men in control of more cash than Latin or Black women control; but these politics seem to me also to ultimately help keep the larger economy in *white* male control.

strenuous in the company of men.[2*] Like men's emotional restraint, women's physical restraint is required by men. But unlike the case of men's emotional restraint, women's physical restraint is not rewarded. What do we get for it? Respect and esteem and acceptance? No. They mock us and parody our mincing steps. We look silly, incompetent, weak, and generally contemptible. Our exercise of this discipline tends to low esteem and low self-esteem. It does not benefit us. It fits in a network of behaviors through which we constantly announce to others our membership in a lower caste and our unwillingness and/or inability to defend our bodily or moral integrity. It is degrading and part of a pattern of degradation.

Acceptable behavior for both groups, men and women, involves a required restraint that seems in itself silly and perhaps damaging. But the social effect is drastically different. The woman's restraint is part of a structure oppressive to women; the man's restraint is part of a structure oppressive to women.

V

One is marked for application of oppressive pressures by one's membership in some group or category. Much of one's suffering and frustration befalls one partly or largely because one is a member or that category. In the case at hand, it is the category, *woman*. Being a woman is a major factor in my not having a better job than I do; being a woman selects me as a likely victim of sexual assault or harassment; it is my being a woman that reduces the power of my anger to a proof of my insanity. If a woman has little or no economic or political power, or achieves little of what she wants to achieve, a major causal factor in this is that she is a woman. For any woman of any race or economic class, being a woman is significantly attached to whatever disadvantages and deprivations she suffers, be they great or small.

None of this is the case with respect to a person's being a man. Simply being a man is not what stands between him and a better job; whatever assaults and harassments he is subject to, being male is not what selects him for victimization; being male is not a factor which would make his anger impotent—quite the opposite. If a man has little or no material or political power, or achieves little of what he wants to achieve, his being male is no part of the explanation. Being male is something he has going *for* him, even if race or class or age or disability is going against him.

Women are oppressed, *as women*. Members of certain racial and/or economic groups and classes, both the males and the females, are oppressed *as* members of those races and/or classes. But men are not oppressed *as men*.

. . . **and isn't it strange that any of us should have been confused and mystified about such a simple thing?**

[2*]Cf. *Let's Take Back Our Space: "Female" and "Male" Body Language as a Result of Patriarchal Structures*, by Marianne Wex (Frauenliteratureverlag Hermine Fees, West Germany, 1979), especially p. 173. This remarkable book presents literally thousands of candid photographs of women and men, in public, seated, standing, and lying down. It vividly demonstrates the very systematic differences in women's and men's postures and gestures.

Oppression

Marilyn Frye

1. In this essay, Marilyn Frye seeks to define and explain oppression. Frye claims that oppression is different from being miserable, having limits or barriers, and being frustrated. Explain. Ultimately, how does Frye define oppression? Offer the fullest definition you can.

2. What is the double bind? Explain and offer examples. She is speaking specifically about women, but your examples could be about other oppressed groups too.

3. Think of a situation that is an example of being caught in the type of birdcage Frye describes. Describe it. What is the bar of the cage? What is the context? Can a person's confinement in such a birdcage be seen only by viewing the larger situation, as Frye claims?

4. Frye says, "If one is looking for an excuse to dilute the word 'oppression,' one can use the fact of social structure as an excuse and say that everyone is oppressed. But if one would rather get clear about what oppression is and is not, one needs to sort out the sufferings, harms, and limitations and figure out which are elements of oppression and which are not" (13). Think of an example you've heard people use to explain that either "everyone is oppressed" or that a powerful group is actually oppressed—using Frye's logic, how might you debate that point?

5. Develop and explain your own metaphor to explain oppression.

My Life as a Man

Elizabeth Gilbert

Elizabeth Gilbert is a journalist and writer of fiction, biography and memoir, including her bestselling Eat, Pray, Love: One Woman's Search for Everything Across Italy, India, and Indonesia *(2006). She has been a frequent contributor to both GQ and Variety. Her memoir of her years as a bartender was the basis for the film* Coyote Ugly *(2000). "My Life as a Man" originally appeared in GQ (2001).*

PRE-READING QUESTIONS

1. What evidence is used to label individuals as feminine or masculine? How confident are you that you can identify someone's gender?
2. Has anyone ever misidentified your gender? Have you ever misidentified someone else's gender? What were your reactions? The other person's?

KEY TERMS

drag

SEE THE THEMATIC TABLE OF CONTENTS, IF YOU WANT TO READ MORE ESSAYS ABOUT:

Masculinity
Social Construction of Gender

My Life as a Man

Elizabeth Gilbert

The first time I was ever mistaken for a boy, I was 6 years old. I was at the county fair with my beautiful older sister, who had the long blond tresses one typically associates with storybook princesses. I had short messy hair, and I had scabs all over my body from falling out of trees. My beautiful sister ordered a snow cone. The lady at the booth asked, "Doesn't your little brother want one, too?"

I was mortified. I cried all day.

The last time I was mistaken for a boy was only a few weeks ago. I was eating in a Denny's with my husband, and the waitress said, "You fellas want some more coffee?"

This time I didn't cry. It didn't even bother me, because I've grown accustomed to people making the mistake. Frankly, I can understand why they do. I'm afraid I'm not the most feminine creature on the planet. I don't exactly wish to hint that Janet Reno and I were separated at birth, but I do wear my hair short, I am tall, I have broad shoulders and a strong jaw, and I have never really understood the principles of cosmetics. In many cultures, this would make me a man already. In some very primitive cultures, this would actually make me a king.

But sometime after the Denny's incident, I decided, *Ah, to hell with it. If you can't beat 'em, join 'em.* What would it take, I began to wonder, for me to actually transform into a man? To live that way for an entire week? To try to fool everyone? . . .

Fortunately, I have plenty of male friends who rally to my assistance, all eager to see me become the best man I can possibly be. And they all have wise counsel to offer about exactly How to Be a Guy:

"Interrupt people with impunity from now on," says Reggie. "Curse recklessly. And never apologize."

"Never talk about your feelings," says Scott. "Only talk about your accomplishments."

"The minute the conversation turns from something that directly involves you," says Bill "let your mind wander and start looking around the room to see if there's anything nearby you can have sex with."

"If you need to win an argument," says David, "just repeat the last thing the guy you're fighting with said to you, but say it much louder."

So I'm thinking about all this, and I'm realizing that I already do all this stuff. I always win arguments, I'm shamefully slow to apologize, I can't imagine how I could possibly curse any more than I already goddamn do, I've spent the better part of my life looking around to see what's available to have sex with, I can't shut up about my accomplishments, and I'm probably interrupting you right this moment.

Another one of my friends warns, "You do this story, people are gonna talk. People might think you're gay." Aside from honestly not caring what people think, I'm not worried about this possibility at all. I'm worried about something else entirely: that this transformation thing might be *too* easy for me to pull off.

What I'm afraid I'll learn is that I'm *already* a man.

My real coach in this endeavor, though, is a woman. Her name is Diane Torr. Diane is a performance artist who has made her life's work the exploration of gender transformation. As a famous drag king, she has been turning herself into a man for twenty years. She is also known for running workshops wherein groups of women gather and become men for a day.

I call Diane and explain my goal, which is not merely to dress up in some silly costume but to genuinely pass as male and to stay in character for a week.

"That's a tough goal," Diane says, sounding dubious. "It's one thing to play with gender for the afternoon, but really putting yourself out there in the world as a man takes a lot of balls, so to speak. . . ."

Diane agrees to give me a private workshop on Monday. She tells me to spend the weekend preparing for my male life and buying new clothes. Before hanging up, I ask Diane a question I never thought I would ever have to ask anybody:

"What should I bring in terms of genitalia?"

This is when she informs me of the ingredients for my penis.

"Of course," I say calmly.

I write *birdseed* on my hand, underline it twice and make a mental note to stay away from the aviary next week.

I SPEND THE WEEKEND INVENTING MY CHARACTER

One thing is immediately clear: I will have to be younger. I'm 31 years old, and I look it, but with my smooth skin, I will look boyish as a man. So I decide I will be 21 years old for the first time in a decade.

As for my character, I decide to keep it simple and become Luke Gilbert—a midwestern kid new to the city, whose entire background is cribbed from my husband, whose life I know as well as my own.

Luke is bright but a slacker. He really doesn't give a damn about his clothes, for instance. Believe me, I know—I'm the one who shopped for Luke all weekend. By Sunday night, Luke owns several pairs of boring Dockers in various shades of khaki, which he wears baggy. He has Adidas sneakers. He has some boxy short-sleeve buttondown shirts in brown plaids. He has a corduroy jacket, a bike messenger's bag, a few baseball caps and clean underwear. He also has, I'm sorry to report, a really skinny neck.

I haven't even met Luke yet, but I'm beginning to get the feeling he's a real friggin' geek.

THE TRANSFORMATION BEGINS PAINLESSLY ENOUGH

It starts with my hair. Rayya, my regular hairdresser, spends the morning undoing all her work of the past months—darkening out my brightest blond highlights, making me drab, brownish, inconsequential; chopping off my sassy Dixie Chick pixie locks and leaving me with a blunt cut.

"Don't wash it all week," Rayya advises. "Get good and greasy; you'll look more like a guy."

Once the hair is done, Diane Torr gets to work on me. She moves like a pro, quick and competent. Together we stuff my condom ("This is the arts-and-crafts portion of the workshop!"), and Diane helps me insert it into my Calvins. She asks if I want my penis to favor the left or right side. Being a traditionalist, I select the right. Diane adjusts me and backs away; I look down and there it is—my semierect penis, bulging slightly against my briefs. I cannot stop staring at it and don't mind saying that it freaks me out to no end. Then she tries to hide my breasts. To be perfectly honest, my breasts are embarrassingly easy to make disappear. Diane expertly binds them down with wide Ace bandages. Breathing isn't easy, but my chest looks pretty flat now—in fact, with a men's undershirt on, I almost look as if I have well-developed pectoral muscles.

But my ass? Ah, here we encounter a more troublesome situation. I don't want to boast, but I have a big, fat, round ass. You could lop off huge chunks of my ass, make a nice osso buco out of it, serve it up to a family of four and still eat the leftovers for a week. This is a woman's ass, unmistakably. But once I'm fully in costume, I turn around before the mirror and see that I'm going to be OK. The baggy, low-slung pants are good ass camouflage, and the boxy plaid shirt completely eliminates any sign of my waist, so I don't have that girlie hourglass thing happening. I'm a little pear-shaped, perhaps, but let us not kid ourselves, people. There are pear-shaped men out there, walking among us every day.

Then Diane starts on my facial transformation. She has brought crepe hair—thin ropes of artificial hair in various colors, which she trims down to a pile of golden brown stubble. I elect, in homage to Tom Waits, to go with just a small soul patch, a minigoatee, right under my bottom lip. Diane dabs my face with spirit gum—a kind of skin-friendly rubber cement—and presses the hair onto me. It makes for a shockingly good effect. I suggest sideburns, too, and we apply these, making me look like every 21-year-old male art student I've ever seen. Then we muss up and darken my eyebrows. A light shadow of brown under my nose gives me a hint of a mustache. When I look in the mirror, I can't stop laughing. *I am a goddamn man, man!*

Well, more or less.

Diane looks me over critically. "Your jaw is good. Your height is good. But you should stop laughing. It makes you look too friendly, too accessible, too feminine." I stop laughing. She stares at me. "Let's see your walk."

I head across the floor, hands in my pockets.

"Not bad," Diane says, impressed.

Well, I've been practicing. I'm borrowing my walk from Tim Goodwin, a guy I went to high school with. Tim was short and slight but an amazing basketball player (we all called him "Tim Godwin"), and he had an athletic, kneeknocking strut that was very cool. There's also a slouch involved in this walk. But it's—and this is hard to explain—a *stiff* slouch. Years of yoga have made me really limber, but as Luke, I need to drop that ease of motion with my body, because men are not nearly as physically free as women. Watch the way a man turns his head: His whole upper torso turns with it. Unless he's a dancer or a baseball pitcher, he's probably operating his entire body on a ramrod, unyielding axis. On the other hand, watch the way a woman drinks from a bottle. She'll probably tilt her whole head back to accommodate the object, whereas a man would probably hold his neck stiff, tilting the bottle at a sharp angle, making the bottle accommodate *him*. Being a man, it seems, is sometimes just about not budging.

Diane goes on to coach my voice, telling me to lower the timbre and narrow the range. She warns me against making statements that come out as questions, which women do constantly (such as when you ask a woman where she grew up and she replies, "Just outside Cleveland?").

But I don't do that begging-for-approval voice anyway, so this is no problem. As I'd suspected, in fact, all this turning-male stuff is coming too easily to me.

But then Diane says, "Your eyes are going to be the real problem. They're too animated, too bright. When you look at people, you're still too engaged and interested. You need to lose that sparkle, because it's giving you away."

The rest of the afternoon, she's on me about my eyes. She says I'm too flirtatious with my eyes, too encouraging, too appreciative, too attentive, too *available*. I need to intercept all those behaviors, Diane says, and erase them. Because all that stuff is "shorthand for girl." Girls typically flirt and engage and appreciate and attend; men typically don't. It's too generous for men to give themselves away in such a manner. Too dangerous, even. Granted, there are men in this world who are engaging, attentive and sparkly eyed, but Luke Gilbert cannot be one of them. Luke Gilbert's looks are so on the border of being feminine already that I can't afford to express any behavior that is "shorthand for girl," or my cover is blown. I can only emit the most stereotypical masculine code, not wanting to offer people even the faintest hint that I'm anything but a man.

Which means that gradually throughout Monday afternoon, I find myself shutting down my entire personality, one degree at a time. It's very similar to the way I had to shut down my range of physical expression, pulling in my gestures and stiffening up my body. Similarly, I must not budge emotionally. I feel as if I'm closing down a factory, silencing all the humming machines of my character, pulling shut the gates, sending home the workers. All my most animated and familiar facial expressions have to go, and with them go all my most animated and familiar emotions. Ultimately, I am left with only two options for expression—boredom and aggression. Only with boredom and aggression do I truly feel male. It's not a feeling I like at all, by the way. In fact, I am amazed by how much I don't like it. We've been laughing and joking and relating all morning, but slowly now, as I turn into Luke, I feel the whole room chill.

Toward the end of the afternoon, Diane gives me her best and most disturbing piece of advice. "Don't look at the world from the surface of your eyeballs," she says. "All your feminine availability emanates from there. Set your gaze back in your head. Try to get the feeling that your gaze originates from two inches behind the surface of your eyeballs, from where your optic nerves begin in your brain. Keep it right there."

Immediately, I get what she's saying. I pull my gaze back. I don't know how I appear from the outside, but the internal effect is appalling. I feel—for the first time in my life—a dense barrier rise before my vision, keeping me at a palpable distance from the world, roping me off from the people in the room. I feel dead eyed. I feel like a reptile. I feel my whole face change, settling into a hard mask.

Everyone in the room steps back. Rayya, my hairdresser, whistles under her breath and says, "Whoa . . . you got the guy vibe happenin' now, Luke."

Slouching and bored, I mutter a stony thanks.

* * *

Diane finally takes me outside, and we stroll down the street together. She has dressed in drag, too. She's now Danny King—a pompous little man who works in a Pittsburgh department store. She seems perfectly at ease on the street, but I feel cagey and nervous out here in the broad daylight, certain that everyone in the world can see that my face is covered with fake hair and rubber cement and discomfort. The only thing that helps me feel even remotely relaxed is the basketball I'm loosely carrying under my arm—a prop so familiar to me in real life that it helps put me at ease in disguise. We head to a nearby basketball court. We have a small crowd following us—my hairdresser, the makeup artist, a photographer. Diane and I pose for photos under the hoop. I set my basketball down, and almost immediately, a young and muscular black guy comes over and scoops it off the pavement.

"Hey," he says to the crowd. "Whose basketball is this?"

Now, if you want to learn how to define your personal space as a man, you could do worse than take lessons from this guy. His every motion is offense and aggression. He leads with his chest and chin, and he's got a hard and cold set of eyes.

"I said, whose basketball is this?" he repeats, warning with his tone that he doesn't want to have to ask again.

"It's hers," says my hairdresser, pointing at me.

"Hers?" The young man looks at me and snorts in disgust. "What are you talkin' about, *hers*? That ain't no *her*. That's a *guy*."

My first gender victory!

But there's no time to celebrate this moment, because this aggressive and intimidating person needs to be dealt with. Now, here's the thing. Everyone on the court is intimidated by this guy, but I am not. In this tense moment, mind you, I have stopped thinking like Luke Gilbert; I'm back to thinking like Liz Gilbert. And Liz Gilbert always thinks she can manage men. I don't know if it's from years of tending bar, or if it's from living in lunatic-filled New York City, or if it's just a ridiculous (and dangerously naive) sense of personal safety, but I have always believed in my heart that I can disarm any man's aggression. I do it by paying close attention to the aggressive man's face and finding the right blend of flirtation, friendliness and confidence to put on my face to set him at ease, to remind him: *You don't wanna hurt me, you wanna like me*. I've done this a million times before. Which is why I'm looking at this scary guy and I'm thinking, *Give me thirty seconds with him and he'll be on my side*.

I step forward. I open up my whole face in a big smile and say teasingly, "Yeah, that's my basketball, man. Why, you wanna play? You think you can take me?"

"You don't know nothin' about this game," he says.

In my flirtiest possible voice, I say, "Oh, I know a *little* somethin' about this game. . . ."

The guy takes a menacing step forward, narrows his eyes and growls, "You don't know *shit* about this game."

This is when I snap to attention. This is when I realize I'm on the verge of getting my face punched. What the hell am I doing? This guy honestly thinks I'm a man! Therefore, my whole cute, tomboyish, I'm-just-one-of-the-guys act is not working. One-of-the-guys doesn't work when you actually *are* one of the guys. I have forgotten that I am Luke Gilbert—a little white loser on a basketball court who has just challenged and pissed off and *flirted* with an already volatile large black man. I have made a very bad choice here. I've only been on the job as a male for a few minutes, but it appears as though I'm about to earn myself a good old-fashioned New York City ass-kicking.

He takes another step forward and repeats, "You don't know shit about nothin'."

"You're right, man," I say. I drop my eyes from his. I lower my voice, collapse my posture, show my submission. I am a stray dog, backing away from a fight, head down, tail tucked. "Sorry, man. I was just kidding. I don't know anything about basketball."

"Yeah, that's right," says the guy, satisfied now that he has dominated me. "You don't know shit."

He drops the ball and walks away. My heart is slamming. I'm angry at my own carelessness and frightened by my newfound helplessness. Luke didn't know how to handle that guy on the court, and Luke almost got thrown a beating as a result (and would have deserved it, too—the moron). Realizing this makes me feel suddenly vulnerable, suddenly aware of how small I've become.

My hands, for instance, which have always seemed big and capable to me, suddenly appear rather dainty when I think of them as a man's hands. My arms, so sturdy only hours before, are now the thin arms of a weenie-boy. I've lost this comfortable feeling I've always carried through the world of being strong and brave. A five-foot-nine-inch, 140-pound woman can be a pretty tough character, after all. But a five-foot-nine-inch, 140-pound man? Kinda small, kinda wussy. . . .

* * *

My world-famously tolerant husband seems to have no trouble with my transformation at first. He unwinds my breast bandages every night before bed and listens with patience to my complaints about my itching beard. In the mornings before work, he binds up my breasts again and lends me his spice-scented deodorant so I can smell more masculine. We vie for mirror space in the bathroom as he shaves off his daily stubble and I apply mine. We eat our cereal together, I take my birth control pills, I pack my penis back into my slacks. . . .

It's all very domestic.

Still, by Wednesday morning, my husband confesses that he doesn't want to hang around with me in public anymore. Not as long as I'm Luke. It's not that he's grossed out by my physical transformation, or threatened by the sexual politics at play, or embarrassed by the possibility of exposure. It's simply this: He is deeply, emotionally unsettled by my new personality.

"I miss you," he says. "It's seriously depressing for me to be around you this way."

What's upsetting to Michael is that as a man, I can't give him what he has become accustomed to getting from me as a woman. And I'm not talking about sex. Sex can always be arranged, even this week. (Although I do make a point now of falling asleep immediately after it's over, just to stay in character.) What Michael hates is that I don't engage him anymore. As Luke, I don't laugh at my husband's jokes or ask him about his day. Hell, as Luke, I don't even have a husband—just another drinking buddy whose jokes and workday concerns I don't really care about. Michael, still seeing his wife under her goatee, keeps thinking I'm mad at him, or—worse—bored by him. But I can't attend to him on this, can't reassure him, or I risk coming across like a girl.

The thing is, I don't like Luke's personality any more than Michael does. As Luke, I feel completely and totally bound—and not just because of the tight bandage wrapped around my chest. I keep thinking back to my drag-king workshop, when Diane Torr talked about "intercepting learned feminine habits." She spoke of those learned feminine habits in slightly disparaging terms. Women, she said, are too attentive, too concerned about the feelings of others, too *available*. This idea of women as lost in empathy is certainly a standard tenet of feminism (Oprah calls it the Disease to Please), and, yes, there are many women who drown in their own overavailability. But I've never personally felt that attentiveness and engagement are liabilities. As a writer—indeed, as a *human being*—I think the most exciting way you can interact with this fantastic and capricious world is by being completely available to it. Peel me wide open; availability is my power. I would so much rather be vulnerable and experience existence than be strong and defend myself from it. And if that makes me a girlie-girl, then so be it—I'll be a goddamn girlie-girl.

Only, this week I'm not a girl at all. I'm Luke Gilbert. And poor Luke, I must say, is completely cut off from the human experience. The guy is looking at the world from a place two inches behind his eyeballs. No wonder my husband hates being around him. I'm not crazy about him myself.

* * *

[Wednesday], I'm walking home alone. Just ahead of me, a blond woman steps out of a bar, alone. She's screamingly sexy. She's got all the props—the long hair, the tiny skirt, the skimpy top, the wobbly stiletto heels, the eternal legs. I walk right behind this woman for several blocks and observe the tsunami she causes on 23rd Street in every man she passes—everyone has to re-act to her somehow. What amazes me, though, is how many of the men end up interacting with *me* after passing *her*. What happens is this: She saunters by, the guy stares at her in astonishment and then makes a comment about her to me because I'm the next man on the scene. So we have a little moment together, the guy and me, in which we share an experience. We get to bond. It's an icebreaker for us.

The best is the older construction worker who checks out the babe, then raises his eyebrows at me and declares: "Fandango!"

"You said it!" I say, but when I walk on by, he seems a little disappointed that I haven't stuck around to talk more about it with him.

This kind of interaction happens more than a dozen times within three blocks. Until I start wondering whether this is actually the game. Until I start suspecting that these guys maybe don't want to talk to the girl at all, that maybe they just desperately want to talk to *one another*.

Suddenly, I see this sexy woman in front of me as being just like sports; she's an excuse for men to try to talk to one another. She's like the Knicks, only prettier—a connection for people who otherwise cannot connect at all. It's a very big job, but I don't know if she even realizes she's doing it.

* * *

[Friday] night, taking a friend's advice, I go out drinking in the East Village, where seven out of ten young men look just like Luke Gilbert. I end up at a bar that is crawling with really cute pierced-nosed girls. I'm wondering whom I should try to pick up when an opportunity falls into my lap. A pretty red-haired girl in a black camisole walks into the bar alone. She has cool tattoos all over her arms. The bouncer says to her, "Hey, Darcy, where's your crowd tonight?"

"Everyone copped out," Darcy says. "I'm flying solo."

"So lemme buy you a drink," I call over from the bar.

"Rum and Coke," she says, and comes over to sit next to me.

Fandango!

We get to talking. Darcy's funny, friendly, from Tennessee. She tells me all about her room-mate problems. She asks me about myself, but I don't share—Luke Gilbert is not available for sharing. Instead, I compliment Darcy on her pretty starfish necklace, which Darcy tells me was a gift from a childhood neighbor who was like a grandmother to her. I ask Darcy about her job, and she tells me she works for a publishing house that prints obscure journals with titles like *Catfish Enthusiast Monthly*.

"Damn, and here I just let my subscription to *Catfish Enthusiast Monthly* run out," I say, and she laughs. Darcy actually does that flirty thing girls do sometimes where they laugh and touch your arm and move closer toward you all at the same time. I know this move. I've been doing this move my whole life. And it is with this move and this touch and this laugh that I lose my desire to play this game anymore, because Darcy, I can tell, actually likes Luke Gilbert. Which is incredible, considering that Luke is a sullen, detached, stiff guy who can't make eye contact with the world. But she still likes him. This should feel like a victory, but all I feel like is a complete shitheel. Darcy is nice. And here I'm lying to her already.

Now I really *am* a guy.

"You know what, Darcy?" I say. "I have to go. I'm supposed to hook up with some friends for dinner."

She looks a little hurt. But not as hurt as she would look if, say, we dated for a month and then she found out the truth about me.

I give her a little kiss good-bye on the cheek.

"You're great," I tell her.

And then I'm done.

UNDOING IT ALL TAKES A FEW DAYS

Rubbing alcohol gets the last of the spirit gum and fake hair off my face. I pluck my eyebrows and put on my softest bra (my skin has become chafed from days of binding and taping). I scatter my penis across the sidewalk for the pigeons. I make an appointment to get my hair lightened again. I go to yoga class and reawaken the idea of movement in my body. I cannot wait to get rid of this gender, which I have not enjoyed. But it's a tricky process, because I'm still walking like Luke, still standing like Luke, still thinking like Luke.

In fact, I don't really get my inner Liz back until the next weekend. It's not until the next Saturday night, when I am sitting at a bar on my own big fat ass, wearing my own girlie jeans, talking to an off-duty New York City fireman, that I really come back into myself. The fireman and I are both out with big groups, but somehow we peel off into our own private conversation. Which quickly gets serious. I ask him to tell me about the crucifix around his neck, and he says he's been leaning on God pretty hard this year. I want to know why. The fireman starts telling me about how his beloved father died this winter, and then his fiancee left him, and now the pressures of his work are starting to kill him, and there are times when he just wishes he could cry but he doesn't want people to see him like that. My guy friends are all playing darts in the corner, but I'm the one sitting here listening to this fireman tell me about how he never cries because his dad was such a hard-ass Irish cop, don'tcha know, because he was raised to hang so tough.

I'm looking right into this guy. I'm not touching him at all, but I'm giving him my entire self. He needs me right now, to tell all this to. He can have me. I've got my eyes locked on him, and I can feel how bad he wants to cry, and with my entire face I am telling this man: *Tell me everything*.

He says, "Maybe I was hard on her, maybe that's why she left me, but I was so worried about my father. . . ."

The fireman digs at his eye with a fist. I hand him a bar napkin. He blows his nose. He keeps talking. I keep listening. He can talk to me all night because I am unbound and I am wide-open. I'm open around the clock, open twenty-four hours a day; I never close. I'm really concerned for this guy, but I'm smiling while he spills his story because it feels so good to catch it. It feels so good to be myself again, to be open for business again—open once more for the rewarding and honest human business of complete *availability*.

My Life as a Man

Elizabeth Gilbert

1. Compare Liz and Luke. List the differences you noted.

2. Why did the interaction on the basketball court become hostile/uncomfortable?

3. Compare Liz's list of masculine traits to your own understanding of masculinity? How does masculinity differ according to class, race, age, etc.?

4. What did Gilbert's transition and experiences illustrate about heterosexuality? What questions remain unanswered by her description of her experience? What questions would you ask her about this experience?

5. Observe behaviors on your campus (e.g., in the student union, library, a dining hall, etc.). What gendered behaviors and interactions do you notice? How are people interacting? What are they doing? Wearing? Write up your list of observations on a separate sheet. Note place, time and duration of your observation.

Based on your observations, what advice would you give to Gilbert for her experiment?

X: A Fabulous Child's Story

Lois Gould

Lois Gould is well known for her best selling novel Such Good Friends *(1970) and her memoir* Mommy Dressing *(1998). She was also a contributor to* The New York Times. *Lois Gould died in 2002.* "X: A Fabulous Child's Story" *first appeared in* Ms. Magazine *in December 1972 and was published as a book in 1978.*

PRE-READING QUESTIONS

1. What do you know about gender?
2. What were your favorite toys as a child? Who were your best friends? What activities did you all like to do? What games did you like to play? As a child were you ever told you could not do something because of your gender? By who? (a teacher, another child, family?) How did that affect your experience of gender?

SEE THE THEMATIC TABLE OF CONTENTS, IF YOU WANT TO READ MORE ESSAYS ABOUT:

Bodies and Genders
Families and Relationships
Social Construction of Gender

X: A Fabulous Child's Story

Lois Gould

Once upon a time, a baby named X was born. This baby was named X so that nobody could tell whether it was a boy or a girl. Its parents could tell, of course, but they couldn't tell anybody else. They couldn't even tell Baby X, at first.

You see, it was all part of a very important Secret Scientific Xperiment, known officially as Project Baby X. The smartest scientists had set up this Xperiment at a cost of Xactly 23 billion dollars and 72 cents, which might seem like a lot for just one baby, even a very important Xperimental baby. But when you remember the prices of things like strained carrots and stuffed bunnies, and popcorn for the movies and booster shots for camp, let alone 28 shiny quarters from the tooth fairy, you begin to see how it adds up.

Also, long before Baby X was born, all those scientists had to be paid to work out the details of the Xperiment, and to write the *Official Instruction Manual* for Baby X's parents and, most important of all, to find the right set of parents to bring up Baby X. These parents had to be selected very carefully. Thousands of volunteers had to take thousands of tests and answer thousands of tricky questions. Almost everybody failed because, it turned out, almost everybody really wanted either a baby boy or a baby girl, and not Baby X at all. Also, almost everybody was afraid that a Baby X would be a lot more trouble than a boy or a girl. (They were probably right, the scientists admitted, but Baby X needed parents who wouldn't *mind* the Xtra trouble.)

There were families with grandparents named Milton and Agatha, who didn't see why the baby couldn't be named Milton or Agatha instead of X, even if it *was* an X. There were families with aunts who insisted on knitting tiny dresses and uncles who insisted on sending tiny baseball mitts. Worst of all, there were families that already had other children who couldn't be trusted to keep the secret. Certainly not if they knew the secret was worth 23 billion dollars and 72 cents—and all you had to do was take one little peek at Baby X in the bathtub to know if it was a boy or a girl.

But, finally, the scientists found the Joneses, who really wanted to raise an X more than any other kind of baby—no matter how much trouble it would be. Ms. and Mr. Jones had to promise they would take equal turns caring for X, and feeding it, and singing it lullabies. And they had to promise never to hire any baby-sitters. The government scientists knew perfectly well that a baby-sitter would probably peek at X in the bathtub, too.

The day the Joneses brought their baby home, lots of friends and relatives came over to see it. None of them knew about the secret Xperiment, though. So the first thing they asked was what kind of a baby X was. When the Joneses smiled and said, "It's an X!" nobody knew what to say. They couldn't say, "Look at her cute little dimples!" And they couldn't say, "Look at his husky little biceps!" And they couldn't even say just plain "kitchy-coo." In fact, they all thought the Joneses were playing some kind of rude joke.

But, of course, the Joneses were not joking. "It's an X" was absolutely all they would say. And that made the friends and relatives very angry. The relatives all felt embarrassed about having an X in the family. "People will think there's something wrong with it!" some of them whispered. "There *is* something wrong with it!" others whispered back.

"Nonsense!" the Joneses told them all cheerfully. "What could possibly be wrong with this perfectly adorable X?"

Nobody could answer that, except Baby X, who had just finished its bottle. Baby X's answer was a loud, satisfied burp.

Clearly, nothing at all was wrong. Nevertheless, none of the relatives felt comfortable about buying a present for a Baby X. The cousins who sent the baby a tiny football helmet would not come and visit any more. And the neighbors who sent a pink-flowered romper suit pulled their shades down when the Joneses passed their house.

The *Official Instruction Manual* had warned the new parents that this would happen, so they didn't fret about it. Besides, they were too busy with Baby X and the hundreds of different Xercises for treating it properly.

Ms. and Mr. Jones had to be Xtra careful about how they played with little X. They knew if they kept bouncing it up in the air and saying how *strong* and *active* it was, they'd be treating it more like a boy than an X. But if all they did was cuddle it and kiss it and tell it how *sweet* and *dainty* it was, they'd be treating it more like a girl than an X.

On page 1,654 of the *Official Instruction Manual*, the scientists prescribed: "plenty of bouncing and plenty of cuddling, *both*. X ought to be strong and sweet and active. Forget about *dainty* altogether."

Meanwhile, the Joneses were worrying about other problems. Toys, for instance. And clothes. On his first shopping trip, Mr. Jones told the store clerk, "I need some clothes and toys for my new baby." The clerk smiled and said, "Well, now, is it a boy or a girl?" "It's an X," Mr. Jones said, smiling back. But the clerk got all red in the face and said huffily, "In *that* case, I'm afraid I can't help you, sir." So Mr. Jones wandered helplessly up and down the aisles trying to find what X needed. But everything in the store was piled up in sections marked "Boys" or "Girls." There were "Boys' Pajamas" and "Girls' Underwear" and "Boys' Fire Engines" and "Girls' Housekeeping Sets." Mr. Jones went home without buying anything for X. That night he and Ms. Jones consulted page 2,326 of the *Official Instruction Manual*. "Buy plenty of everything!" it said firmly.

So they bought plenty of sturdy blue pajamas in the Boys' Department and cheerful flowered underwear in the Girls' Department. And they bought all kinds of toys. A boy doll that made pee-pee and cried, "Pa-pa." And a girl doll that talked in three languages and said, "I am the Pres-i-dent of Gen-er-al Mo-tors." They also bought a storybook about a brave princess who rescued a handsome prince from his ivory tower, and another one about a sister and brother who grew up to be a baseball star and a ballet star, and you had to guess which was which.

The head scientists of Project Baby X checked all their purchases and told them to keep up the good work. They also reminded the Joneses to see page 4,629 of the *Manual*, where it said, "Never make Baby X feel *embarrassed* or *ashamed* about what it wants to play with. And if X gets dirty climbing rocks, never say 'Nice little Xes don't get dirty climbing rocks.'"

Likewise, it said, "If X falls down and cries, never say 'Brave little Xes don't cry.' Because, of course, nice little Xes *do* get dirty, and brave little Xes do cry. No matter how dirty X gets, or how hard it cries, don't worry. It's all part of the Xperiment."

Whenever the Joneses pushed Baby X's stroller in the park, smiling strangers would come over and coo: "Is that a boy or a girl?" The Joneses would smile back and say, "It's an X." The strangers would stop smiling then, and often snarl something nasty—as if the Joneses had snarled at *them*.

By the time X grew big enough to play with other children, the Joneses' troubles had grown bigger, too. Once a little girl grabbed X's shovel in the sandbox, and zonked X on the head with it. "Now, now, Tracy," the little girl's mother began to scold, "little girls mustn't hit little—" and she turned to ask X, "Are you a little boy or a little girl, dear?"

Mr. Jones who was sitting near the sandbox, held his breath and crossed his fingers.

X smiled politely at the lady, even though X's head had never been zonked so hard in its life. "I'm a little X," X replied.

"You're a what?" the lady exclaimed angrily. "You're a little b-r-a-t, you mean!"

"But little girls mustn't hit little Xes, either!" said X, retrieving the shovel with another polite smile. "What good does hitting do, anyway?"

X's father, who was still holding his breath, finally let it out, uncrossed his fingers, and grinned back at X.

And at their next secret Project Baby X meeting, the scientists grinned, too. Baby X was doing fine.

But then it was time for X to start school. The Joneses were really worried about this, because school was even more full of rules for boys and girls, and there were no rules for Xes. The teacher would tell boys to form one line, and girls to form another line. There would be boys' games and girls' games, and boys' secrets and girls' secrets. The school library would have a list of recommended books for girls, and a different list of recommended books for boys. There would even be a bathroom marked BOYS and another one marked GIRLS. Pretty soon boys and girls would hardly talk to each other. What would happen to poor little X?

The Joneses spent weeks consulting their *Instruction Manual* (there were 249/Z> pages of advice under "First Day of School"), and attending urgent special conferences with the smart scientists of Project Baby X.

The scientists had to make sure that X's mother had taught X how to throw and catch a ball properly, and that X's father had been sure to teach X what to serve at a doll's tea party. X had to know how to shoot marbles and how to jump rope and, most of all, what to say when the Other Children asked whether X was a Boy or a Girl.

Finally, X was ready. The Joneses helped X button on a nice new pair of red-and-white checked overalls, and sharpened six pencils for X's nice new pencil box, and marked X's name clearly on all the books in its nice new book bag. X brushed its teeth and combed its hair, which just about covered its ears, and remembered to put a napkin in its lunchbox.

The Joneses had asked X's teacher if the class could line up alphabetically, instead of forming separate lines for boys and girls. And they had asked if X could use the principal's bathroom, because it wasn't marked anything except BATHROOM. X's teacher promised to take care of all those problems. But nobody could help X with the biggest problem of all—Other Children.

Nobody in X's class had ever known an X before. What would they think? How would X make friends?

You couldn't tell what X was by studying its clothes—overalls don't even button right-to-left, like girls' clothes, or left-to-right, like boys' clothes. And you couldn't guess whether X had a girl's short haircut or a boy's long haircut. And it was very hard to tell by the games X liked to play. Either X played ball very well for a girl, or else X played house very well for a boy.

Some of the children tried to find out by asking X tricky questions, like "Who's your favorite sports star?" That was easy. X had two favorite sports stars: a girl jockey named Robyn Smith and a boy archery champion named Robin Hood. Then they asked, "What's your favorite TV program?" And that was even easier. X's favorite TV program was "Lassie," which stars a girl dog played by a boy dog.

When X said that its favorite toy was a doll, everyone decided that X must be a girl. But then X said that the doll was really a robot, and that X had computerized it, and that it was programmed to bake fudge brownies and then clean up the kitchen. After X told them that, the other children gave up guessing what X was. All they knew was they'd sure like to see X's doll.

After school, X wanted to play with the other children. "How about shooting some baskets in the gym?" X asked the girls. But all they did was make faces and giggle behind X's back.

"How about weaving some baskets in the arts and crafts room?" X asked the boys. But they all made faces and giggled behind X's back too.

That night, Ms. and Mr. Jones asked X how things had gone at school. X told them sadly that the lessons were okay, but otherwise school was a terrible place for an X. It seemed as if Other Children would never want an X for a friend.

Once more, the Joneses reached for their *Instruction Manual.* Under "Other Children," they found the following message: "What did you Xpect? *Other Children* have to obey all the silly boy-girl rules, because their parents taught them to. Lucky X—you don't have to stick to the rules at all! All you have to do is be yourself. P.S. We're not saying it'll be easy."

X liked being itself. But X cried a lot that night, partly because it felt afraid. So X's father held X tight, and cuddled it, and couldn't help crying a little, too. And X's mother cheered them both up by reading an Xciting story about an enchanted prince called Sleeping Handsome, who woke up when Princess Charming kissed him.

The next morning, they all felt much better, and little X went back to school with a brave smile and a clean pair of red-and-white checked overalls.

There was a seven-letter-word spelling bee in class that day. And a seven-lap boys' relay race in the gym. And a seven-layer-cake baking contest in the girls' kitchen corner. X won the spelling bee. X also won the relay race. And X almost won the baking contest, except it forgot to light the oven. Which only proves that nobody's perfect.

One of the Other Children noticed something else, too. He said: "Winning or losing doesn't seem to count to X. X seems to have fun being good at boys' skills *and* girls' skills."

"Come to think of it," said another one of the Other Children, "maybe X is having twice as much fun as we are!"

So after school that day, the girl who beat X at the baking contest gave X a big slice of her prize winning cake. And the boy X beat in the relay race asked X to race him home.

From then on, some really funny things began to happen. Susie, who sat next to X in class, suddenly refused to wear pink dresses to school any more. She insisted on wearing red-and-white checked overalls—just like X's. Overalls, she told her parents, were much better for climbing monkey bars.

Then Jim, the class football nut, started wheeling his little sister's doll carriage around the football field. He'd put on his entire football uniform, except for the helmet. Then he'd put the helmet *in* the carriage, lovingly tucked under an old set of shoulder pads. Then he'd start jogging around the field, pushing the carriage and singing "Rock-a-bye Baby" to his football helmet. He told his family that X did the same thing, so it must be okay. After all X was now the team's star quarterback.

Susie's parents were horrified by her behavior, and Jim's parents were worried sick about his. But the worst came when the twins, Joe and Peggy, decided to share everything with each other. Peggy used Joe's hockey skates, and his microscope, and took half his newspaper route. Joe used Peggy's needlepoint kit, and her cookbooks, and took two of her three baby-sitting jobs. Peggy started running the lawn mower, and Joe started running the vacuum cleaner.

Their parents weren't one bit pleased with Peggy's wonderful biology experiments, or with Joe's terrific needlepoint pillows. They didn't care that Peggy mowed the lawn better, and that Joe vacuumed the carpet better. In fact, they were furious. It's all that little X's fault, they agreed. Just because X doesn't know what it is, or what it's supposed to be, it wants to get everybody *else* mixed up, too!

Peggy and Joe were forbidden to play with X any more. So was Susie, and then Jim, and then *all* the Other Children. But it was too late; the Other Children stayed mixed up and happy and free, and refused to go back to the way they'd been before X.

Finally, Joe and Peggy's parents decided to call an emergency meeting of the school's Parents' Association, to discuss "The X Problem." They sent a report to the principal stating that X was a "disruptive influence." They demanded immediate action. The Joneses, they said, should be *forced* to tell whether X was a boy or a girl. And then X should be *forced* to behave like whichever it was. If the Joneses refused to tell, the Parents' Association said, then X must take an Xamination. The school psychiatrist must Xamine it physically and mentally, and issue a full report. If X's test showed it was a boy, it would have to obey all the boys' rules. If it proved to be a girl, X would have to obey all the girls' rules.

And if X turned out to be some kind of mixed-up misfit, then X should be Xpelled from the school. Immediately!

The principal was very upset. Disruptive influence? Mixed-up misfit? But X was an Xcellent student. All the teachers said it was a delight to have X in their classes. X was president of the student council. X had won first prize in the talent show, and second prize in the art show, and honorable mention in the science fair, and six athletic events on field day, including the potato race.

Nevertheless, insisted the Parents' Association, X is a Problem Child. X is the Biggest Problem Child we have ever seen!

So the principal reluctantly notified X's parents that numerous complaints about X's behavior had come to the school's attention. And that after the psychiatrist's Xamination, the school would decide what to do about X.

The Joneses reported this at once to the scientists, who referred them to page 85,759 of the *Instruction Manual*. "Sooner or later," it said, "X will have to be Xamined by a psychiatrist. This may be the only way any of us will know for sure whether X is mixed up—or whether everyone else is."

The night before X was to be Xamined, the Joneses tried not to let X see how worried they were. "What if—?" Mr. Jones would say. And Ms. Jones would reply, "No use worrying." Then a few minutes later, Ms. Jones would say, "What if—?" and Mr. Jones would reply, "No use worrying."

X just smiled at them both, and hugged them hard and didn't say much of anything. X was thinking. What if—? And then X thought: No use worrying.

At Xactly 9 o'clock the next day, X reported to the school psychiatrist's office. The principal, along with a committee from the Parents' Association, X's teacher, X's classmates, and Ms. and

Mr. Jones, waited in the hall outside. Nobody knew the details of the tests X was to be given, but everybody knew they'd be *very* hard, and that they'd reveal Xactly what everyone wanted to know about X, but were afraid to ask.

It was terribly quiet in the hall. Almost spooky. Once in a while, they would hear a strange noise inside the room. There were buzzes. And a beep or two. And several bells. An occasional light would flash under the door. The Joneses thought it was a white light, but the principal thought it was blue. Two or three children swore it was either yellow or green. And the Parents' Committee missed it completely.

Through it all, you could hear the psychiatrist's low voice, asking hundreds of questions, and X's higher voice, answering hundreds of answers.

The whole thing took so long that everyone knew it must be the most complete Xamination anyone had ever had to take. Poor X, the Joneses thought. Serves X right, the Parents' Committee thought. I wouldn't like to be in X's overalls right now, the children thought.

At last, the door opened. Everyone crowded around to hear the results. X didn't look any different; in fact, X was smiling. But the psychiatrist looked terrible. He look as if he was crying! "What happened?" everyone began shouting. Had X done something disgraceful? "I wouldn't be a bit surprised!" muttered Peggy and Joe's parents. "Did X flunk the *whole* test?" cried Susie's parents. "Or just the most important part?" yelled Jim's parents.

"Oh, dear," sighed Mr. Jones.

"Oh, dear," sighed Ms. Jones.

"*Sssh*," ssshed the principal. "The psychiatrist is trying to speak."

Wiping, his eyes and clearing his throat, the psychiatrist began, in a hoarse whisper. "In my opinion," he whispered—you could tell he must be very upset—"in my opinion, young X here—"

"Yes? Yes?" shouted a parent impatiently.

"*Sssh!*" ssshed the principal.

"Young *Sssh* here, I mean young X," said the doctor, frowning, "is just about—"

"Just about *what*? Let's have it!" shouted another parent.

". . . just about the *least* mixed-up child I've ever Xamined!" said the psychiatrist.

"Yay for X!" yelled one of the children. And then the others began yelling, too. Clapping and cheering and jumping up and down.

"*SSSH!*" SSShed the principal, but nobody did.

The Parents' Committee was angry and bewildered. How *could* X have passed the whole Xamination? Didn't X have an *identity* problem? Wasn't X mixed up at *all*? Wasn't X *any* kind of a misfit? How could it *not* be, when it didn't even *know* what it was? And why was the psychiatrist crying?

Actually, he had stopped crying and was smiling politely through his tears. "Don't you see?" he said. "I'm crying because it's wonderful! X has absolutely no identity problem! X isn't one bit mixed up! As for being a misfit—ridiculous! X knows perfectly well what it is! Don't you, X?" The doctor winked, X winked back.

"But what *is* X?" shrieked Peggy and Joe's parents. "*We* still want to know what it is!"

"Ah, yes," said the doctor, winking again. "Well, don't worry. You'll all know one of these days. And you won't need me to tell you."

"What? What does he mean?" some of the parents grumbled suspiciously.

Susie and Peggy and Joe all answered at once. "He means that by the time X's sex matters, it won't be a secret any more!"

With that, the doctor began to push through the crowd toward X's parents. "How do you do," he said, somewhat stiffly. And then he reached out to hug them both. "If I ever have an X of my own," he whispered, "I sure hope you'll lend me your instruction manual."

Needless to say, the Joneses were very happy. The Project Baby X scientists were rather pleased, too. So were Susie, Jim, Peggy, Joe, and all the Other Children. The Parents' Association wasn't, but they had promised to accept the psychiatrist's report, and not make any more trouble. They even invited Ms. and Mr. Jones to become honorary members, which they did.

Later that day, all X's friends put on their red-and-white checked overalls and went over to see X. They found X in the back yard, playing with a very tiny baby that none of them had ever seen before. The baby was wearing very tiny red-and-white checked overalls.

"How do you like our new baby?" X asked the Other Children proudly.

"It's got cute dimples," said Jim.

"It's got husky biceps, too," said Susie.

"What kind of baby is it?" asked Joe and Peggy.

X frowned at them. "Can't you tell?" Then X broke into a big, mischievous grin. *"It's a Y!"*

X: A Fabulous Child's Story

Lois Gould

1. How are children socialized into their genders? What is the role of parenting, schooling and other children in this regard?

2. What does this story demonstrate about the social construction of gender?

3. If you were to meet X, how would you treat this individual?

4. "X" is a 1970s fantasy story. If you were the author, would you give this story a different ending? Why or why not? What do you think would be different about X's experience if this story were written today?

5. How does recognizing gender as a social construct help us achieve gender justice? After thinking about the Xperiment in this story, what ideas about gender would you want to share with prospective parents, elementary school teachers, toy companies, etc.?

6. Go to parenting.com, parents.com, or parenting.org. Look at the titles of ten articles. What trends do you notice? Do these articles reinforce biological or cultural expectations of sex and gender? Do they support a gender binary or gender non-conformity? Write a letter to the editors with tips for parenting based on what you read in X.

"It's Only a Penis"
Rape, Feminism, and Difference

Christine Helliwell

Christine Helliwell is a professor in the Anthropology Department at the Australian National University, where she received her PhD. The author of more than a dozen essays, her work focuses on the Borneo Dayak people of Indonesia, most specifically the Gerai. This essay first appeared in Signs: Journal of Women in Culture and Society (2000).

PRE-READING QUESTIONS:

1. What have you been taught about rape?
2. Is it possible to have a society without rape? What would that look like?

KEY TERMS

difference
dimorphism
feminism
heterosexualization of desire
object
rape
rape-free culture
rape-prone culture
sexualization of violence
subject
"third-world difference"
universalization of rape

SEE THE THEMATIC TABLE OF CONTENTS,
IF YOU WANT TO READ MORE ESSAYS ABOUT:

Bodies and Genders
Feminism and Social Movements
Gendered Violence
Sexual Assault and Sexual Consent
Social Construction of Gender

"It's Only a Penis"
Rape, Feminism, and Difference

Christine Helliwell

In 1985 and 1986 I carried out anthropological fieldwork in the Dayak community of Gerai in Indonesian Borneo. One night in September 1985, a man of the village climbed through a window into the freestanding house where a widow lived with her elderly mother, younger (unmarried) sister, and young children. The widow awoke, in darkness, to feel the man inside her mosquito net, gripping her shoulder while he climbed under the blanket that covered her and her youngest child as they slept (her older children slept on mattresses nearby). He was whispering, "be quiet, be quiet!" She responded by sitting up in bed and pushing him violently, so that he stumbled backward, became entangled with her mosquito net, and then, finally free, moved across the floor toward the window. In the meantime, the woman climbed from her bed and pursued him, shouting his name several times as she did so. His hurried exit through the window, with his clothes now in considerable disarray, was accompanied by a stream of abuse from the woman and by excited interrogations from wakened neighbors in adjoining houses.

I awoke the following morning to raucous laughter on the longhouse verandah outside my apartment where a group of elderly women gathered regularly to thresh, winnow, and pound rice. They were recounting this tale loudly, and with enormous enjoyment, to all in the immediate vicinity. As I came out of my door, one was engaged in mimicking the man climbing out the window, sarong falling down, genitals askew. Those others working or lounging near her on the verandah—both men and women—shrieked with laughter.

When told the story, I was shocked and appalled. An unknown man had tried to climb into the bed of a woman in the dead, dark of night? I knew what this was called: attempted rape. The woman had seen the man and recognized him (so had others in the village, wakened by her shouting). I knew what he deserved: the full weight of the law. My own fears about being a single woman alone in a strange place, sleeping in a dwelling that could not be secured at night, bubbled to the surface. My feminist sentiments poured out. "How can you laugh?" I asked my women friends; "this is a very bad thing that he has tried to do." But my outrage simply served to fuel the hilarity. "No, not bad," said one of the old women (a particular friend of mine), "simply stupid."

I felt vindicated in my response when, two hours later, the woman herself came onto the verandah to share betel nut and tobacco and to broadcast the story. Her anger was palpable, and she shouted for all to hear her determination to exact a compensation payment from the man.

Thinking to obtain information about local women's responses to rape, I began to question her. Had she been frightened? I asked. Of course she had—Wouldn't I feel frightened if I awoke in the dark to find an unknown person inside my mosquito net? Wouldn't I be angry? Why then, I asked, hadn't she taken the opportunity, while he was entangled in her mosquito net, to kick him hard or to hit him with one of the many wooden implements near at hand? She looked shocked. Why would she do that? she asked—after all, he hadn't hurt her. No, but he had wanted to, I replied. She looked at me with puzzlement. Not able to find a local word for *rape* in my vocabulary, I scrabbled to explain myself: "He was trying to have sex with you," I said, "although you didn't want to. He was trying to hurt you." She looked at me, more with pity than with puzzlement now, although both were mixed in her expression. "Tin [Christine], it's only a penis," she said. "How can a penis hurt anyone?"

RAPE, FEMINISM, AND DIFFERENCE

A central feature of many feminist writings about rape in the past twenty years is their concern to eschew the view of rape as a natural function of male biology and to stress instead its bases in society and culture. It is curious, then, that so much of this work talks of rape in terms that suggest—either implicitly or explicitly—that it is a universal practice. To take only several examples: Pauline Bart and Patricia O'Brien tell us that "every female from nine months to ninety years is at risk" (1985, 1); Anna Clark argues that "all women know the paralyzing fear of walking down a dark street at night. . . . It seems to be a fact of life that the fear of rape imposes a curfew on our movements" (1987, 1); Catharine MacKinnon claims that "sexuality is central to women's definition and forced sex is central to sexuality," so "rape is indigenous, not exceptional, to women's social condition" (1989b, 172) and "all women live all the time under the shadow of the threat of sexual abuse" (1989a, 340); Lee Madigan and Nancy Gamble write of "the global terrorism of rape" (1991, 21–22); and Susan Brison asserts that "the fact that all women's lives are restricted by sexual violence is indisputable" (1993, 17). The potted "world histories" of rape—which attempt to trace the practice in a range of different societies against a single historical/evolutionary timeline—found in a number of feminist writings on the topic, further illustrate this universalizing tendency.[1] Just as I, an anthropologist trained to be particularly sensitive to the impact of cultural difference, nevertheless took for granted the occurrence of rape in a social and cultural context that I knew to be profoundly different from my own, so most other feminists also unwittingly assume that the practice occurs in all human societies.[2] This is particularly puzzling given that Peggy Reeves Sanday, for one, long ago demonstrated that while rape occurs widely throughout the world, it is by no means a human universal: some societies can indeed be classified as rape free (1981).

There are two general reasons for this universalization of rape among Western feminists. The first of these has to do with the understanding of the practice as horrific by most women in Western societies. In these settings, rape is seen as "a fate worse than, or tantamount to, death" (S. Marcus 1992, 387): a shattering of identity that, for instance, left one North American survivor feeling "not quite sure whether I had died and the world went on without me, or whether I was alive in a totally alien world" (Brison 1993, 10). While any form of violent attack may have

[1]For recent examples of such histories, see Madigan and Gamble 1991, 11ff.; McColgan 1996, 12–27.
[2]There are some exceptions to this. For example, Peggy Sanday's work on rape among the Minangkabau (1986) and within U.S. college fraternities (1990b) emphasizes very much its contextualized character. In fact, Sanday is one of the few feminists who has attempted to formulate a more general theory concerning the conditions under which rape occurs and under which it does not occur (1981; 1986; 1990b, 8).

severe emotional consequences for its victims, the *sexualization* of violence in rape greatly inten-
sifies those consequences for women in Western societies: "To show power and anger through
rape—as opposed to mugging or assault—men are calling on lessons women learn from society,
from history and religion, to defile, degrade and shame in addition to inflicting physical pain.
Rapists have learned, *as have their victims*, that to rape is to do something worse than to assault"
(Gordon and Riger 1989, 45; see also Koss and Harvey 1991). Clearly, the intermeshing of sexuality and personal identity in contemporary Western societies—such that Michel Foucault refers
to sex as "that secret which seems to underlie all that we are" (1978, 155)—imbues the practice
of rape with particular horror for most victims from those societies, since there it involves a
violation of personhood itself.[3]

Significantly, almost one-third of the respondents in Bart and O'Brien's sample of U.S.
women subject to rape attempts were more afraid of being raped by their attackers than they
were of being murdered and/or mutilated by them (1985, 52–53)—an extraordinarily large
number given that American women are reported to fear murder more than any other crime
(Gordon and Riger 1989, 2).[4] Rape is the second most feared crime among women in America,
a situation that is no doubt exacerbated by the frequency with which it occurs there.[5] Margaret
Gordon and Stephanie Riger (1989) have documented at length the way fear of rape—"the
female fear" or "this special fear," as they call it—pervades the lives and shapes the actions of
American women. So deep is this fear for many Western women that they anticipate the possibility of rape everywhere: rape comes to be understood simply as part of the "natural" human
condition. Susan Griffin puts it eloquently: "I have never been free of the fear of rape. From a
very early age I, like most women, have thought of rape as part of my natural environment—
something to be feared and prayed against like fire and lightning. I never asked why men raped;
I simply thought it one of the many mysteries of human nature" (1986, 3). Since feminists are,
undoubtedly, as subject to this fear as any other Western women, our tendency to universalize
rape is almost overwhelming.

In addition, because within Western feminist discourse rape is depicted as a shockingly bar-
baric practice—"illuminat[ing] gendered relations of power in their rawest, most brutal forms"

---

[3]It is clear from the ethnographic record that while for women in many non-Western societies the experience of rape is similar to that
of most Western women, this is not the case in all societies. Material from, e.g., Mehinaku (Gregor 1990) and some Papua New Guinea
societies suggests that rape takes on rather different meanings and significances in these settings and, in particular, that rape is not
everywhere experienced by women victims in the deeply traumatic terms taken for granted by most Western feminist writers on the
topic. Indeed, there is evidence to suggest that, even within specific Western contexts, rape can mean rather different things to different
people: Bourque 1989, for instance, has shown that within a single community in southern California, definitions of rape vary enormously, both between men and women and between different women. It is important to point out in this context that to acknowledge
the social and cultural variability of the meaning of rape is not to deny its horror or invalidate its trauma for most women victims in
the West. The work of such disparate thinkers as Maurice Merleau-Ponty, Foucault, and Pierre Bourdie has demonstrated that bodily
(including emotional) responses are largely socially constituted; the fact that they are therefore not universally shared renders them
no less real for those who experience them. Iris Marion Young's classic account (1990) of how Western women's oppression is lived in
their bodily experience, for instance, makes very clear the connection between social institutions and practices and the bodily/emotional
responses of individuals.
[4]Twenty-nine women out of ninety-two were more afraid of being raped by their attackers than of being murdered and/or mutilated
by them. Forty-seven women were more afraid of being murdered and/or mutilated, and sixteen were unclear on this point (Bart and
O'Brien 1985, 53). Bart and O'Brien suggest that women who are more afraid of being raped than of being murdered and/or mutilated
are more likely to avoid rape when attacked by a potential rapist.
[5]Madigan and Gamble state that an estimated 15 to 40 percent of women (presumably of American women) are "victims of attempted
or completed rapes during their lifetimes" (1991, 4; see also Russell 1984; Bart and O'Brien 1985, 129–30; Kilpatrick et al. 1987; Koss
and Harvey 1991, 22–29). Koss and Harvey cite a study showing that one in 3.6 American college women has been subject to rape or
attempted rape in her lifetime (1991, 24). While the frequency rates are lower in most other Western countries, they are nonetheless
high; McColgan, e.g., refers to a 1982 study in London that found that one woman in every six had been raped and a further one in five
had been subject to attempted rape (1996, 94).

(Dubinsky 1993, 8)—there is a tendency to view it as atavistic. Because the practice is widespread in "civilized" Western countries, it is assumed to pervade all other societies as well, since these latter are understood as located closer to the savagery end of the evolutionary ladder. This relates very closely to what Chandra Mohanty has described as "the third world difference": "that stable ahistorical something" that, in many feminist accounts, oppresses the women of Third World countries in addition to their oppression by men (1991, 53). Under this logic, practices deemed oppressive to women that are not commonly found in the West, such as clitoridectomy and *sati*, are explained as resulting from the barbarism of Third World peoples, while oppressive practices that are common in the West, such as rape, are explained in universalistic terms.[6] The related tendency within Western iconography to sexualize black female bodies (see Gilman 1985) means that rape is readily assumed to be a characteristic of "other"—especially black—societies. In fact, the link between this racist iconography and the frequency with which white men rape black women in countries like the United States should lead us to be extremely wary of this kind of assumption. Feminists cannot sidestep this problem by claiming that apparently universalizing statements about rape are meant to refer to Western societies only, since the assumption that unmarked statements should automatically be read in this way is itself suggestive of a form of racism. This is a point to which Western feminists, of all people, should be particularly sensitive, having ourselves been engaged in a protracted battle to fracture universalizing masculinist discourses.

A second, equally deep-seated reason for the feminist tendency to universalize rape stems from Western feminism's emphasis on difference between men and women and from its consequent linking of rape and difference. Two types of difference are involved here. The first of these is difference in social status and power; thus rape is linked quite explicitly, in contemporary feminist accounts, to patriarchal social forms. Indeed, this focus on rape as stemming from difference in social position is what distinguishes feminist from other kinds of accounts of rape (see Ellis 1989, 10). In this view, inequality between men and women is linked to men's desire to possess, subjugate, and control women, with rape constituting a central means by which the freedom of women is limited and their continued submission to men ensured. For this reason, rape has assumed a significant role within many feminist narratives, with Carole Pateman's account of the social contract as based on an originary rape of a woman by a man providing perhaps the best-known example (1988). Since many feminists continue to believe that patriarchy is universal—or, at the very least, to feel deeply ambivalent on this point—there is a tendency among us to believe that rape, too, is universal.[7]

However, the view of women as everywhere oppressed by men has been extensively critiqued within the anthropological literature. A number of anthropologists have argued that in some societies, while men and women may perform different roles and occupy different spaces, they are nevertheless equal in value, status, and power.[8] In addition, Marilyn Strathern, for

---

[6]Kathleen Barry's recent book on prostitution provides a good example of this kind of approach. Without providing any historical or ethnographic evidence whatsoever, she claims that in "pre-industrial and feudal societies" (the first of four progessive historical "stages of sexual exploitation"), "women's reduction to sex is a fact of their status as the property of their husbands. Under such conditions women are governed by marital relations of power through the exploitation of their unpaid labor in the home, their reproduction, and their sexuality. . . . Men may sexually exploit their wives, take concubines, and buy prostitutes with impunity as the privilege of male domination that services their promiscuity. By contrast, as women are sexual property of men, any sexual act outside of their marriage, including rape and forced prostitution, is usually considered infidelity and the victims are severely punished" (Barry 1995, 51).

[7]Among "radical" feminists such as Andrea Dworkin and Catharine MacKinnon this belief reaches its most extreme version, in which all sexual intercourse between a man and a woman is viewed as akin to rape (Dworkin 1987; MacKinnon 1989a, 1989b).

[8]Leacock 1978 and Bell 1983 are well-known examples. Sanday 1990a and Marcus 1992 are more recent examples, on Minangkabau and Turkish society, respectively.

one, has pointed out that notions such as "inequality" and "domination" cannot necessarily be applied in societies with very different conceptions of agency and personhood: "To argue that what happens to women qua women is a function of what happens to men qua men is not to postulate that women's concerns are relative to or subsumed by those of men but that neither can be understood without comprehending the relationship between them" (1988, 34; see also Strathern 1987). As Strathern sees it, the Western tendency to distinguish between subject and object makes it impossible for Westerners to recognize that in some societies (in this case, Melanesian ones) a person (whether male or female) is, at the same time, both subject and object. Feminist distinctions between male subjects and female objects—and corresponding notions of asymmetry—thus do not make sense in these contexts (Strathern 1988). Viewed in this light, feminist claims concerning the universality of rape begin to look even more problematic.[9]

But there is a second type of difference between men and women that also, albeit largely implicitly, underlies the assumption that rape is universal, and it is the linkage between this type of difference and the treatment of rape in feminist accounts with which I am largely concerned in this article. I refer to the assumption by most Western feminists writing on rape that men and women have different bodies and, more specifically, different genitalia: that they are, in other words, differently sexed. Furthermore, it is taken for granted in most feminist accounts that these differences render the former biologically, or "naturally," capable of penetrating and therefore brutalizing the latter and render the latter "naturally" able to be brutalized. While this assumption was quite explicit in earlier feminist accounts of rape—in particular, in Susan Brownmiller's (1975) argument that men rape primarily because they are biologically equipped with the "tools" (penises) to do so—it is largely implicit in more recent feminist work, where the concern is to eschew biological explanations and to stress instead the social bases of rape.[10] Rape of women by men is thus assumed to be universal because the same "biological" bodily differences between men and women are believed to exist everywhere.

Unfortunately, the assumption that preexisting bodily difference between men and women underlies rape has blinded feminists writing on the subject to the ways the practice of rape itself creates and inscribes such difference. This seems particularly true in contemporary Western societies where the relationship between rape and bodily/genital dimorphism appears to be an extremely intimate one. Judith Butler (1990, 1993) has argued (following Foucault 1978) that the Western emphasis on sexual difference is a product of the heterosexualization of desire within Western societies over the past few centuries, which "requires and institutes the production of discrete and asymmetrical oppositions between 'feminine' and 'masculine,' where these are understood as expressive attributes of 'male' and 'female'" (1990, 17).[11] The practice of rape in Western contexts can only properly be understood with reference to this heterosexual matrix, to the division of humankind into two distinct—and in many respects opposed—types of body

---

[9]MacKinnon suggests, for instance, that Khalka Mongol men's assertion (as quoted by Sanday) that "our women never resist" evokes a society in which sex can be equated with rape (1989a, 322). This suggestion clearly assumes that the individuated "subject" of Western experience is found also among the Khalka Mongol, such that the observer can separate out the "autonomous" interests of husband and wife and thus describe sexual relations between them in the familiar Western terms of "consent" and "resistance." While any categorization of Khalka Mongol society as "rape free" cannot be based simply on male claims of this type, categorization of it as "rape prone" purely on this basis is equally absurd, since it assumes that these kinds of male claims serve the same function here as they often do in the United States: namely, to legitimate male objectification of women. Work such as Strathern's throws into question precisely this kind of assumption.

[10]Some contemporary feminist accounts, however, are more explicit in their adoption of this kind of position. Aileen McColgan, e.g., states that most rapists "are not armed with . . . anything other than their fists, their penises and their superior strength" (1996, 9).

[11]See Laqueur 1990 for a historical account of this process.

(and hence types of person).[12] While it is certainly the case that rape is linked in contemporary Western societies to disparities of power and status between men and women, it is the particular discursive form that those disparities take—their elaboration in terms of the discourse of sex— that gives rape its particular meaning and power in these contexts.

Sharon Marcus has already argued convincingly that the act of rape "feminizes" women in Western settings, so that "the entire female body comes to be symbolized by the vagina, itself conceived of as a delicate, perhaps inevitably damaged and pained inner space" (1992, 398). I would argue further that the *practice* of rape in these settings—both its possibility and its actualization—not only feminizes women but masculinizes men as well.[13] This masculinizing character of rape is very clear in, for instance, Sanday's ethnography of fraternity gang rape in North American universities (1990b) and, in particular, in material on rape among male prison inmates. In the eyes of these rapists the act of rape marks them as "real men" and marks their victims as not men, that is, as feminine.[14] In this iconography, the "masculine" body (along with the "masculine" psyche), is viewed as hard, penetrative, and aggressive, in contrast to the soft, vulnerable, and violable "feminine" sexuality and psyche. Rape both reproduces and marks the pronounced sexual polarity found in these societies.

Western understandings of gender difference have almost invariably started from the presumption of a presocial bodily difference between men and women ("male" and "female") that is then somehow acted on by society to produce gender. In particular, the possession of either male genitals or female genitals is understood by most Westerners to be not only the primary marker of gender identity but, indeed, the underlying cause of that identity. Most feminist models of gender, while wishing to draw attention to the socially constructed character of difference, have nevertheless assumed—however reluctantly—that gender ultimately relates "back" to sex, that is, to the differences between "male" and "female" bodies. Yet this assumption is problematic in light of both feminist challenges to the notion that "sex" is given (and therefore universal) (Butler 1990, 1993) and historical research suggesting that dimorphic "sexing" of bodies is a relatively recent phenomenon in West European history (Trumbach 1989, 1993; Laqueur 1990; van der Meer 1993). This kind of model is especially problematic for using with cross-cultural material, such as that described below.[15]

I seek to do two things in this article. First, in providing an account of a community in which rape does not occur, I aim to give the lie to the widespread assumption that rape is universal and thus to invite Western feminists to interrogate the basis of our own tendency to take its

---

[12]On the equation of body and person within Western (especially feminist) thought, see Moore 1994.

[13]See Plaza 1980: "[Rape] is very sexual in the sense that [it] frequently a sexual activity, but especially in the sense that it opposes men and women: it is *social sexing* which is latent in rape. . . . Rape is sexual essentially because it rests on the very social difference between the sexes" (31).

[14]The material on male prison inmates is particularly revealing in this respect. As an article by Stephen Donaldson, a former prisoner and the president of the U.S. advocacy group Stop Prisoner Rape, makes clear, "hooking up" with another prisoner is the best way for a prisoner to avoid sexual assaults, particularly gang rapes. Hooking up involves entering a sexual liaison with a senior partner ("jocker," "man," "pitcher," "daddy") in exchange for protection. In this arrangement, the rules are clear: the junior partner gives up his autonomy and comes under the authority of the senior partner; he is often expected by the senior partner "to be as feminine in appearance and behaviour as possible," including shaving his legs, growing long hair, using a feminine nickname, and performing work perceived as feminine (laundry, cell cleaning, giving backrubs, etc.) (Donaldson 1996, 17, 20). See also the extract from Jack Abbott's prison letters in Halperin 1993 (424–25).

[15]Henrietta Moore has pointed out some of the problems with the conventional sex/gender model. These include its assumption that difference lies between bodies (whereas in many societies gender differences are understood to reside within individual bodies) and its stress on the body as the ultimate repository of identity, which relates to the Western belief in the unified, continuous person located in an individual body (a belief that is by no means universal) (Moore 1994, chaps. 1 and 2).

universality for granted.[16] The fundamental question is this: Why does a woman of Gerai see a penis as lacking the power to harm her, while I, a white Australian/New Zealand woman, am so ready to see it as having the capacity to defile, to humiliate, to subjugate and, ultimately, to destroy me?

Second, by exploring understandings of sex and gender in a community that stresses identity, rather than difference, between men and women (including men's and women's bodies), I aim to demonstrate that Western beliefs in the "sexed" character of bodies are not "natural" in basis but, rather, are a component of specifically Western gendering and sexual regimes. And since the practice of rape in Western societies is profoundly linked to these beliefs, I will suggest that it is an inseparable part of such regimes. This is not to say that the practice of rape is always linked to the kind of heterosexual regime found in the West; even the most cursory glance at any list of societies in which the practice occurs indicates that this is not so.[17] But it is to point out that we will be able to understand rape only ever in a purely localized sense, in the context of the local discourses and practices that are both constitutive of and constituted by it. In drawing out the implications of the Gerai stress on identity between men and women for Gerai gender and sexual relations, I hope to point out some of the possible implications of the Western emphasis on gender difference for Western gender and sexual relations—including the practice of rape.

GENDER, SEX, AND PROCREATION IN GERAI

Gerai is a Dayak community of some seven hundred people in the Indonesian province of Kalimantan Barat (West Borneo).[18] In the twenty months I spent in the community, I heard of no cases of either sexual assault or attempted sexual assault (and since this is a community in which privacy as we understand it in the West is almost nonexistent—in which surveillance by neighbors is at a very high level [see Helliwell 1996]—I would certainly have heard of any such cases had they occurred). In addition, when I questioned men and women about sexual assault, responses ranged from puzzlement to outright incredulity to horror.

While relations between men and women in Gerai can be classified as relatively egalitarian in many respects, both men and women nevertheless say that men are "higher" than women (Helliwell 1995, 364). This is especially the case in the context of formal community-wide functions such as village meetings and moots to settle legal disputes. While women are not required to remain silent on such occasions, their voices carry less authority than those of men, and, indeed, legal experts in the community (all men) told me that a woman's evidence in a moot is worth seven-tenths of a man's (see also Tsing 1990). In addition, a husband is granted a degree of formal authority over his wife that she does not have over him; thus a wife's disobedience of her husband is theoretically a punishable offense under *adat*, or local law. I have noted elsewhere

[16]While I am primarily concerned here with the feminist literature (believing that it contains by far the most useful and insightful work on rape), it needs to be noted that many other (nonfeminist) writers also believe rape to be universal. See, e.g., Ellis 1989; Palmer 1989.

[17]For listings of "rape-prone" societies, see Minturn, Grosse, and Haider 1969; Sanday 1981.

[18]I carried out anthropological fieldwork in Gerai from March 1985 to February 1986 and from June 1986 to January 1987. The fieldwork was funded by an Australian National University Ph.D. scholarship and carried out under the sponsorship of Lembaga Ilmu Pengetahuan Indonesia. At the time that I was conducting my research a number of phenomena were beginning to have an impact on the community—these had the potential to effect massive changes in the areas of life discussed in this article. These phenomena included the arrival of a Malaysian timber company in the Gerai region and the increasing frequency of visits by Malay, Bugis, Chinese, and Batak timber workers to the community; the arrival of two American fundamentalist Protestant missionary families to live and proselytize in the community; and the establishment of a Catholic primary school in Gerai, resulting in a growing tendency among parents to send their children (both male and female) to attend Catholic secondary school in a large coastal town several days' journey away.

that Gerai people stress the ideal of *diri*, literally meaning "standing" or "to stand," according to which each rice group should take primary responsibility for itself in all spheres of life and make its own decisions on matters concerning its members (Helliwell 1995). It is on the basis of their capacity to stand that rice groups within the community are ranked against one another. The capacity to stand is predicated primarily on the ability to produce rice surpluses: yet, significantly, although men and women work equally at rice-field work, it is only men who occasionally are individually described as standing. As in some other societies in the same region (Ilongot, Wana), Gerai people link men's higher status to their greater bravery.[19] This greater bravery is demonstrated, they say, by the fact that it is men who *pat* (cut down the large trees to make a rice field), who burn off the rice field to prepare for planting, and who enter deep primary jungle in search of game and jungle products such as aloe wood—all notoriously dangerous forms of work.

This greater status and authority does not, however, find expression in the practice of rape, as many feminist writings on the subject seem to suggest that it should. This is because the Gerai view of men as "higher" than women, although equated with certain kinds of increased potency vis-a-vis the world at large, does not translate into a conception of that potency as attached to and manifest through the penis—of men's genitals as able to brutalize women's genitals.

Shelly Errington has pointed out that a feature of many of the societies of insular Southeast Asia is a stress on sameness, even identity, between men and women (1990, 35, 39), in contrast to the Western stress on difference between the passive "feminine" object and the active, aggressive "masculine" subject.[20] Gerai understandings of gender fit Errington's model very well. In Gerai, men and women are not understood as fundamentally different types of persons: there is no sense of a dichotomized masculinity and femininity. Rather, men and women are seen to have the same kinds of capacities and proclivities, but with respect to some, men are seen as "more so" and with respect to others, women are seen as "more so." Men are said to be braver and more knowledgeable about local law (*adat*), while women are said to be more persistent and more enduring. All of these qualities are valued. Crucially, in terms of the central quality of nurturance (perhaps the most valued quality in Gerai), which is very strongly marked as feminine among Westerners, Gerai people see no difference between men and women. As one (female) member of the community put it to me: "We all must nurture because we all need."[21] The capacity both to nurture and to need, particularly as expressed through the cultivation of rice as a member of a rice group, is central to Gerai conceptions of personhood: rice is the source of life, and its (shared) production humanizes and socializes individuals (Helliwell, forthcoming). Women and men have identical claims to personhood based on their equal contributions to rice production (there is no notion that women are somehow diminished as persons even though they may be seen as less "high"). As in Strathern's account of Hagen (1988), the perceived mutuality of rice-field work in Gerai renders inoperable any notion of either men or women as autonomous individual subjects.

[19]On the Ilongot, see Rosaldo 1980a; on the Wana, see Atkinson 1990.
[20]The Wana, as described by Jane Atkinson (1990), provide an excellent example of a society that emphasizes sameness. Emily Martin points out that the explicit Western opposition between the "natures" of men and women is assumed to occur even at the level of the cell, with biologists commonly speaking of the egg as passive and immobile and the sperm as active and aggressive even though recent research indicates that these descriptions are erroneous and that they have led biologists to misunderstand the fertilization process (1991). See also Lloyd 1984 for an excellent account of how (often latent) conceptions of men and women as having opposed characteristics are entrenched in the history of Western philosophical thought.
[21]The nurture-need dynamic (that I elsewhere refer to as the "need-share dynamic") is central to Gerai sociality. Need for others is expressed through nurturing them; such expression is the primary mark of a "good" as opposed to a "bad" person. See Helliwell (forthcoming) for a detailed discussion.

It is also important to note that while men's bravery is linked to a notion of their greater physical strength, it is not equated with aggression—aggression is not valued in most Gerai contexts.[22] As a Gerai man put it to me, the wise man is the one "who fights when he has to, and runs away when he can"; such avoidance of violence does not mark a man as lacking in bravery. This does not mean that in certain contexts male warriorship—the ability to fight and even to take heads—is not valorized; on the contrary, the most popular myths in Gerai are those that tell of the legendary warrior hero (and headhunter without peer) Koling. However, Gerai people make a clear distinction between the fantastic world of the heroes of the past and the mundane world in which the present man of Gerai must make his way.[23] While it is recognized that a man will sometimes need to fight—and skill and courage in fighting are valued—aggression and hotheadedness are ridiculed as the hallmarks of a lazy and incompetent man. In fact, physical violence between adults is uncommon in Gerai, and all of the cases that I did witness or hear about were extremely mild.[24] Doubtless the absence of rape in the community is linked to this devaluing of aggression in general. However, unlike a range of other forms of violence (slapping, beating with a fist, beating with an implement, knifing, premeditated killing, etc.), rape is not named as an offense and accorded a set punishment under traditional Gerai law. In addition, unlike these other forms of violence, rape is something that people in the community find almost impossible to comprehend ("How would he be able to do such a thing?" one woman asked when I struggled to explain the concept of a man attempting to put his penis into her against her will). Clearly, then, more is involved in the absence of rape in Gerai than a simple absence of violence in general.

Central to all of the narratives that Gerai people tell about themselves and their community is the notion of a "comfortable life": the achievement of this kind of life marks the person and the household as being of value and constitutes the norm to which all Gerai people aspire. Significantly, the content of such a life is seen as identical for both men and women: it is marked by the production of bountiful rice harvests each year and the successful raising of a number of healthy children to maturity. The core values and aspirations of men and women are thus identical; of the many life histories that I collected while in the community—all of which are organized around this central image—it is virtually impossible to tell those of men from those of women. Two points are significant in this respect. First, a "comfortable life" is predicated on the notion of a partnership between a man and a woman (a conjugal pair). This is because while men and women are seen to have the same basic skills and capacities, men are seen to be "better" at certain kinds of work and women to be "better" at other kinds. Second, and closely related to this, the Gerai notion of men's and women's work does not constitute a rigid division of labor: both men and women say that theoretically women can perform all of the work routinely carried

[22]In this respect, Gerai is very different from, e.g., Australia or the United States, where, as Michelle Rosaldo has pointed out, aggression is linked to success, and women's constitution as lacking aggression is thus an important element of their subordination (1980b, 416; see also Myers 1988, 600).

[23]The practice of headhunting—seeking out enemies in order to sever their heads, which were then brought back to one's own village and treated with ritual reverence—was, in the past, widely found among Borneo Dayak groups. Gerai people claim that their not-too-distant ancestors practiced headhunting, but my own sense is that they are more likely to have been the hunted than the hunters. While in many respects Gerai resembles some of the "nonviolent" societies found throughout the region—including the Semai (Dentan 1968, 1978) and Chewong (Howell 1989) of Peninsular Malaysia and the Buid (Gibson 1986) of Mindoro in the Philippines—its celebration of violence in certain specified contexts marks it as rather different from many of them. Howell, for instance, claims that none of the indigenous peoples of Peninsular Malaysia "has any history of warfare, either recorded by the outside world or represented in myths and legends" (1989, 35), while Gibson notes that the Buid language "lacks words expressing a positive evaluation of courage or the reciprocation of violence" (1986, 107–8). Gerai people are, in fact, very similar in this respect to another Borneo Dayak people, the Bidayuh, who also valorize male violence in myth but tend to devalue and avoid it in everyday life and who also have a tradition of headhunting but are likely to have been hunted rather than hunters (Geddes 1957).

[24]See Helliwell 1996, 142–43, for an example of a "violent" altercation between husband and wife.

out by men, and men can perform all of the work routinely carried out by women. However, men are much better at men's work, and women are much better at women's work. Again, what we have here is a stress on *identity* between men and women at the expense of radical difference.

This stress on identity extends into Gerai bodily and sexual discourses. A number of people (both men and women) assured me that men sometimes menstruate; in addition, menstrual blood is not understood to be polluting, in contrast to how it is seen in many societies that stress more strongly the difference between men and women. While pregnancy and childbirth are spoken of as "women's work," many Gerai people claim that under certain circumstances men are also able to carry out this work—but, they say, women are "better" at it and so normally undertake it. In line with this claim, I collected a Gerai myth concerning a lazy woman who was reluctant to take on the work of pregnancy and childbirth. Her husband instead made for himself a lidded container out of bark, wood, and rattan ("like a betel nut container"), which he attached around his waist beneath his loincloth and in which he carried the growing fetus until it was ready to be born. On one occasion when I was watching a group of Gerai men cut up a boar, one, remembering an earlier conversation about the capacity of men to give birth, pointed to a growth in the boar's body cavity and said with much disapproving shaking of the head: "Look at this. He wants to carry his child. He's stupid." In addition, several times I saw fathers push their nipples into the mouths of young children to quieten them; while none of these fathers claimed to be able to produce milk, people nevertheless claimed that some men in the community were able to lactate, a phenomenon also attested to in myth. Men and women are thought to produce the same genital fluid, and this is linked in complex ways to the capacity of both to menstruate. All of these examples demonstrate the community's stress on bodily identity between men and women.

Furthermore, in Gerai, men's and women's sexual organs are explicitly conceptualized as the same. This sexual identity became particularly clear when I asked several people who had been to school (and hence were used to putting pencil to paper) to draw men's and women's respective organs for me: in all cases, the basic structure and form of each were the same. One informant, endeavoring to convince me of this sameness, likened both to wooden and bark containers for holding valuables (these vary in size but have the same basic conical shape, narrower at the base and wider at the top). In all of these discussions, it was reiterated that the major difference between men's and women's organs is their location: inside the body (women) and outside the body (men).[25] In fact, when I pressed people on this point, they invariably explained that it makes no sense to distinguish between men's and women's genitalia themselves; rather, it is location that distinguishes between penis and vulva.[26]

Heterosexuality constitutes the normative sexual activity in the community and, indeed, I was unable to obtain any information about homosexual practices during my time there. In line with the stress on sameness, sexual intercourse between a man and a woman in Gerai is understood as an equal coming together of fluids, pleasures, and life forces. The same stress also underlies beliefs about conception. Gerai people believe that repeated acts of intercourse between the same two people are necessary for conception, since this "prepares" the womb for

[25]I have noted elsewhere that the inside-outside distinction is a central one within this culture (Helliwell 1996).

[26]While the Gerai stress on the sameness of men's and women's sexual organs seems, on the face of it, to be very similar to the situation in Renaissance Europe as described by Laqueur 1990, it is profoundly different in at least one respect: in Gerai, women's organs are not seen as emasculated versions of men's—"female penises"—as they were in Renaissance Europe. This is clearly linked to the fact that, in Gerai, as we have already seen, *people* is not synonymous with *men*, and women are not relegated to positions of emasculation or abjection, as was the case in Renaissance Europe.

pregnancy. The fetus is deemed to be created through the mingling of equal quantities of fluids and forces from both partners. Again, what is seen as important here is not the fusion of two different types of bodies (male and female) as in Western understandings; rather, Gerai people say, it is the similarity of the two bodies that allows procreation to occur. As someone put it to me bluntly: "If they were not the same, how could the fluids blend? It's like coconut oil and water: they can't mix!"

What needs to be stressed here is that both sexual intercourse and conception are viewed as involving a mingling of similar bodily fluids, forces, and so on, rather than as the penetration of one body by another with a parallel propulsion of substances from one (male) body only into the other, very different (female) one. Nor is there anything in Gerai understandings that equates with the Western notion of conception as involving an aggressive active male cell (the sperm) seeking out and penetrating a passive, immobile female cell (the egg) (Martin 1991). What Gerai accounts of both sexual intercourse and conception stress are tropes of identity, mingling, balance, and reciprocity. In this context it is worth noting that many Gerai people were puzzled by the idea of gender-specific "medicine" to prevent contraception—such as the injectable or oral contraceptives promoted by state-run health clinics in the area. Many believed that, because both partners play the same role in conception, it should not matter whether husband or wife received such medicine (and indeed, I knew of cases where husbands had taken oral contraceptives meant for their wives). This suggests that such contraceptive regimes also serve (like the practice of rape) to reinscribe sex difference between men and women (see also Tsing 1993, 104–20).

When I asked why, if conception is predicated on the mingling of two similar bodies, two men or two women could not also come together to create a child, the response was that a man and a woman "fit" with one another (sedang). But while there is some sense of physical compatibility being suggested here, Gerai people were adamant that what is more important in constituting "fit" is the role of each individual's "life force" (semongan') and its intimate connection to particular forms of work. The semongan' is the spiritual essence or force that animates the person, that gives the person his or her individual life. Without his or her semongan', a human being cannot live (this is true of all other elements in the universe as well), and thus when a person dies, the semongan' is understood to have left the body and journeyed away. In turn, an individual's semongan' is centrally linked to the kind of work he or she routinely performs—particularly during the rice-cultivation cycle, which is understood as the source of life itself in Gerai.

While Gerai people stress sameness over difference between men and women, they do, nevertheless, see them as being different in one important respect: their life forces are, they say, oriented differently ("they face different ways," it was explained to me). This different orientation means that women are "better" at certain kinds of work and men are "better" at other kinds of work—particularly with respect to rice-field work. Gerai people conceive of the work of clearing large trees for a new rice field as the definitive man's work and regard the work of selecting and storing the rice seed for the following year's planting—which is correlated in fundamental ways with the process of giving birth—as the definitive woman's work. Because women are perceived to lack appropriate skills with respect to the first, and men are perceived to lack appropriate skills with respect to the second, Gerai people say that to be viable a household must contain both adult males and adult females. And since a "comfortable life" is marked by success in production not only of rice but also of children, the truly viable household must contain at least one conjugal pair. The work of both husband and wife is seen as necessary for the adequate nurturance of the child and successful rearing to adulthood (both of which depend on the successful cultivation of rice). Two women or two men would not be able to provide adequately for a child since they would not be able to produce consistently successful rice harvests; while such a household might be able to select seed, clear a rice field, and so grow rice in some rudimentary fashion, its lack of expertise at one of these tasks would render it perennially poor and its children perennially unhealthy, Gerai people say. For this reason, households with adults of only one gender are greatly pitied by Gerai people, and single parents seek to marry or remarry as quickly as they can. It is the mingling of the respective life forces of a man and a woman, then—linked, as they are, to the work skills of each—that primarily enables conception. It is this, Gerai people say, that allows the child's *semongan'* to come into being. Mingling of the parental bodily fluids, in turn, creates the child's bodily substance, but this substance must be animated in some prior sense by a life force, or the child will die.

Gender difference in Gerai, then, is not predicated on the character of one's body, and especially of one's genitalia, as in many Western contexts. Rather, it is understood as constituted in the differential capacity to perform certain kinds of work, a capacity assigned long before one's bodily being takes shape.[27] In this respect it is important to note that Gerai ontology rests on a belief in predestination, in things being as they should (see Helliwell 1995). In this understanding, any individual's *semongan'* is linked in multifarious and unknowable ways to the cosmic order, to the "life" of the universe as a whole. Thus the new fetus is predestined to become someone "fitted" to carry out either men's work or women's work as part of the maintenance of a universal balance. Bodies with the appropriate characteristics—internal or external genitalia, presence or absence of breasts, and so on—then develop in line with this prior destiny. At first sight this may not seem enormously different from Western conceptions of gender, but the difference is in fact profound. While, for Westerners, genitalia, as significant of one's role in the procreative process, are absolutely fundamental in determining one's identity, in Gerai the work that one performs is seen as fundamental, and genitalia, along with other bodily characteristics, are relegated to a kind of secondary, derivative function.

Gerai understandings of gender were made quite clear through circumstances surrounding my own gender classification while in the community. Gerai people remained very uncertain about my gender for some time after I arrived in the community because (as they later told me) "I did not . . . walk like a woman, with arms held out from the body and hips slightly swaying; I was "brave," trekking from village to village through the jungle on my own; I had bony kneecaps; I did not know how to tie a sarong in the appropriate way for women; I could not distinguish different varieties of rice from one another; I did not wear earrings; I had short hair; I was tall" (Helliwell 1993, 260). This was despite the fact that people in the community knew from my first few days with them both that I had breasts (this was obvious when the sarong that I wore clung to my body while I bathed in the river) and that I had a vulva rather than a penis and testicles (this was obvious from my trips to defecate or urinate in the small stream used for that purpose, when literally dozens of people would line the banks to observe whether I performed these functions differently from them). As someone said to me at a later point, "Yes, I saw that you had a vulva, but I thought that Western men might be different."

My eventual, more definitive classification as a woman occurred largely fortuitously. My initial research proposal focused on the creation of subjectivity and sociality through work and, accordingly, as soon as I arrived in the community, I began accompanying people to work in the rice fields. Once I had negotiated a longhouse apartment of my own in which to live (several weeks after arrival), I also found myself, in concert with all other households in the community,

---

[27]In this respect Gerai is similar to a number of other peoples in this region (e.g., Wana, Ilongot), for whom difference between men and women is also seen as primarily a matter of the different kinds of work that each performs.

preparing and cooking rice at least twice daily. These activities rapidly led to a quest for information concerning rice itself, particularly concerning the different strains, how they are cultivated, and what they are used for. As I learned to distinguish types of rice and their uses, I became more and more of a woman (as I realized later), since this knowledge—including the magic that goes with it—is understood by Gerai people as foundational to femininity. However, while people eventually took to referring to me as a woman, for many in the community my gender identity remained deeply ambiguous, partly because so many of my characteristics and behaviors were more like those of a man than a woman, but also, and more importantly, because I never achieved anything approaching the level of knowledge concerning rice-seed selection held by even a girl child in Gerai.

In fact, Gerai people talk of two kinds of work as defining a woman: the selection and storage of rice seed and the bearing of children.[28] But the first of these is viewed as prior, logically as well as chronologically. People are quite clear that in the womb either "someone who can cut down the large trees for a ricefield is made, or someone who can select and store rice." When I asked if it was not more important whether or not someone could bear a child, it was pointed out to me that many women do not bear children (there is a high rate of infertility in the community), but all women have the knowledge to select and store rice seed. In fact, at the level of the rice group the two activities of "growing" rice and "growing" children are inseparable: a rice group produces rice in order to raise healthy children, and it produces children so that they can in turn produce the rice that will sustain the group once their parents are old and frail (Helliwell, forthcoming). For this reason, any Gerai couple unable to give birth to a child of their own will adopt one, usually from a group related by kinship. The two activities of growing rice and growing children are constantly talked about together, and the same imagery is used to describe the development of a woman's pregnancy and the development of rice grains on the plant. Indeed, the process of pregnancy and birth is seen as intimately connected to the process of rice selection and storage. As one woman explained to me, "It is because we know how to hold the seed in the storage baskets that we are able to hold it in our wombs." But just as the cultivation of rice is seen as in some sense prior to the cultivation of children, so it is said that "knowledge about childbirth comes from knowledge about rice seed."

Gerai, then, lacks the stress on bodily—and especially genital—dimorphism that most feminist accounts of rape assume. Indeed, the reproductive organs themselves are not seen as "sexed." In a sense it is problematic even to use the English categories *woman* and *man* when writing of this community, since these terms are saturated with assumptions concerning the priority of biological (read, bodily) difference. In the Gerai context, it would be more accurate to deal with the categories of, on the one hand, "those responsible for rice selection and storage" and, on the other, "those responsible for cutting down the large trees to make a ricefield." There is no discursive space in Gerai for the distinction between an active, aggressive, penetrating male sexual organ (and sexuality) and a passive, vulnerable, female one. Indeed, sexual intercourse in Gerai is understood by both men and women to stem from mutual "need" on the part of the two partners; without such need, people say, sexual intercourse cannot occur, because the requisite balance is lacking. Since, as I have described at length elsewhere (Helliwell, forthcoming), a relationship of "needing" is always reciprocal (it is almost inconceivable, in Gerai terms, to need someone who does not need you in return, and the consequences of unreciprocated needing are dire for both individual and rice group), the sexual act is understood as preeminently mutual in

---

[28]In Gerai, pregnancy and birth are seen not as semimystical "natural" processes, as they are for many Westerners, but simply as forms of work, linked very closely to the work of rice production.

its character, including in its initiation. The idea of having sex with someone who does not need you to have sex with them—and so the idea of coercing someone into sex—is thus almost unthinkable to Gerai people. In addition, informants asserted that any such action would destroy the individual's spiritual balance and that of his or her rice group and bring calamity to the group as a whole.[29]

In this context, a Gerai man's astonished and horrified question "How can a penis be taken into a vagina if a woman doesn't want it?" has a meaning very different from that of the same statement uttered by a man in the West. In the West, notions of radical difference between men and women—incorporating representations of normative male sexuality as active and aggressive, normative female sexuality as passive and vulnerable, and human relationships (including acts of sexual intercourse) as occurring between independent, potentially hostile, agents—would render such a statement at best naive, at worst misogynist. In Gerai, however, the stress on identity between men and women and on the sexual act as predicated on mutuality validates such a statement as one of straightforward incomprehension (and it should be noted that I heard similar statements from women). In the Gerai context, the penis, or male genitalia in general, is not admired, feared, or envied, nor is the phallus a central signifier in the way postulated by Lacanians. In fact, Gerai people see men's sexual organs as more vulnerable than women's for the simple reason that they are outside the body, while women's are inside. This reflects Gerai understandings of "inside" as representing safety and belonging, while "outside" is a place of strangers and danger, and it is linked to the notion of men as braver than women.[30] In addition, Gerai people say, because the penis is "taken into" another body, it is theoretically at greater risk during the sexual act than the vagina. This contrasts, again, quite markedly with Western understandings, where women's sexual organs are constantly depicted as more vulnerable during the sexual act—as liable to be hurt, despoiled, and so on (some men's anxieties about *vagina dentata* not withstanding). In Gerai a penis is "only a penis": neither a marker of dimorphism between men and women in general nor, in its essence, any different from a vagina.

CONCLUSIONS

The Gerai case suggests that, in some contexts at least, the practice of rape is linked to sexual dimorphism and, indeed, that in these contexts discourses of rape (including the act of rape itself) reinscribe such dimorphism. While the normative sexual practice in Gerai is heterosexual (between men and women), it is not accompanied by a heterosexual regulatory regime in the sense meant by Foucault (1978) in his discussion of the creation of sex as part of the heterosexualization of desire in the West, nor is it part of what Butler terms "the heterosexual matrix" (Butler 1990, 1993). The notion of "heterosexualization" as used by these thinkers refers to far more than the simple establishment of sexual relations between men and women as the normative ideal; it denotes the entire governmental regime that accompanies this normative ideal in Western contexts. Gerai stresses sameness between men and women more than difference, and such difference as occurs is based on the kinds of work people perform. Although this process certainly naturalizes a division between certain kinds of tasks—and the capacity to perform those tasks effectively—clearly, it does not involve sex or sexed bodies in the way Westerners

[29]Sanday 1986 makes a similar point about the absence of rape among the Minangkabau. See Helliwell (forthcoming) for a discussion of the different kinds of bad fate that can afflict a group through the actions of its individual members.
[30]In Gerai, as in nearby Minangkabau (Sanday 1986), vulnerability is respected and valued rather than despised.

normally understand those terms—as a naturalized difference between bodies (located primarily in the genitals) that translates into two profoundly different types of person. In this context, sexual assault by a man on a woman is almost unthinkable (both by women and by men).

With this background, I return now to the case with which I began this article—and, particularly, to the great differences between my response to this case and that of the Gerai woman concerned. On the basis of my own cultural assumptions concerning the differences—and particularly the different sexual characters—of men and women, I am inclined (as this case showed me) to read any attempt by a man to climb into a woman's bed in the night without her explicit consent as necessarily carrying the threat of sexual coercion and brutalization. This constant threat has been inscribed onto my body as part of the Western cultural process whereby I was "girled" (to use Butler's felicitous term [1993, 7]), or created as a gendered being in a context where male and female sexualities are perceived as penetrative and aggressive and as vulnerable and self-protective, respectively. The Gerai woman, in contrast, has no fear of coerced sexual intercourse when awakened in the dark by a man. She has no such fear because in the Gerai context "girling" involves the inscription of sexual sameness, of a belief that women's sexuality and bodies are no less aggressive and no more vulnerable than men's.

In fact, in the case in question, the intruding man did expect to have intercourse with the woman.[31] He claimed that the woman had already agreed to this through her acceptance of his initiatory gifts of soap.[32] The woman, however, while privately agreeing that she had accepted such gifts, claimed that no formal agreement had yet been reached. Her anger, then, did not stem from any belief that the man had attempted to sexually coerce her ("How would he be able to do such a thing?"). Because the term "to be quiet" is often used as a euphemism for sexual intercourse in Gerai, she saw the man's exhortation that she "be quiet" as simply an invitation to engage in sex with him, rather than the implicit threat that I read it to be.[33] Instead, her anger stemmed from her conviction that the correct protocols had not been followed, that the man ought to have spoken with her rather than taking her acceptance of the soap as an unequivocal expression of assent. She was, as she put it, letting him know that "you have sexual relations together when you talk together. Sexual relations cannot be quiet."[34]

---

[31]The man left the community on the night that this event occurred and went to stay for several months at a nearby timber camp. Community consensus—including the view of the woman concerned—was that he left because he was ashamed and distressed, not only as a result of having been sexually rejected by someone with whom he thought he had established a relationship but also because his adulterous behavior had become public, and he wished to avoid an airing of the details in a community moot. Consequently, I was unable to speak to him about the case. However, I did speak to several of his close male kin (including his married son), who put his point of view to me.

[32]The woman in this particular case was considerably younger than the man (in fact, a member of the next generation). In such cases of considerable age disparity between sexual partners, the older partner (whether male or female) is expected to pay a fine in the form of small gifts to the younger partner, both to initiate the liaison and to enable its continuance. Such a fine rectifies any spiritual imbalance that may result from the age imbalance and hence makes it safe for the relationship to proceed. Contrary to standard Western assumptions, older women appear to pay such fines to younger men as often as older men pay them to younger women (although it was very difficult to obtain reliable data on this question, since most such liaisons are adulterous and therefore highly secretive). While not significant in terms of value (women usually receive such things as soap and shampoo, while men receive tobacco or cigarettes), these gifts are crucial in their role of "rebalancing" the relationship. It would be entirely erroneous to subsume this practice under the rubric of "prostitution."

[33]Because Gerai adults usually sleep surrounded by their children, and with other adults less than a meter or two away (although the latter are usually inside different mosquito nets), sexual intercourse is almost always carried out very quietly.

[34]In claiming that "sexual relations cannot be quiet," the woman was playing on the expression "be quiet" (meaning to have sexual intercourse) to make the point that while adulterous sex may need to be even "quieter" than legitimate sex, it should not be so "quiet" as to preclude dialogue between the two partners. Implicit here is the notion that in the absence of such dialogue, sex will lack the requisite mutuality.

Yet, this should not be taken to mean that the practice of rape is simply a product of discourse: that brutality toward women is restricted to societies containing particular, dimorphic representations of male and female sexuality and that we simply need to change the discourse in order to eradicate such practices.[35] Nor is it to suggest that a society in which rape is unthinkable is for that reason to be preferred to Western societies. To adopt such a position would be still to view the entire world through a sexualized Western lens. There are, in fact, horrific things that may be done to women in places such as Gerai—things that are no less appalling in their implications for the fact that they do not involve the sexualized brutality of rape. In Gerai, for instance, while a woman does not fear rape, she does fear an enemy's bewitchment of her rice seed (the core of her gendered identity in this context) and the subsequent failure of the seed to sprout, resulting in hunger and illness for herself and her rice group. In extreme cases, bewitchment of rice seed can lead to malignancy of the growing fetus inside the woman; her subsequent death in childbirth, killed by her own "seed"; and her resultant transformation into a particularly vile kind of demon. Gerai women live constantly with the fear of this bewitchment (much as Western women live with the fear of rape), and even talking of it (always in whispers) reduces them to a state of terror.[36] The fact that this kind of attack can be carried out on a woman by either a woman or a man, and that it strikes not at her alone but at her rice group as a whole, marks it as belonging to a very different gendering regime from that which operates in the West. But it is no less horrific in its implications for that.

In order to understand the practice of rape in countries like Australia and the United States, then—and so to work effectively for its eradication there—feminists in these countries must begin to relinquish some of our most ingrained presumptions concerning difference between men and women and, particularly, concerning men's genitalia and sexuality as inherently brutalizing and penetrative and women's genitalia and sexuality as inherently vulnerable and subject to brutalization. Instead, we must begin to explore the ways rape itself *produces* such experiences of masculinity and femininity and so inscribes sexual difference onto our bodies. In a recent article, Moira Gatens asks of other feminists, "Why concede to the penis the power to push us around, destroy our integrity, 'scribble on us,' invade our borders and boundaries, and . . . occupy us in our (always already) conquered 'privacy'?" (1996, 43). This article echoes her lament. The tendency among many Western feminists writing on rape to accept as a seeming fact of nature the normative Western iconography of sexual difference leads them to reproduce (albeit unwittingly) the very discursive framework of Western rapists themselves, with their talk of "tools" and "holes," the very discursive framework in which rape is possible and which it reinscribes. For rape imposes difference as much as it is produced by difference. In fact, the highly racialized character of rape in many Western contexts suggests that the practice serves to police not simply sexual boundaries but racial ones as well. This is hardly surprising, given the history of the present "heterosexual matrix" in the West: as Stoler (1989, 1995) has demonstrated, the process of heterosexualization went hand-in-hand with that of colonialism. As a result, in contemporary Western settings sexual othering is inextricably entangled with racial othering. Unfortunately, in universalizing rape, many Western feminists risk naturalizing these othering processes and so contributing to a perpetuation of the very practices they seek to eradicate.

---

[35]Foucualt, e.g., once suggested (in a debate in French reprinted in *La Folie Encerclee* [see Plaza 1980]) that an effective way to deal with rape would be to decriminalize it in order to "desexualize" it. For feminist critiques of his suggestion, see Plaza 1980; de Lauretis 1987; Woodhull 1988.

[36]Men fear a parallel form of bewitchment that causes death while engaged in the definitive "men's work" of cutting down large trees to make a rice field. Like women's death in childbirth, this is referred to as an "evil death" (*mati jat*) and is believed to involve the transformation of the man into an evil spirit.

REFERENCES

Atkinson, Jane Monnig. 1990. "How Gender Makes a Difference in Wana Society." In *Power and Difference: Gender in Island Southeast Asia*, ed. Jane Monnig Atkinson and Shelly Errington, 59–93. Stanford, Calif.: Stanford University Press.

Barry, Kathleen. 1995. *The Prostitution of Sexuality*. New York and London: New York University Press.

Bart, Pauline B., and Patricia H. O'Brien. 1985. *Stopping Rape: Successful Survival Strategies*. New York: Pergamon.

Bell, Diane. 1983. *Daughters of the Dreaming*. Melbourne: McPhee Gribble.

Bourque, Linda B. 1989. *Defining Rape*. Durham, N.C., and London: Duke University Press.

Brison, Susan J. 1993. "Surviving Sexual Violence: A Philosophical Perspective." *Journal of Social Philosophy* 24(1):5–22.

Brownmiller, Susan. 1975. *Against Our Will: Men, Women, and Rape*. New York: Simon & Schuster.

Butler, Judith. 1990. *Gender Trouble: Feminism and the Subversion of Identity*. New York and London: Routledge.

———. 1993. *Bodies That Matter: On the Discursive Limits of "Sex."* New York and London: Routledge.

Clark, Anna. 1987. *Women's Silence, Men's Violence: Sexual Assault in England, 1770–1845*. London and New York: Pandora.

de Lauretis, Teresa. 1987. "The Violence of Rhetoric: Considerations on Representation and Gender." In her *Technologies of Gender: Essays on Theory, Film and Fiction*, 31–50. Bloomington and Indianapolis: Indiana University Press.

Dentan, Robert Knox. 1968. *The Semai: A Nonviolent People of Malaya*. New York: Holt, Rinehart & Winston.

———. 1978. "Notes on Childhood in a Nonviolent Context: The Semai Case (Malaysia)." In *Learning Non-Aggression: The Experience of Non-Literate Societies*, ed. Ashley Montagu, 94–143. New York: Oxford University Press.

Donaldson, Stephen. 1996. "The Deal behind Bars." *Harper's* (August): 17–20.

Dubinsky, Karen. 1993. *Improper Advances: Rape and Heterosexual Conflict in Ontario, 1880–1929*. Chicago and London: University of Chicago Press.

Dworkin, Andrea. 1987. *Intercourse*. London: Secker & Warburg.

Ellis, Lee. 1989. *Theories of Rape: Inquiries into the Causes of Sexual Aggression*. New York: Hemisphere.

Errington, Shelly. 1990. "Recasting Sex, Gender, and Power: A Theoretical and Regional Overview." In *Power and Difference: Gender in Island Southeast Asia*, ed. Jane Monnig Atkinson and Shelly Errington, 1–58. Stanford, Calif.: Stanford University Press.

Foucault, Michel. 1978. *The History of Sexuality*. Vol. 1, *An Introduction*. Harmondsworth: Penguin.

Gatens, Moira. 1996. "Sex, Contract, and Genealogy." *Journal of Political Philosophy* 4(1):29–44.

Geddes, W R. 1957. *Nine Dayak Nights*. Melbourne and New York: Oxford University Press.

Gibson, Thomas. 1986. *Sacrifice and Sharing in the Philippine Highlands: Religion and Society among the Buid of Mindoro*. London and Dover: Athlone.

Gilman, Sander L. 1985. "Black Bodies, White Bodies: Toward an Iconography of Female Sexuality in Late Nineteenth-Century Art, Medicine, and Literature." In *"Race," Writing, and Difference*, ed. Henry Louis Gates, Jr., 223–40. Chicago and London: University of Chicago Press.

Gordon, Margaret T., and Stephanie Riger. 1989. *The Female Fear*. New York: Free Press.

Gregor, Thomas. 1990. "Male Dominance and Sexual Coercion." In *Cultural Psychology: Essays on Comparative Human Development*, ed. James W Stigler, Richard A. Shweder, and Gilbert Herdt, 477–95. Cambridge: Cambridge University Press.

Griffin, Susan. 1986. *Rape: The Politics of Consciousness.* San Francisco: Harper & Row.

Halperin, David M. 1993. "Is There a History of Sexuality?" In *The Lesbian and Gay Studies Reader*, ed. Henry Abelove, Michele Barale, and David M. Halperin, 416–31. New York and London: Routledge.

Helliwell, Christine 1993. "Women in Asia: Anthropology and the Study of Women." In *Asia's Culture Mosaic*, ed. Grant Evans, 260–86. Singapore: Prentice Hall.

———. 1995. "Autonomy as Natural Equality: Inequality in 'Egalitarian' Societies." *Journal of the Royal Anthropological Institute 1(2):359–75.*

———. 1996. "Space and Sociality in a Dayak Longhouse." In *Things as They Are: New Directions in Phenomenological Anthropology*, ed. Michael Jackson, 128–48. Bloomington and Indianapolis: Indiana University Press.

———. Forthcoming. *"Never Stand Alone": A Study of Borneo Sociality.* Williamsburg: Borneo Research Council.

Howell, Signe. 1989. *Society and Cosmos: Chewong of Peninsular Malaysia.* Chicago and London: University of Chicago Press.

Kilpatrick, Dean G., Benjamin E. Saunders, Lois J. Veronen, Connie L. Best, and Judith M. Von. 1987. "Criminal Victimization: Lifetime Prevalence, Reporting to Police, and Psychological Impact." *Crime and Delinquency* 33(4):479–89.

Koss, Mary P., and Mary R. Harvey. 1991. *The Rape Victim: Clinical and Community Interventions.* 2d ed. Newbury Park, Calif.: Sage.

Laqueur, Thomas. 1990. *Making Sex: Body and Gender from the Greeks to Freud.* Cambridge, Mass., and London: Harvard University Press.

Leacock, Eleanor. 1978. "Women's Status in Egalitarian Society: Implications for Social Evolution." *Current Anthropology* 19(2):247—75.

Lloyd, Genevieve. 1984. *The Man of Reason: "Male" and "Female" in Western Philosophy.* London: Methuen.

MacKinnon, Catharine A. 1989a. "Sexuality, Pornography, and Method: 'Pleasure under Patriarchy.' " *Ethics* 99:314–46.

———. 1989b. *Toward a Feminist Theory of the State.* Cambridge, Mass., and London: Harvard University Press.

Madigan, Lee, and Nancy C. Gamble. 1991. *The Second Rape: Society's Continued Betrayal of the Victim.* New York: Lexington.

Marcus, Julie. 1992. *A World of Difference: Islam and Gender Hierarchy in Turkey.* Sydney: Allen & Unwin.

Marcus, Sharon. 1992. "Fighting Bodies, Fighting Words: A Theory and Politics of Rape Prevention." In *Feminists Theorize the Political*, ed. Judith Butler and Joan W Scott, 385–403. New York and London: Routledge.

Martin, Emily 1991. "The Egg and the Sperm: How Science Has Constructed a Romance Based on Stereotypical Male-Female Roles." *Signs: Journal of Women in Culture and Society* 16(3):485–501.

McColgan, Aileen. 1996. *The Case for Taking the Date Out of Rape.* London: Pandora.

Minturn, Leigh, Martin Grosse, and Santoah Haider. 1969. "Cultural Patterning of Sexual Beliefs and Behaviour." *Ethnology* 8(3):301–18.

Mohanty, Chandra Talpade. 1991. "Under Western Eyes: Feminist Scholarship and Colonial Discourses." In *Third World Women and the Politics of Feminism*, ed. Chandra Talpade Mohanty, Ann Russo, and Lourdes Torres, 51–80. Bloomington and Indianapolis: Indiana University Press.

Moore, Henrietta L. 1994. *A Passion for Difference: Essays in Anthropology and Gender*. Cambridge and Oxford: Polity.

Myers, Fred R. 1988. "The Logic and Meaning of Anger among Pintupi Aborigines." *Man* 23(4):589–610.

Palmer, Craig. 1989. "Is Rape a Cultural Universal? A Re-Examination of the Ethnographic Data." *Ethnology* 28(1):1–16.

Pateman, Carole. 1988. *The Sexual Contract*. Cambridge: Polity.

Plaza, Monique. 1980. "Our Costs and Their Benefits." *m/f*4:28–39.

Rosaldo, Michelle Z. 1980a. *Knowledge and Passion: Ilongot Notions of Self and Social Life*. Cambridge: Cambridge University Press.

———. 1980b. "The Use and Abuse of Anthropology: Reflections on Feminism and Cross-cultural Understanding." *Signs* 5(3):389–417.

Russell, Diana E. H. 1984. *Sexual Exploitation: Rape, Child Abuse, and Workplace Harassment*. Beverly Hills, Calif.: Sage.

Sanday, Peggy Reeves. 1981. "The Socio-Cultural Context of Rape: A Cross-Cultural Study." *Journal of Social Issues* 37(4):5–27.

———. 1986. "Rape and the Silencing of the Feminine." In *Rape*, ed. Sylvana Tomaselli and Roy Porter, 84–101. Oxford: Blackwell.

———. 1990a. "Androcentric and Matrifocal Gender Representations in Minangkabau Ideology." In *Beyond the Second Sex: New Directions in the Anthropology of Gender*, ed. Peggy Reeves Sanday and Ruth Gallagher Goodenough, 141–68. Philadelphia: University of Pennsylvania Press.

———. 1990b. *Fraternity Gang Rape: Sex, Brotherhood, and Privilege on Campus*. New York and London: New York University Press.

Stoler, Ann Laura. 1989. "Carnal Knowledge and Imperial Power: Gender, Race, and Morality in Colonial Asia." In *Gender at the Crossroads of Knowledge: Feminist Anthropology in the Postmodern Era*, ed. Micaela di Leonardo, 51–101. Berkeley and Los Angeles: University of California Press.

———. 1995. *Race and the Education of Desire: Foucault's* History of Sexuality *and the Colonial Order of Things*. Durham, N.C., and London: Duke University Press.

Strathern, Marilyn 1987. "Conclusion." In *Dealing with Inequality: Analysing Gender Relations in Melanesia and Beyond*, ed. Marilyn Strathern, 278–302. Cambridge: Cambridge University Press.

———. 1988. *The Gender of the Gift: Problems with Women and Problems with Society in Melanesia*. Berkeley and Los Angeles: University of California Press.

Trumbach, Randolph. 1989. "Gender and the Homosexual Role in Modern Western Culture: The Eighteenth and Nineteenth Centuries Compared." In *Homosexuality, Which Homosexuality?* ed. Dennis Altman, 149–69. Amsterdam: An Dekker/Schorer; London: GMP.

———. 1993. "London's Sapphists: From Three Sexes to Four Genders in the Making of Modern Culture." *In Third Sex, Third Gender: Beyond Sexual Dimorphism in Culture and History*, ed. Gilbert Herdt, 111–36. New York: Zone.

Tsing, Anna Lowenhaupt. 1990. "Gender and Performance in Meratus Dispute Settlement." In *Power and Difference: Gender in Island Southeast Asia*, ed. Jane Monnig Atkinson and Shelly Errington, 95–125. Stanford, Calif.: Stanford University Press.

———. 1993. *In the Realm of the Diamond Queen: Marginality in an Out-of-the-Way Place.* Princeton, N.J.: Princeton University Press.

van der Meer, Theo. 1993. "Sodomy and the Pursuit of a Third Sex in the Early Modern Period." In *Third Sex, Third Gender: Beyond Sexual Dimorphism in Culture and History*, ed. Gilbert Herdt, 137–212. New York: Zone.

Woodhull, Winifred. 1988. "Sexuality, Power, and the Question of Rape." In *Feminism and Foucault: Reflections on Resistance*, ed. Irene Diamond and Lee Quinby, 167–76. Boston: Northeastern University Press.

Young, Iris Marion. 1990. "Throwing like a Girl: A Phenomenology of Feminine Body Comportment, Motility, and Spatiality." In her *Throwing like a Girl and Other Essays in Feminist Philosophy and Social Theory*, 141–59. Bloomington and Indianapolis: Indiana University Press.

'It's Only a Penis'
Rape, Feminism, and Difference

Christine Helliwell

1. What happened when Helliwell was researching the Dayak community of Gerai in Indonesian Borneo? Describe the incident.

2. How did Helliwell interpret what happened that night? Why? Why did the women of the Dayak community interpret it differently?

3. According to Helliwell, how do western feminists explain gender difference? How do western feminists explain rape? How are feminist explanations of gender difference and rape connected?

4. List the other differences Helliwell found between western ideas and experiences of gender and those of the Dayak community.

5. Explain the reasons western feminists assume that rape is a universal problem. What is the impact of this assumption on the way western feminists perceive the world?

6. Imagine that a group of women from the Gerai community is coming to campus to talk about creating a global campaign to end sexual assault. Create a flyer or advertisement to convince people to attend the event.

"Race and Gender"

bell hooks

bell hooks is a renowned writer and activist who has written over 25 books about race, gender, education, and community. She earned her BA in English from Stanford University in 1973 and her MA in English from the University of Wisconsin–Madison in 1976. In 1983, she earned her doctorate in literature from the University of California, Santa Cruz. In 2004, hooks joined the faculty at Berea College as a distinguished professor-in-residence.

PREREADING QUESTIONS

1. Who is feminism for? Who benefits from feminism?
2. How has feminism impacted the contemporary US workforce?
3. What does genuine sisterhood look like?

KEY TERMS

Antiracist struggle
Consumer capitalism
Liberation
Privilege
Solidarity
White Supremacist Capitalist Patriarchy

SEE THE THEMATIC TABLE OF CONTENTS, IF YOU WANT TO READ MORE ESSAYS ABOUT:

Feminism and Social Movements
Privilege, Identities, and Intersectionalities

Race and Gender

bell hooks essay

No intervention changed the face of American feminism more than the demand that feminist thinkers acknowledge the reality of race and racism. All white women in this nation know that their status is different from that of black women/women of color. They know this from the time they are little girls watching television and seeing only their images, and looking at magazines and seeing only their images. They know that the only reason nonwhites are absent/invisible is because they are not white. All white women in this nation know that whiteness is a privileged category. The fact that white females may choose to repress or deny this knowledge does not mean they are ignorant: it means that they are in denial.

No group of white women understood the differences in their status and that of black women more than the group of politically conscious white females who were active in civil rights struggle. Diaries and memoirs of this period in American history written by white women document this knowledge. Yet many of these individuals moved from civil rights into women's liberation and spearheaded a feminist movement where they suppressed and denied the awareness of difference they had seen and heard articulated firsthand in civil rights struggle. Just because they participated in anti-racist struggle did not mean that they had divested of white supremacy, of notions that they were superior to black females, more informed, better educated, more suited to "lead" a movement.

In many ways they were following in the footsteps of their abolitionist ancestors who had demanded that everyone (white women and black people) be given the right to vote, but, when faced with the possibility that black males might gain the right to vote while they were denied it on the basis of gender, they chose to ally themselves with men, uniting under the rubric of white supremacy. Contemporary white females witnessing the militant demand for more rights for black people chose that moment to demand more rights for themselves. Some of these individuals claim that it was working on behalf of civil rights that made them aware of sexism and sexist oppression. Yet if this was the whole picture one might think their newfound political awareness of difference would have carried over into the way they theorized contemporary feminist movement.

They entered the movement erasing and denying difference, not playing race alongside gender, but eliminating race from the picture. Foregrounding gender meant that white women could take center stage, could claim the movement as theirs, even as they called on all women to join. The utopian vision of sisterhood evoked in a feminist movement that initially did not take racial difference or anti-racist struggle seriously did not capture the imagination of most black women/women of color. Individual black women who were active in the movement from its inception for the most part stayed in their place. When the feminist movement began racial integration was still rare. Many black people were learning how to interact with whites on the basis of being peers for the first time in their lives. No wonder individual black women choosing feminism were reluctant to introduce their awareness of race. It must have felt so awesome to have white women evoke sisterhood in a world where they had mainly experienced white women as exploiters and oppressors.

A younger generation of black females/women of color in the late '70s and early '80s challenged white female racism. Unlike our older black women allies we had for the most part been educated in predominantly white settings. Most of us had never been in a subordinated position in relation to a white female. Most of us had not been in the workforce. *We had never been in our place.* We were better positioned to critique racism and white supremacy within the women's movement. Individual white women who had attempted to organize the movement around the banner of common oppression evoking the notion that women constituted a sexual class/caste were the most reluctant to acknowledge differences among women, differences that overshadowed all the common experiences female shared. Race was the most obvious difference.

In the '70s I wrote the first draft of *Ain't I a Woman: Black Women and Feminism.* I was 19 years old. I had never worked a full-time job. I had come from a racially segregated small town in the south to Stanford University. While I had grown up resisting patriarchal thinking, college was the place where I embraced feminist politics. It was there as the only black female present in feminist classrooms, in consciousness-raising, that I began to engage race and gender theoretically. It was there that I began to demand recognition of the way in which racist biases were shaping feminist thinking and call for change. At other locations individual black women/women of color were making the same critique.

In those days white women who were unwilling to tace the reality of racism and racial difference accused us of being traitors by introducing race. Wrongly they saw us as deflecting focus away from gender. In reality, we were demanding that we look at the status of females realistically, and that realistic understanding serve as the foundation for a real feminist politic. Our intent was not to diminish the vision of sisterhood. We sought to put in place a concrete politics of solidarity that would make genuine sisterhood possible. We knew that there could no real sisterhood between white women and women of color if white women were not able to divest of white supremacy, if feminist movement were not fundamentally anti-racist.

Critical interventions around race did not destroy the women's movement; it became stronger. Breaking through denial about race helped women face the reality of difference on all levels. And we were finally putting in place a movement that did not place the class interests of privileged women, especially white women, over that of all other women. We put in place a vision of sisterhood where all our realities could be spoken. There has been no contemporary movement for social justice where individual participants engaged in the dialectical exchange that occurred among feminist thinkers about race which led to the re-thinking of much feminist theory and practice. The fact that participants in the feminist movement could face critique and challenge while still remaining wholeheartedly committed to a vision of justice, of liberation, is a testament to the movement's strength and power. It shows us that no matter how misguided feminist thinkers have been in the past, the will to change, the will to create the context for struggle and liberation, remains stronger than the need to hold on to wrong beliefs and assumptions.

For years I witnessed the reluctance of white feminist thinkers to acknowledge the importance of race. I witnessed their refusal to divest of white supremacy, their unwillingness to acknowledge that an anti-racist feminist movement was the only political foundation that would make sisterhood be a reality. And I witnessed the revolution in consciousness that occurred as individual women began to break free of denial, to break free of white supremacist thinking. These awesome changes restore my faith in feminist movement and strengthen the solidarity I feel towards all women.

Overall feminist thinking and feminist theory has benefited from all critical interventions on the issue of race. The only problematic arena has been that of translating theory into practice. While individual white women have incorporated an analysis of race into much feminist scholarship, these insights have not had as much impact on the day to day relations between white women and women of color. Anti-racist interactions between women are difficult in a society that remains racially segregated. Despite diverse work settings a vast majority of folks still socialize only with people of their own group. Racism and sexism combined create harmful barriers between women. So far feminist strategies to change this have not been very useful.

Individual white women and women of color who have worked through difficulties to make the space where bonds of love and political solidarity can emerge need to share the methods and strategies that we have successfully employed. Almost no attention is given the relationship between girls of different races. Biased feminist scholarship which attempts to show that white girls are somehow more vulnerable to sexist conditioning than girls of color simply perpetuates the white supremacist assumption that white females require and deserve more attention to their concerns and ills than other groups. Indeed while girls of color may express different behavior than their white counterparts they are not only internalizing sexist conditioning, they are far more likely to be victimized by sexism in ways that are irreparable.

Feminist movement, especially the work of visionary black activists, paved the way for a reconsideration of race and racism that has had positive impact on our society as a whole. Rarely do mainstream social critiques acknowledge this fact. As a feminist theorist who has written extensively about the issue of race and racism within feminist movement, I know that there remains much that needs to be challenged and changed, but it is equally important to celebrate the enormous changes that have occurred. That celebration, understanding our triumphs and using them as models, means that they can become the sound foundation for the building of a mass-based anti-racist feminist movement.

Selection from Feminism is For Everybody

bell hooks

1. In this selection, bell hooks articulates some of the challenges of feminist theorizing about work, particularly the relationship between work and liberation. According to hooks, what types of work would be key to liberation?

2. As part of advancing feminist theorizing, hooks calls for "a way to rethink work." What would that look like? Include examples to illustrate.

3. This selection includes hooks's critique of feminists who had participated in antiracist struggle but had not divested of white supremacy. What does she mean? Explain and offer examples that illustrate.

4. How have visionary black feminist activists paved the way for reconsideration of race and racism? Include examples that explain.

5. What are some of the concrete actions that can be taken to move toward "a mass-based anti-racist feminist movement"?

Privilege, Power, Difference, and Us

Allan G. Johnson

Allan G. Johnson *is a sociologist, public speaker, nonfiction author and novelist. He earned his PhD from the University of Michigan and taught for more than twenty years. In 1995 he left higher education to devote his attention to social justice workshops and writing. He has written dozens of articles, five scholarly books, and two novels. This excerpt is from* The Gender Knot: Unraveling Our Patriarchal Legacy *(1997).*

PRE-READING QUESTIONS

1. In your own words, define privilege.
2. Do you think privilege is difficult to discuss? Why or why not?

KEY TERMS

difference
Equal Rights Amendment
individualism
oppression
path of least resistance
power
privilege
resistance
sexism
social system

SEE THE THEMATIC TABLE OF CONTENTS, IF YOU WANT TO READ MORE ESSAYS ABOUT:

Masculinity
Privilege, Identities, and Intersectionalities

Privilege, Power, Difference, and Us

Allan G. Johnson*

To do something about the trouble around difference, we have to talk about it, but most of the time we don't, because it feels too risky. This is true for just about everyone, but especially for members of privileged categories, for whites, for men, and for heterosexuals. As Paul Kivel writes, for example, "Rarely do we whites sit back and listen to people of color without interrupting, without being defensive, without trying to regain attention to ourselves, without criticizing or judging."

The discomfort, defensiveness, and fear come in part from not knowing how to talk about privilege without feeling vulnerable to anger and blame. They will continue until we find a way to reduce the risk of talking about privilege. The key to reducing the risk is to understand what makes talking about privilege *seem* risky. I don't mean that risk is an illusion. There is no way to do this work without the possibility that people will feel uncomfortable or frightened or threatened. But the risk isn't nearly as big as it seems, for like the proverbial (and mythical) human fear of the strange and unfamiliar, the problem begins with how people *think* about things and who they are in relation to them.

INDIVIDUALISM, OR THE MYTH THAT EVERYTHING IS SOMEBODY'S FAULT

We live in a society that encourages us to think that the social world begins and ends with individuals. It's as if an organization or a society is just a collection of people, and everything that happens in it begins with what each one thinks, feels, and intends. If you understand people, the reasoning goes, then you also understand social life. It's an appealing way to think because it's grounded in our experience as individuals, which is what we know best. But it's also misleading, because it boxes us into a narrow and distorted view of reality. In other words, it isn't true.

If we use individualism to explain sexism, for example, it's hard to avoid the idea that sexism exists simply because men *are* sexist—men have sexist feelings, beliefs, needs, and motivations that lead them to behave in sexist ways. If sexism produces evil consequences, it's because men *are* evil, hostile, and malevolent toward women. In short, everything bad in the world is seen as somebody's fault, which is why talk about privilege so often turns into a game of hot potato.

Individualistic thinking keeps us stuck in the trouble by making it almost impossible to talk seriously about it. It encourages women, for example, to blame and distrust men. It sets men up to feel personally attacked if anyone mentions gender issues, and to define those issues as a "women's problem." It also encourages men who don't think or behave in overtly sexist ways—the ones most likely to become part of the solution—to conclude that sexism has nothing to do with them, that it's just a problem for "bad" men. The result is a kind of paralysis: people either talk about sexism in the most superficial, unthreatening, trivializing, and even stupid way ("The Battle of the Sexes," *Men Are from Mars, Women Are from Venus*) or they don't talk about it at all.

Breaking the paralysis begins with realizing that the social world consists of a lot more than individuals. We are always participating in something larger than ourselves—what sociologists call social systems—and systems are more than collections of people. A university, for example, is a social system, and people participate in it. But the people aren't the university and the university isn't the people. This means that to understand what happens in it, we have to look at both the university and how individual people participate in it. If patterns of racism exist in a society, for example, the reason is never just a matter of white people's personalities, feelings, or intentions. We also have to understand how they participate in particular kinds of behavior, and what consequences it produces.

INDIVIDUALS, SYSTEMS, AND PATHS OF LEAST RESISTANCE

To see the difference between a system and the people who participate in it, consider a game like Monopoly. I used to play Monopoly, but I don't anymore because I don't like the way I behave when I do. Like everyone else, as a Monopoly player I try to take everything from the other players—all their money, all their property—which then forces them out of the game. The point of the game is to ruin everyone else and be the only one left in the end. When you win, you feel good, because you're *supposed* to feel good. Except that one day I realized that I felt good about winning—about taking everything from everyone else—even when I played with my children, who were pretty young at the time. But there didn't seem to be much point to playing without trying to win, because winning is what the game is *about*. Why land on a property and not buy it, or own a property and not improve it, or have other players land on your property and not collect the rent? So I stopped playing.

And it worked, because the fact is that I don't behave in such greedy ways when I'm not playing Monopoly, even though it's still me, Allan, in either case. So what's all this greedy behavior about? Do we behave in greedy ways simply because we *are* greedy? In a sense, the answer is yes, in that greed is part of the human repertoire of possible motivations, just like compassion, altruism, or fear. But how, then, do I explain the absence of such behavior when I'm not playing Monopoly? Clearly, the answer has to include both me as an individual human being who's capable of making all kinds of choices *and* something about the social situation in which I make those choices. It's not one or the other; it's both in relation to each other.

If we think of Monopoly as a social system—as "something larger than ourselves that we participate in"—then we can see how people and systems come together in a dynamic relationship that produces the patterns of social life, including problems around difference and privilege. People are indisputably the ones who make social systems happen. If no one plays Monopoly, it's just a box full of stuff with writing inside the cover. When people open it up and identify themselves as players, however, Monopoly starts to *happen*. This makes people very important, but we shouldn't confuse that with Monopoly itself. We aren't Monopoly and Monopoly isn't us. I can describe the game and how it works without saying anything about the personal characteristics of all the people who play it or might play it.

People make Monopoly happen, but *how?* How do we know what to do? How do we choose from the millions of things that, as human beings, we *could* do at any given moment? The answer is the other half of the dynamic relation between individuals and systems. As we sit around the table, we make Monopoly happen from one minute to the next. But our participation in the game also shapes how *we* happen as people—what we think and feel and do. This doesn't mean that systems control us in a rigid and predictable way. Instead, systems load the odds in certain directions by offering what I call "paths of least resistance" for us to follow.

In every social situation, we have an almost limitless number of choices we might make. Sitting in a movie theater, for example, we could go to sleep, sing, eat dinner, undress, dance, take out a flashlight and read the newspaper, carry on loud conversations, dribble a basketball up and down the aisles—these are just a handful of the millions of behaviors people are capable of. All of these possible paths vary in how much resistance we run into if we try to follow them. We discover this as soon as we choose paths we're not supposed to. Jump up and start singing, for example, and you'll quickly feel how much resistance the management and the rest of the audience offer up to discourage you from going any further. By comparison, the path of least resistance is far more appealing, which is why it's the one we're most likely to choose.

The odds are loaded toward a path of least resistance in several ways. We often choose a path because it's the only one we see. When I get on an elevator, for example, I turn and face front along with everyone else. It rarely occurs to me to do it another way, such as facing the rear. If I did, I'd soon feel how some paths have more resistance than others.

I once tested this idea by walking to the rear of an elevator and standing with my back toward the door. As the seconds ticked by, I could feel people looking at me, wondering what I was up to, and actually wanting me to turn around. I wasn't saying anything or doing anything to anyone. I was only standing there minding my own business. But that wasn't all that I was doing, for I was also violating a social norm that makes facing the door a path of least resistance. The path is there all the time—it's built in to riding the elevator as a social situation—but the path wasn't clear until I stepped onto a different one and felt the greater resistance rise up around it.

Similar dynamics operate around issues of difference and privilege. In many corporations, for example, the only way to get promoted is to have a mentor or sponsor pick you out as a promising person and bring you along by teaching you what you need to know and acting as an advocate who opens doors and creates opportunities. In a society that separates and privileges people by gender and race, there aren't many opportunities to get comfortable with people across difference. This means that senior managers will feel drawn to employees who resemble them, which usually means those who are white, straight, and male.

Managers who are white and/or male probably won't realize they're following a path of least resistance that shapes their choice until they're asked to mentor an African American woman or someone else they don't resemble. The greater resistance toward the path of mentoring across difference may result from something as subtle as feeling "uncomfortable" in the other person's presence. But that's all it takes to make the relationship ineffective or to ensure that it never happens in the first place. And as each manager follows the system's path to mentor and support those who most resemble them, the patterns of white dominance and male dominance in the system as a whole are perpetuated, regardless of what people consciously feel or intend.

In other cases, people know alternative paths exist but they stick to the path of least resistance anyway, because they're afraid of what will happen if they don't. Resistance can take many forms, ranging from mild disapproval to being fired from a job, beaten up, run out of town, imprisoned, tortured, or killed. When managers are told to lay off large numbers of workers, for example, they may hate the assignment and feel a huge amount of distress. But the path of *least* resistance is to do what they're told, because the alternative may be for them to lose their own jobs. To make it less unpleasant, they may use euphemisms like "downsizing" and "outplacement" to soften the painful reality of people losing their jobs. (Note in this example how the path of least resistance isn't necessarily an easy path to follow.)

In similar ways, a man may feel uncomfortable when he hears a friend tell a sexist joke, and feel compelled to object in some way. But the path of least resistance in that situation is to go along and avoid the risk of being ostracized or ridiculed for challenging his friend and making *him* feel uncomfortable. The path of least resistance is to smile or laugh or just remain silent.

What we experience as social life happens through a complex dynamic between all kinds of systems—families, schools, workplaces, communities, entire societies—and the choices people make as they participate in them and help make them happen. How we experience the world and ourselves, our sense of other people, and the ongoing reality of the systems themselves all arise, take shape, and happen through this dynamic. In this way, social life produces a variety of consequences, including privilege and oppression. To understand that and what we can do to change it, we have to see how systems are organized in ways that encourage people to follow paths of least resistance. The existence of those paths and the choice we make to follow them are keys to what creates and perpetuates all the forms that privilege and oppression can take in people's lives.

WHAT IT MEANS TO BE INVOLVED IN PRIVILEGE AND OPPRESSION

Individuals and systems are connected to each other rough a dynamic relationship. If we use this relationship as a model for thinking about the world and ourselves, it's easier to bring problems like racism, sexism, and heterosexism out into the open and talk about them. In particular, it's easier to see the problems in relation to us, and to see ourselves in relation to them.

If we think the world is just made up of individuals, then a white woman who's told she's "involved" in racism is going to think you're telling her she's a racist person who harbors ill will toward people of color. She's using an individualistic model of the world that limits her to interpreting words like *racist* as personal characteristics, personality flaws. Individualism divides the world up into different kinds of people—good people and bad, racists and nonracists, "good guys" and sexist pigs. It encourages us to think of racism, sexism, and heterosexism as diseases that infect people and make them sick. And so we look for a "cure" that will turn diseased, flawed individuals into healthy, "good" ones, or at least isolate them so that they can't infect others. And if we can't cure them, then we can at least try to control their behavior.

But what about everyone else? How do we see *them* in relation to the trouble around difference? What about the vast majority of whites, for example, who tell survey interviewers that they aren't racist and don't hate or even dislike people of color? Or what about the majority of men who say they favor an Equal Rights Amendment to the US Constitution? From an individualistic perspective, if you aren't consciously or openly prejudiced or hurtful, then you aren't part of the problem. You might show disapproval of "bad" people and even try to help out the people who are hurt by them. Beyond that, however, the trouble doesn't have anything to do with you so far as you can see. If your feelings and thoughts and outward behavior are good, then *you* are good, and that's all that matters.

Unfortunately, that isn't all that matters. There's more, because patterns of oppression and privilege are rooted in systems that we all participate in and make happen. Those patterns are built into paths of least resistance that people feel drawn to follow every day, regardless of whether they think about where they lead or the consequences they produce. When male professors take more seriously students who look like themselves, for example, they don't have to be self-consciously sexist in order to help perpetuate patterns of gender privilege. They don't have to be bad people in order to play a "game" that produces oppressive consequences. It's the same as when people play Monopoly—it always ends with someone winning and everyone else losing, *because that's how the game is set up to work as a system.* The only way to change the outcome is to change how we see and play the game and, eventually, the *system itself* and its paths of least resistance. If we have a vision of what we want social life to look like, we have to create paths that lead in that direction.

Of course there are people in the world who have hatred in their hearts—such as neo-Nazi skinheads who make a sport of harassing and killing blacks or homosexuals—and it's important not to minimize the damage they do. Paradoxically, however, even though they cause a lot of trouble, they aren't the key to understanding privilege or to doing something about it. They are participating in something larger than themselves that, among other things, steers them toward certain targets for their rage. It's no accident that their hatred is rarely directed at privileged groups, but instead those who are culturally devalued and excluded. Hate-crime perpetrators may have personality disorders that bend them toward victimizing *someone*, but their choice of whom to victimize isn't part of a mental illness. That's something they have to learn, and culture is everyone's most powerful teacher. In choosing their targets, they follow paths of least resistance built into a society that everyone participates in, that everyone makes happen, regardless of how they feel or what they intend.

So if I notice that someone plays Monopoly in a ruthless way, it's a mistake to explain that simply in terms of their personality. I also have to ask how a system like Monopoly rewards ruthless behavior more than other games we might play. I have to ask how it creates conditions that make such behavior appear to be the path of least resistance, normal and unremarkable. And since I'm playing the game, too, I'm one of the people who make it happen as a system, and its paths must affect me, too.

My first reaction might be to deny that I follow that path. I'm not a ruthless person or anything close to it. But this misses the key difference between systems and the people who participate in them: We don't have to be ruthless *people* in order to support or follow paths of least resistance that lead to behavior with ruthless *consequences*. After all, we're all trying to win, because that's the point of the game. However gentle and kind I am as I take your money when you land on my Boardwalk with its four houses, take it I will, and gladly, too. "Thank you," I say in my most sincerely unruthless tone, or even "Sorry," as I drive you out of the game by taking your last dollar and your mortgaged properties. Me, ruthless? Not at all. I'm just playing the game the way it's supposed to be played. And even if I don't try hard to win, the mere fact that I play the game supports its existence and makes it possible, especially if I remain silent about the consequences it produces. Just my going along makes the game appear normal and acceptable, which reinforces the paths of least resistance for everyone else.

This is how most systems work and how most people participate in them. It's also how systems of privilege work. Good people with good intentions make systems happen that produce all kinds of injustice and suffering for people in culturally devalued and excluded groups. Most of the time, people don't even know the paths are there in the first place, and this is why it's important to raise awareness that everyone is always following them in one way or another. If you weren't following a path of least resistance, you'd certainly know it, because you'd be on an alternative path with greater resistance that would make itself felt. In other words, if you're not going along with the system, it won't be long before people notice and let you know it. All you have to do is show up for work wearing "inappropriate" clothes to see how quickly resistance can form around alternative paths.

The trouble around difference is so pervasive, so long-standing, so huge in its consequences for so many millions of people that it can't be written off as the misguided doings of a small minority of people with personality problems. The people who get labeled as bigots, misogynists, or homophobes are all following racist, sexist, heterosexist paths of least resistance that are built into the entire society.

In a way, "bad people" are like ruthless Monopoly players who are doing just what the game calls for even if their "style" is a bit extreme. Such extremists may be the ones who grab the headlines, but they don't have enough power to create and sustain trouble of this magnitude. The trouble appears in the daily workings of every workplace, every school and university, every government agency, every community. It involves every major kind of social system, and since systems don't exist without the involvement of people, there's no way to escape being involved in the trouble that comes out of them. If we participate in systems the trouble comes out of, and if those systems exist only through our participation, then this is enough to involve us in the trouble itself.

Reminders of this reality are everywhere. I see it, for example, every time I look at the label in a piece of clothing. I just went upstairs to my closet and noted where each of my shirts was made. Although each carries a US brand name, only three were made here; the rest were made in the Philippines, Thailand, Mexico, Taiwan, Macao, Singapore, or Hong Kong. And although each cost me twenty to forty dollars, it's a good bet that the people who actually made them—primarily women—were paid pennies for their labor performed under terrible conditions that can sometimes be so extreme as to resemble slavery.

The only reason people exploit workers in such horrible ways is to make money in a capitalist system. To judge from the contents of my closet, that clearly includes *my* money. By itself, that fact doesn't make me a bad person, because I certainly don't intend that people suffer for the sake of my wardrobe. But it does mean that I'm involved in their suffering because I participate in a system that produces that suffering. As someone who helps make the system happen, however, I can also be a part of the solution.

But isn't the difference I could make a tiny one? The question makes me think of the devastating floods of 1993 along the Mississippi and Missouri rivers. The news was full of powerful images of people from all walks of life working feverishly side by side to build dikes to hold back the raging waters that threatened their communities. Together, they filled and placed thousands of sandbags. When the waters receded, much had been lost, but a great deal had been saved as well. I wonder how it felt to be one of those people. I imagine they were proud of their effort and experienced a satisfying sense of solidarity with the people they'd worked with. The sandbags each individual personally contributed were the tiniest fraction of the total, but each felt part of the group effort and was proud to identify with the consequences it produced. They didn't have to make a big or even measurable difference to feel involved.

It works that way with the good things that come out of people pulling together in all the systems that make up social life. It also works that way with the bad things, with each sandbag adding to the problem instead of the solution. To perpetuate privilege and oppression, we don't even have to do anything consciously to support it. Just our silence is crucial for ensuring its future, for the simple fact is that no system of social oppression can continue to exist without most people choosing to remain silent about it. If most whites spoke out about racism; if most men talked about sexism; if most heterosexuals came out of their closet of silence and stood openly against heterosexism, it would be a critical first step toward revolutionary change. But the vast majority of "good" people are silent on these issues, and it's easy for others to read their silence as support.

As long as we participate in social systems, we don't get to choose whether to be involved in the consequences they produce. We're involved simply through the fact that we're here. As such, we can only choose *how* to be involved, whether to be just part of the problem or also to be part of the solution. That's where our power lies, and also our responsibility.

Privilege, Power, Difference and Us

Allan G. Johnson

1. What is the path of least resistance? How does the path of least resistance impact our daily choices?

2. Why is it important to examine both individual and systemic dimensions of privilege?

3. Compare Johnson's framework for analyzing privilege with other discussions about privilege you have had in this class or elsewhere. What is unique about Johnson's perspective?

4. Think of a personal example where you followed the path of least resistance. What choices did you make in that situation about your own behavior? Why did you make the choices you did? What might the outcome have been if you acted differently?

5. Imagine a difficult conversation about privilege that you may face in the future, one in which you might be tempted to take the path of least resistance. Consider a family dinner with immediate and extended family or a debate on social media that you might have with friends or family. Describe the situation here:

Now create a plan for handling this imagined situation. How do you hope to react? What actions do you hope you are able to take?

More than a Few Good Men

Jackson Katz

Jackson Katz is an anti-sexist male activist, educator, author, filmmaker and social theorist. He minored in Women's Studies as an undergraduate at Amherst and earned his PhD at UCLA. Drawing on his research and activism about violence and masculinity, he has created or co-created several educational videos including Tough Guise *(2000),* Tough Guise 2 *(2013),* Wrestling with Manhood *(2002)* and Spin the Bottle *(2004). He also wrote* The Macho Paradox: Why Some Men Hurt Women and How All Men Can Help *(2006) from which this essay comes.*

PRE-READING QUESTIONS:

1. What is the role of men in ending domestic and sexual violence? What are men's responsibilities in ending domestic and sexual violence?
2. What do you think is the role of men in feminism?

KEY TERMS

big tent approach
gendered violence prevention
National Organization for Men Against Sexism (NOMAS)
Venn diagram
White Ribbon Campaign

SEE THE THEMATIC TABLE OF CONTENTS, IF YOU WANT TO READ MORE ESSAYS ABOUT:

Feminism and Social Movements
Gendered Violence
Masculinity

More Than a Few Good Men

Jackson Katz

"As long as we take the view that these are problems for women alone to solve, we cannot expect to reverse the high incidence of rape and child abuse . . . and domestic violence. We do know that many men do not abuse women and children; and that they strive always to live with respect and dignity. But until today the collective voice of these men has never been heard, because the issue has not been regarded as one for the whole nation. From today those who inflict violence on others will know they are being isolated and cannot count on other men to protect them. From now on all men will hear the call to assume their responsibility for solving this problem."—President Nelson Mandela, 1997, National Men's March, Pretoria, South Africa

Since the very beginning of the women-led movements against domestic and sexual violence in the 1970s, there have been men who personally, professionally, and politically supported the work of those women. In addition, over the past several decades there have been repeated attempts by men to create organizations and targeted initiatives to address men's roles in ending men's violence against women. Some of the early efforts were undertaken by groups of concerned men who responded to the challenge from women's organizations to educate, politicize, and organize other men. Some of these men chose to volunteer in supportive roles with local rape crisis centers or battered women's programs. Others contributed to the development of the fledgling batterer intervention movement in the late 1970s and 1980s. Some of the better known programs for batterers were Emerge in Cambridge, Massachusetts; RAVEN (Rape and Violence End Now) in St. Louis, Missouri; and Men Stopping Violence in Atlanta, Georgia. Still other men created political and activist educational organizations, like the National Organization for Men Against Sexism (NOMAS), which has held "Men and Masculinity" conferences annually since 1975; the Oakland Men's Project in the San Francisco Bay Area; Men Stopping Rape in Madison, Wisconsin; DC Men Against Rape; and Real Men, an anti-sexist men's organization I co-founded in Boston in 1988.

The rapidly growing field of "men's work" also produced community centers that combine batterer-intervention and counseling services for men with educational outreach and social activism. One of the groundbreaking programs in this field is the Men's Resource Center of Western Massachusetts, founded in Amherst in 1982. In the 1990s anti-sexist men's initiatives in the U.S. and around the world increased dramatically. One of the most visible has been the White Ribbon Campaign, an activist educational campaign founded by a group of men in Canada in 1991. They started the WRC in response to a horrific incident on December 6, 1989, at the University of Montreal, where an armed twenty-five-year-old man walked into a classroom, separated the women from the men and proceeded to shoot the women. Before he finished his rampage, he had murdered fourteen women in cold blood—and shaken up an entire country.

The significance of the white ribbon—which has been adopted on hundreds of college campuses and communities in the U.S. as well as a number of other countries—is that men wear it to make a visible and public pledge "never to commit, condone, nor remain silent about violence against women."

Despite these notable efforts over the past thirty years, the movement of men committed to ending men's violence against women has only recently picked up significant momentum. There are more men doing this work in the United States and around the world than ever before. Halfway through the first decade of the twenty-first century there is reason for optimism, especially about the emergence of a new generation of anti-sexist men. But there are nowhere near enough men yet involved to make a serious dent in this enormous problem. Several key challenges lie ahead:

- How to increase dramatically the number of men who make these issues a priority in their personal and professional lives
- How to expand the existing infrastructure of men's anti-rape and domestic violence prevention groups, and other campus and community-based initiatives
- How to institutionalize gender violence prevention education at every level of the educational system
- How to build multiracial and multiethnic coalitions that unite men across differences around their shared concerns about sexist violence and the sexual exploitation of children
- How to insure that federal, state, and local funding for efforts to reduce gender violence are maintained and expanded in the coming years
- And finally, how to make it socially acceptable—even cool—for men to become vocal and public allies of women in the struggle against all forms of men's violence against women and children

A "BIG TENT" APPROACH

As I have made clear in this book, there is much that we can do to prevent men's violence against women—if we find the collective will in male culture to make it a priority. I am convinced that millions of men in our society are deeply concerned about the abuse, harassment, and violence we see—and fear—in the lives of our daughters, mothers, sisters, and lovers. In fact, a recent poll conducted for Lifetime Television found that 57 percent of men aged sixteen to twenty-four believe gender violence is an "extremely serious" problem. A 2000 poll conducted by the Family Violence Prevention Fund found that one-quarter of men would do more about the issue if they were asked. And some compelling social norms research on college campuses suggests that one of the most significant factors in a man's decision to intervene in an incident is his perception of how other men would act in a similar situation. Clearly, a lot of men are uncomfortable with other men's abusive behaviors, but they have not figured out what to do about it—or have not yet mustered the courage to act on their own. So there is great potential to increase dramatically the number of men who commit personal time, money, and institutional clout to the effort to reduce men's violence against women. But in order to achieve this we need to think outside the box about how to reach into the mainstream of male culture and social power.

One promising approach employs elements of what might be called "big tent" movement building. The big tent concept comes from politics, where it has been used most famously to describe efforts to unite various constituencies and single-issue special-interest groups under the Republican Party label. A number of questions arise when this concept is applied to gender violence prevention: How do we attract individuals and organizations not known for their advocacy of the issues of men's violence? What are some of the necessary compromises required in order to broaden the coalition of participating individuals and groups? What are some of the costs and benefits of engaging new partners, who might not have the depth of experience or the ideological affinities of the majority of women and men currently in the movement?

Growing pains always accompany growth. A bigger movement will inevitably create new conflicts. One way to think about the question of broadening the base of the movement is to consider the concept embodied in the geometric model of the Venn diagram. The Venn diagram captures the idea that coalition building involves identifying shared objectives between groups with different interests, not creating a perfect union between fully compatible partners. The diagram consists of two overlapping circles. In this case we might say that one circle represents the needs and interests of the battered women's and rape crisis movements. The other circle represents any men's organization that has not historically been part of these movements. Clearly, there are large areas where the circles do not overlap. But the big tent approach does not dwell on the areas of disconnection. It focuses on the center area, where there are points of agreement and shared objectives. If individuals and groups of men and women can agree that reducing men's violence against women is an urgent objective, then perhaps they can agree for the moment to table their other differences.

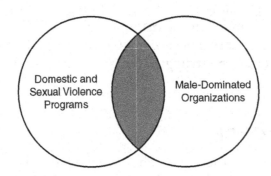

CHALLENGES

There are obvious downsides to incautiously expanding the big tent. Take, for example, the costs and benefits of working with men in the sports culture. Many women in domestic and sexual violence advocacy have long seen the benefit to partnering with athletic teams or utilizing high-profile male athletes in public service campaigns. But some of these same women worry about the potential risks inherent in such collaboration. They fear that a male athlete who speaks out publicly against men's violence could undermine the integrity of the movement if his private behavior does not match his public rhetoric. Happily, in recent years this fear has begun to dissipate as more male athletes speak out, in part because with increased men's participation there is less pressure on any one man to be the "perfect" poster child for anti-violence efforts. We can also never lose sight of the fact that professional sports teams are not social justice organizations. They are businesses that sometimes have huge investments in players. Say a team takes a public stand against men's violence, and then at some point one of its star players is arrested for domestic violence or sexual assault. Is the team likely to respond based on what they think is best for the community, or for their own bottom line?

   The participation of faith-based organizations in the big tent presents significant opportunities, but comes with its own unique set of challenges. As the Rev. Dr. Marie Fortune, a pioneer in
the movements against domestic and sexual violence and founder of the Faith Trust Institute in
Seattle, Washington, points out, "Millions of men participate in faith-based communities whose
leaders, often male, typically enjoy significant moral authority and shape in important ways the
values and behaviors of men in their congregations." There are male clergy in every denomina-
tion who are strong allies of women in the domestic and sexual violence prevention movements.
But many clergy and religious leaders have received no training on the issue of men's violence
against women. To this day many male clergy are reluctant to take strong public stands on issues
of sexual and domestic violence. What further complicates matters is that many religious traditions have "reflected and reinforced," in the words of Rev. Fortune, "patriarchal values that have
been at the core of violence against women." But perhaps even more troubling are the clergy
sex abuse scandals that have become routine in recent years. It is plain to see that even men with
impeccable religious credentials can be private hypocrites.
   The participation of faith-based organizations in gender violence prevention also raises the
question of how much ideological incompatibility is tolerable in the quest for big tent inclusive-
ness. Can feminist religious and secular leaders work in coalition with religious leaders who have
resisted the advancement of women in the family and the pulpit? Can progressive religious and
secular leaders who support full sexual equality work side by side with religious leaders who oppose gay civil rights?
   Similar questions arise about an organization like the Boy Scouts. Scouting plays an important role in the lives of millions of boys and adolescent males. Many local Boy Scout chapters
have participated in events of domestic violence and sexual assault awareness month. But if the
Scouts went a step further and made participation in gender violence prevention a major nationwide organizational goal, they could have a tremendous impact, especially since the Scouts have
a presence in many communities where there is currently little male participation in domestic
and sexual violence programs. But many progressive organizations refuse to work with the Boy
Scouts because their official policy discriminates against openly gay scouts and scoutmasters.
Does their anti-gay stance make the Boy Scouts an unacceptable coalition partner in the struggle against teen-relationship abuse and sexual assault?
   Until now most men in the movement to end men's violence against women have been
profeminist and politically liberal or progressive. But this does not preclude them from framing
one aspect of the gender-violence issue in language about crime and punishment that resonates
with conservatives. In fact, many politically conservative men have played an important role in
this fight—particularly men in law enforcement, the military, and government. After all, domestic and sexual violence are more than social problems; they are crimes. Nonetheless, millions
of abusive men continue to receive suspended sentences, probation, and other light penalties,
which signals that their crimes are not taken seriously. In order to be effective, decisive action
is required by police, prosecutors, and judges. The goal of punishment is to send the message
to would-be perps that the price for transgression is steep. Conservative as well as progressive
men who take the idea of personal responsibility seriously should support policies that hold
law-breakers accountable, and advocacy that strengthens the community's desire to do so. But
a criminal justice approach is also fraught with potential problems. For one thing, there are not
enough jail cells to house all the men who could be prosecuted for domestic and sexual violence. As I have discussed, class bias and racism are factors in any discussion about the criminal
justice system. Efforts to attract conservative men's support by emphasizing a law enforcement
approach might exact too high a cost—and jeopardize the increased participation of people of

color who are concerned about both gender violence *and* the over-representation of men in color in the "prison industrial complex." In addition, since most gender violence—including the vast majority of rape—is currently not reported, it is questionable how effective a criminal justice approach can be.

MEN AND WOMEN

The special challenge of gender violence prevention politics is that women's trust of men is not a given. Some women are understandably wary of men's motivations and skeptical about their commitment to gender justice. As increasing numbers of men get involved, they worry that men might try to "take over" the movement, or take it in a direction that suits men's needs rather than women's. Women are always eager to see whether men "walk their talk." For example, an administrator in a domestic-violence agency recently told me about a talented young man who had applied for a youth outreach position. He seemed to know the issues really well, she explained, and he grasped some of the subtle racial and ethnic issues involved in this work. He also had an engaging personal style. But he had not yet mastered the "micro-politics" of how to interact with women in positions of leadership. He often cut off women co-presenters, or talked over them in an effort to prove his knowledge. Was it worth the risk of hiring him?

For their part, some men are well-meaning but oblivious to the sensitivities required for effective inter-gender collaboration on an issue where women have historically been the leaders. For example, I have heard stories too many times about earnest young men on college campuses who were inspired to start anti-rape groups, but neglected first to check in with women who were already engaged in rape prevention work, like the director of the campus women's center. These sorts of political missteps can cause unnecessary tension and discord at the earliest stages and can undermine successful coalition-building.

Even so, there are numerous examples across the country of men and women working together to create and sustain sexual and domestic violence prevention initiatives. In fact, many successful college men's anti-violence programs have actually been started by women. Among the more well-known are Men Against Violence at Louisiana State University, begun by Dr. Luoluo Hong, and the Fraternity Anti-Violence Education Project at West Chester University in Pennsylvania, led by Dr. Deborah Mahlstedt.

WHAT CAN MEN DO?

At a small state college in the Northeast, a controversy erupted in early 2005 when the editors of the student newspaper distributed a sex survey across campus that included a question about which professor on campus they would most like to "get it on with." The person chosen was the coordinator of the women's studies program, who responded with a lengthy letter to the editor in which she wrote that it was "offensive and hurtful" to be disrespected by students in this way, and as a professional it undermined her ability to do her job. In her letter she posed a number of questions for an alternative survey, including one to men which asked, "What are you willing to do to help reduce rape and sexual assault among college students?" In response, a male columnist for the student newspaper wrote dismissively: "I will not rape anyone. Is there anything more I should add to this?" The student's response might have been glib and a bit obnoxious, but he spoke for a lot of men. Many of them have never even considered the wide range of choices men have to reduce rape and sexual assault, and every other type of gender violence. What follows is a brief discussion about how men can be effective anti-sexist agents, both as individuals and in their various public and private leadership roles within institutions.

Have the Courage to Look Inward

One of the most important steps any man can take if he wants to be an ally to women in the struggle against gender violence is to be honest with himself. A key requirement for men to become effective anti-sexist agents is their willingness to examine their own attitudes and behaviors about women, sex, and manhood. This is similar to the sort of introspection required of anti-racist whites. It is not an easy process, especially when men start to see that they have inadvertently perpetuated sexism and violence through their personal actions, or their participation in sexist practices in male culture. Because defensiveness is the enemy of introspection, it is vital that men develop ways to transcend their initial defensive reactions about men's mistreatment of women and move toward a place where they are grounded enough to do something about it.

Support Survivors

In a social climate where women who report sexual and domestic violence are often disbelieved and called "accusers," it is crucial that men personally and publicly support survivors—girls and boys, women and men. This can mean the offer of a supportive ear in a conversation, or a shoulder for a friend to cry on. It can also mean challenging others—men and women—who seek to discredit victims' accounts of their victimization. For example, when a girl or woman reports a sexual assault and her alleged attacker is a popular guy with a network of supporters, people often rally around him—even when they have nothing more than his word to go on that she is lying. Sadly, some of them try to smear her character and reputation. It is not fair to assume the man's guilt; he is entitled to a presumption of innocence until proven guilty. But alleged victims are entitled to a presumption as well—the presumption that they are telling the truth about what was done to them. They also have the right to be treated with respect, and to expect the people around them to defend their integrity if it is ever questioned.

Seek Help

Men who are emotionally, physically, or sexually abusive to women and girls need to seek help now. But first they have to acknowledge to themselves that they have a problem. I once gave a speech about men's violence against women at a big state university in the West. After the event was over, a blond-haired college student in jeans and a T-shirt approached me in the main lobby of the student center. His voice quivered as he said, "I just realized that I have done bad things to women." He did not elaborate, nor did I ask him to. But I could tell he had a troubled conscience by the look in his eyes, and because he waited nearly half an hour to talk to me. The question of what to do about men who have been abusive will take on ever greater urgency as more men become involved in the movement against gender violence. Many men who were formerly abusive to women have become effective professionals in batterer intervention programs. They share their personal stories and serve as models for how men can grow and change. This is crucial because millions of men have committed mild or severe acts of cruelty toward women and children, and whether they were charged with and convicted of a crime or not, we have to figure out ways to integrate most of them back into our families and communities. Of course, sometimes this is easier said than done. For example, in recent years families in communities across the U.S. have faced the challenge of living in neighborhoods alongside convicted child molesters. This raises another set of questions: When do the rights of children and their parents to be free from the threat of sexual abuse and violence out-weigh the rights of men (or women) who have served their sentences and are seeking to rebuild their lives? If a man has committed acts of sexual or domestic violence, should those acts define him for the rest of his life?

Refuse to Condone Sexist and Abusive Behavior
by Friends, Peers, and Coworkers

As I have argued in this book, if we want to dramatically increase the number of men who make men's violence against women a priority, it is not useful to engage them as perpetrators or potential perpetrators. Instead, it makes sense to enlist them as empowered bystanders who can do something to confront abusive peers, or who can help to create a climate in male peer culture that discourages some men's sexist attitudes and behaviors. This is often easier said than done, because it can be quite awkward for men to confront each other about how they talk about and treat women. Consider an experience I had when I was in my early thirties at a wedding of an old friend of mine. A few minutes after I was introduced to the best man at a cocktail reception the day before the wedding, he confidently told me and a group of other guys a tasteless joke about battered women. I was not sure how to react. If I said something, I feared that it could create a chill between us, and this was the first day of a long weekend. But if I did not say something, I feared my silence might imply approval of the joke. I felt similar to how I would have felt if a white friend had told a racist joke. There was an added concern: How could I—or anyone else—know the full context of his joke-telling? The guy may have been personally harmless, but at the very least his gender politics were suspect, and at the worst he also may have been a closeted batterer who was subtly seeking public approval for his private behavior. I managed to mutter a feeble objection, something like, "Surely you have other topics to joke about." But I never told the guy how I really felt.

Sometimes men who take a strong stand against gender violence can face serious interpersonal consequences for their efforts. Mike LaRiviere, a police officer who is deeply committed to domestic and sexual violence prevention, trains police across the country in domestic violence policies and procedures. He recounts an incident many years ago when he was relatively new to his small-city New England police force. He and his more senior partner answered a domestic violence call, and when they arrived at the apartment it was obvious that the man had assaulted the woman. Mike thought it was clear they should make an arrest, both for the victim's safety and to hold the man accountable for what he had done. But the senior partner had another idea.

He just wanted to tell the guy to cool down. Mike and he had a hushed but heated conversation in another room about what to do. They finally arrested the man, but for the next five or six months, Mike's partner barely spoke with him. The atmosphere in the squad car was tense and chilly, which in police work can be dangerous as well as unpleasant, because you can never be certain that someone who seethes with resentment will always have your back.

In spite of how difficult it can be for men to challenge each other about sexism, it does happen. In fact, it might happen more often than many people realize. In any case, it is important for men to hear each other's stories about this type of intervention, so they can see that other men feel as they do and so they can get potentially useful ideas. I heard one such story about a bachelor party road trip that Al Emerick, a leader of Men Against Violence Against Women in Jacksonville, Florida, took a couple of years ago with some friends. They were a group of well-off white guys in their thirties who had been playing poker together for nine years. There were four married men in the car along with the groom, and the discussion came up about strip clubs. The best man was ready to drop a pile of one-dollar bills on some "fine ladies' asses." Al said he would not be joining them, and the guys immediately got on him. "Whattya gay?" "What's the big deal, the wife's not here." "Cut loose." Because the guys had known Al for quite some time, they knew he was no prude, nor were his objections based on his religious beliefs. But they did know he had been working with a men's group that was affiliated with the local domestic violence shelter. He told them he did not want to take part because he had a problem with the objectification of women—even when it is voluntary. As he tells it, this group of friends spent two hours in an "intense but wonderful" conversation about sexism, domestic violence, male privilege, power, and control. In the course of the conversation Al fielded a range of predictable challenges like: "I'm not an abuser because I look at chicks." He countered with questions like, "What about men in the audience who might be abusers or rapists? By us being there and supporting the action, aren't we reinforcing their behaviors?" In the end, they never went to the strip clubs. Since that event, they have had further conversations about these issues, and according to Al, one of the guys has even offered to help produce a public service announcement for the anti-sexist men's group.

Make Connections between Men's Violence against Women and Other Issues

Gender violence contributes to a wide range of social problems that include youth violence, homelessness, divorce, alcoholism, and the transmission of HIV/AIDS. Men who care about these problems need to educate themselves about the relationship between gender violence and these issues, and then integrate this understanding in their work and daily life.

Perhaps nowhere are the effects of gender violence more pronounced than with HIV/AIDS, the global pandemic that has already killed twenty million people and infected forty-five million. Across the world, there is an inextricable linkage between men's violence against women and transmission of the virus. Forms of gender violence that are fueling transmission include sexual coercion and rape, men's refusal to wear condoms, and married or monogamous men's solicitation of prostitutes followed by unprotected sex with their wives or partners. Gender violence also takes the form of civil and customary laws that perpetuate male privilege and prerogative and deny women's human rights. This might include civil and customary laws that do not recognize marital rape or the dangers of early marriage, as well as systematic prohibitions against females inheriting wealth and property—a reality that ultimately forces millions of widows and daughters to lives of abject poverty and economic dependence on men. But according to M.I.T. research fellow and United Nations consultant Miriam Zoll, while heterosexual transmission may be the primary route of HIV/AIDS infection today, few HIV-prevention programs actually address the underlying gender, power, and sexual dynamics between men and women that contribute to infection, including violence. In a 2004 report entitled "Closing the HIV/AIDS Prevention Gender Gap?" Zoll surveyed men's and women's attitudes about gender and sexuality on several continents. She found that men and women's cultural definitions and perceptions of masculinity and femininity often reinforced men's power over women in ways that make sexually transmitted infections more likely. In the report, Zoll featured the work of men and women who are implementing promising gender-based prevention strategies. For example, Dean Peacock is a white South African who lived for many years in the U.S., where he worked in San Francisco as a facilitator in a batterer intervention program. Peacock returned to South Africa a couple of years ago to lead HIV prevention work with men in a program called Men As Partners, sponsored by Engender Health and Planned Parenthood of South Africa. As Zoll reports, from his unique vantage point Peacock observed with groups of men in prevention trainings in South Africa many of the same ideas about masculinity that he encountered with batterers in the U.S.: "A real man doesn't negotiate with a woman." "A real man doesn't use condoms." "A real man doesn't worry about his health status." "A real man doesn't get tested." "A real man has sex with multiple partners." Even so, Peacock says that men in South Africa with whom he has worked are very open to gender equitable work. "The paradox of the HIV/AIDS epidemic is that it has opened the door to gender equality. We say to these men, 'If you work with us, your life will become richer.' We appeal to them as moral agents. We ask them, 'What is your responsibility to take this to the community, to challenge other men's behaviors, to confront men who are violent, to confront other men who are placing their partners at risk?'"

Contribute Financial Resources

Men with significant financial resources need to think creatively about what they can do to help support the growing number of domestic and sexual-assault prevention initiatives that target boys and men. This is the cutting edge of prevention work, and the field is new enough that a small number of wealthy men could make an enormous impact. Ted Waitt, founder of the Gateway Computer Company, has been one of the early leaders in this area. Philanthropic individuals and organizations can and should continue to fund services for women and girls who are victims and survivors of men's violence, especially when state and federal funds are being cut; funds that target work with men and boys should never compete with funds for direct services for women and girls. But they should not have to, because the pool of available resources should increase as more influential men get involved and bring new ideas and energy to the task of preventing men's violence against women.

Be Creative and Entrepreneurial

A number of enterprising men have used their imagination and creativity to raise other men's awareness of sexism, and to challenge the sexist attitudes and behaviors of men around them. Any list of these individuals is necessarily subjective and abbreviated, but I would nonetheless people to each other, is a former federal prosecutor with extensive experience prosecuting domestic violence, sexual assault, rape, child abuse, and hate crimes. He formerly served as special counsel to the Violence Against Women Office at the United States Department of Justice and is an expert in the federal civil rights of people with disabilities.

Start Anti-Sexist Men's Groups

The power of individuals to catalyze change increases exponentially when they work together to create new institutions and organizations. A growing number of organizations have made significant contributions in recent years to gender violence prevention efforts with men and boys. Some of these groups have paid staff and operate along the lines of traditional non-profit educational organizations; others are more grass roots and volunteer-oriented. It is not possible to provide anything close to a comprehensive list of these various initiatives, but consider a handful of examples from around the country: The Washington, D.C.-based group Men Can Stop Rape regularly conducts anti-rape trainings with high school, college, and community organizations. Their "strength campaign" posters and other materials have been widely circulated. The Institute on Domestic Violence in the African American Community, headed by Dr. Oliver Williams, regularly brings together scholars and activists to discuss issues of particular interest to men (and women) of color, such as the potential role of the hip-hop generation in preventing men's violence against women. The anti-rape men's group One in Four has chapters on dozens of college campuses. In 1999, a group of men in the famous fishing town of Gloucester, Massachusetts—carpenters and clergy, bartenders and bankers—started Gloucester Men Against

Domestic Abuse. They march annually in the town's popular Fourth of July parade and sponsor a billboard that says "Strong Men Don't Bully," a public testimonial of sorts that features the names of five hundred Gloucester men. The Men's Leadership Forum in San Diego, California, is a high-profile annual conference held on Valentine's Day. Since 2001, MLF has brought together a diverse group of men and boys (and women) from across the city to learn how men in business, labor unions, the sports culture, education, the faith community, and the human services can contribute to ending men's violence against women. Some men are politicized about sexism out of concern for their daughters, or as a result of things that have happened to them. One of the most effective organizations that addresses these concerns is Dads and Daughters, a Duluth, Minnesota-based advocacy group led by Joe Kelly. Part of the mission of DADS is to mobilize concerned fathers to challenge companies whose marketing is sexist and exploitative—especially when it involves the sexualization of young girls or adolescents, or treats men's violence against women as a joke.

In addition to some of these now well-established organizations, anti-sexist men on college campuses and in local communities have worked—often in collaboration with women's centers or domestic and sexual violence programs—to educate men and boys about the role men can play in confronting and interrupting other men's abusive behaviors. One venue for this collaboration has been the proliferating number of V-Day events held on college campuses. While V-Day is woman-centered, male students have played all sorts of supportive roles, such as organizing outreach efforts to men and coproducing and promoting performances of the Eve Ensler play *The Vagina Monologues.*

Some anti-sexist men's efforts have been ad hoc and customized to fit the needs and experiences of various communities. For example, in 2003 a group of Asian American men in Seattle organized to support the local chapter of the National Asian Pacific American Women's Forum in their opposition to a restaurant that was promoting "naked sushi" nights, where patrons took sushi off the bodies of semi-nude models wrapped in cellophane. And in the summer of 2004, a group of men (and women) in the "punk, indie, alternative" music scene organized a Different Kind of Dude Fest in Washington, D.C. Along the lines of the Riot Girrls and Girlfest, Hawaii, they sought to use art as an organizing tool. Their goal was to call attention to the ways in which progressive political punk culture, while promising liberation from other forms of social conformity and oppression, nonetheless helped to perpetuate sexism and patriarchal domination. The organizers of the music festival also explicitly affirmed the need for men to be allies of feminists in the fight for gender justice and social equality.

Champion Institutional Reform

Men who hold positions of power in government, non-profit organizations, business, and labor unions can do much to prevent men's violence against women if they take two critical steps: 1.) Recognize domestic and sexual violence prevention as a leadership issue for men, and 2.) Start to think creatively about how they can push their institutions to address it. The problem is that many men in positions of institutional authority do not yet see gender violence prevention in this way. That is why I strongly suggest that public or private institutions who want to begin serious primary prevention initiatives first arrange trainings for men in positions of senior leadership—and the more senior, the better. If done well, gender violence prevention training for men can be transformative. Men often come out of such trainings with an entirely new sensibility about their professional and personal responsibilities to women and children, as well as to other men. This is important because in the long term, dramatic reductions in the incidence of men's violence against women in the U.S. and around the world will only come about when people with power—which often means *men* in power—make gender violence issues a priority. Among other things, this means that male leaders must set and maintain a tone—in educational institutions, corporations, the military—where sexist and abusive behavior is considered unacceptable and unwelcome, not only because women don't like it but because other men will not stand for it. This sounds good, but people often ask me how to get powerful men to take these issues seriously. For example, how do you convince male legislators, educational administrators, business leaders, or military commanders to attend gender violence prevention training? There are a variety of strategies, but the bottom line is that they do not necessarily have to be motivated—at least initially—by altruism or concerns about social justice. They need instead to be persuaded that prevention is a widely shared institutional goal, and that it is their responsibility to be as knowledgeable and proactive about these issues as possible.

Think and Act Locally and Globally

The focus of this book has been mostly on the U.S., but obviously men's violence against women is an issue everywhere in the world. Since 9/11, many Americans have learned what many people around the world have long known—in the modern era, what happens in foreign cultures thousands of miles away can affect people right here at home, sometimes in ways that are impossible to predict. That is the irrevocable reality of the global environment in which we now live. As I have maintained throughout, gender violence is best seen not as aberrational behavior perpetrated by a few bad men but as an expression of much more deeply seated structures of male dominance and gender inequality. This is much easier to see when you are looking at someone else's culture. For example, in radical fundamentalist Islamic countries, women have few rights, and in many instances men's violence against them is legal and even expected—especially when they defy male authority. In other words, men's violence against women functions in some cultures to maintain a highly authoritarian, even fascistic male power structure. In that sense, gender violence is clearly a political crime with potentially far-reaching consequences. As a result, the way that men in distant lands treat women—individually and as a group—cannot be dismissed as a private family or cultural matter. It has too much bearing on political developments that could affect all of us—like the possibility of nuclear war, or the constant threat of terrorist attacks.

At the same time, it is tempting for some Americans to hear and read about the way men mistreat women in foreign cultures and attribute that mistreatment to cultural deficiencies and even barbarism. But it is important to remember that by world standards, the incidence of men's violence against women here in the U.S. is embarrassingly high. No doubt many American men would be offended to hear people in other countries speculating about the shortcomings of American men—and the inferiority of the culture that produced them.

Fortunately, the growing movement of men who are speaking out about men's violence against women is international in scope. There are anti-sexist men's initiatives in scores of countries across the world. In addition, one of the most promising developments in the history of international human rights law is the growing international movement to identify men's violence against women as a human rights issue. A pivotal moment in that movement came in 2001, when the United Nations war crimes tribunal named rape and sexual slavery as war crimes. And today, a number of international organizations—most prominently Amnesty International—have begun to focus on gender violence and link the physical and sexual exploitation of women to a host of other social and political problems. One of the major challenges for American anti-sexist men in the coming years will be to make connections between men's violence against women in the U.S. with violence around the world, and to support efforts everywhere to reduce men's violence and advance gender equality—not only because it is the right thing to do, but also because it is arguably in our national interest.

What's in It for Men?

Men who occupy positions of influence in boys' lives—fathers, grandfathers, older brothers, teachers, coaches, religious leaders—need to teach them that men of integrity value women and do not tolerate other men's sexism or abusive behavior. Obviously they have to lead by example. But that is not enough. In a cultural climate where the objectification of women and girls has accelerated, and boys are exposed to ever more graphic displays of brutality toward women disguised as "entertainment," men need to preemptively provide clear guidelines for boys' behavior. This does not always have to be defined in negative terms, e.g., "Don't hit women." It can be framed as a positive challenge to young men, especially if they aspire to something more special than being "one of the guys" at all costs.

In fact, when I give talks about men's violence against women to groups of parents, I am often asked by parents of sons if there is something positive we can offer young men as a substitute for what we are taking away from them. "We constantly say to our kids, 'Don't do this, don't do that, I wish you wouldn't listen to this music.' We tell them they shouldn't treat girls a certain way, they shouldn't act tough. We spend a lot of time telling our sons what they shouldn't be. It's so negative. Why shouldn't they just tune us out? What's in it for them?"

My answer is really quite simple, and it is as true for the fathers as it is for the sons. When we ask men to reject sexism and the abuse of women, we are not taking something away from them. In fact, we are giving them something very valuable—a vision of manhood that does not depend on putting down others in order to lift itself up. When a man stands up for social justice, non-violence, and basic human rights—for women as much as for men—he is acting in the best traditions of our civilization. That makes him not only a better man, but a better human being.

Name _____   Date _____

Course & section: _____   Instructor _____

More than a Few Good Men

Jackson Katz

1. Name some examples of male-dominated organizations. What are the points of agreement and shared objectives between movements to end domestic and sexual violence and male-dominated organizations?

2. What does Katz mean by the Big Tent Approach? How does he think it can be applied to reading the mainstream of male culture and social power?

3. What are some of the challenges to the Big Tent Approach? What are additional barriers to building a larger movement?

4. What can men who want to work to end domestic and sexual violence *do*?

5. What can athletics, housing, or Greek life on your campus do to join the movement to end domestic and sexual violence?

Pick one organization and identify the overlap between the objectives of that organization and the objectives of the movement to end domestic and sexual violence. What is this organization currently doing with regard to ending domestic and sexual violence? Write them a letter outlining what they can do and how they might be involved.

Uses of the Erotic
The Erotic as Power

Audre Lorde

Audre Lorde was a black lesbian feminist activist, poet and essayist who challenged white feminists to acknowledge the deep rooms of racism. She is famous for her poetry, essays and her memoirs including The Cancer Journals and Zami: a New Spelling of My Name *(1983). Her life and struggle with breast cancer are documented in the film* A Litany for Survival: The Life and Work of Audre Lorde *(1995). Lorde succumbed to breast cancer in 1992. This piece comes from her collected essays,* Sister Outsider *(1984).*

PRE-READING QUESTIONS:

1. What cautions or lessons did you learn when growing up regarding your sexuality?
2. How often do we truly love what we are doing (school, work, volunteering, etc.) even at its most difficult?

KEY TERMS

Eros
the Erotic
pornography
power
women-identified-women

SEE THE THEMATIC TABLE OF CONTENTS, IF YOU WANT TO READ MORE ESSAYS ABOUT:

Bodies and Genders
Sexualities
Social Construction of Gender

Uses of the Erotic
The Erotic as Power

Audre Lorde

There are many kinds of power, used and unused, acknowledged or otherwise. The erotic is a resource within each of us that lies in a deeply female and spiritual plane, firmly rooted in the power of our unexpressed or unrecognized feeling. In order to perpetuate itself, every oppression must corrupt or distort those various sources of power within the culture of the oppressed that can provide energy for change. For women, this has meant a suppression of the erotic as a considered source of power and information within our lives.

We have been taught to suspect this resource, vilified, abused, and devalued within western society. On the one hand, the superficially erotic has been encouraged as a sign of female inferiority; on the other hand, women have been made to suffer and to feel both contemptible and suspect by virtue of its existence.

It is a short step from there to the false belief that only by the suppression of the erotic within our lives and consciousness can women be truly strong. But that strength is illusory, for it is fashioned within the context of male models of power.

As women, we have come to distrust that power which rises from our deepest and nonrational knowledge. We have been warned against it all our lives by the male world, which values this depth of feeling enough to keep women around in order to exercise it in the service of men, but which fears this same depth too much to examine the possibilities of it within themselves. So women are maintained at a distant/inferior position to be psychically milked, much the same way ants maintain colonies of aphids to provide a life-giving substance for their masters.

But the erotic offers a well of replenishing and provocative force to the woman who does not fear its revelation, nor succumb to the belief that sensation is enough.

The erotic has often been misnamed by men and used against women. It has been made into the confused, the trivial, the psychotic, the plasticized sensation. For this reason, we have often turned away from the exploration and consideration of the erotic as a source of power and information, confusing it with its opposite, the pornographic. But pornography is a direct denial of the power of the erotic, for it represents the suppression of true feeling. Pornography emphasizes sensation without feeling.

The erotic is a measure between the beginnings of our sense of self and the chaos of our strongest feelings. It is an internal sense of satisfaction to which, once we have experienced it, we know we can aspire. For having experienced the fullness of this depth of feeling and recognizing its power, in honor and self-respect we can require no less of ourselves.

It is never easy to demand the most from ourselves, from our lives, from our work. To encourage excellence is to go beyond the encouraged mediocrity of our society is to encourage excellence. But giving in to the fear of feeling and working to capacity is a luxury only the unintentional can afford, and the unintentional are those who do not wish to guide their own destinies.

This internal requirement toward excellence which we learn from the erotic must not be misconstrued as demanding the impossible from ourselves nor from others. Such a demand incapacitates everyone in the process. For the erotic is not a question only of what we do; it is a question of how acutely and fully we can feel in the doing. Once we know the extent to which we are capable of feeling that sense of satisfaction and completion, we can then observe which of our various life endeavors bring us closest to that fullness.

The aim of each thing which we do is to make our lives and the lives of our children richer and more possible. Within the celebration of the erotic in all our endeavors, my work becomes a conscious decision—a longed-for bed which I enter gratefully and from which I rise up empowered.

Of course, women so empowered are dangerous. So we are taught to separate the erotic demand from most vital areas of our lives other than sex. And the lack of concern for the erotic root and satisfactions of our work is felt in our disaffection from so much of what we do. For instance, how often do we truly love our work even at its most difficult?

The principal horror of any system which defines the good in terms of profit rather than in terms of human need, or which defines human need to the exclusion of the psychic and emotional components of that need—the principal horror of such a system is that it robs our work of its erotic value, its erotic power and life appeal and fulfillment. Such a system reduces work to a travesty of necessities, a duty by which we earn bread or oblivion for ourselves and those we love. But this is tantamount to blinding a painter and then telling her to improve her work, and to enjoy the act of painting. It is not only next to impossible, it is also profoundly cruel.

As women, we need to examine the ways in which our world can be truly different. I am speaking here of the necessity for reassessing the quality of all the aspects of our lives and of our work, and of how we move toward and through them.

The very word *erotic* comes from the Greek word *eros*, the personification of love in all its aspects—born of Chaos, and personifying creative power and harmony. When I speak of the erotic, then, I speak of it as an assertion of the lifeforce of women; of that creative energy empowered, the knowledge and use of which we are now reclaiming in our language, our history, our dancing, our loving, our work, our lives.

There are frequent attempts to equate pornography and eroticism, two diametrically opposed uses of the sexual. Because of these attempts, it has become fashionable to separate the spiritual (psychic and emotional) from the political, to see them as contradictory or antithetical. "What do you mean, a poetic revolutionary, a meditating gunrunner?" In the same way, we have attempted to separate the spiritual and the erotic, thereby reducing the spiritual to a world of flattened affect, a world of the ascetic who aspires to feel nothing. But nothing is farther from the truth. For the ascetic position is one of the highest fear, the gravest immobility. The severe abstinence of the ascetic becomes the ruling obsession. And it is one not of self-discipline but of self-abnegation.

The dichotomy between the spiritual and the political is also false, resulting from an incomplete attention to our erotic knowledge. For the bridge which connects them is formed by the erotic—the sensual—those physical, emotional, and psychic expressions of what is deepest and strongest and richest within each of us, being shared: the passions of love, in its deepest meanings.

Beyond the superficial, the considered phrase, "It feels right to me," acknowledges the strength of the erotic into a true knowledge, for what that means is the first and most powerful guiding light toward any understanding. And understanding is a handmaiden which can only wait upon, or clarify, that knowledge, deeply born. The erotic is the nurturer or nursemaid of all our deepest knowledge.

The erotic functions for me in several ways, and the first is in providing the power which comes from sharing deeply any pursuit with another person. The sharing of joy, whether physical, emotional, psychic, or intellectual, forms a bridge between the sharers which can be the basis for understanding much of what is not shared between them, and lessens the threat of their difference.

Another important way in which the erotic connection functions is the open and fearless underlining of my capacity for joy. In the way my body stretches to music and opens into response, hearkening to its deepest rhythms, so every level upon which I sense also opens to the erotically satisfying experience, whether it is dancing, building a bookcase, writing a poem, examining an idea.

That self-connection shared is a measure of the joy which I know myself to be capable of feeling, a reminder of my capacity for feeling. And that deep and irreplaceable knowledge of my capacity for joy comes to demand from all of my life that it be lived within the knowledge that such satisfaction is possible, and does not have to be called *marriage*, nor *god*, nor *an afterlife*.

This is one reason why the erotic is so feared, and so often relegated to the bedroom alone, when it is recognized at all. For once we begin to feel deeply all the aspects of our lives, we begin to demand from ourselves and from our life-pursuits that they feel in accordance with that joy which we know ourselves to be capable of. Our erotic knowledge empowers us, becomes a lens through which we scrutinize all aspects of our existence, forcing us to evaluate those aspects honestly in terms of their relative meaning within our lives. And this is a grave responsibility, projected from within each of us, not to settle for the convenient, the shoddy, the conventionally expected, nor the merely safe.

During World War II, we bought sealed plastic packets of white, uncolored margarine, with a tiny, intense pellet of yellow coloring perched like a topaz just inside the clear skin of the bag. We would leave the margarine out for a while to soften, and then we would pinch the little pellet to break it inside the bag, releasing the rich yellowness into the soft pale mass of margarine. Then taking it carefully between our fingers, we would knead it gently back and forth, over and over, until the color had spread throughout the whole pound bag of margarine, thoroughly coloring it.

I find the erotic such a kernel within myself. When released from its intense and constrained pellet, it flows through and colors my life with a kind of energy that heightens and sensitizes and strengthens all my experience.

We have been raised to fear the *yes* within ourselves, our deepest cravings. But, once recognized, those which do not enhance our future lose their power and can be altered. The fear of our desires keeps them suspect and indiscriminately powerful, for to suppress any truth is to give it strength beyond endurance. The fear that we cannot grow beyond whatever distortions we may find within ourselves keeps us docile and loyal and obedient, externally defined, and leads us to accept many facets of our oppression as women.

When we live outside ourselves, and by that I mean on external directives only rather than from our internal knowledge and needs, when we live away from those erotic guides from within ourselves, then our lives are limited by external and alien forms, and we conform to the needs of a structure that is not based on human need, let alone an individual's. But when we begin to live from within outward, in touch with the power of the erotic within ourselves, and allowing that power to inform and illuminate our actions upon the world around us, then we begin to be responsible to ourselves in the deepest sense. For as we begin to recognize our deepest feelings, we begin to give up, of necessity, being satisfied with suffering and self-negation, and with the numbness which so often seems like their only alternative in our society. Our acts against oppression become integral with self, motivated and empowered from within.

In touch with the erotic, I become less willing to accept powerlessness, or those other supplied states of being which are not native to me, such as resignation, despair, self-effacement, depression, self-denial.

And yes, there is a hierarchy. There is a difference between painting a back fence and writing a poem, but only one of quantity. And there is, for me, no difference between writing a good poem and moving into sunlight against the body of a woman I love.

This brings me to the last consideration of the erotic. To share the power of each other's feelings is different from using another's feelings as we would use a kleenex. When we look the other way from our experience, erotic or otherwise, we use rather than share the feelings of those others who participate in the experience with us. And use without consent of the used is abuse.

In order to be utilized, our erotic feelings must be recognized. The need for sharing deep feeling is a human need. But within the european-american tradition, this need is satisfied by certain proscribed erotic comings-together. These occasions are almost always characterized by a simultaneous looking away, a pretense of calling them something else, whether a religion, a fit, mob violence, or even playing doctor. And this misnaming of the need and the deed give rise to that distortion which results in pornography and obscenity – the abuse of feeling.

When we look away from the importance of the erotic in the development and sustenance of our power, or when we look away from ourselves as we satisfy our erotic needs in concert with others, we use each other as objects of satisfaction rather than share our joy in the satisfying, rather than make connection with our similarities and our differences. To refuse to be conscious of what we are feeling at any time, however comfortable that might seem, is to deny a large part of the experience, and to allow ourselves to be reduced to the pornographic, the abused, and the absurd.

The erotic cannot be felt secondhand. As a Black lesbian feminist, I have a particular feeling, knowledge, and understanding for those sisters with whom I have danced hard, played, or even fought. This deep participation has often been the forerunner for joint concerted actions not possible before.

But this erotic charge is not easily shared by women who continue to operate under an exclusively european-american male tradition. I know it was not available to me when I was trying to adapt my consciousness to this mode of living and sensation.

Only now, I find more and more women-identified women brave enough to risk sharing the erotic's electrical charge without having to look away, and without distorting the enormously powerful and creative nature of that exchange. Recognizing the power of the erotic within our lives can give us the energy to pursue genuine change within our world, rather than merely settling for a shift of characters in the same weary drama.

For not only do we touch our most profoundly creative source, but we do that which is female and self-affirming in the face of a racist, patriarchal, and anti-erotic society.

Uses of the Erotic
The Erotic as Power

Audre Lorde

1. How have women been taught to misidentify/misuse the erotic?

2. How does Audre Lorde define the pornographic? How does she distinguish it from the erotic?

3. What does Lorde mean by power? What does Lorde mean by powerlessness? Why are empowered women perceived as dangerous?

4. What is Lorde asking us to do?

5. What power is there in recognizing the erotic? What would it look like for you to claim the power of the erotic? To say yes to yourself? To respond to internal rather than external directives?

White Privilege
Unpacking the Invisible Knapsack

Peggy McIntosh

Peggy McIntosh is a Senior Research Scientist and former Associate Director of the Wellesley College Centers for Women. She received her PhD from Harvard. McIntosh's work focuses on feminism, anti-racism and education. This essay was originally presented at a Virginia Women's Studies Conference in 1986 and has since been widely anthologized.

PRE-READING QUESTIONS

1. What is race? What is racism?
2. Define privilege in your own words.

KEY TERMS

complicity in oppression
heterosexual privilege
male privilege
oppression
power
race privilege
systemic privilege
white privilege

SEE THE THEMATIC TABLE OF CONTENTS, IF YOU WANT TO READ MORE ESSAYS ABOUT:

Privilege, Identities and Intersectionalities

White Privilege
Unpacking the Invisible Knapsack

Peggy McIntosh

"I was taught to see racism only in individual acts of meanness, not in invisible systems conferring dominance on my group "

Through work to bring materials from women's studies into the rest of the curriculum, I have often noticed men's unwillingness to grant that they are overprivileged, even though they may grant that women are disadvantaged. They may say they will work to women's statues, in the society, the university, or the curriculum, but they can't or won't support the idea of lessening men's. Denials that amount to taboos surround the subject of advantages that men gain from women's disadvantages. These denials protect male privilege from being fully acknowledged, lessened, or ended.

Thinking through unacknowledged male privilege as a phenomenon, I realized that, since hierarchies in our society are interlocking, there are most likely a phenomenon, I realized that, since hierarchies in our society are interlocking, there was most likely a phenomenon of while privilege that was similarly denied and protected. As a white person, I realized I had been taught about racism as something that puts others at a disadvantage, but had been taught not to see one of its corollary aspects, white privilege, which puts me at an advantage.

I think whites are carefully taught not to recognize white privilege, as males are taught not to recognize male privilege. So I have begun in an untutored way to ask what it is like to have white privilege. I have come to see white privilege as an invisible package of unearned assets that I can count on cashing in each day, but about which I was "meant" to remain oblivious. White privilege is like an invisible weightless knapsack of special provisions, maps, passports, codebooks, visas, clothes, tools, and blank checks.

Describing white privilege makes one newly accountable. As we in women's studies work to reveal male privilege and ask men to give up some of their power, so one who writes about having white privilege must ask, "having described it, what will I do to lessen or end it?"

After I realized the extent to which men work from a base of unacknowledged privilege, I understood that much of their oppressiveness was unconscious. Then I remembered the frequent charges from women of color that white women whom they encounter are oppressive. I began to understand why we are just seen as oppressive, even when we don't see ourselves that way. I began to count the ways in which I enjoy unearned skin privilege and have been conditioned into oblivion about its existence.

My schooling gave me no training in seeing myself as an oppressor, as an unfairly advantaged person, or as a participant in a damaged culture. I was taught to see myself as an individual whose moral state depended on her individual moral will. My schooling followed the pattern my colleague Elizabeth Minnich has pointed out: whites are taught to think of their lives as morally neutral, normative, and average, and also ideal, so that when we work to benefit others, this is seen as work that will allow "them" to be more like "us."

DAILY EFFECTS OF WHITE PRIVILEGE

I decided to try to work on myself at least by identifying some of the daily effects of white privilege in my life. I have chosen those conditions that I think in my case attach somewhat more to skin-color privilege than to class, religion, ethnic status, or geographic location, though of course all these other factors are intricately intertwined. As far as I can tell, my African American coworkers, friends, and acquaintances with whom I come into daily or frequent contact in this particular time, place and time of work cannot count on most of these conditions.

1. I can if I wish arrange to be in the company of people of my race most of the time.
2. I can avoid spending time with people whom I was trained to mistrust and who have learned to mistrust my kind or me.
3. If I should need to move, I can be pretty sure of renting or purchasing housing in an area which I can afford and in which I would want to live.
4. I can be pretty sure that my neighbors in such a location will be neutral or pleasant to me.
5. I can go shopping alone most of the time, pretty well assured that I will not be followed or harassed.
6. I can turn on the television or open to the front page of the paper and see people of my race widely represented.
7. When I am told about our national heritage or about "civilization," I am shown that people of my color made it what it is.
8. I can be sure that my children will be given curricular materials that testify to the existence of their race.
9. If I want to, I can be pretty sure of finding a publisher for this piece on white privilege.
10. I can be pretty sure of having my voice heard in a group in which I am the only member of my race.
11. I can be casual about whether or not to listen to another person's voice in a group in which s/he is the only member of his/her race.
12. I can go into a music shop and count on finding the music of my race represented, into a supermarket and find the staple foods which fit with my cultural traditions, into a hairdresser's shop and find someone who can cut my hair.
13. Whether I use checks, credit cards or cash, I can count on my skin color not to work against the appearance of financial reliability.
14. I can arrange to protect my children most of the time from people who might not like them.
15. I do not have to educate my children to be aware of systemic racism for their own daily physical protection.
16. I can be pretty sure that my children's teachers and employers will tolerate them if they fit school and workplace norms; my chief worries about them do not concern others' attitudes toward their race.
17. I can talk with my mouth full and not have people put this down to my color.

18. I can swear, or dress in second hand clothes, or not answer letters, without having people attribute these choices to the bad morals, the poverty or the illiteracy of my race.
19. I can speak in public to a powerful male group without putting my race on trial.
20. I can do well in a challenging situation without being called a credit to my race.
21. I am never asked to speak for all the people of my racial group.
22. I can remain oblivious of the language and customs of persons of color who constitute the world's majority without feeling in my culture any penalty for such oblivion.
23. I can criticize our government and talk about how much I fear its policies and behavior without being seen as a cultural outsider.
24. I can be pretty sure that if I ask to talk to the "person in charge", I will be facing a person of my race.
25. If a traffic cop pulls me over or if the IRS audits my tax return, I can be sure I haven't been singled out because of my race.
26. I can easily buy posters, post-cards, picture books, greeting cards, dolls, toys and children's magazines featuring people of my race.
27. I can go home from most meetings of organizations I belong to feeling somewhat tied in, rather than isolated, out-of-place, outnumbered, unheard, held at a distance or feared.
28. I can be pretty sure that an argument with a colleague of another race is more likely to jeopardize her/his chances for advancement than to jeopardize mine.
29. I can be pretty sure that if I argue for the promotion of a person of another race, or a program centering on race, this is not likely to cost me heavily within my present setting, even if my colleagues disagree with me.
30. If I declare there is a racial issue at hand, or there isn't a racial issue at hand, my race will lend me more credibility for either position than a person of color will have.
31. I can choose to ignore developments in minority writing and minority activist programs, or disparage them, or learn from them, but in any case, I can find ways to be more or less protected from negative consequences of any of these choices.
32. My culture gives me little fear about ignoring the perspectives and powers of people of other races.
33. I am not made acutely aware that my shape, bearing or body odor will be taken as a reflection on my race.
34. I can worry about racism without being seen as self-interested or self-seeking.
35. I can take a job with an affirmative action employer without having my co-workers on the job suspect that I got it because of my race.
36. If my day, week or year is going badly, I need not ask of each negative episode or situation whether it had racial overtones.
37. I can be pretty sure of finding people who would be willing to talk with me and advise me about my next steps, professionally.
38. I can think over many options, social, political, imaginative or professional, without asking whether a person of my race would be accepted or allowed to do what I want to do.
39. I can be late to a meeting without having the lateness reflect on my race.
40. I can choose public accommodation without fearing that people of my race cannot get in or will be mistreated in the places I have chosen.
41. I can be sure that if I need legal or medical help, my race will not work against me.
42. I can arrange my activities so that I will never have to experience feelings of rejection owing to my race.

43. If I have low credibility as a leader I can be sure that my race is not the problem.
44. I can easily find academic courses and institutions which give attention only to people of my race.
45. I can expect figurative language and imagery in all of the arts to testify to experiences of my race.
46. I can chose blemish cover or bandages in "flesh" color and have them more or less match my skin.
47. I can travel alone or with my spouse without expecting embarrassment or hostility in those who deal with us.
48. I have no difficulty finding neighborhoods where people approve of our household.
49. My children are given texts and classes which implicitly support our kind of family unit and do not turn them against my choice of domestic partnership.
50. I will feel welcomed and "normal" in the usual walks of public life, institutional and social.

ELUSIVE AND FUGITIVE

I repeatedly forgot each of the realizations on this list until I wrote it down. For me white privilege has turned out to be an elusive and fugitive subject. The pressure to avoid it is great, for in facing it I must give up the myth of meritocracy. If these things are true, this is not such a free country; one's life is not what one makes it; many doors open for certain people through no virtues of their own.

In unpacking this invisible knapsack of white privilege, I have listed conditions of daily experience that I once took for granted. Nor did I think of any of these perquisites as bad for the holder. I now think that we need a more finely differentiated taxonomy of privilege, for some of these varieties are only what one would want for everyone in a just society, and others give license to be ignorant, oblivious, arrogant, and destructive.

I see a pattern running through the matrix of white privilege, a patter of assumptions that were passed on to me as a white person. There was one main piece of cultural turf; it was my own turn, and I was among those who could control the turf. My skin color was an asset for any move I was educated to want to make. I could think of myself as belonging in major ways and of making social systems work for me. I could freely disparage, fear, neglect, or be oblivious to anything outside of the dominant cultural forms. Being of the main culture, I could also criticize it fairly freely.

In proportion as my racial group was being made confident, comfortable, and oblivious, other groups were likely being made unconfident, uncomfortable, and alienated. Whiteness protected me from many kinds of hostility, distress, and violence, which I was being subtly trained to visit, in turn, upon people of color.

For this reason, the word "privilege" now seems to me misleading. We usually think of privilege as being a favored state, whether earned or conferred by birth or luck. Yet some of the conditions I have described here work systematically to over empower certain groups. Such privilege simply confers dominance because of one's race or sex.

EARNED STRENGTH, UNEARNED POWER

I want, then, to distinguish between earned strength and unearned power conferred privilege can look like strength when it is in fact permission to escape or to dominate. But not all of the privileges on my list are inevitably damaging. Some, like the expectation that neighbors will be decent to you, or that your race will not count against you in court, should be the norm in a just society. Others, like the privilege to ignore less powerful people, distort the humanity of the holders as well as the ignored groups.

We might at least start by distinguishing between positive advantages, which we can work to spread, and negative types of advantage, which unless rejected will always reinforce our present hierarchies. For example, the feeling that one belongs within the human circle, as Native Americans say, should not be seen as privilege for a few. Ideally it is an unearned entitlement. At present, since only a few have it, it is an unearned advantage for them. This paper results from a process of coming to see that some of the power that I originally say as attendant on being a human being in the United States consisted in unearned advantage and conferred dominance.

I have met very few men who truly distressed about systemic, unearned male advantage and conferred dominance. And so one question for me and others like me is whether we will be like them, or whether we will get truly distressed, even outraged, about unearned race advantage and conferred dominance, and, if so, what we will do to lessen them. In any case, we need to do more work in identifying how they actually affect our daily lives. Many, perhaps most, of our white students in the United States think that racism doesn't affect them because they are not people of color; they do not see "whiteness" as a racial identity. In addition, since race and sex are not the only advantaging systems at work, we need similarly to examine the daily experience of having age advantage, or ethnic advantage, or physical ability, or advantage related to nationality, religion, or sexual orientation.

Difficulties and angers surrounding the task of finding parallels are many. Since racism, sexism, and heterosexism are not the same, the advantages associated with them should not be seen as the same. In addition, it is hard to disentangle aspects of unearned advantage that rest more on social class, economic class, race, religion, sex, and ethnic identity that on other factors. Still, all of the oppressions are interlocking, as the members of the Combahee River Collective pointed out in their "Black Feminist Statement" of 1977.

One factor seems clear about all of the interlocking oppressions. They take both active forms, which we can see, and embedded forms, which as a member of the dominant groups one is taught not to see. In my class and place, I did not see myself as a racist because I was taught to recognize racism only in individual acts of meanness by members of my group, never in invisible systems conferring unsought racial dominance on my group from birth.

Disapproving of the system won't be enough to change them. I was taught to think that racism could end if white individuals changed their attitude. But a "white" skin in the United States opens many doors for whites whether or not we approve of the way dominance has been conferred on us. Individual acts can palliate but cannot end, these problems.

To redesign social systems we need first to acknowledge their colossal unseen dimensions. The silences and denials surrounding privilege are the key political surrounding privilege are the key political tool here. They keep the thinking about equality or equity incomplete, protecting unearned advantage and conferred dominance by making these subject taboo. Most talk by whites about equal opportunity seems to me now to be about equal opportunity to try to get into a position of dominance while denying that systems of dominance exist.

It seems to me that obliviousness about white advantage, like obliviousness about male advantage, is kept strongly inculturated in the United States so as to maintain the myth of meritocracy, the myth that democratic choice is equally available to all. Keeping most people unaware that freedom of confident action is there for just a small number of people props up those in power and serves to keep power in the hands of the same groups that have most of it already.

Although systemic change takes many decades, there are pressing questions for me and, I imagine, for some others like me if we raise our daily consciousness on the perquisites of being light-skinned. What will we do with such knowledge? As we know from watching men, it is an open question whether we will choose to use unearned advantage, and whether we will use any of our arbitrarily awarded power to try to reconstruct power systems on a broader base.

Name _____   Date _____

Course & section: _____   Instructor _____

White Privilege
Unpacking the Invisible Knapsack

Peggy McIntosh

1. How is the author using knapsack as a metaphor? Why is the knapsack *invisible*?

2. What are the day-to-day effects of white privilege? How are they connected to the unseen dimensions of social systems?

3. Identify three day-to-day privileges listed by McIntosh that seemed most striking to you. Why?

4. How will you answer McIntosh's call to lessen or end privilege?

5. Create a list of privileges derived from one or more of these identity-based categories: gender, sexuality, ability, class, nationality or location, and age.

'Dude, You're a Fag': Adolescent Masculinity and the Fag Discourse

C. J. Pascoe

C. J. Pascoe is an associate professor of sociology and David M. and Nancy Petrone faculty scholar at the University of Oregon where she teaches courses on sexuality, masculinity, social psychology, and gender. Her research focuses on youth, masculinity, gender, sexuality, and new media and has been featured in *The New York Times, The Wall Street Journal,* and on NPR's *All Things Considered.*

PREREADING QUESTIONS

1. What is masculinity? How do you know?
2. What is homophobia?

KEY TERMS

Penetrated masculinity
Subordinated masculinity
Specter of the faggot

SEE THE THEMATIC TABLE OF CONTENTS, IF YOU WANT TO READ MORE ESSAYS ABOUT:

Homophobia
Masculinity
Privilege, Identities, and Intersectionalities
Social Construction of Gender

'Dude, You're a Fag': Adolescent Masculinity and the Fag Discourse

C. J. Pascoe

'There's a faggot over there! There's a faggot over there! Come look!' yelled Brian, a senior at River High School, to a group of 10-year-old boys. Following Brian, the 10 year olds dashed down a hallway. At the end of the hallway Brian's friend, Dan, pursed his lips and began sashaying towards the 10-year-olds. He minced towards them, swinging his hips exaggeratedly and wildly waving his arms. To the boys Brian yelled, 'Look at the faggot! Watch out! He'll get you!' In response the 10-year-olds raced back down the hallway screaming in terror. (From author's fieldnotes)

The relationship between adolescent masculinity and sexuality is embedded in the specter of the faggot. Faggots represent a penetrated masculinity in which 'to be penetrated is to abdicate power' (Bersani, 1987: 212). Penetrated men symbolize a masculinity devoid of power, which, in its contradiction, threatens both psychic and social chaos. It is precisely this specter of penetrated masculinity that functions as a regulatory mechanism of gender for contemporary American adolescent boys.

Feminist scholars of masculinity have documented the centrality of homophobic insults to masculinity (Lehne, 1998; Kimmel, 2001) especially in school settings (Wood, 1984; Smith, 1998; Burn, 2000; Plummer, 2001; Kimmel, 2003). They argue that homophobic teasing often characterizes masculinity in adolescence and early adulthood, and that anti-gay slurs tend to primarily be directed at other gay boys.

This article both expands on and challenges these accounts of relationships between homophobia and masculinity. Homophobia is indeed a central mechanism in the making of contemporary American adolescent masculinity. This article both critiques and builds on this finding by (1) pointing to the limits of an argument that focuses centrally on homophobia, (2) demonstrating that the fag is not only an identity linked to homosexual boys[1] but an identity that can temporarily adhere to heterosexual boys as well and (3) highlighting the racialized nature of the fag as a disciplinary mechanism.

'Homophobia' is too facile a term with which to describe the deployment of 'fag' as an epithet. By calling the use of the word 'fag' homophobia – and letting the argument stop with that point – previous research obscures the gendered nature of sexualized insults (Plummer, 2001). Invoking homophobia to describe the ways in which boys aggressively tease each other overlooks the powerful relationship between masculinity and this sort of insult. Instead, it seems incidental in this conventional line of argument that girls do not harass each other and are not

---

[1] While the term 'homosexual' is laden with medicalized and normalizing meanings, I use it instead of 'gay' because 'gay' in the world of River High has multiple meanings apart from sexual practices or identities.

C.J. Pascoe, *Sexualities: Studies in Culture and Society*, *** Volume 8 (3), pp. 329–346, Copyright © 2005 by SAGE Publications. Reprinted by permisison of SAGE Publications, Ltd

harassed in this same manner.[2] This framing naturalizes the relationship between masculinity and homophobia, thus obscuring the centrality of such harassment in the formation of a gendered identity for boys in a way that it is not for girls.

'Fag' is not necessarily a static identity attached to a particular (homosexual) boy. Fag talk and fag imitations serve as a discourse with which boys discipline themselves and each other through joking relationships.[3] Any boy can temporarily become a fag in a given social space or interaction. This does not mean that those boys who identify as or are perceived to be homosexual are not subject to intense harassment. But becoming a fag has as much to do with failing at the masculine tasks of competence, heterosexual prowess and strength or an anyway revealing weakness or femininity, as it does with a sexual identity. This fluidity of the fag identity is what makes the specter of the fag such a powerful disciplinary mechanism. It is fluid enough that boys police most of their behaviors out of fear of having the fag identity permanently adhere and definitive enough so that boys recognize a fag behavior and strive to avoid it.

The fag discourse is racialized. It is invoked differently by and in relation to white boys' bodies than it is by and in relation to African-American boys' bodies. While certain behaviors put all boys at risk for becoming temporarily a fag, some behaviors can be enacted by African-American boys without putting them at risk of receiving the label. The racialized meanings of the fag discourse suggest that something more than simple homophobia is involved in these sorts of interactions. An analysis of boys' deployments of the specter of the fag should also extend to the ways in which gendered power works through racialized selves. It is not that this gendered homophobia does not exist in African-American communities. Indeed, making fun of 'Negro faggotry seems to be a rite of passage among contemporary black male rappers and film-makers' (Riggs, 1991: 253). However, the fact that 'white women and men, gay and straight, have more or less colonized cultural debates about sexual representation' (Julien and Mercer, 1991: 167) obscures varied systems of sexualized meanings among different racialized ethnic groups (Almaguer, 1991; King, 2004).

THEORETICAL FRAMING

The sociology of masculinity entails a 'critical study of men, their behaviors, practices, values and perspectives' (Whitehead and Barrett, 2001: 14). Recent studies of men emphasize the multiplicity of masculinity (Connell, 1995) detailing the ways in which different configurations of gender practice are promoted, challenged or reinforced in given social situations. This research on how men do masculinities has explored gendered practices in a wide range of social institutions, such as families (Coltrane, 2001) schools (Skelton, 1996; Parker, 1996; Mac an Ghaill, 1996; Francis and Skelton, 2001), workplaces (Cooper, 2000), media (Craig, 1992), and sports (Messner, 1989; Edly and Wetherel, 1997; Curry, 2004). Many of these studies have developed specific typologies of masculinities: gay, Black, Chicano, working class, middle class, Asian, gay Black, gay Chicano, white working class, militarized, transnational business, New Man, negotiated, versatile, healthy, toxic, counter, and cool masculinities, to name a few (Messner, 2004). In this sort of model the fag could be (and often has been) framed as a type of subordinated masculinity attached to homosexual adolescent boys' bodies.

[2]Girls do insult one another based on sexualized meanings. But in my own research I found that girls and boys did not harass girls in this manner with the same frequency that boys harassed each other through engaging in joking about the fag.
[3]I use discourse in the Foucauldian sense, to describe truth producing practices, not just text or speech (Foucault, 1978).

Heeding Timothy Carrigan's admonition that an 'analysis of masculinity needs to be related as well to other currents in feminism' (Carrigan et al., 1987: 64), in this article I integrate queer theory's insights about the relationships between gender, sexuality, identities and power with the attention to men found in the literature on masculinities. Like the sociology of gender, queer theory destabilizes the assumed naturalness of the social order (Lemert, 1996). Queer theory is a 'conceptualization which sees sexual power as embedded in different levels of social life' and interrogates areas of the social world not usually seen as sexuality (Stein and Plummer, 1994). In this sense queer theory calls for sexuality to be looked at not only as a discrete arena of sexual practices and identities, but also as a constitutive element of social life (Warner, 1993; Epstein, 1996).

While the masculinities' literature rightly highlights very real inequalities between gay and straight men (see for instance Connell, 1995), this emphasis on sexuality as inhered in static identities attached to male bodies, rather than major organizing principles of social life (Sedgwick, 1990), limits scholars' ability to analyze the myriad ways in which sexuality, in part, constitutes gender. This article does not seek to establish that there are homosexual boys and heterosexual boys and the homosexual ones are marginalized. Rather this article explores what happens to theories of gender if we look at a *discourse* of sexualized identities in addition to focusing on seemingly static identity categories inhabited by men. This is not to say that gender is reduced only to sexuality, indeed feminist scholars have demonstrated that gender is embedded in and constitutive of a multitude of social structures – the economy, places of work, families and schools. In the tradition of post-structural feminist theorists of race and gender who look at 'border cases' that explode taken-for-granted binaries of race and gender (Smith, 1994), queer theory is another tool which enables an integrated analysis of sexuality, gender and race.

As scholars of gender have demonstrated, gender is accomplished through day-to-day interactions (Fine, 1987; Hochschild, 1989; West and Zimmerman, 1991; Thorne, 1993). In this sense gender is the 'activity of managing situated conduct in light of normative conceptions of attitudes and activities appropriate for one's sex category' (West and Zimmerman, 1991: 127). Similarly, queer theorist Judith Butler argues that gender is accomplished interactionally through 'a set of repeated acts within a highly rigid regulatory frame that congeal over time to produce the appearance of substance, of a natural sort of being' (Butler, 1999: 43). Specifically she argues that gendered beings are created through processes of citation and repudiation of a 'constitutive outside' (Butler, 1993: 3) in which is contained all that is cast out of a socially recognizable gender category. The 'constitutive outside' is inhabited by abject identities, unrecognizably and unacceptably gendered selves. The interactional accomplishment of gender in a Butlerian model consists, in part, of the continual iteration and repudiation of this abject identity. Gender, in this sense, is 'constituted through the force of exclusion and abjection, on which produces a constitutive outside to the subject, an abjected outside, which is, after all, 'inside' the subject as its own founding repudiation' (Butler, 1993: 3). This repudiation creates and reaffirms a 'threatening specter' (Butler, 1993: 3) of failed, unrecognizable gender, the existence of which must be continually repudiated through interactional processes.

I argue that the 'fag' position is an 'abject' position and, as such, is a 'threatening specter' constituting contemporary American adolescent masculinity. The fag discourse is the interactional process through which boys name and repudiate this abjected identity. Rather than analyzing the fag as an identity for homosexual boys, I examine uses of the discourse that imply that any boy can become a fag, regardless of his actual desire or self-perceived sexual orientation. The threat of the abject position infuses the faggot with regulatory power. This article provides empirical data to illustrate Butler's approach to gender and indicates that it might be a useful addition to the sociological literature on masculinities through highlighting one of the ways in which a masculine gender identity is accomplished through interaction.

METHOD

Research site

I conducted fieldwork at a suburban high school in north-central California which I call River High.[4] River High is a working class, suburban 50-year-old high school located in a town called Riverton. With the exception of the median household income and racial diversity (both of which are elevated due to Riverton's location in California), the town mirrors national averages in the percentages of white collar workers, rates of college attendance, and marriages, and age composition (according to the 2000 census). It is a politically moderate to conservative, religious community. Most of the students' parents commute to surrounding cities for work.

On average Riverton is a middle-class community. However, students at River are likely to refer to the town as two communities: 'Old Riverton' and 'New Riverton'. A busy highway and railroad tracks bisect the town into these two sections. River High is literally on the 'wrong side of the tracks', in Old Riverton. Exiting the freeway, heading north to Old Riverton, one sees a mix of 1950s-era ranch-style homes, some with neatly trimmed lawns and tidy gardens, others with yards strewn with various car parts, lawn chairs and appliances. Old Riverton is visually bounded by smoke-puffing factories. On the other side of the freeway New Riverton is characterized by wide sidewalk-lined streets and new walled-in home developments. Instead of smokestacks, a forested mountain, home to a state park, rises majestically in the background. The teens from these homes attend Hillside High, River's rival.

River High is attended by 2000 students. River High's racial/ethnic breakdown roughly represents California at large: 50 percent white, 9 percent African-American, 28 percent Latino and 6 percent Asian (as compared to California's 46, 6, 32, and 11 percent respectively, according to census data and school records). The students at River High are primarily working class.

Research

I gathered data using the qualitative method of ethnographic research. I spent a year and a half conducting observations, formally interviewing 49 students at River High (36 boys and 13 girls), one male student from Hillside High, and conducting countless informal interviews with students, faculty and administrators. I concentrated on one school because I explore the richness rather than the breadth of data (for other examples of this method see Willis, 1981; MacLeod, 1987; Eder et al., 1995; Ferguson, 2000).

I recruited students for interviews by conducting presentations in a range of classes and hanging around at lunch, before school, after school and at various events talking to different groups of students about my research, which I presented as 'writing a book about guys'. The interviews usually took place at school, unless the student had a car, in which case he or she met me at one of the local fast food restaurants where I treated them to a meal. Interviews lasted anywhere from half an hour to two hours.

The initial interviews I conducted helped me to map a gendered and sexualized geography of the school, from which I chose my observation sites. I observed a 'neutral' site – a senior

---

[4]The names of places and respondents have been changed.

government classroom, where sexualized meanings were subdued. I observed three sites that students marked as 'fag' sites – two drama classes and the Gay/Straight Alliance. I also observed two normatively 'masculine' sites – auto-shop and weightlifting.[5] I took daily field notes focusing on how students, faculty and administrators negotiated, regulated and resisted particular meanings of gender and sexuality. I attended major school rituals such as Winter Ball, school rallies, plays, dances and lunches. I would also occasionally 'ride along' with Mr Johnson (Mr J.), the school's security guard, on his battery-powered golf cart to watch which, how and when students were disciplined. Observational data provided me with more insight to the interactional processes of masculinity than simple interviews yielded. If I had relied only on interview data I would have missed the interactional processes of masculinity which are central to the fag discourse.

Given the importance of appearance in high school, I gave some thought as to how I would present myself, deciding to both blend in and set myself apart from the students. In order to blend in I wore my standard graduate student gear – comfortable, baggy cargo pants, a black t-shirt or sweater and tennis shoes. To set myself apart I carried a messenger bag instead of a back-pack, didn't wear makeup, and spoke slightly differently than the students by using some slang, but refraining from uttering the ubiquitous 'hecka' and 'hella'.

The boys were fascinated by the fact that a 30-something white 'girl' (their words) was interested in studying them. While at first many would make sexualized comments asking me about my dating life or saying that they were going to 'hit on' me, it seemed eventually they began to forget about me as a potential sexual/romantic partner. Part of this, I think, was related to my knowledge about 'guy' things. For instance, I lift weights on a regular basis and as a result the weightlifting coach introduced me as a 'weight-lifter from U.C. Berkeley' telling the students they should ask me for weight-lifting advice. Additionally, my taste in movies and television shows often coincided with theirs. I am an avid fan of the movies 'Jackass' and 'Fight Club', both of which contain high levels of violence and 'bathroom' humor. Finally, I garnered a lot of points among boys because I live off a dangerous street in a nearby city famous for drug deals, gang fights and frequent gun shots.

WHAT IS A FAG?

'Since you were little boys you've been told, "hey, don't be a little faggot,"' explained Darnell, an African-American football player, as we sat on a bench next to the athletic field. Indeed, both the boys and girls I interviewed told me that 'fag' was the worst epithet one guy could direct at another. Jeff, a slight white sophomore, explained to me that boys call each other fag because 'gay people aren't really liked over here and stuff.' Jeremy, a Latino Junior told me that this insult literally reduced a boy to nothing, 'To call someone gay or fag is like the lowest thing you can call someone. Because that's like saying that you're nothing.'

Most guys explained their or other's dislike of fags by claiming that homophobia is just part of what it means to be a guy. For instance Keith, a white soccer-playing senior, explained, 'I think guys are just homophobic.' However, it is not just homophobia, it is *a gendered* homophobia. Several students told me that these homophobic insults only applied to boys and not girls. For example, while Jake, a handsome white senior, told me that he didn't like gay people, he quickly added, 'Lesbians, okay that's *good.*' Similarly Cathy, a popular white cheerleader, told me 'Being

---

[5]Auto-shop was a class in which students learned how to build and repair cars. Many of the students in this course were looking into careers as mechanics.

a lesbian is accepted because guys think "oh that's cool."' Darnell, after telling me that boys were told not to be faggots, said of lesbians, 'They're [guys are] fine with girls. I think it's the guy part that they're like ewwww!' In this sense it is not strictly homophobia, but a gendered homophobia that constitutes adolescent masculinity in the culture of this school. However, it is clear, according to these comments, that lesbians are 'good' because of their place in heterosexual male fantasy not necessarily because of some enlightened approach to same-sex relationships. It does however, indicate that using only the term homophobia to describe boys' repeated use of the word 'fag' might be a bit simplistic and misleading.

Additionally, girls at River High rarely deployed the word 'fag' and were never called 'fags'. I recorded girls uttering 'fag' only three times during my research. In one instance, Angela, a Latina cheerleader, teased Jeremy, a well-liked white senior involved in student government, for not ditching school with her, 'You wouldn't 'cause you're a faggot.' However, girls did not use this word as part of their regular lexicon. The sort of gendered homophobia that constitutes adolescent masculinity does not constitute adolescent femininity. Girls were not called dykes or lesbians in any sort of regular or systematic way. Students did tell me that 'slut' was the worst thing a girl could be called. However, my field notes indicate that the word 'slut' (or its synonym 'ho') appears one time for every eight times the word 'fag' appears. Even when it does occur, 'slut' is rarely deployed as a direct insult against another girl.

Highlighting the difference between the deployment of 'gay' and 'fag' as insults brings the gendered nature of this homophobia into focus. For boys and girls at River High 'gay' is a fairly common synonym for 'stupid'. While this word shares the sexual origins of 'fag', it does not *consistently* have the skew of gender-loaded meaning. Girls and boys often used 'gay' as an adjective referring to inanimate objects and male or female people, whereas they used 'fag' as a noun that denotes only un-masculine males. Students used 'gay' to describe anything from someone's clothes to a new school rule that the students did not like, as in the following encounter:

> In auto-shop Arnie pulled out a large older version black laptop computer and placed it on his desk. Behind him Nick said 'That's a gay laptop! It's five inches thick!'

A laptop can be gay, a movie can be gay or a group of people can be gay. Boys used 'gay' and 'fag' interchangeably when they refer to other boys, but 'fag' does not have the non-gendered attributes that 'gay' sometimes invokes.

While its meanings are not the same as 'gay', 'fag' does have multiple meanings which do not necessarily replace its connotations as a homophobic slur, but rather exist alongside. Some boys took pains to say that 'fag' is not about sexuality. Darnell told me 'It doesn't even have anything to do with being gay.' J.L., a white sophomore at Hillside High (River High's cross-town rival) asserted 'Fag, seriously, it has nothing to do with sexual preference at all. You could just be calling somebody an idiot you know?' I asked Ben, a quiet, white sophomore who wore heavy metal t-shirts to auto-shop each day, 'What kind of things do guys get called a fag for?' Ben answered 'Anything . . . literally, anything. Like you were trying to turn a wrench the wrong way, "dude, you're a fag!" Even if a piece of meat drops out of your sandwich, "you fag!"' Each time Ben said 'you fag' his voice deepened as if he were imitating a more masculine boy. While Ben might rightly *feel* like a guy could be called a fag for 'anything . . . literally, anything', there are actually specific behaviors which, when enacted by most boys, can render him more vulnerable to a fag epithet. In this instance Ben's comment highlights the use of 'fag' as a generic insult for incompetence, which in the world of River High, is central to a masculine identity. A boy could get called a fag for exhibiting any sort of behavior defined as non-masculine (although not necessarily behaviors aligned with femininity) in the world of River High: being stupid, incompetent, dancing, caring too much about clothing, being too emotional or expressing interest (sexual or platonic) in other guys. However, given the extent of its deployment and the laundry list of behaviors that could get a boy in trouble it is no wonder that Ben felt like a boy could be called 'fag' for 'anything'.

One-third (13) of the boys I interviewed told me that, while they may liberally insult each other with the term, they would not actually direct it at a homosexual peer. Jabes, a Filipino senior, told me

> I actually say it [fag] quite a lot, except for when I'm in the company of an actual homosexual person. Then I try not to say it at all. But when I'm just hanging out with my friends I'll be like, 'shut up, I don't want you hear you any more, you stupid fag'.

Similarly J.L. compared homosexuality to a disability, saying there is 'no way' he'd call an actually gay guy a fag because

> There's people who are the retarded people who nobody wants to associate with. I'll be so nice to those guys and I hate it when people make fun of them. It's like, 'bro do you realize that they can't help that?' And then there's gay people. They were born that way.

According to this group of boys, gay is a legitimate, if marginalized, social identity. If a man is gay, there may be a chance he could be considered masculine by other men (Connell, 1995). David, a handsome white senior dressed smartly in khaki pants and a white button-down shirt said, 'Being gay is just a lifestyle. It's someone you choose to sleep with. You can still throw around a football and be gay.' In other words there is a possibility, however slight, that a boy can be gay and masculine. To be a fag is, by definition, the opposite of masculine, whether or not the word is deployed with sexualized or non-sexualized meanings. In explaining this to me, Jamaal, an African-American junior, cited the explanation of popular rap artist, Eminem,

> Although I don't like Eminem, he had a good definition of it. It's like taking away your title. In an interview they were like, 'you're always capping on gays, but then you sing with Elton John.' He was like 'I don't mean gay as in gay'.

This is what Riki Wilchins calls the 'Eminem Exception. Eminem explains that he doesn't call people "faggot" because of their sexual orientation but because they're weak and unmanly' (Wilchins, 2003). This is precisely the way in which this group of boys at River High uses the term 'faggot'. While it is not necessarily acceptable to be gay, at least a man who is gay can do other things that render him acceptably masculine. A fag, by the very definition of the word, indicated by students' usages at River High, cannot be masculine. This distinction between 'fag' as an un-masculine and problematic identity and 'gay' as a possibly masculine, although marginalized, sexual identity is not limited to a teenage lexicon, but is reflected in both psychological discourses (Sedgwick, 1995) and gay and lesbian activism.

BECOMING A FAG

'The ubiquity of the word faggot speaks to the reach of its discrediting capacity' (Corbett, 2001: 4). It is almost as if boys cannot help but shout it out on a regular basis – in the hallway, in class, across campus as a greeting, or as a joke. In my fieldwork I was amazed by the way in which the word seemed to pop uncontrollably out of boys' mouths in all kinds of situations. To quote just one of many instances from my fieldnotes:

> Two boys walked out of the P.E. locker room and one yelled 'fucking faggot!' at no one in particular.

This spontaneous yelling out of a variation of fag seemingly apropos of nothing happened repeatedly among boys throughout the school.

The fag discourse is central to boys' joking relationships. Joking cements relationships between boys (Kehily and Nayak, 1997; Lyman, 1998) and helps to manage anxiety and discomfort (Freud, 1905). Boys invoked the specter of the fag in two ways: through humorous imitation and through lobbing the epithet at one another. Boys at River High imitated the fag by acting out an exaggerated 'femininity', and/or by pretending to sexually desire other boys. As indicated by the introductory vignette in which a predatory 'fag' threatens the little boys, boys at River High link these performative scenarios with a fag identity. They lobbed the fag epithet at each other in a verbal game of hot potato, each careful to deflect the insult quickly by hurling it toward someone else. These games and imitations make up a fag discourse which highlights the fag not as a static but rather as a fluid identity which boys constantly struggle to avoid.

In imitative performances the fag discourse functions as a constant reiteration of the fag's existence, affirming that the fag is out there; at any moment a boy can become a fag. At the same time these performances demonstrate that the boy who is invoking the fag is *not* a fag. By invoking it so often, boys remind themselves and each other that at any point they can become fags if they are not sufficiently masculine.

> Mr McNally, disturbed by the noise outside of the classroom, turned to the open door saying 'We'll shut this unless anyone really wants to watch sweaty boys playing basketball.' Emir, a tall skinny boy, lisped 'I wanna watch the boys play!' The rest of the class cracked up at his imitation.

Through imitating a fag, boys assure others that they are not a fag by immediately becoming masculine again after the performance. They mock their own performed femininity and/or same-sex desire, assuring themselves and others that such an identity is one deserving of derisive laughter. The fag identity in this instance is fluid, detached from Emir's body. He can move in and out of this 'abject domain' while simultaneously affirming his position as a subject.

Boys also consistently tried to put another in the fag position by lobbing the fag epithet at one another.

> Going through the junk-filled car in the auto-shop parking lot, Jay poked his head out and asked 'Where are Craig and Brian?' Neil, responded with 'I think they're over there', pointing, then thrusting his hips and pulling his arms back and forth to indicate that Craig and Brian might be having sex. The boys in auto-shop laughed.

This sort of joke temporarily labels both Craig and Brian as faggots. Because the fag discourse is so familiar, the other boys immediately understand that Neil is indicating that Craig and Brian are having sex. However these are not necessarily identities that stick. Nobody actually thinks Craig and Brian are homosexuals. Rather the fag identity is a fluid one, certainly an identity that no boy wants, but one that a boy can escape, usually by engaging in some sort of discursive contest to turn another boy into a fag. However, fag becomes a hot potato that no boy wants to be left holding. In the following example, which occurred soon after the 'sex' joke, Brian lobs the fag epithet at someone else, deflecting it from himself:

> Brian initiated a round of a favorite game in auto-shop, the 'cock game'. Brian quietly, looking at Josh, said, 'Josh loves the cock,' then slightly louder, 'Josh loves the cock.' He continued saying this until he was yelling 'JOSH LOVES THE COCK!' The rest of the boys laughed hysterically as Josh slinked away saying 'I have a bigger dick than all you mother fuckers!'

These two instances show how the fag can be mapped, momentarily, on to one boy's body and how he, in turn, can attach it to another boy, thus deflecting it from himself. In the first instance Neil makes fun of Craig and Brian for simply hanging out together. In the second instance

Brian goes from being a fag to making Josh into a fag, through the 'cock game'. The 'fag' is transferable. Boys move in and out of it by discursively creating another as a fag through joking interactions. They, somewhat ironically, can move in and out of the fag position by transforming themselves, temporarily, into a fag, but this has the effect of reaffirming their masculinity when they return to a heterosexual position after imitating the fag.

These examples demonstrate boys invoking the trope of the fag in a discursive struggle in which the boys indicate that they know what a fag is – and that they are not fags. This joking cements bonds between boys as they assure themselves and each other of their masculinity through repeated repudiations of a non-masculine position of the abject.

RACING THE FAG

The fag trope is not deployed consistently or identically across social groups at River High. Differences between white boys' and African-American boys' meaning making around clothes and dancing reveal ways in which the fag as the abject position is racialized.

Clean, oversized, carefully put together clothing is central to a hip-hop identity for African-American boys who identify with hip-hop culture.[6] Richard Majors calls this presentation of self a 'cool pose' consisting of 'unique, expressive and conspicuous styles of demeanor, speech, gesture, clothing, hairstyle, walk, stance and handshake', developed by African-American men as a symbolic response to institutionalized racism (Majors, 2001: 211). Pants are usually several sizes too big, hanging low on a boy's waist, usually revealing a pair of boxers beneath. Shirts and sweaters are similarly oversized, often hanging down to a boy's knees. Tags are frequently left on baseball hats worn slightly askew and sit perched high on the head. Meticulously clean, unlaced athletic shoes with rolled up socks under the tongue complete a typical hip-hop outfit.

This amount of attention and care given to clothing for white boys not identified with hip-hop culture (that is, most of the white boys at River High) would certainly cast them into an abject, fag position. White boys are not supposed to appear to care about their clothes or appearance, because only fags care about how they look. Ben illustrates this:

Ben walked in to the auto-shop classroom from the parking lot where he had been working on a particularly oily engine. Grease stains covered his jeans. He looked down at them, made a face and walked toward me with limp wrists, laughing and lisping in a in a high pitch sing-song voice 'I got my good panths all dirty!'

Ben draws on indicators of a fag identity, such as limp wrists, as do the boys in the introductory vignette to illustrate that a masculine person certainly would not care about having dirty clothes. In this sense, masculinity, for white boys, becomes the carefully crafted appearance of not caring about appearance, especially in terms of cleanliness.

However, African-American boys involved in hip-hop culture talk frequently about whether or not their clothes, specifically their shoes, are dirty:

In drama class both Darnell and Marc compared their white Adidas basketball shoes. Darnell mocked Marc because black scuff marks covered his shoes, asking incredulously 'Yours are a week old and they're dirty – I've had mine for a month and they're not dirty!' Both laughed.

Monte, River High's star football player echoed this concern about dirty shoes when looking at the fancy red shoes he had lent to his cousin the week before, told me he was frustrated because

---

[6]While there are several white and Latino boys at River High who identify with hip-hop culture, hip-hop is identified by the majority of students as an African-American cultural style.

after his cousin used them, the 'shoes are hella scuffed up'. Clothing, for these boys, does not indicate a fag position, but rather defines membership in a certain cultural and racial group (Perry, 2002).

Dancing is another arena that carries distinctly fag associated meanings for white boys and masculine meanings for African-American boys who participate in hip-hop culture. White boys often associate dancing with 'fags'. J.L. told me that guys think ''nSync's gay' because they can dance. 'nSync is an all white male singing group known for their dance moves. At dances white boys frequently held their female dates tightly, locking their hips together. The boys never danced with one another, unless engaged in a round of 'hot potato'. White boys often jokingly danced together in order to embarrass each other by making someone else into a fag:

> Lindy danced behind her date, Chris. Chris's friend, Matt, walked up and nudged Lindy aside, imitating her dance moves behind Chris. As Matt rubbed his hands up and down Chris's back, Chris turned around and jumped back startled to see Matt there instead of Lindy. Matt cracked up as Chris turned red.

However dancing does not carry this sort of sexualized gender meaning for all boys at River High. For African-American boys dancing demonstrates membership in a cultural community (Best, 2000). African-American boys frequently danced together in single sex groups, teaching each other the latest dance moves, showing off a particularly difficult move or making each other laugh with humorous dance moves. Students recognized K.J. as the most talented dancer at the school. K.J. is a sophomore of African-American and Filipino descent who participated in the hip-hop culture of River High. He continually wore the latest hip-hop fashions. K.J. was extremely popular. Girls hollered his name as they walked down the hall and thrust urgently written love notes folded in complicated designs into his hands as he sauntered to class. For the past two years K.J. won first place in the talent show for dancing. When he danced at assemblies the room reverberated with screamed chants of 'Go K.J.! Go K.J! Go K.J.!' Because dancing for African-American boys places them within a tradition of masculinity, they are not at risk of becoming a fag for this particular gendered practice. Nobody called K.J. a fag. In fact in several of my interviews boys of multiple racial/ethnic backgrounds spoke admiringly of KJ.'s dancing abilities.

IMPLICATIONS

These findings confirm previous studies of masculinity and sexuality that position homophobia as central to contemporary definitions of adolescent masculinity. These data extend previous research by unpacking multi-layered meanings that boys deploy through their uses of homophobic language and joking rituals. By attending to these meanings I reframe the discussion as one of a fag discourse, rather than simply labeling this sort of behavior as homophobia. The fag is an 'abject' position, a position outside of masculinity that actually constitutes masculinity. Thus, masculinity, in part becomes the daily interactional work of repudiating the 'threatening specter' of the fag.

The fag extends beyond a static sexual identity attached to a gay boy. Few boys are permanently identified as fags; most move in and out of fag positions. Looking at 'fag' as a discourse rather than a static identity reveals that the term can be invested with different meanings in different social spaces. 'Fag' may be used as a weapon with which to temporarily assert one's masculinity by denying it to others. Thus 'fag' becomes a symbol around which contests of masculinity take place.

The fag epithet, when hurled at other boys, may or may not have explicit sexual meanings, but it always has gendered meanings. When a boy calls another boy a fag, it means he is not a man, not necessarily that he is a homosexual. The boys in this study know that they are not supposed to call homosexual boys 'fags' because that is mean. This, then has been the limited success of the mainstream gay rights movement. The message absorbed by some of these teenage boys is that 'gay men can be masculine, just like you.' Instead of challenging gender inequality, this particular discourse of gay rights has reinscribed it. Thus we need to begin to think about how gay men may be in a unique position to challenge gendered as well as sexual norms.

This study indicates that researchers who look at the intersection of sexuality and masculinity need to attend to the ways in which racialized identities may affect how 'fag' is deployed and what it means in various social situations. While researchers have addressed the ways in which masculine identities are racialized (Connell, 1995; Ross, 1998; Bucholtz, 1999; Davis, 1999; Price, 1999; Ferguson, 2000; Majors, 2001) they have not paid equal attention to the ways in which 'fag' might be a racialized epithet. It is important to look at when, where and with what meaning 'the fag' is deployed in order to get at how masculinity is defined, contested, and invested in among adolescent boys.

Research shows that sexualized teasing often leads to deadly results, as evidenced by the spate of school shootings in the 1990s (Kimmel, 2003). Clearly the fag discourse affects not just homosexual teens, but all boys, gay and straight. Further research could investigate these processes in a variety of contexts: varied geographic locations, sexualized groups, classed groups, religious groups and age groups.

REFERENCES

Almaguer, Tomas (1991) 'Chicano Men: A Cartography of Homosexual Identity and Behavior', *Differences* 3: 75–100.

Bersani, Leo (1987) 'Is the Rectum a Grave?' *October* 43: 197–222.

Best, Amy (2000) *Prom Night: Youth, Schools and Popular Culture*. New York: Routledge.

Bucholtz, Mary (1999) '"You Da Man": Narrating the Racial Other in the Production of White Masculinity', *Journal of Sociolinguistics* 3/4: 443–60.

Burn, Shawn M. (2000) 'Heterosexuals' Use of "Fag" and "Queer" to Deride One Another: A Contributor to Heterosexism and Stigma', *Journal of Homosexuality* 40: 1–11.

Butler, Judith (1993) *Bodies that Matter*. Routledge: New York.

Butler, Judith (1999) *Gender Trouble*. New York: Routledge.

Carrigan, Tim, Connell, Bob and Lee, John (1987) 'Toward a New Sociology of Masculinity', in Harry Brod (ed.) *The Making of Masculinities: The New Men's Studies*, pp. 188–202. Boston, MA: Allen & Unwin.

Coltrane, Scott (2001) 'Selling the Indispensable Father', paper presented at *Pushing the Boundaries Conference: New Conceptualizations of Childhood and Motherhood*, Philadelphia.

Connell, R.W. (1995) *Masculinities*. Berkeley: University of California Press.

Cooper, Marianne (2000) 'Being the "Go-To Guy": Fatherhood, Masculinity and the Organization of Work in Silicon Valley', *Qualitative Sociology* 23: 379–405.

Corbett, Ken (2001) 'Faggot = Loser', *Studies in Gender and Sexuality* 2: 3–28.

Craig, Steve (1992) *Men, Masculinity and the Media*. Newbury Park: Sage.

Curry, Timothy J. (2004) 'Fraternal Bonding in the Locker Room: A Profeminist Analysis of Talk about Competition and Women', in Michael Messner and Michael Kimmel (eds) *Men's Lives*. Boston, MA: Pearson.

Davis, James E. (1999) 'Forbidden Fruit, Black Males' Constructions of Transgressive Sexualities in Middle School', in William J. Letts IV and James T. Sears (eds) *Queering Elementary*

Education: Advancing the Dialogue about Sexualities and Schooling, pp. 49 ff. Lanham, MD: Rowan & Littlefield.

Eder, Donna, Evans, Catherine and Parker, Stephen (1995) *School Talk: Gender and Adolescent Culture*. New Brunswick, NJ: Rutgers University Press.

Edly, Nigel and Wetherell, Margaret (1997) 'Jockeying for Position: The Construction of Masculine Identities', *Discourse and Society* 8: 203–17.

Epstein, Steven (1996) 'A Queer Encounter', in Steven Seidman (ed.) *Queer Theory/Sociology*, pp. 188–202. Cambridge, MA: Blackwell.

Ferguson, Ann (2000) *Bad Boys: Public Schools in the Making of Black Masculinity*. Ann Arbor: University of Michigan Press.

Fine, Gary (1987) *With the Boys: Little League Baseball and Preadolescent Culture*. Chicago, IL: University of Chicago Press.

Foucault, Michel (1978) *The History of Sexuality, Volume I*. New York: Vintage Books.

Francis, Becky and Skelton, Christine (2001) 'Men Teachers and the Construction of Heterosexual Masculinity in the Classroom', *Sex Education* 1: 9–21.

Freud, Sigmund (1905) *The Basic Writings of Sigmund Freud*, (translated and edited by A.A. Brill). New York: The Modern Library.

Hochschild, Arlie (1989) *The Second Shift*. New York: Avon.

Julien, Isaac and Mercer, Kobena (1991) 'True Confessions: A Discourse on Images of Black Male Sexuality', in Essex Hemphill (ed.) *Brother to Brother: New Writings by Black Gay Men*, pp. 167–73. Boston, MA: Alyson Publications.

Kehily, Mary Jane and Nayak, Anoop (1997) 'Lads and Laughter: Humour and the Production of Heterosexual Masculinities', *Gender and Education* 9: 69–87.

Kimmel, Michael (2001) 'Masculinity as Homophobia: Fear, Shame, and Silence in the Construction of Gender Identity', in Stephen Whitehead and Frank Barrett (eds) *The Masculinities Reader*, pp. 266–187. Cambridge: Polity.

Kimmel, Michael (2003) 'Adolescent Masculinity, Homophobia, and Violence: Random School Shootings, 1982–2001', *American Behavioral Scientist* 46: 1439–58.

King, D. L. (2004) *Double Lives on the Down Low*. New York: Broadway Books.

Lehne, Gregory (1998) 'Homophobia among Men: Supporting and Defining the Male Role', in Michael Kimmel and Michael Messner (eds) *Men's Lives*, pp. 237–149. Boston, MA: Allyn and Bacon.

Lemert, Charles (1996) 'Series Editor's Preface', in Steven Seidman (ed.) *Queer Theory/Sociology*. Cambridge, MA: Blackwell.

Lyman, Peter (1998) 'The Fraternal Bond as a Joking Relationship: A Case Study of the Role of Sexist Jokes in Male Group Bonding', in Michael Kimmel and Michael Messner (eds) *Men's lives*, pp. 171–93. Boston, MA: Allyn and Bacon.

Mac an Ghaill, Martain (1996) 'What about the Boys – School, Class and Crisis Masculinity', *Sociological Review* 44: 381–97.

MacLeod, Jay (1987) *Ain't No Makin It: Aspirations and Attainment in a Low Income Neighborhood*. Boulder, CO: Westview Press.

Majors, Richard (2001) 'Cool Pose: Black Masculinity and Sports', in Stephen Whitehead and Frank Barrett (eds) *The Masculinities Reader*, pp. 208–17. Cambridge: Polity.

Messner, Michael (1989) 'Sports and the Politics of Inequality', in Michael Kimmel and Michael Messner (eds) *Men's Lives*. Boston, MA: Allyn and Bacon.

Messner, Michael (2004) 'On Patriarchs and Losers: Rethinking Men's Interests', paper presented at Berkeley *Journal of Sociology* Conference, Berkeley.

Parker, Andrew (1996) 'The Construction of Masculinity within Boys' Physical Education', *Gender and Education* 8: 141–57.

Perry, Pamela (2002) *Shades of White: White Kids and Racial Identities in High School.* Durham, NC: Duke University Press.

Plummer, David C. (2001) 'The Quest for Modern Manhood: Masculine Stereotypes, Peer Culture and the Social Significance of Homophobia', *Journal of Adolescence* 24: 15–23.

Price, Jeremy (1999) 'Schooling and Racialized Masculinities: The Diploma, Teachers and Peers in the Lives of Young, African-American Men', *Youth and Society* 31: 224–63.

Riggs, Marlon (1991) 'Black Macho Revisited: Reflections of a SNAP! Queen', in Essex Hemphill (ed.) *Brother to Brother: New Writings by Black Gay Men*, pp. 153–260. Boston, MA: Alyson Publications.

Ross, Marlon B. (1998) 'In Search of Black Men's Masculinities', *Feminist Studies* 24: 599–626.

Sedgwick, Eve K. (1990) *Epistemology of the Closet.* Berkeley: University of California Press.

Sedgwick, Eve K. (1995) '"Gosh, Boy George, You Must be Awfully Secure in Your Masculinity!" in Maurice Berger, Brian Wallis and Simon Watson (eds) *Constructing Masculinity*, pp. 11–20. New York: Routledge.

Skelton, Christine (1996) 'Learning to be Tough: The Fostering of Maleness in One Primary School', *Gender and Education* 8: 185–97.

Smith, George W. (1998) 'The Ideology of "Fag": The School Experience of Gay Students', *The Sociological Quarterly* 39: 309–35.

Smith, Valerie (1994) 'Split Affinities: The Case of Interracial Rape', in Anne Herrmann and Abigail Stewart (eds) *Theorizing Feminism*, pp. 155–70. Boulder, CO: Westview Press.

Stein, Arlene and Plummer, Ken (1994) ' "I Can't Even Think Straight": "Queer" Theory and the Missing Sexual Revolution in Sociology', *Sociological Theory* 12: 178 ff.

Thorne, Barrie (1993) *Gender Play: Boys and Girls in School.* New Brunswick, NJ: Rutgers University Press.

Warner, Michael (1993) 'Introduction', in Michael Warner (ed.) *Fear of a Queer Planet: Queer Politics and Social Theory*, pp. vii–xxxi. Minneapolis: University of Minnesota Press.

West, Candace and Zimmerman, Don (1991) 'Doing Gender', in Judith Lorber (ed.) *The Social Construction of Gender*, pp. 102–21. Newbury Park: Sage.

Whitehead, Stephen and Barrett, Frank (2001) 'The Sociology of Masculinity', in Stephen Whitehead and Frank Barrett (eds) *The Masculinities Reader*, pp. 472–6. Cambridge: Polity.

Wilchins, Riki (2003) 'Do You Believe in Fairies?' *The Advocate*, 4 February.

Willis, Paul (1981) *Learning to Labor: How Working Class Kids Get Working Class Jobs.* New York: Columbia University Press.

Wood, Julian (1984) 'Groping Toward Sexism: Boy's Sex Talk', in Angela McRobbie and Mica Nava (eds) *Gender and Generation.* London: Macmillan Publishers.

"Dude You're A Fag": Adolescent Masculinity and the Fag Discourse

C. J. Pascoe

1. In this essay, C. J. Pascoe analyzes ways that adolescent enact masculinity in a working-class U.S. setting. According to Pascoe, how does contemporary American adolescent masculinity operate? How does it relate to sexuality? Include examples to illustrate.

2. What is the specter of the faggot? Explain and offer examples. How does it function to confine ideas about masculinity? How does it relate to gendered power?

3. Pascoe says that "fag discourse is racialized." Explain and offer examples that illustrate how fag discourse operates in relation to race.

4. Think of examples of contemporary contests of masculinity. Describe one. How does it compare to Pascoe's adolescent examples?

5. How does Pascoe's analysis fit with the claim that gender is socially constructed? What examples do you think are most useful to show how the social construction of gender operates?

Swept Awake! Negotiating Passion on Campus

Bonnie Pfister

Bonnie Pfister is content manager for ImaginePittsburgh.com, an online magazine promoting Pittsburg. She earned a dual Bachelor of Arts degree in Magazine Journalism and International Relations from Syracuse University. A former reporter for the Pittsburg Tribune-Review *Pfister has contributed to* The Nation, The New York Times *and written articles for the Associated Press. This piece originally appeared in* On the Issues: Progressive Women's Quarterly.

PRE-READING QUESTIONS

1. What and how do you learn about the topic of sexual offense on your campus?
2. What do you know about your campus' sexual offense policy? What questions do you have about it?

KEY TERMS

Antioch Sexual Offense Policy
backlash
Clery Act
consent
secondary survivor
sexual offense policy
Campus Sexual Assault Victims Bill of Rights

SEE THE THEMATIC TABLE OF CONTENTS, IF YOU WANT TO READ MORE ESSAYS ABOUT:

Gender and Public Policy
Gendered Violence
Sexual Assault and Sexual Consent

Swept Awake! Negotiating Passion on Campus

Bonnie Pfister

With the introduction of their "Sexual Offense Policy" in 1992, Ohio's Antioch College took a dramatic—and controversial—step to establish firmer rules of sexual conduct on their campus. This policy, requiring ongoing verbal consent throughout every stage of a sexual encounter, is based on the premise that clear communication is necessary for healthy, consensual sex, and a college administration should take active steps to create the safest environment possible. This 1994 essay, from On the Issues: The Progressive Women's Quarterly, examines Antioch's policy and discusses other activism against sexual violence taking place on college campuses.

What's an activist to do when everyone from George Will to "Saturday Night Live" satirizes your work and accuses you of infantilizing women and taking the fun out of sex?

"I find it exciting," says Jodi Gold, coordinator of STAAR, Students Together Against Acquaintance Rape at the University of Pennsylvania in Philadelphia. "You don't get a backlash until you've ruffled some feathers. It means we've really pushed the envelope and things are happening."

The backlash has all but obscured the radical importance of student efforts to develop new—fairer—rules for sexual liaisons. The emerging new code includes the apparently controversial idea that potential lovers should *ask* before foisting sexual attention on their partners, and that partners should clearly *answer* "yes" or "no." In other words: people should communicate about their desires before making love, rather than waiting to be "swept away" by overwhelming passion.

While a deadpan legalistic approach to sex is easy to ridicule, Jodi Gold believes that the real reason media coverage of today's campus activism is so highly critical is that Americans are still scared silly by its sexual frankness—a frankness that today's generation of young people desperately needs.

"Sexuality is perhaps the most defining issue for today's students," says Alan Guskin, president of Antioch College in Ohio for nine years, and a supporter of the often-mocked Sexual Offense Policy, the student-written rules for sexual conduct at the college, which have been in place since fall 1992.

"Men and women students come to the campus with a very different consciousness about sexuality," notes Dr. Guskin. "The women have learned they have a right to determine how their bodies are used, but many of the young men still think the central question is how to get women to do what they want." The best way to deal with the situation, says Guskin, is for women and men to learn to communicate with each other. "The policy gives no specific checklist or statements. But there is a sense of how you should behave."

The Antioch policy says verbal consent is needed before all sexual contact, and that consent is an on-going process that can be withdrawn at any time. Students who are sleeping or unconscious or incapacitated by alcohol or drugs are not considered capable of consent. The policy also defines offenses as unwanted touching, verbal harassment, and non-disclosure of sexually transmitted disease, including HIV, and defines punishments for violations of various parts of the policy. All students are required to attend an educational workshop on consent and sexual offense each academic year.

Guskin notes that the media swarming over the campus for two and a half months reporting on the controversial policy accomplished more student education on the issue than the college's past five years of effort.

The policy emerged when thirty feminists disrupted a campus government meeting in November 1990 demanding institutional rules to deal with rape, says Bethany Saltman, Antioch '93 and member of the original group, the Womyn of Antioch. Even at this tiny (650 students last fall) alternative college, the administration seemed to prefer to keep rape reports under wraps. Faced with vehement, relentless protest and a flurry of local news attention, the administration reluctantly accepted the feminists' demand to remove any accused perpetrator from campus within twenty-four hours of a reported rape. But the rule was adopted on the condition that a committee of concerned staff and students would work to retool the policy while the administration consulted lawyers about its constitutionality. Womyn of Antioch demanded the policy out of strength, not weakness, notes Saltman. "We get to say who touches us, and where."

The policy has been criticized as a return to the 1950s that disempowers women by viewing them as damsels in distress and spells the death of *amour*.

Perhaps the critics are upset because they're embarrassed, says Elizabeth Sullivan, Antioch '93, now of Seattle. "It's still very hard for people to be explicit about sexual intimacy. The policy limits certain options, such as casual, thoughtless sex, while encouraging other options, such as accountability, sexual equality, and living in a community with a reduced fear of harassment or coerced sex."

Sullivan notes that critics act as though, without this policy, there is no social context influencing students' interactions at all. "Most of us acquire a whole set of norms and attitudes before we become sexual with other people. We learn who is an acceptable partner, we learn unspoken codes of how to proceed, and we develop a set of expectations about what sex should be," says Sullivan. In an intentional community like Antioch, people can choose to restructure that context.

Some students from other campuses who have adopted the Antioch rules as their own, don't understand what all the fuss is about. Matthew Mizel, a student at Stanford (CA), likens the current resistance to people's initial embarrassment about asking a partner to use a condom during the early years of the AIDS crisis. "Why do people feel asking is not romantic?" asks Mizel. "All it does is clarify things. For me, it's not a romantic situation until I know the woman is comfortable."

As a letter writer to *The New Yorker* noted, asking permission, as in—"may I kiss the hollow of your neck?"—does not have to be devoid of *amour*.

Students should be relieved to discard the old stereotypes that "masculine sexuality is dangerous, passionate, reckless, and that the woman is passive and just laying back there," according to Mizel.

Callie Cary, an Antioch spokeswoman, herself out of college for less than a decade, scoffs at the idea that the asking-before-you-touch policy infantilizes women. "The assumption that this policy is about women saying no to men is based on the idea that men initiate sex all the time. But I know there are men on this campus who feel the women are very aggressive."

ACTIVISM ON OTHER CAMPUSES

While Antioch's policy contains the most detailed rules for sexual correctness to date, feminist actions on a number of campuses have expanded from helping rape victims *after* the fact to including a preventive approach. These efforts by female—and male—students are cropping up at conservative, co-ed universities like Syracuse (NY) and Vanderbilt (TN), as well as traditionally liberal women's colleges, such as Barnard (NY) and Mount Holyoke (MA). Private schools such as Stanford and Duke (NC) Universities boast dynamic men's groups examining why men rape and striving to prevent it, while students at public Evergreen State (WA) and Rutgers University (NJ) are reaching out to local high school girls with educational programs. On black college campuses the emphasis is on how the negative depiction of women in rap music discourages fair treatment in the sexual arena.

Most student organizers express some reservations over Antioch's policy—some hate it, while others herald it as swinging the pendulum dramatically to the side of open communication about sex—so far, in fact, that they might not need to adopt such a radical approach at their own schools (phew!).

"I would love to address the Antioch policy, but from what I can gather from other people on our committee, it would be suicide for us to consider it here," says Melinda Lewis, a sophomore at Vanderbilt University in Nashville and president of Students For Women's Concerns. After speaking in spring 1992 with rape survivors who felt revictimized by the school's judicial system, Lewis returned in the fall to push for a new sexual assault policy. Although she is sensitive to Katie Roiphe-inspired charges of "victim feminism," she counters that the term does not accurately describe the activism—or the problems—she sees around her.

RATS IN THE IVORY TOWERS

At Lehigh University (PA), Jeanne Clery was robbed, sodomized and murdered in her dorm bed by a student she had never met. Jeanne's own actions that night—it is believed that she left her door unlocked for her roommate's convenience—made it clear that students are often shockingly oblivious to the dangers around them. At the time, in 1986, Lehigh students regularly propped open outside doors to allow friends to come and go easily. Lehigh had "studied" the security problem for eleven years but taken no action until after Jeanne's death, according to Lynda Getchis of Security on Campus, a group founded by Clery's parents.

After this incident, then-freshman Congressman Jim Ramstad (R-MN) joined forces with Clery's parents and crafted the Campus Sexual Assault Victims Bill of Rights. Signed into law in 1990, it requires that all post-secondary schools that receive federal funding publish annual reports about crime statistics on campus, institute policies to deal with sexual assault and offer rape awareness educational programs.

For 1991, the first year statistics were collected, 2,300 American campuses reported 30 murders, 1,000 rapes, and more than 1,800 robberies, according to *The Chronicle of Higher Education*. Most campus crime (78%) is student-on-student. While the crime incidence on campus is lower than that of the country as a whole, student and parent perceptions of the campus as a safe haven make the crime levels seem more shocking.

There is much controversy about just how many women experience sexual assault at college—the figures range from a scary 1 in 25 to a horrifying 1 in 4. But even the smallest estimates amount to a large threat to women's safety.

So it's no wonder that student activists are increasingly pressing their colleges to own up to the reality of crime and to codify, in writing, the kind of campus they want. The demands usually include more stringent acquaintance rape policies and mandatory peer education for students of both genders.

In the past five years, student activists have increasingly focused on university policies, notes Claire Kaplan, sexual assault education coordinator at the University of Virginia. "This strategy can be construed as students asking for protection, but it is not a throwback to *in loco parentis*. The institution has a contract with the student—the same kind of contract that could result in a third party suit against employers or landlords who fail to provide adequate protection against crime on their premises."

Today's students are also coming of age in a litigious, capitalist culture and many adopt a consumerist creed: "I pay a lot of money to go to this school, I deserve to be protected from assault and, at the very least, informed of its incidence on campus."

COMING OF AGE IN THE '90S

Today's young activists have a point of view so different from those of the 1960s and '70s, that commentators have had difficulty making the connections. In the '60s it was college men who had their lives on the line with the threat of being drafted to serve in the unpopular war in Vietnam. But today it is the women, and threat of rape, that's the flashpoint.

And unlike the rebels of the '60s and '70s who were trying to tear down repressive rules, institutions and social establishments, the generation growing up in the no-rules '90s is striving to build up a foundation of acceptable personal conduct and institutionalized norms.

At Evergreen State College in Olympia, WA, the administration had spent two years, with no end in sight, developing an anti-rape protocol. In the spring of 1993, rage at slow adjudication of a rape charge boiled over into graffiti hits around campus. The scribblers named names and proclaimed, "Rape Me and I'll Kill You," said Nina Fischer, a member of the Rape Response Coalition. The university protocol went into effect last fall, and students plan to take their rape awareness workshops to local high schools this spring.

Radical approaches are less popular at a school like North Carolina State University in Raleigh, says Brian Ammons, a founder of that school's REAL-Men (Rape Education and Active Leadership). Originally active as the male-involvement voice in crafting a campus sex offense protocol, Ammons formed the group to examine male socialization and responsibility in a rape culture. In fact, at NCSU, it was REAL-Men that organized last fall's Take Back the Night march. The resident women's group, Help, Education and Activism on Rape (HEAR-Women) developed out of that.

"In some ways it was easier for a group of men to come together to offer some legitimacy on the issue," Ammons says. "Women on our campus are afraid to speak up about a lot of things. The fear of being labeled a feminist and being alienated here is very real."

WHITE WOMEN'S FEMINISM?

Melinda Lewis, an African American, is a sophomore at Vanderbilt and president of Students For Women's Concerns, a predominantly white feminist group. "People question my involvement," she says. "The rape issue is perceived as something with which only Anglo, middle-class women are concerned. But that's a misguided notion. Women of color are raped and assaulted much more frequently than Anglo women."

Jennifer Lipton, a Barnard College student involved in rewriting sexual offense policy for the Columbia-Barnard community amidst administrator recalcitrance, agrees that the perception of acquaintance rape as a "white women's issue" flies in the face of reality. At the rape crisis center at St. Luke's-Roosevelt Hospital nearby, where she is a volunteer, most of the survivors she sees are women of color, most very poor, some homeless.

"Their concerns are very different," Lipton says. "If their perpetrator is also black, they wonder if they should report it to the police. They are very aware of the racism of the judicial system, and worried about what it will do to their own community if they turn in this man. They also know that, as poor black women, society doesn't really value what they say."

However at many African American colleges, date rape is a significantly less prominent gender concern than how women are depicted in rap music and advertising, reports Dionne Lyne, a student at the all-women Spelman College in Atlanta and member of the new campus organization SISTERS (Sisters in Solidarity to Eradicate Sexism). There's also anger at the persistent reference to certain Pan-Hellenic parties as "Greek Freaks," because of the use of "freak" as a disparaging term depicting black women as nymphomaniacs.

"There is a silence on the issue, a sense of, 'Yeah, it happens but we really don't want to know about it.' It reinforces the [idea] that these things happen to bad women, and we're just going to assume that we are all striving to be Spelman women, who are finer than that," Lyne says.

Spelman and brother school Morehouse College frequently co-sponsor educational programs about acquaintance rape, but Lyne says many women get the sense that Morehouse men are lecturing them about the issue, as if the men don't have a thing or two of their own to learn about date rape. Morehouse organizations have frequently scheduled their programs on Spelman's campus rather than their own, and fill the room with women and just one or two men.

Thomas Prince, associate director of counseling at Morehouse, counters that there are numerous anti-rape programs on the men's campus for co-ed groups, but his description of them seemed to indicate upon whom the responsibility is placed.

"We cover the FBI statistics, . . . talk about the things that might be contributing to the rise of acquaintance rapes and what to do if it happens to you. [That is] . . . what women can do if they find themselves in that situation," Prince said.

Prince states that there is no student group specifically organizing around this problem at Morehouse, and felt the Antioch policy did not encompass the way African-American men and women communicate about sex. "The language used around African American males is different," Prince said. "They have their own way of communicating verbally."

MEN AGAINST RAPE

Some male activists are just as disturbed as their female counterparts with men's penchants during educational programs, for doggedly questioning the technical definition of rape or assault, rather than focusing on the nature of sexual relationships themselves.

"It's always coming up: 'What if this happens? Is this rape? How about that—is that rape?'" said James Newell, a senior at Syracuse University and president of the five-year-old coed student group SCARED (Students Concerned About Rape Education). "Men feel victimized by groups like ours. But we are not a group that's against sex."

Examining male expectations of sex is one tactic used at Duke University in Durham, NC, by the four-year-old student group Men Acting for Change (MAC). Pornography as sex education for men is a focal point of at least one of the eight-session course on men and gender issues, a topic that precedes the class on rape, says Jason Schultz, a MAC co-founder who graduated in spring 1993.

While most of the women activists interviewed praised the men's organizations that are working against sexual violence, many expressed reservations and some suspicions about token support from other men's groups. One woman who asked not to be named criticized a men's group on her campus whose sole pro-feminist action is an annual day-long wearing of white ribbons to signify opposition to sexual assault. "Frankly I think it's a very shallow and trivial way of responding," she said.

Kelly Wall, a founder of HEAR-Women at North Carolina State, expressed irritation that the most visible anti-rape presence on campus before HEAR was comprised of men.

The REAL-Men group is aware of the apparent irony of the situation. "We're very conscious of what our place is. We don't want to take over the issue," Ammons says. Although his group does deal with "secondary survivors" (men who are grappling with their feelings about the rape of a lover, friend or relative), it is with some hesitation that they discuss the issues of male survivors of sexual offense.

Anti-rape activist Matthew Mizel at Stanford University says he sometimes feels his motivation questioned. Mizel founded Stanford Men's Collective in fall 1992 to discuss where rape comes from and how to stop it by examining men's own behavior. A talkative, outgoing senior easily recognized on campus by his long blond hair, Mizel says the praise he gets from women for his work generates curiosity and the occasional impression that he's doing it to "get laid."

"Men have asked if I'm trying to gain points with women and be some kind of super-heterosexual. . . . And some women have asked if I'm gay—as if there was no chance that I'm just a regular person who cares about this issue," Mizel said.

These young men make it clear that anti-rape work is not just a woman's thing, and that the most progressive voices among college students are determined to rewrite the sexual code to fit the needs of their generation.

And they agree that a rewrite is necessary. At the University of Virginia, Claire Kaplan described a seminar in which several fraternity men asserted: "When you get to a certain point during sex you can't stop," an attitude she thought had long since fallen to the wayside. "That's why the Antioch policy was created," she notes. "There is still the attitude, 'don't talk, just do.'"

Name _____   Date _____

Course & section: _____   Instructor _____

Swept Awake! Negotiating Passion on Campus

Bonnie Pfister

1. What are some of the criticisms of the Antioch Sexual Offense Policy?

2. Describe sexual assault activism on the different campuses discussed in this essay. What are the similarities and differences in their approaches? How do they address race and gender?

3. Are there alternative solutions to those proposed by Antioch? What kinds of actions/support would you like to see for men on your campus?

4. Search your campus' website for Clery Act, sexual offense, and sexual assault. What did you learn? Are there student organizations that address sexual assault on your campus?

5. What changes to your campus policies would you suggest after reading this essay? How does your school define sexual assault? Sexual consent? What are the procedures for reporting a violation of these policies on your campus?

Homophobia
A Weapon of Sexism

Suzanne Pharr

Suzanne Pharr describes herself as a "Political Handywoman," whose goal is social and economic justice. Her work focuses on racism, sexism and homophobia and the intersections of these forms of oppression and discrimination. Her books include In the Time of the Right: Reflections on Liberation *(1996) and* Homophobia: A Weapon of Sexism *(1997) from which this excerpt comes. Her books are available to read in their entirety for free on her blog.*

PRE-READING QUESTIONS

1. Define homophobia. Define sexism. Are they connected? If so, how?
2. What would the world be like without homophobia?

KEY TERMS

backlash
compulsory heterosexuality
economic inequity
Equal Rights Amendment
heterosexism
heterosexual privilege
homophobia
internalized sexism
lesbian baiting
misogyny

National Coalition Against Domestic
   Violence (NCADV)
patriarchy
racism
sexism
sickness theory
sin theory
U.S. Department of Justice
violence as a means to control
women's liberation movement

SEE THE THEMATIC TABLE OF CONTENTS, IF YOU WANT TO READ MORE ESSAYS ABOUT:

Feminism and Social Movements
Gendered Violence
Homophobia
LGBTQ Studies

Homophobia
A Weapon of Sexism

Suzanne Pharr

HOMOPHOBIA: A WEAPON OF SEXISM

HOMOPHOBIA—The irrational fear and hatred of those who love and sexually desire those of the same sex. Though I intimately knew its meaning, the word homophobia was unknown to me until the late 1970s, and when I first heard it, I was struck by how difficult it is to say, what an ugly word it is, equally as ugly as its meaning. Like racism and anti-Semitism, it is a word that calls up images of loss of freedom, verbal and physical violence, death.

In my life I have experienced the effects of homophobia through rejection by friends, threats of loss of employment, and threats upon my life; and I have witnessed far worse things happening to other lesbian and gay people: loss of children, beatings, rape, death. Its power is great enough to keep ten to twenty percent of the population living lives of fear (if their sexual identity is hidden) or lives of danger (if their sexual identity is visible) or both. And its power is great enough to keep the remaining eighty to ninety percent of the population trapped in their own fears.

Long before I had a word to describe the behavior, I was engaged in a search to discover the source of its power, the power to damage and destroy lives. The most common explanations were that to love the same sex was either abnormal (sick) or immoral (sinful).

My exploration of the sickness theory led me to understand that homosexuality is simply a matter of sexual identity, which, along with heterosexual identity, is formed in ways that no one conclusively understands. The American Psychological Association has said that it is no more abnormal to be homosexual than to be lefthanded. It is simply that a certain percentage of the population *is*. It is not healthier to be heterosexual or righthanded. What is unhealthy—and sometimes a source of stress and sickness so great it can lead to suicide—is homophobia, that societal disease that places such negative messages, condemnation, arid violence on gay men and lesbians that we have to struggle throughout our lives for self-esteem.

The sin theory is a particularly curious one because it is expressed so often and with such hateful emotion both from the pulpit and from laypeople who rely heavily upon the Bible for evidence. However, there is significant evidence that the approximately eight references to homosexuality in the Bible are frequently read incorrectly, according to Dr. Virginia Ramey Mollenkott in an essay in *Christianity and Crisis:*

Much of the discrimination against homosexual persons is justified by a common misreading of the Bible. Many English translations of the Bible contain the word homosexual in extremely negative contexts. But the fact is that the word *homosexual* does not occur anywhere in the Bible. No extant text, no manuscript, neither Hebrew nor Greek, Syriac, nor Aramaic, contains the word. The terms *homosexual* and *heterosexual* were not developed in any language until the 1890's, when for the first time the awareness developed that there are people with a lifelong, constitutional orientation toward their own sex. Therefore the use of the word *homo-sexuality* by certain English Bible translators is an example of the extreme bias that endangers the human and civil rights of homosexual persons. *(pp. 383–4, Nov. 9, 1987)*

Dr. Mollenkott goes on to add that two words in I Corinthians 6:9 and one word in Timothy 1:10 have been used as evidence to damn homosexuals but that well into the 20th century the first of these was understood by everyone to mean masturbation, and the second was known to refer to male prostitutes who were available for hire by either women or men. There are six other Biblical references that are thought by some to refer to homosexuals but each of these is disputed by contemporary scholars. For instance, the sin in the Sodom and Gomorrah passage (Genesis 19: 1–10) is less about homosexuality than it is about inhospitality and gang rape. The law of hospitality was universally accepted and Lot was struggling to uphold it against what we assume are heterosexual townsmen threatening gang rape to the two male angels in Lot's home. While people dwell on this passage as a condemnation of homosexuality, they bypass what I believe is the central issue or, if you will, *sin:* Lot's offering his two virgin daughters up to the men to be used as they desired for gang rape. Here is a perfectly clear example of devaluing and dehumanizing and violently brutalizing women.

The eight Biblical references (and not a single one by Jesus) to alleged homosexuality are very small indeed when compared to the several hundred references (and many by Jesus) to money and the necessity for justly distributing wealth. Yet few people go on a rampage about the issue of a just economic system, using the Bible as a base.

Finally, I came to understand that homosexuality, hetero-sexuality, bi-sexuality are *morally neutral*. A particular sexual identity is not an indication of either good or evil. What is important is not the gender of the two people in relationship with each other but the content of that relationship. Does that relationship contain violence, control of one person by the other? Is the relationship a growthful place for the people involved? It is clear that we must hold all relationships, whether opposite sex or same sex, to these standards.

The first workshops that I conducted were an effort to address these two issues, and I assumed that if consciousness could be raised about the invalidity of these two issues then people would stop feeling homophobic and would understand homophobia as a civil rights issue and work against it. The workshops took a high moral road, invoking participants' compassion, understanding, and outrage at injustice.

The eight-hour workshops raised consciousness and increased participants' commitment to work against homophobia as one more oppression in a growing list of recognized oppressions, but I still felt something was missing. I felt there was still too much unaccounted for power in homophobia even after we looked at the sick and sinful theories, at how it feels to be a lesbian in a homophobic world, at why lesbians choose invisibility, at how lesbian existence threatens male dominance. All of the pieces seemed available but we couldn't sew them together into a quilt.

As I conducted more workshops over the years I noticed several important themes that led to the final piecing together:

1. Women began to recognize that economics was a central issue connecting various oppressions;
2. Battered women began talking about how they had been called lesbians by their batterers;

3. Both heterosexual and lesbian women said they valued the workshops because in them they were given the rare opportunity to talk about their own sexuality and also about sexism in general.

Around the same time (1985–86), the National Coalition Against Domestic Violence (NCADV) entered into a traumatic relationship with the U.S. Department of Justice (DOJ), requesting a large two-year grant to provide domestic violence training and information nationally. At the time the grant was to be announced, NCADV was attacked by conservative groups such as the Heritage Foundation as a "pro-lesbian, pro-feminist, anti-family" organization. In response to these attacks, the DOJ decided not to award a grant; instead they formulated a "cooperative agreement" that allowed them to monitor and approve all work, and they assured conservative organizations that the work would not be pro-lesbian and anti-family. The major issue between NCADV and the DOJ became whether NCADV would let an outside agency define and control its work, and finally, during never-ending concern from the DOJ about "radical" and "lesbian" issues, the agreement was terminated by NCADV at the end of the first year. Throughout that year, there were endless statements and innuendoes from the DOJ and some members of NCADV's membership about NCADV's lesbian leadership and its alleged concern for only lesbian issues. Many women were damaged by the crossfire, NCADV's work was stopped for a year, and the organization was split from within. It was lesbian baiting at its worst.

As one of NCADV's lesbian leadership during that onslaught of homophobic attacks, I was still giving homophobia workshops around the country, now able to give even more personal witness to the virulence of the hatred and fear of lesbians and gay men within both institutions and individuals. It was a time of pain and often anger for those of us committed to creating a world free of violence, and it was a time of deep distress for those of us under personal attack. However, my mother, like many mothers, had always said, "All things work for the good" and sure enough, it was out of the accumulation of these experiences that the pieces began coming together to make a quilt of our understanding.

On the day that I stopped reacting to attacks and gave my time instead to visioning, this simple germinal question came forth for the workshops: "What will the world be like without homophobia in it—for everyone, female and male, whatever sexual identity?" Simple though the question is, it was at first shocking because those of us who work in the anti-violence movement spend most of our time working with the damaging, negative results of violence and have little time to vision. It is sometimes difficult to create a vision of a world we have never experienced, but without such a vision, we cannot know clearly what we are working toward in our social change work.

From this question, answer led to answer until a whole appeared of our collective making, from one workshop to another.

Here are some of the answers women have given:

- Kids won't be called tomboys or sissies; they'll just be who they are, able to do what they wish.
- People will be able to love anyone, no matter what sex; the issue will simply be whether or not she/he is a good human being, compatible, and loving.
- Affection will be opened up between women and men, women and women, men and men, and it won't be centered on sex; people won't fear being called names if they show affection to someone who isn't a mate or potential mate.
- If affection is opened up, then isolation will be broken down for all of us, especially for those who generally experience little physical affection, such as unmarried old people.

- Women will be able to work whatever jobs we want without being labeled masculine.
- There will be less violence if men do not feel they have to prove and assert their manhood. Their desire to dominate and control will not spill over from the personal to the level of national and international politics and the use of bigger and better weapons to control other countries.
- People will wear whatever clothes they wish, with the priority being comfort rather than the display of femininity or masculinity.
- There will be no gender roles.

It is at this point in the workshops—having imagined a world without homophobia—that the participants see the analysis begin to fall into place. Someone notes that all the things we have been talking about relate to sexual gender roles. It's rather like the beginning of a course in Sexism 101. The next question is "Imagine the world with no sex roles—sexual identity, which may be in flux, but no sexual gender roles." Further: imagine a world in which opportunity is not determined by gender or race. Just the imagining makes women alive with excitement because it is a vision of freedom, often just glimpsed but always known deep down as truth. Pure joy.

We talk about what it would be like to be born in a world in which there were no expectations or treatment based on gender but instead only the expectation that each child, no matter what race or sex, would be given as many options and possibilities as society could muster. Then we discuss what girls and boys would be like at puberty and beyond if sex role expectations didn't come crashing down on them with girls' achievement levels beginning to decline thereafter; what it would be for women to have the training and options for economic equity with men; what would happen to issues of power and control, and therefore violence, if there were real equality. To have no prescribed sex roles would open the possibility of equality. It is a discussion women find difficult to leave. Freedom calls.

PATRIARCHY—an enforced belief in male dominance and control—is the ideology and sexism the system that holds it in place. The catechism goes like this: Who do gender roles serve? Men and the women who seek power from them. Who suffers from gender roles? Women most completely and men in part. How are gender roles maintained? By the weapons of sexism: economics, violence, homophobia.

Why then don't we ardently pursue ways to eliminate gender roles and therefore sexism? It is my profound belief that all people have a spark in them that yearns for freedom, and the history of the world's atrocities—from the Nazi concentration camps to white dominance in South Africa to the battering of women—is the story of attempts to snuff out that spark. When that spark doesn't move forward to full flame, it is because the weapons designed to control and destroy have wrought such intense damage over time that the spark has been all but extinguished.

Sexism, that system by which women are kept subordinate to men, is kept in place by three powerful weapons designed to cause or threaten women with pain and loss. As stated before, the three are economics, violence, and homophobia. The stories of women battered by men, victims of sexism at its worst, show these three forces converging again and again. When battered women tell why they stayed with a batterer or why they returned to a batterer, over and over they say it was because they could not support themselves and their children financially, they had no skills for jobs, they could not get housing, transportation, medical care for their children. And how were they kept controlled? Through violence and threats of violence, both physical and verbal, so that they feared for their lives and the lives of their children and doubted their own abilities and self-worth. And why were they beaten? Because they were not good enough, were not "real women," were dykes, or because they stood up to him as no "real woman" would.

And the male batterer, with societal backing, felt justified, often righteous, in his behavior—for his part in keeping women in their place.

ECONOMICS must be looked at first because many feminists consider it to be the root cause of sexism. Certainly the United Nations study released at the final conference of the International Decade on Women, held in Nairobi, Kenya, in 1985, supports that belief: of the world's population, women do 75% of the work, receive 10% of the pay and own 1% of the property. In the United States it is also supported by the opposition of the government to the idea of comparable worth and pay equity, as expressed by Ronald Reagan who referred to pay equity as "a joke." Obviously, it is considered a dangerous idea. Men profit not only from women's unpaid work in the home but from our underpaid work within horizontal female segregation such as clerical workers or upwardly mobile tokenism in the workplace where a few affirmative action promotions are expected to take care of all women's economic equality needs. Moreover, they profit from women's bodies through pornography, prostitution, and international female sexual slavery. And white men profit from both the labor of women and of men of color. Forced economic dependency puts women under male control and severely limits women's options for self-determination and self-sufficiency.

This truth is borne out by the fact that according to the National Commission on Working Women, on average, women of all races working year round earn only 64 cents to every one dollar a man makes. Also, the U.S. Census Bureau reports that only 9 percent of working women make over $25,000 a year. There is fierce opposition to women gaining employment in the nontraditional job market, that is, those jobs that traditionally employ less than 25 percent women. After a woman has gained one of these higher paying jobs, she is often faced with sexual harassment, lesbian baiting, and violence. It is clear that in the workplace there is an all-out effort to keep women in traditional roles so that the only jobs we are "qualified" for are the low-paid ones.

Actually, we have to look at economics not only as the root cause of sexism but also as the underlying, driving force that keeps all the oppressions in place. In the United States, our economic system is shaped like a pyramid, with a few people at the top, primarily white males, being supported by large numbers of unpaid or low-paid workers at the bottom. When we look at this pyramid, we begin to understand the major connection between sexism and racism because those groups at the bottom of the pyramid are women and people of color. We then begin to understand why there is such a fervent effort to keep those oppressive systems (racism and sexism and all the ways they are manifested) in place to maintain the unpaid and low-paid labor.

Susan DeMarco and Jim Hightower, writing for *Mother Jones*, report that *Forbes* magazine indicated that "the 400 richest families in America last year had an average net worth of $550 million each. These and less than a million other families—roughly one percent of our population—are at the prosperous tip of our society. In 1976, the wealthiest 1 percent of America's families owned 19.2 percent of the nation's total wealth. (This sum of wealth counts all of America's cash, real estate, stocks, bonds, factories, art, personal property, and anything else of financial value.) By 1983, those at this 1 percent tip of our economy owned 34.3 percent of our wealth. *Today, the top 1 percent of Americans possesses more net wealth than the bottom 90 percent.*" (My italics.) (*May, 1988, pp. 32–33*)

In order for this top-heavy system of economic inequity to maintain itself, the 90 percent on the bottom must keep supplying cheap labor. A very complex, intricate system of institutionalized oppressions is necessary to maintain the status quo so that the vast majority will not demand its fair share of wealth and resources and bring the system down. Every institution—schools, banks, churches, government, courts, media, etc—as well as individuals must be enlisted in the campaign to maintain such a system of gross inequity.

What would happen if women gained the earning opportunities and power that men have? What would happen if these opportunities were distributed equitably, no matter what sex one was, no matter what race one was born into, and no matter where one lived? What if educational and training opportunities were equal? Would women spend most of our youth preparing for marriage? Would marriage be based on economic survival for women? What would happen to issues of power and control? Would women stay with our batterers? If a woman had economic independence in a society where women had equal opportunities, would she still be thought of as owned by her father or husband?

Economics is the great controller in both sexism and racism. If a person can't acquire food, shelter, and clothing and provide them for children, then that person can be forced to do many things in order to survive. The major tactic, worldwide, is to provide unrecompensed or inadequately recompensed labor for the benefit of those who control wealth. Hence, we see women performing unpaid labor in the home or filling low-paid jobs, and we see people of color in the lowest-paid jobs available.

The method is complex: limit educational and training opportunities for women and for people of color and then withhold adequate paying jobs with the excuse that people of color and women are incapable of filling them. Blame the economic victim and keep the victim's self-esteem low through invisibility and distortion within the media and education. Allow a few people of color and women to succeed among the profit-makers so that blaming those who don't "make it" can be intensified. Encourage those few who succeed in gaining power now to turn against those who remain behind rather than to use their resources to make change for all. Maintain the myth of scarcity—that there are not enough jobs, resources, etc., to go around—among the middleclass so that they will not unite with laborers, immigrants, and the unemployed. The method keeps in place a system of control and profit by a few and a constant source of cheap labor to maintain it.

If anyone steps out of line, take her/his job away. Let homelessness and hunger do their work. The economic weapon works. And we end up saying, "I would do this or that—be openly who I am, speak out against injustice, work for civil rights, join a labor union, go to a political march, etc.—if I didn't have this job. I can't afford to lose it." We stay in an abusive situation because we see no other way to survive.

In the battered women's movement abusive relationships are said to be about power and control and the way out of them is through looking at the ways power and control work in our lives, developing support, improving self-esteem, and achieving control over our decisions and lives. We have yet to apply these methods successfully to our economic lives. Though requiring massive change, the way there also lies open for equality and wholeness. But the effort will require at least as much individual courage and risk and group support as it does for a battered woman to leave her batterer, and that requirement is very large indeed. Yet battered women find the courage to leave their batterers every day. They walk right into the unknown. To break away from economic domination and control will require a movement made up of individuals who possess this courage and ability to take risks.

VIOLENCE is the second means of keeping women in line, in a narrowly defined place and role. First, there is the physical violence of battering, rape, and incest. Often when battered women come to shelters and talk about their lives, they tell stories of being not only physically beaten but also raped and their children subjected to incest. Work in the women's anti-violence movement during almost two decades has provided significant evidence that each of these acts, including rape and incest, is an attempt to seek power over and control of another person. In each case, the victim is viewed as an object and is used to meet the abuser's needs. The violence is used to wreak punishment and to demand compliance or obedience.

Violence against women is directly related to the condition of women in a society that refuses us equal pay, equal access to resources, and equal status with males. From this condition comes men's confirmation of their sense of ownership of women, power over women, and assumed right to control women for their own means. Men physically and emotionally abuse women because they *can*, because they live in a world that gives them permission. Male violence is fed by their sense of their *right* to dominate and control, and their sense of superiority over a group of people who, because of gender, they consider inferior to them.

It is not just the violence but the threat of violence that controls our lives. Because the burden of responsibility has been placed so often on the potential victim, as women we have curtailed our freedom in order to protect ourselves from violence. Because of the threat of rapists, we stay on alert, being careful not to walk in isolated places, being careful where we park our cars, adding incredible security measures to our homes—massive locks, lights, alarms, if we can afford them—and we avoid places where we will appear vulnerable or unprotected while the abuser walks with freedom. Fear, often now so commonplace that it is unacknowledged, shapes our lives, reducing our freedom.

As Bernice Reagan of the musical group Sweet Honey in the Rock said at the 1982 National Coalition Against Domestic Violence conference, women seem to carry a genetic memory that women were once burned as witches when we stepped out of line. To this day, mothers pass on to their daughters word of the dangers they face and teach them the ways they must limit their lives in order to survive.

Part of the way sexism stays in place is the societal promise of survival, false and unfulfilled as it is, that women will not suffer violence if we attach ourselves to a man to protect us. A woman without a man is told she is vulnerable to external violence and, worse, that there is something wrong with her. When the male abuser calls a woman a lesbian, he is not so much labeling her a woman who loves women as he is warning her that by resisting him, she is choosing to be outside society's protection from male institutions and therefore from wide-ranging, unspecified, ever-present violence. When she seeks assistance from woman friends or a battered women's shelter, he recognizes the power in woman bonding and fears loss of her servitude and loyalty: the potential loss of his control. The concern is not affectional/sexual identity: the concern is disloyalty and the threat is violence.

The threat of violence against women who step out of line or who are disloyal is made all the more powerful by the fact that women do not have to do anything—they may be paragons of virtue and subservience—to receive violence against our lives: the violence still comes. It comes because of the woman-hating that exists throughout society. Chance plays a larger part than virtue in keeping women safe. Hence, with violence always a threat to us, women can never feel completely secure and confident. Our sense of safety is always fragile and tenuous.

Many women say that verbal violence causes more harm than physical violence because it damages self-esteem so deeply. Women have not wanted to hear battered women say that the verbal abuse was as hurtful as the physical abuse: to acknowledge that truth would be tantamount to acknowledging that *virtually every woman is a battered woman*. It is difficult to keep strong against accusations of being a bitch, stupid, inferior, etc., etc. It is especially difficult when these individual assaults are backed up by a society that shows women in textbooks, advertising, TV programs, movies, etc., as debased, silly, inferior, and sexually objectified, and a society that gives tacit approval to pornography. When we internalize these messages, we call the result "low self-esteem," a therapeutic individualized term. It seems to me we should use the more political expression: when we internalize these messages, we experience *internalized sexism*, and we experience it in common with all women living in a sexist world. The violence against us is supported by a society in which woman-hating is deeply imbedded.

In "Eyes on the Prize," a 1987 Public Television documentary about the Civil Rights Movement, an older white woman says about her youth in the South that it was difficult to be anything different from what was around her when there was no vision for another way to be. Our society presents images of women that say it is appropriate to commit violence against us. Violence is committed against women because we are seen as inferior in status and in worth. It has been the work of the women's movement to present a vision of another way to be.

Every time a woman gains the strength to resist and leave her abuser, we are given a model of the importance of stepping out of line, of moving toward freedom. And we all gain strength when she says to violence, "Never again!" Thousands of women in the last fifteen years have resisted their abusers to come to this country's 1100 battered women's shelters. There they have sat down with other women to share their stories, to discover that their stories again and again are the same, to develop an analysis that shows that violence is a statement about power and control, and to understand how sexism creates the climate for male violence. Those brave women are now a part of a movement that gives hope for another way to live in equality and peace.

HOMOPHOBIA works effectively as a weapon of sexism because it is joined with a powerful arm, heterosexism. Heterosexism creates the climate for homophobia with its assumption that the world is and must be heterosexual and its display of power and privilege as the norm. Heterosexism is the systemic display of homophobia in the institutions of society. Heterosexism and homophobia work together to enforce compulsory heterosexuality and that bastion of patriarchal power, the nuclear family. The central focus of the rightwing attack against women's liberation is that women's equality, women's self-determination, women's control of our own bodies and lives will damage what they see as the crucial societal institution, the nuclear family. The attack has been led by fundamentalist ministers across the country. The two areas they have focused on most consistently are abortion and homosexuality, and their passion has led them to bomb women's clinics and to recommend deprogramming for homosexuals and establishing camps to quarantine people with AIDS. To resist marriage and/or heterosexuality is to risk severe punishment and loss.

It is not by chance that when children approach puberty and increased sexual awareness they begin to taunt each other by calling these names: "queer' "faggot' "pervert?" It is at puberty that the full force of society's pressure to conform to heterosexuality and prepare for marriage is brought to bear. Children know what we have taught them, and we have given clear messages that those who deviate from standard expectations are to be made to get back in line. The best controlling tactic at puberty is to be treated as an outsider, to be ostracized at a time when it feels most vital to be accepted. Those who are different must be made to suffer loss. It is also at puberty that misogyny begins to be more apparent, and girls are pressured to conform to societal norms that do not permit them to realize their full potential. It is at this time that their academic achievements begin to decrease as they are coerced into compulsory heterosexuality and trained for dependency upon a man, that is, for economic survival.

There was a time when the two most condemning accusations against a woman meant to ostracize and disempower her were "whore" and "lesbian?" The sexual revolution and changing attitudes about heterosexual behavior may have led to some lessening of the power of the word *whore*, though it still has strength as a threat to sexual property and prostitutes are stigmatized and abused. However, the word *lesbian* is still fully charged and carries with it the full threat of loss of power and privilege, the threat of being cut asunder, abandoned, and left outside society's protection.

To be a lesbian is to be *perceived* as someone who has stepped out of line, who has moved out of sexual/economic dependence on a male, who is woman-identified. A lesbian is perceived as someone who can live without a man, and who is therefore (however illogically) against men. A lesbian is perceived as being outside the acceptable, routinized order of things. She is seen as someone who has no societal institutions to protect her and who is not privileged to the protection of individual males. Many heterosexual women see her as someone who stands in contradiction to the sacrifices they have made to conform to compulsory heterosexuality. A lesbian is perceived as a threat to the nuclear family, to male dominance and control, to the very heart of sexism.

Gay men are perceived also as a threat to male dominance and control, and the homophobia expressed against them has the same roots in sexism as does homophobia against lesbians. Visible gay men are the objects of extreme hatred and fear by heterosexual men because their breaking ranks with male heterosexual solidarity is seen as a damaging rent in the very fabric of sexism. They are seen as betrayers, as traitors who must be punished and eliminated. In the beating and killing of gay men we see clear evidence of this hatred. When we see the fierce homophobia expressed toward gay men, we can begin to understand the ways sexism also affects males through imposing rigid, dehumanizing gender roles on them. The two circumstances in which it is legitimate for men to be openly physically affectionate with one another are in competitive sports and in the crisis of war. For many men, these two experiences are the highlights of their lives, and they think of them again and again with nostalgia. War and sports offer a cover of all-male safety and dominance to keep away the notion of affectionate openness being identified with homosexuality. When gay men break ranks with male roles through bonding and affection outside the arenas of war and sports, they are perceived as not being "real men," that is, as being identified with women, the weaker sex that must be dominated and that over the centuries has been the object of male hatred and abuse. Misogyny gets transferred to gay men with a vengeance and is increased by the fear that their sexual identity and behavior will bring down the entire system of male dominance and compulsory heterosexuality.

If lesbians are established as threats to the status quo, as outcasts who must be punished, homophobia can wield its power over all women through lesbian baiting. Lesbian baiting is an attempt to control women by labeling us as lesbians because our behavior is not acceptable, that is, when we are being independent, going our own way, living whole lives, fighting for our rights, demanding equal pay, saying no to violence, being self-assertive, bonding with and loving the company of women, assuming the right to our bodies, insisting upon our own authority, making changes that include us in society's decision-making; lesbian baiting occurs when women are called lesbians because we resist male dominance and control. And it has little or nothing to do with one's sexual identity.

To be named as lesbian threatens all women, not just lesbians, with great loss. And any woman who steps out of role risks being called a lesbian. To understand how this is a threat to all women, one must understand that any woman can be called a lesbian and there is no real way she can defend herself: there is no way to credential one's sexuality. ("The Children's Hour," a Lillian Heilman play, makes this point when a student asserts two teachers are lesbians and they have no way to disprove it.) She may be married or divorced, have children, dress in the most feminine manner, have sex with men, be celibate—but there are lesbians who do all those things. *Lesbians look like all women and all women look like lesbians.* There is no guaranteed method of identification, and as we all know, sexual identity can be kept hidden. (The same is true for men. There is no way to prove their sexual identity, though many go to extremes to prove heterosexuality.) Also, women are not necessarily born lesbian. Some seem to be, but others become lesbians later in life after having lived heterosexual lives. Lesbian baiting of heterosexual women would not work if there were a definitive way to identify lesbians (or heterosexuals.)

We have yet to understand clearly how sexual identity develops. And this is disturbing to some people, especially those who are determined to discover how lesbian and gay identity is formed so that they will know where to start in eliminating it. (Isn't it odd that there is so little concern about discovering the causes of heterosexuality?) There are many theories: genetic makeup, hormones, socialization, environment, etc. But there is no conclusive evidence that indicates that heterosexuality comes from one process and homosexuality from another.

We do know, however, that sexual identity can be in flux, and we know that sexual identity means more than just the gender of people one is attracted to and has sex with. To be a lesbian has as many ramifications as for a woman to be heterosexual. It is more than sex, more than just the bedroom issue many would like to make it: it is a woman-centered life with all the social interconnections that entails. Some lesbians are in long-term relationships, some in short-term ones, some date, some are celibate, some are married to men, some remain as separate as possible from men, some have children by men, some by alternative insemination, some seem "feminine" by societal standards, some "masculine," some are doctors, lawyers and ministers, some laborers, housewives and writers: what all share in common is a sexual/affectional identity that focuses on women in its attractions and social relationships.

If lesbians are simply women with a particular sexual identity who look and act like all women, then the major difference in living out a lesbian sexual identity as opposed to a heterosexual identity is that as lesbians we live in a homophobic world that threatens and imposes damaging loss on us for being who we are, for choosing to live whole lives. Homophobic people often assert that homosexuals have the choice of not being homosexual; that is, we don't have to act out our sexual identity. In that case, I want to hear heterosexuals talk about their willingness not to act out their sexual identity, including not just sexual activity but heterosexual social interconnections and heterosexual privilege. It is a question of wholeness. It is very difficult for one to be denied the life of a sexual being, whether expressed in sex or in physical affection, and to feel complete, whole. For our loving relationships with humans feed the life of the spirit and enable us to overcome our basic isolation and to be interconnected with humankind.

If, then, any woman can be named a lesbian and be threatened with terrible losses, what is it she fears? Are these fears real? Being vulnerable to a homophobic world can lead to these losses:

- *Employment.* The loss of job leads us right back to the economic connection to sexism. This fear of job loss exists for almost every lesbian except perhaps those who are self-employed or in a business that does not require societal approval. Consider how many businesses or organizations you know that will hire and protect people who are openly gay or lesbian.
- *Family.* Their approval, acceptance, love.
- *Children.* Many lesbians and gay men have children, but very, very few gain custody in court challenges, even if the other parent is a known abuser. Other children may be kept away from us as though gays and lesbians are abusers. There are written and unwritten laws prohibiting lesbians and gays from being foster parents or from adopting children. There is an irrational fear that children in contact with lesbians and gays will become homosexual through influence or that they will be sexually abused. Despite our knowing that 95 percent of those who sexually abuse children are heterosexual men, there are no

policies keeping heterosexual men from teaching or working with children, yet in almost every school system in America, visible gay men and lesbians are not hired through either written or unwritten law.

- *Heterosexual privilege and protection.* No institutions, other than those created by lesbians and gays—such as the Metropolitan Community Church, some counseling centers, political organizations such as the National Gay and Lesbian Task Force, the National Coalition of Black Lesbians and Gays, the Lambda Legal Defense and Education Fund, etc.,—affirm homosexuality and offer protection. Affirmation and protection cannot be gained from the criminal justice system, mainline churches, educational institutions, the government.

- *Safety.* There is nowhere to turn for safety from physical and verbal attacks because the norm presently in this country is that it is acceptable to be overtly homophobic. Gay men are beaten on the streets; lesbians are kidnapped and "deprogrammed?" The National Gay and Lesbian Task Force, in an extended study, has documented violence against lesbians and gay men and noted the inadequate response of the criminal justice system. One of the major differences between homophobia/heterosexism and racism and sexism is that because of the Civil Rights Movement and the women's movement racism and sexism are expressed more covertly (though with great harm); because there has not been a major, visible lesbian and gay movement, it is permissible to be overtly homophobic in any institution or public forum. Churches spew forth homophobia in the same way they did racism prior to the Civil Rights Movement. Few laws are in place to protect lesbians and gay men, and the criminal justice system is wracked with homophobia.

- *Mental health.* An overtly homophobic world in which there is full permission to treat lesbians and gay men with cruelty makes it difficult for lesbians and gay men to maintain a strong sense of well-being and self-esteem. Many lesbians and gay men are beaten, raped, killed, subjected to aversion therapy, or put in mental institutions. The impact of such hatred and negativity can lead one to depression and, in some cases, to suicide. The toll on the gay and lesbian community is devastating.

- *Community.* There is rejection by those who live in homophobic fear, those who are afraid of association with lesbians and gay men. For many in the gay and lesbian community, there is a loss of public acceptance, a loss of allies, a loss of place and belonging.

- *Credibility.* This fear is large for many people: the fear that they will no longer be respected, listened to, honored, believed. They fear they will be social outcasts.

The list goes on and on. But any one of these essential components of a full life is large enough to make one deeply fear its loss. A black woman once said to me in a workshop, "When I fought for Civil Rights, I always had my family and community to fall back on even when they didn't fully understand or accept what I was doing. I don't know if I could have borne losing them. And you people don't have either with you. It takes my breath away?"

What does a woman have to do to get called a lesbian? Almost anything, sometimes nothing at all, but certainly anything that threatens the status quo, anything that steps out of role, anything that asserts the rights of women, anything that doesn't indicate submission arid subordination. Assertiveness, standing up for oneself, asking for more pay, better working conditions, training for and accepting a non-traditional (you mean a man's?) job, enjoying the company of women, being financially independent, being in control of one's life, depending first and foremost upon oneself, thinking that one can do whatever needs to be done, but above all, working for the rights and equality of women.

In the backlash to the gains of the women's liberation movement, there has been an increased effort to keep definitions man-centered. Therefore, to work on behalf of women must mean to work against men. To love women must mean that one hates men. A very effective attack has been made against the word *feminist* to make it a derogatory word. In current backlash usage, *feminist* equals *man-hater* which equals *lesbian*. This formula is created in the hope that women will be frightened away from their work on behalf of women. Consequently, we now have women who believe in the rights of women and work for those rights while from fear deny that they are feminists, or refuse to use the word because it is so "abrasive."

So what does one do in an effort to keep from being called a lesbian? She steps back into line, into the role that is demanded of her, tries to behave in such a way that doesn't threaten the status of men, and if she works for women's rights, she begins modifying that work. When women's organizations begin doing significant social change work, they inevitably are lesbian-baited; that is, funders or institutions or community members tell us that they can't work with us because of our "man-hating attitudes" or the presence of lesbians. We are called too strident, told we are making enemies, not doing good.

The battered women's movement has seen this kind of attack: the pressure has been to provide services only, without analysis of the causes of violence against women and strategies for ending it. To provide only services without political analysis or direct action is to be in an approved "helping" role; to analyze the causes of violence against women is to begin the work toward changing an entire system of power and control. It is when we do the latter that we are threatened with the label of man-hater or lesbian. For my politics, if a women's social change organization has not been labeled lesbian or communist, it is probably not doing significant work; it is only "making nice."

Women in many of these organizations, out of fear of all the losses we are threatened with, begin to modify our work to make it more acceptable and less threatening to the male-dominated society which we originally set out to change. The work can no longer be radical (going to the root cause of the problem) but instead must be reforming, working only on the symptoms and not the cause. Real change for women becomes thwarted and stopped. The word *lesbian* is instilled with the power to halt our work and control our lives. And we give it its power with our fear.

In my view, homophobia has been one of the major causes of the failure of the women's liberation movement to make deep and lasting change. (The other major block has been racism.) We were fierce when we set out but when threatened with the loss of heterosexual privilege, we began putting on brakes. Our best-known nationally distributed women's magazine was reluctant to print articles about lesbians, began putting a man on the cover several times a year, and writing articles about women who succeeded in a man's world. We worried about our image, our being all right, our being "real women" despite our work. Instead of talking about the elimination of sexual gender roles, we stepped back and talked about "sex role stereotyping" as the issue. Change around the edges for middleclass white women began to be talked about as successes. We accepted tokenism and integration, forgetting that equality for all women, for all people—and not just equality of white middleclass women with white men—was the goal that we could never put behind us.

But despite backlash and retreats, change is growing from within. The women's liberation movement is beginning to gain strength again because there are women who are talking about liberation for all women. We are examining sexism, racism, homophobia, classism, anti-Semitism, ageism, ableism, and imperialism, and we see everything as connected. This change in point of view represents the third wave of the women's liberation movement, a new direction that does not get mass media coverage and recognition. It has been initiated by women of color and lesbians who were marginalized or rendered invisible by the white heterosexual leaders of earlier efforts. The first wave was the 19th and early 20th century campaign for the vote; the second, beginning in the 1960s, focused on the Equal Rights Amendment and abortion rights. Consisting of predominantly white middleclass women, both failed in recognizing issues of equality and empowerment for all women. The third wave of the movement, multi-racial and multi-issued, seeks the transformation of the world for us all. We know that we won't get there until everyone gets there; that we must move forward in a great strong line, hand in hand, not just a few at a time.

We know that the arguments about homophobia originating from mental health and Biblical/religious attitudes can be settled when we look at the sexism that permeates religious and psychiatric history. The women of the third wave of the women's liberation movement know that *without the existence of sexism, there would be no homophobia.*

Finally, we know that as long as the word lesbian can strike fear in any woman's heart, then work on behalf of women can be stopped; the only successful work against sexism must include work against homophobia.

Homophobia
A Weapon of Sexism

Suzanne Pharr

1. How do the sickness theory and the sin theory explain homosexuality?

2. Explain how Pharr comes to the conclusion that homosexuality, heterosexuality and bisexuality are simply a matter of identity and are morally neutral.

3. Explain the role of patriarchy, economics, violence, and homophobia in upholding sexism. Draw a concept map connecting the processes.

4. How are all people harmed by homophobia? Provide examples.

5. Pharr argues that homophobia results in real losses for lesbians and provides a list of the many ways that this happens. Find a current example from United States that illustrates one of the categories of loss that she discusses and explain how this example fits.

Claiming an Education

Adrienne Rich

Adrienne Rich *was a feminist poet and essayist. Many of her essays are collected in three books:* On Lies, Secrets and Silence, Of Woman Born *and* Blood, Bread and Poetry. *Her works of poetry include:* A Change of World, The Diamond Cutters and Other Poems, Diving into the Wreck *and* The Dream of A Common Language. *Rich passed away in 2012. "Claiming an Education" is a convocation speech delivered at Douglas College in 1977; it appears in* On Lies, Secrets and Silence *(1979).*

PRE-READING QUESTIONS

1. What have you learned about women's history and experiences thus far in your education?
2. What do you think education for women was like before the 1970s?

KEY TERMS

claiming an education
intellectual contract
subjectivity

SEE THE THEMATIC TABLE OF CONTENTS, IF YOU WANT TO READ MORE ESSAYS ABOUT:

Education
Feminism and Social Movements

Claiming an Education

Adrienne Rich

For this convocation, I planned to separate my remarks into two parts: some thoughts about you, the women students here, and some thoughts about us who teach in a women's college. But ultimately, those two parts are indivisible. If university education means anything beyond the processing of human beings into expected roles, through credit hours, tests, and grades (and I believe that in a women's college especially it *might* mean much more), it implies an ethical and intellectual contract between teacher and student. This contract must remain intuitive, dynamic, unwritten; but we must turn to it again and again if learning is to be reclaimed from the depersonalizing and cheapening pressures of the present-day academic scene.

The first thing I want to say to you who are students, is that you cannot afford to think of being here to *receive* an education; you will do much better to think of yourselves as being here to *claim* one. One of the dictionary definitions of the verb "to claim" is: *to take as the rightful owner; to assert in the face of possible contradiction.* "To receive" is *to come into possession of; to act as receptacle or container for; to accept as authoritative or true.* The difference is that between acting and being acted-upon, and for women it can literally mean the difference between life and death.

One of the devastating weaknesses of university learning, of the store of knowledge and opinion that has been handed down through academic training, has been its almost total erasure of women's experience and thought from the curriculum, and its exclusion of women as members of the academic community. Today, with increasing numbers of women students in nearly every branch of higher learning, we still see very few women in the upper levels of faculty and administration in most institutions. Douglass College itself is a women's college in a university administered overwhelmingly by men, who in turn are answerable to the state legislature, again composed predominantly of men. But the most significant fact for you is that what you learn here, the very texts you read, the lectures you hear, the way your studies are divided into categories and fragmented one from the other—all this reflects, to a very large degree, neither objective reality, nor an accurate picture of the past, nor a group of rigorously tested observations about human behavior. What you can learn here (and I mean not only at Douglass but any college in any university) is how *men* have perceived and organized their experience, their history, their ideas of social relationships, good and evil, sickness and health, etc. When you read or hear about "great issues," "major texts," "the mainstream of Western thought," you are hearing about what men, above all white men, in their male subjectivity, have decided is important.

Black and other minority peoples have for some time recognized that their racial and ethnic experience was not accounted for in the studies broadly labeled human; and that even the sciences can be racist. For many reasons, it has been more difficult for women to comprehend our exclusion, and to realize that even the sciences can be sexist. For one thing, it is only within the last hundred years that higher education has grudgingly been opened up to women at all, even to white, middle-class women. And many of us have found ourselves poring eagerly over books with titles like: *The Descent of Man; Man and His Symbols; Irrational Man; The Phenomenon of Man; The Future of Man; Man and the Machine; From Man to Man; May Man Prevail?; Man, Science and Society;* or *One-Dimensional Man*—books pretending to describe a "human" reality that does not include over one-half the human species.

Less than a decade ago, with the rebirth of a feminist movement in this country, women students and teachers in a number of universities began to demand and set up women's studies courses—to *claim* a woman-directed education. And, despite the inevitable accusations of "unscholarly," "group therapy," "faddism," etc., despite backlash and budget cuts, women's studies are still growing, offering to more and more women a new intellectual grasp on their lives, new understanding of our history, a fresh vision of the human experience, and also a critical basis for evaluating what they hear and read in other courses, and in the society at large.

But my talk is not really about women's studies, much as I believe in their scholarly, scientific, and human necessity. While I think that any Douglass student has everything to gain by investigating and enrolling in women's studies courses, I want to suggest that there is a more essential experience that you owe yourselves, one which courses in women's studies can greatly enrich, but which finally depends on you, in all your interactions with yourself and your world. This is the experience of *taking responsibility toward yourselves*. Our upbringing as women has so often told us that this should come second to our relationships and responsibilities to other people. We have been offered ethical models of the self-denying wife and mother; intellectual models of the brilliant but slapdash dilettante who never commits herself to anything the whole way, or the intelligent woman who denies her intelligence in order to seem more "feminine," or who sits in passive silence even when she disagrees inwardly with everything that is being said around her.

Responsibility to yourself means refusing to let others do your thinking, talking, and naming for you; it means learning to respect and use your own brains and instincts; hence, grappling with hard work. It means that you do not treat your body as a commodity with which to purchase superficial intimacy or economic security; for our bodies and minds are inseparable in this life, and when we allow our bodies to be treated as objects, our minds are in mortal danger. It means insisting that those to whom you give your friendship and love are able to respect your mind. It means being able to say, with Charlotte Bronte's *Jane Eyre:* "I have an inward treasure born with me, which can keep me alive if all the extraneous delights should be withheld or offered only at a price I cannot afford to give."

Responsibility to yourself means that you don't fall for shallow and easy solutions—predigested books and ideas, weekend encounters guaranteed to change your life, taking "gut" courses instead of ones you know will challenge you, bluffing at school and life instead of doing solid work, marrying early as an escape from real decisions, getting pregnant as an evasion of already existing problems. It means that you refuse to sell your talents and aspirations short, simply to avoid conflict and confrontation. And this, in turn, means resisting the forces in society which say that women should be nice, play safe, have low professional expectations, drown in love and forget about work, live through others, and stay in the places assigned to us. It means that we insist on a life of meaningful work, insist that work be as meaningful as love and friendship in our lives. It means, therefore, the courage to be "different"; not to be continuously available to others when we need time for ourselves and our work; to be able to demand of others—parents, friends, roommates, teachers, lovers, husbands, children—that they respect our sense of purpose and our integrity as persons. Women everywhere are finding the courage to do this, more and more, and we are finding that courage both in our study of women in the past who possessed it, and in each other as we look to other women for comradeship, community, and challenge. The difference between a life lived actively, and a life of passive drifting and dispersal of energies, is an immense difference. Once we begin to feel committed to our lives, responsible to ourselves, we can never again be satisfied with the old, passive way.

Now comes the second part of the contract. I believe that in a women's college you have the right to expect your faculty to take you seriously. The education of women has been a matter of debate for centuries, and old, negative attitudes about women's role, women's ability to think and take leadership, are still rife both in and outside the university. Many male professors (and I don't mean only at Douglass) still feel that teaching in a women's college is a second-rate career. Many tend to eroticize their women students—to treat them as sexual objects—instead of demanding the best of their minds. (At Yale a legal suit [*Alexander* v. *Yale*] has been brought against the university by a group of women students demanding a stated policy against sexual advances toward female students by male professors.) Many teachers, both men and women, trained in the male-centered tradition, are still handing the ideas and texts of that tradition on to students without teaching them to criticize its antiwoman attitudes, its omission of women as part of the species. Too often, all of us fail to teach the most important thing, which is that clear thinking, active discussion, and excellent writing are all necessary for intellectual freedom, and that these require *hard work*. Sometimes, perhaps in discouragement with a culture which is both antiintellectual and antiwoman, we may resign ourselves to low expectations for our students before we have given them half a chance to become more thoughtful, expressive human beings. We need to take to heart the words of Elizabeth Barrett Browning, a poet, a thinking woman, and a feminist, who wrote in 1845 of her impatience with studies which cultivate a "passive recipiency" in the mind, and asserted that "women want to be made to *think actively*: their apprehension is quicker than that of men, but their defect lies for the most part in the logical faculty and in the higher mental activities." Note that she implies a defect which can be remedied by intellectual training; *not* an inborn lack of ability.

I have said that the contract on the student's part involves that you demand to be taken seriously so that you can also go on taking yourself seriously. This means seeking out criticism, recognizing that the most affirming thing anyone can do for you is demand that you push yourself further, show you the range of what you *can* do. It means rejecting attitudes of "take-it-easy," "why-be-so-serious," "why-worry-you'll-probably-get-married-anyway." It means assuming your share of responsibility for what happens in the classroom, because that affects the quality of your daily life here. It means that the student sees herself engaged *with* her teachers in an active, ongoing struggle for a real education. But for her to do this, her teachers must be committed to the belief that women's minds and experience are intrinsically valuable and indispensable to any civilization worthy the name; that there is no more exhilarating and intellectually fertile place in the academic world today than a women's college—*if* both students and teachers in large enough numbers are trying to fulfill this contract. The contract is really a pledge of mutual seriousness about women, about language, ideas, methods, and values. It is our shared commitment toward a world in which the inborn potentialities of so many women's minds will no longer be wasted, raveled-away, paralyzed, or denied.

Claiming an Education

Adrienne Rich

1. This essay is a speech that Adrienne Rich gave in 1977. Does this essay seem dated to you? In what ways? Which of Rich's points still seem relevant?

2. What is the difference between claiming an education and receiving an education?

3. What responsibilities does the university have to students? To the public? Community? What does it mean to you for faculty to take you seriously?

4. What changes would you recommend to the general education curriculum or to the course offerings in your chosen major in your quest to claim your education?

5. Draw up a contract for yourself. What will you do to claim your education in this class? This semester? What do you expect from yourself? What do you have a right to expect from your peers in this classroom? Your professors? Your university? What can you do to make sure those things happen?

From "Compulsory Heterosexuality and Lesbian Existence"

Adrienne Rich

Adrienne Rich was a feminist poet and essayist. Many of her essays are collected in three books: *On Lies, Secrets and Silence, Of Woman Born,* and *Blood, Bread and Poetry.* Her works of poetry include *A Change of World, The Diamond Cutters and Other Poems, Diving into the Wreck,* and *The Dream of a Common Language.* Rich passed away in 2012. "Compulsory Heterosexuality and Lesbian Existence" originally appeared in the feminist journal *Signs* in 1980; it is also included in *Blood, Bread and Poetry,* a collection of her essays (1986).

PRE-READING QUESTIONS

1. What do you think the concept compulsory heterosexuality means?
2. How might heterosexuality be compulsory in our culture?

KEY TERMS

characteristics of male power
compulsory heterosexuality
lesbian continuum
lesbian existence
woman identification
woman identified woman

SEE THE THEMATIC TABLE OF CONTENTS, IF YOU WANT TO READ MORE ESSAYS ABOUT:

Homophobia
LGBTQ Studies
Feminism and Social Movements
Privilege, Identities, and Intersectionalities
Sexualities
Social Construction of Gender

Compulsory Heterosexuality and Lesbian Existence (1980)

Adrienne Rich

FOREWORD

I want to say a little about the way "Compulsory Heterosexuality" was originally conceived and the context in which we are now living. It was written in part to challenge the erasure of lesbian existence from so much of scholarly feminist literature, an erasure which I felt (and feel) to be not just anti-lesbian, but anti-feminist in its consequences, and to distort the experience of heterosexual women as well. It was not written to widen divisions but to encourage heterosexual feminists to examine heterosexuality as a political institution which disempowers women—and to change it. I also hoped that other lesbians would feel the depth and breadth of woman identification and woman bonding that has run like a continuous though stifled theme through the heterosexual experience, and that this would become increasingly a politically activating impulse, not simply a validation of personal lives. I wanted the essay to suggest new kinds of criticism, to incite new questions in classrooms and academic journals, and to sketch, at least, some bridge over the gap between *lesbian* and *feminist*. I wanted, at the very least, for feminists to find it less possible to read, write, or teach from a perspective of unexamined heterocentricity.

Within the three years since I wrote "Compulsory Heterosexuality"—with this energy of hope and desire—the pressures to conform in a society increasingly conservative in mood have become more intense. The New Right's messages to women have been, precisely, that we are the emotional and sexual property of men, and that the autonomy and equality of women threaten the family, religion, and state. The institutions by which women have traditionally been controlled—patriarchal motherhood, economic exploitation, the nuclear family, compulsory heterosexuality—are being strengthened by legislation, religious fiat, media imagery, and efforts at censorship. In a worsening economy, the single mother trying to support her children confronts the feminization of poverty which Joyce Miller of the National Coalition of Labor Union Women has named one of the major issues of the 1980s. The lesbian, unless in disguise, faces discrimination in hiring and harassment and violence in the street. Even within feminist-inspired institutions such as battered-women's shelters and Women's Studies programs, open lesbians are fired and others warned to stay in the closet. The retreat into sameness—assimilation for those who can manage it—is the most passive and debilitating of responses to political repression, economic insecurity, and a renewed open season on difference.

I want to note that documentation of male violence against women—within the home especially—has been accumulating rapidly in this period (see pages 30–31[41], note 9). At the same time, in the realm of literature which depicts woman bonding and woman identification as essential for female survival, a steady stream of writing and criticism has been coming from women of color in general and lesbians of color in particular—the latter group being even more profoundly erased in academic feminist scholarship by the double bias of racism and homophobia.[1]

There has recently been an intensified debate on female sexuality among feminists and lesbians, with lines often furiously and bitterly drawn, with *sadomasochism* and *pornography* as key words which are variously defined according to who is talking. The depth of women's rage and fear regarding sexuality and its relation to power and pain is real, even when the dialogue sounds simplistic, self-righteous, or like parallel monologues.

Because of all these developments, there are parts of this essay that I would word differently, qualify, or expand if I were writing it today. But I continue to think that heterosexual feminists will draw political strength for change from taking a critical stance toward the ideology which *demands* heterosexuality, and that lesbians cannot assume that we are untouched by that ideology and the institutions founded upon it. There is nothing about such a critique that requires us to think of ourselves as victims, as having been brainwashed or totally powerless. Coercion and compulsion are among the conditions in which women have learned to recognize our strength. Resistance is a major theme in this essay and in the study of women's lives, if we know what we are looking for.

I

I have chosen to use the term *lesbian existence* and *lesbian continuum* because the word *lesbianism* has a clinical and limiting ring. *Lesbian existence* suggests both the fact of the historical presence of lesbians and our continuing creation of the meaning of that existence. I mean the term *lesbian continuum* to include a range—through each woman's life and throughout history—of women-identified experience, not simply the fact that a woman has had or consciously desired genital sexual experience with another woman. If we expand it to embrace many more forms of primary intensity between and among women, including the sharing of a rich inner life, the bonding against male tyranny, the giving and receiving of practical and political support, if we can also hear it in such associations as *marriage resistance* and the "haggard" behavior identified in Mary

---

[1]See for example, Paula Gunn Allen, *The Sacred Hoop: Recovering the Feminine in American Indian Traditions* (Boston: Beacon, 1986); Beth Brant, ed., *A Gathering of Spirit: Writing and Art by North American Indian Women* (Montpelier, Vt.: Sinister Wisdom Books, 1984); Gloria Anzaldúa and Cherríe Moraga, eds., *This Bridge Called My Back: Writings by Radical Women of Color* (Watertown, Mass.: Persephone, 1981; distributed by Kitchen Table/Women of Color Press, Albany, N.Y.) J.R. Roberts, *Black Lesbians: An Annotated Bibliography* (Tallahassee, Fla.: Naiad, 1981); Barbara Smith, ed., *Home Girls: A Black Feminist Anthology* (Albany, N.Y.: Kitchen Table/ Women of Color Press, 1984). As Lorraine Bethel and Barbara Smith pointed out in *Conditions 5: The Black Women's Issue* (1980), a great deal of fiction by Black women depicts primary relationships between women. I would like to cite here the work of Ama Ata Aidoo, Toni Cade Bambara, Buchi Emecheta, Bessie Head, Zora Neale Hurston, Alice Walker. Donna Allegra, Red Jordan Arobateau, Audre Lorde, Ann Allen Shockley, among others, write directly as Black lesbians. For fiction by other lesbians of color, see Elly Bulkin, ed., *Lesbian Fiction: An Anthology* (Watertown, Mass.; Persephone, 1981).

See also, for accounts of contemporary Jewish-lesbian existence, Evelyn Torton Beck, ed., *Nice Jewish Girls: A Lesbian Anthology* (Watertown, Mass.; Persephone, 1982; distributed by Crossing Press, Trumansburg, N.Y. 14886); Alice Bloch, *Lifetime Guarantee* (Watertown, Mass.; Persephone, 1982); and Melanie Kaye-Kantrowitz and Irena Klepfisz, eds., *The Tribe of Dina: A Jewish Women's Anthology* (Montpelier, Vt.: Sinister Wisdom Books, 1986).

The earliest formulation that I know of heterosexuality as an institution was in the lesbian-feminist paper *The Furies*, founded in 1971. For a collection of articles from that paper, see Nancy Myron and Charlotte Bunch, eds., *Lesbianism and the Women's Movement* (Oakland, Calif.: Diana Press, 1975; distributed by Crossing Press, Trumansburg, N.Y. 14886).

Daly (obsolete meanings: "intractable," "willful," "wanton," and "unchaste," "a woman reluctant to yield to wooing"),[2] we begin to grasp breadths of female history and psychology which have lain out of reach as a consequence of limited, mostly clinical, definitions of *lesbianism*.

Lesbian existence comprises both the breaking of a taboo and the rejection of a compulsory way of life. It is also a direct or indirect attack on male right of access to women. But it is more than these, although we may first begin to perceive it as a form of naysaying to patriarchy, an act of resistance. It has, of course, included isolation, self-hatred, breakdown, alcoholism, suicide, and intrawoman violence; we romanticize at our peril what it means to love and act against the grain, and under heavy penalties; and lesbian existence has been lived (unlike, say, Jewish or Catholic existence) without access to any knowledge of a tradition, a continuity, a social underpinning. The destruction of records and memorabilia and letters documenting the realities of lesbian existence must be taken very seriously as a means of keeping heterosexuality compulsory for women, since what has been kept from our knowledge is joy, sensuality, courage, and community, as well as guilt, self-betrayal, and pain.[3]

Lesbians have historically been deprived of a political existence through "inclusion" as female versions of male homosexuality. To equate lesbian existence with male homosexuality because each is stigmatized is to erase female reality once again. Part of the history of lesbian existence is, obviously, to be found where lesbians, lacking a coherent female community, have shared a kind of social life and common cause with homosexual men. But there are differences: women's lack of economic and cultural privilege relative to men; qualitative differences in female and male relationships—for example, the patterns of anonymous sex among male homosexuals, and the pronounced ageism in male homosexual standards of sexual attractiveness. I perceive the lesbian experience as being, like motherhood, a profoundly *female* experience, with particular oppressions, meanings, and potentialities we cannot comprehend as long as we simply bracket it with other sexually stigmatized existences. Just as the term *parenting* serves to conceal the particular and significant realty of being a parent who is actually a mother, the term *gay* may serve the purpose of blurring the very outlines we need to discern, which are of crucial value for feminism and for the freedom of women as a group.[4]

As the term *lesbian* has been held to limiting, clinical associations in its patriarchal definition, female friendship and comradeship have been set apart from the erotic, this limiting the erotic itself. But as we deepen and broaden the range of what we define as lesbian existence, as we delineate a lesbian continuum, we begin to discover the erotic in female terms: as that which is unconfined to any single part of the body or solely to the body itself; as an energy not only diffuse but, as Audre Lorde has described it, omnipresent in "the sharing of joy, whether physical, emotional, psychic," and in the sharing of work; as the empowering joy which "makes us less willing to accept powerlessness, or those other supplied states of being which are not native to me, such as resignation, despair, self-effacement, depression, self-denial."[5] In another context,

---

[2]Daly, *Gyn/Ecology*, p.15.

[3]"In a hostile world in which women are not supposed to survive except in relation with and in service to men, entire communities of women were simply erased. History tends to bury what it seeks to reject" (Blanche W. Cook, "'Women Alone Stir My Imagination': Lesbianism and the Cultural Tradition," *Signs: Journal of Women in Culture and Society* 4, no. 4 [Summer 1979]: 719–720). The Lesbian Herstory Archives in New York City is one attempt to preserve contemporary documents on lesbian existence—a project of enormous value and meaning, working against the continuing censorship and obliteration of relationships, networks, communities in other archives and elsewhere in the culture.

[4][A.R., 1986: The shared historical and spiritual "crossover" functions of lesbians and gay men in cultures past and present are traced by Judy Grahn in *Another Mother Tongue: Gay Words, Gay Worlds* (Boston: Beacon, 1984.) I know think we have much to learn both from the uniquely female aspects of lesbian existence and from the complex "gay" identity we share with gay men.]

[5]Audre Lorde, "Uses of the Erotic: The Erotic as Power," in *Sister Outsider* (Trumansburg, N.Y.: Crossing Press, 1984).

writing of women and work, I quoted the autobiographical passage in which the poet H.D. described how her friend Bryher supported her in persisting with the visionary experience which was to shape her mature work:

> I knew that this experience, this writing-on-the-wall before me, could not be shared with anyone except the girl who stood so bravely there beside me. This girl said without hesitation, "Go on." It was she really who had the detachment and integrity of the Pythoness of Delphi. But it was I, battered and dissociated ... who was seeing the pictures, and who was reading the writing or granted the inner vision. Or perhaps, in some sense, we were "seeing" it together, for without her, admittedly, I could not have gone on.[6]

If we consider the possibility that all women—from the infant suckling at her mother's breast, to the grown woman experiencing orgasmic sensations while suckling her own child, perhaps recalling her mother's milk smell in her own, to two women like Virginia Woolf's Chloe and Olivia, who share a laboratory,[7] to the woman dying at ninety, touched and handled by women— exist on a lesbian continuum, we can see ourselves as moving in and out of this continuum, whether we identify ourselves as lesbian or not.

We can then connect aspects of woman identification as diverse as the impudent, intimate girl friendships of eight or nine year olds and the banding together of those women of the twelfth and fifteenth centuries known as the Beguines who "shared houses, rented to one another, bequeathed houses to their room-mates ... in cheap subdivided houses in the artisans' area of town," who "practiced Christian virtue on their own, dressing and living simply and not associating with men," who earned their livings as spinsters, bakers, nurses, or ran schools for young girls, and who managed—until the Church forced them to disperse—to live independent both of marriage and of conventual restrictions.[8] It allows us to connect these women with the more celebrated "Lesbians" of the women's school around Sappho of the seventh century B.C., with the secret sororities and economic networks reported among African women, and with the Chinese marriage-resistance sisterhoods—communties of women who refused marriage or who, if married, often refused to consummate their marriages and soon left their husbands, the only women in China who were not footbound and who, Agnes Smedley tells us, welcomed the births of daughters and organzied successful women's strikes in the silk mills.[9] It allows us to connect and compare disparate individual instances of marriage resistance: for example, the strategies available to Emily Dickinson, a nineteenth-century white woman genius, with the strategies available to Zora Neale Hurston, a twentieth-century Black woman genius. Dickinson never married, had tenuous intellectual friendships with men, lived self-convented in her genteel father's house in Amherst, and wrote a lifetime of passionate letters to her sister-in-law Sue Gilbert and a smaller group of such letters to her friend Kate Scott Anthon. Hurston married twice but soon left each husband, scrambled her way from Florida to Harlem to Columbia University to Haiti and finally back to Florida, moved in and out of white patronage and poverty, professional success, and failure; her survival relationships were all with women, beginning with

---

[6]Adrienne Rich, "Conditions for Work: The Common World of Women" in *On Lies, Secrets, and Silence*, p. 209; H.D., *Tribute to Freud* (Oxford: Carcanet, 1971), pp. 50–54.

[7]Woolf, *A Room of One's Own*, p. 126.

[8]Gracia Clark, "The Beguines: A Mediaeval Women's Community," *Quest: A Feminist Quarterly* 1, no. 4 (1975): 73–80.

[9]See Denise Paulmé, ed., *Women of Tropical Africa* (Berkeley: University of California Press, 1963), pp. 7, 266–267. Some of these sororities are described as "a kind of defensive syndicate against the male element," their aims being "to offer concerted resistance to an oppressive patriarchate," "independence in relation to ones' husband with regard to motherhood, mutual aid, satisfaction of personal revenge." See also Audre Lorde, "Scratching the Surface: Some Notes on Barriers to Women and Loving," in *Sister Outsider*, pp. 45–52.; Marjorie Topley, "Marriage Resistance in Rural Kwangtung," in *Women in Chinese Society*, ed. M. Wolf and R. Witke (Stanford, Calif.: Stanford University Press, 1978), pp. 67–89; Agnes Smedley, *Portraits of Chinese Women in Revolution*, ed. J. MacKinnon and S. MacKinnon (Old Westbury, N.Y.: Feminist Press, 1976), pp. 103–110.

her mother. Both of these women in their vastly different circumstances were marriage resisters, committed to their own work and selfhood, and were later characterized as "apolitical." Both were drawn to men of intellectual quality; for both of them women provided the ongoing fascination and sustenance of life.

If we think of heterosexuality as *the* natural emotional and sensual inclination for women, lives as these are seen as deviant, as pathological, or as emotionally and sensually deprived. Or, in more recent and permissive jargon, they are banalized as "life styles." And the work of such women, whether merely the daily work of individual or collective survival and resistance or the work of the writer, the activist, the reformer, the anthropologist, or the artist—the work of self-creation—is undervalued, or seen as the bitter fruit of "penis envy" or the sublimation of repressed eroticism or the meaningless rant of a "man-hater." But when we turn the lens of vision and consider the degree to which and the methods whereby heterosexual "preference" has actually been imposed on women, not only can we understand differently the meaning of individual lives and work, but we can begin to recognize a central fact of women's history: that women have always resisted male tyranny. A feminism of action, often though not always without a theory, has constantly re-emerged in every culture and in every period. We can then begin to study women's struggle against powerlessness, women's radical rebellion, not just in male-defined "concrete revolutionary situations"[10] but in all the situations male ideologies have not perceived as revolutionary—for example, the refusal of some women to produce children, aided at great risk by other women;[11] the refusal to produce a higher standard of living and leisure for men (Leghorn and Parker show how both are part of women's unacknowledged, unpaid, and un-unionized economic contribution). We can no longer have patience with Dinnerstein's view that women have simply collaborated with men in the "sexual arrangements" of history. We begin to observe behavior, both in history and in individual biography, that has hitherto been invisible or misnamed, behavior which often constitutes, given the limits of the counterforce exerted in a given time and place, radical rebellion. And we can connect these rebellions and the necessity for them with the physical passion of woman for woman which is central to lesbian existence: the erotic sensuality which as been, precisely, the most violently erased fact of female experience.

Heterosexuality has been both forcibly and subliminally imposed on women. Yet everywhere women have resisted it, often at the cost of physical torture, imprisonment, psychosurgery, social ostracism, and extreme poverty. "Compulsory heterosexuality" was named as one of the "crimes against women" by the Brussels International Tribunal on Crimes against Women in 1976. Two pieces of testimony from two very different cultures reflect the degree to which persecution of lesbians is a global practice here and now. A report from Norway relates:

> A lesbian in Oslo was in a heterosexual marriage that didn't work, so she stared taking tranquillizers and ended up at the health sanatorium for treatment and rehabilitation. . . . The moment she said in family group therapy that she believed she was a lesbian, the doctor told her she was not. He knew from "looking into her eyes," he said. She had the eyes of a woman who wanted sexual intercourse with her husband. So she was subjected to so-called "couch therapy." She was put into a comfortably heated room, naked, on a bed, and for an hour her husband was to . . . try to excite her sexually. . . . The ideal was that the touching was always to end with sexual intercourse. She felt stronger and stronger aversion. She threw up and sometimes ran out of the room to avoid this "treatment." The more strongly she asserted that she was a lesbian, the more violent the forced heterosexual intercourse became. This treatment went on for about six months. She escaped from the hospital, but

---

[10]See Rosalind Petchesky, "Dissolving the Hyphen: A Report on Marxist-Feminist Groups 1–5," in *Capitalist Patriarchy and the Case for Socialist Feminism*, ed. Zillah Eisenstein (New York: Monthly Review Press, 1979), p. 387.

[11][A.R., 1986: See Angela Davis, *Women, Race and Class* (New York: Random House, 1981), p. 102; Orlando Patterson, *Slavery and Social Death: A Comparative Study* (Cambridge: Harvard University Press, 1982), p. 133.]

she was brought back. Again she escaped. She has not been there since. In the end she realized that she had been subjected to forcible rape for six months.

And from Mozambique:

> I am condemned to a life of exile because I will not deny that I am a lesbian, that my primary commitments are, and will always be to other women. In the new Mozambique, lesbianism is considered a left-over from colonialism and decadent Western civilization. Lesbians are sent to rehabilitation camps to learn through self-criticism the correct line about themselves. . . . If I am forced to denounce my own love for women, if I therefore denounce myself, I could go back to Mozambique and join forces in the exciting and hard struggle of rebuilding a nation, including the struggle for the emancipation of Mozambiquan women. As it is, I either risk the rehabilitation camps, or remain in exile.[12]

Nor can it be assumed that women like those in Carroll Smith-Rosenberg's study, who married, stayed married, yet dwelt in a profoundly female emotional and passional world, "preferred" or "chose" heterosexuality. Women have married because it was necessary, in order to survive economically, in order to have children who would not suffer economic deprivation or social ostracism, in order to remain respectable, in order to do what was expected of women, because coming out of "abnormal" childhoods they wanted to feel "normal," and because heterosexual romance has been represented as the great female adventure, duty, and fulfillment. We may faithfully or ambivalently have obeyed the institution, but our feelings—and our sensuality—have not been tamed or contained with in it. There is no statistical documentation of the numbers of lesbians who have remained in heterosexual marriages for most of their lives. But in a letter to the early lesbian publication *The Ladder*, the playwright Lorraine Hansberry had this to say:

> I suspect that that problem of the married woman who would prefer emotional-physical relationships with other women is proportionally much higher than a similar statistic for men. (A statistic surely no one will ever really have.) This because of the estate of women being what it is, how could we ever begin to guess the numbers of women who are not prepared to risk a life alien to what they have been taught all their lives to believe was their "natural" destiny—AND—their only expectation for ECONOMIC security. It seems to be that this is why the question has an immensity that it does not have for male homosexuals. . . . A woman of strength and honesty may, if she chooses, sever her marriage and marry a new male mate and society will be upset that the divorce rate is rising so—but there are few places in the United States, in any event, where she will be anything remotely akin to an "outcast." Obviously this is not true for a woman who would end her marriage to take up life with another woman.[13]

This *double life*—this apparent acquiescence to an institution founded on male interest and prerogative—has been characteristic of female experience: in motherhood and in many kinds of heterosexual behavior, including the rituals of courtship; the pretense of asexuality by the nineteenth-century wife; the simulation of orgasm by the prostitute, the courtesan, the twentieth-century "sexually liberated" woman.

Meridel LeSueur's documentary novel of the depression, *The Girl*, is arresting as a study of female double life. The protagonist, a waitress in a St. Paul working-class speakeasy, feels herself passionately attracted to the young man Butch, but her survival relationships are with Clara, an older waitress and prostitute, with Belle, whose husband owns the bar, and with Amelia, a union activist. For Clara and Belle and the unnamed protagonist, sex with men is in one sense

[12]Russell and van de Ven, pp. 42–43, 56–57.
[13]I am indebted to Jonathan Katz's *Gay American History* (*op. cit.*) for bringing to my attention Hansberry's letters to *The Ladder* and to Barbara Grier for supplying me with copies of relevant pages from *The Ladder*, quoted here by permission of Barbara Grier. See also the reprinted series of *The Ladder*, ed. Jonathan Katz *et al.* (New York: Arno, 1975), and Deirdre Carmody, "Letters by Eleanor Roosevelt Detail Friendship with Lorena Hickok," *New York Times* (October 21, 1979).

an escape from the bedrock misery of daily life, a flare of intensity in the gray, relentless, often brutal web of day-to-day existence:

> It was like having a magnet pulling me. It was exciting and powerful and frightening. He was after me too and when he found me I would run, or be petrified, just standing in front of him like a zany. And he told me not to be wandering with Clara to the Marigold where we danced with strangers. He said he would knock the shit out of me. Which made me shake and tremble, but it was better than being a husk full of suffering and not knowing why.[14]

Throughout the novel the theme of double life emerges; Belle reminisces about her marriage to bootlegger Hoinck:

> You know, when I had that black eye and said I hit it on the cupboard, well he did it the bastard, and then he says don't tell anybody. . . . He's nuts, that's what he is, nuts, and I don't see why I live with him, why I put up with him a minute on this earth. But listen kid, she said, I'm telling you something. She looked at me and her face was wonderful. She said, Jesus Christ, Goddam him I love him that's why I'm hooked like this all my life, Goddam him I love him.[15]

After the protagonist has her first sex with Butch, her women friends care for her bleeding, give her whiskey, and compare notes.

> My luck, the first time and I got into trouble. He gave me a little money and I come to St. Paul where for ten bucks they'd stick a huge vet's needle into you and you start it and then you were on your own. . . . I never had no child. I've just had Hoinck to mother, and a hell of a child he is.[16]
>
> Later they made me go back to Clara's room to lie down. . . . Clara lay down beside me and put her arms around me and wanted me to tell her about it but she wanted to tell about herself. She said she started it when she was twelve with a bunch of boys in an old shed. She said nobody had paid any attention to her before and she became very popular. . . . They like it so much, she said, why shouldn't you give it to them and get presents and attention? I never cared anything for it and neither did my mama. But it's the only thing you got that's valuable.[17]

Sex is thus equated with attention from the male, who is charismatic though brutal, infantile, or unreliable. Yet it is the women who make life endurable for each other, give physical affection without causing pain, share, advise, and stick by each other. *(I am trying to find my strength through women—without my friends, I could not survive.)* LeSueur's *The Girl* parallels Toni Morrison's remarkable *Sula*, another revelation of female double life:

> Nel was the one person who had wanted nothing from her, who had accepted all aspects of her. . . . Nel was one of the reasons Sula had drifted back to Medallion. . . . The men . . . had merged into one large personality: the same language of love, the same entertainments of love, the same cooling of love. Whenever she introduced her private thoughts into their rubbings and goings, they hooded their eyes. They taught her nothing but love tricks, shared nothing but worry, gave nothing but money. She had been looking all along for a friend, and it took her a while to discover that a lover was not a comrade and could never be—for a woman.

But Sula's last thought at the second of her death is "Wait'll I tell Nel." And after Sula's death, Nel looks back on her own life:

> "All that time, all that time, I thought I was missing Jude." And the loss pressed down on her chest and came up into her throat. "We was girls together," she said as though explaining something. "O Lord, Sula," she

---

[14]Meridel LeSueur, *The Girl* (Cambridge, Mass: West End Press, 1978), pp. 10–11. LeSueur describes, in an afterword, how this book was drawn from the writings and oral narration of women in the Workers Alliance who met as a writers' group during the depression.
[15]*Ibid.*, p. 20.
[16]*Ibid.*, pp. 53–54.
[17]*Ibid.*, p. 55.

cried, "Girl, girl, girlgirlgirl!" It was a fine cry—loud and long—but it had no bottom and it had no top, just circles and circles of sorrow.[18]

The Girl and *Sula* are both novels which examine what I am calling the lesbian continuum, in contrast to the shallow or sensational "lesbian scenes" in recent commercial fiction.[19] Each shows us woman identification untarnished (till the end of LeSueur's novel) by romanticism; each depicts the competition of heterosexual compulsion for women's attention, the diffusion and frustration of female bonding that might, in a more conscious form, reintegrate love and power.

---

[18]Toni Morrison, *Sula* (New York: Bantam, 1973), pp. 103–104, 149. I am indebted to Lorraine Bethel's essay "'This is a Conscious Pain': Zora Neale Hurston and the Black Female Literary Tradition," in *All the Women Are White, All the Blacks Are Men, but Some of Us are Brave: Black Women's Studies*, ed. Gloria T. Hull, Patricia Bell Scott, and Barbara Smith (Old Westbury, N.Y.: Feminist Press, 1982).
[19]See Maureen Brady and Judith McDaniel, "Lesbians in the Mainstream: The Image of Lesbians in Recent Commercial Fiction," *Conditions 6* (1979): 82–105.

Name _____   Date _____

Course & section: _____   Instructor _____

Compulsory Heterosexuality

Adrienne Rich

1. In this essay, Adrienne Rich seeks to define and explain compulsory heterosexuality, lesbian existence, and the lesbian continuum. How does she define the lesbian continuum?

2. What does Rich mean by the term *compulsory heterosexuality*?

3. As you might guess, Rich's reclaiming and redefining of the term *lesbian and lesbian existence* was (and still is) controversial. What is controversial about this? What also might be liberating? Is this a case of reverse discourse?

4. Though she isn't using the term, Rich is using an intersectional analysis to discuss lesbianism. How so? To help build this answer, consider the definition of intersectionality in the text book and apply it to her analysis here.

5. What connections do you see between this essay and Audre Lorde's essay "The Uses of the Erotic"?

The Chilly Climate

Subtle Ways in Which Women Are Often Treated Differently at Work and in Classrooms

Bernice R. Sandler

Bernice R. Sandler is a Senior Scholar at the Women's Research and Education Institute in Washington DC. She earned an EdD from the University of Maryland. Because she focuses on making both education and the workplace more equitable for women, she is considered "The Godmother of Title IX." "The Chilly Climate" first appeared in the newsletter About Women on Campus *in 1999. The material was drawn from* The Chilly Classroom Climate: A Guide to Improve the Education of Women *(1996) by Bernice R. Sandler, Lisa A Silverberg and Roberta M. Hall, published by the National Association for Women in Education, Washington, D.C.*

PRE-READING QUESTIONS

1. What have been your most influential experiences in your education? Provide an example.
2. How might someone's gender affect their educational experiences?

KEY TERMS

chilly climate
devaluation
microinequity
internalized stereotypes
outsider experience
stereotyping
women and men of color

SEE THE THEMATIC TABLE OF CONTENTS, IF YOU WANT TO READ MORE ESSAYS ABOUT:

Education
Privilege, Identities and Intersectionalities

The Chilly Climate
Subtle Ways in Which Women Are Often Treated Differently at Work and in Classrooms

Bernice R. Sandler

The word "women" as used here includes all women. However, for women of color, disabled women, lesbians and older women these behaviors may be exacerbated and these women may experience other forms of differential behavior as well. Additionally, other "outsiders" such as men of color, persons for whom English is a second language, and those from working class backgrounds often experience many of the same behaviors described here.

Most of the behaviors are what has been described as "microinequities," a term coined by Mary Rowe of Massachusetts Institute of Technology. They describe the small everyday inequities through which individuals are often treated differently because of their gender, race, age, or other "outsider" status. Taken by itself, a microinequity may have a minuscule effect, if it has any at all, and is typically not noticed by the person it happens to or by the person who asserts it. Yet when these behaviors occur again and again, and especially if they are not noticed or understood, they often have a damaging cumulative effect, creating an environment that is indeed chilly—an environment that dampens women's self-esteem, confidence, aspirations and their participation.

Because overt behaviors are more easily recognized, they have generally been omitted from this article. Those that are included here are the types of behaviors that are typically minimized by the person engaging in the behavior. Some of the behaviors below may fit in more than one category.

BEHAVIORS THAT COMMUNICATE LOWER EXPECTATIONS FOR WOMEN

Asking women easier, more factual questions, men the harder, open-ended ones that require critical thinking.

Grouping women in ways which indicate they have less status or are less capable.

Doubting women's work and accomplishments: "Did you really do that without any help from someone else?"

This article appeared in the Summer 1999 issue *About Women on Campus, Vol. 8, Number 3* published by the Association of American Colleges and Universities. Virtually all of the material was drawn from *The Chilly Classroom Climate: A Guide to Improve the Education of Women,* by Bernice R. Sandler, Lisa A Silverberg and Roberta M. Hall, published by the now defunct National Association for Women in Education, Washington, D.C. in 1996. The book is no longer in print. Sandler is a Senior Scholar at the Women's Research and Education Institute; the article also appears on her web site, www.bernicesandler.com.

Expecting less of women in the future.

Calling males "men" and women "girls" or "gals" which implies that women are not as serious or as capable as men.

YIELDING TO THE INFLUENCE OF INTERNALIZED STEREOTYPES

Using examples that reflect stereotypes.

Addressing women in ways that reinforce stereotypes and social roles rather than intellectual ones, for instance, calling women "honey."

Focusing on a woman's appearance, personal qualities and relationships rather than on her accomplishments: "I'd like you to meet our new charming colleague" rather than "I'd like you to meet the new hot-shot we just hired."

Judging women by their physical appearance and downgrading those who are not "attractive."

Describing women by their physical characteristics, such as a "blonde."

Using a different vocabulary to describe similar behavior or accomplishments, such as "angry man" but "bitchy woman."

Expressing stereotypes that discourage women from pursuing professional careers, such as "Women are naturally more caring and men are naturally more aggressive."

Assigning classroom tasks according to stereotyped roles. Women are assigned to be the note-takers.

Falling back on disparaging stereotyped words when angry or annoyed with females: "Look here, sweetie," and "Don't talk back to me, little girl."

EXCLUDING WOMEN FROM PARTICIPATION IN MEETINGS AND CONVERSATIONS

Ignoring women while recognizing men, even when women clearly volunteer to participate by raising their hands.

Addressing a group as if there were no women present: "When you were a boy..." Interrupting women more than men or allowing their peers to interrupt them.

Women may be more vulnerable when interrupted—they may not participate again for the rest of a meeting.

TREATING MEN AND WOMEN DIFFERENTLY WHEN THEIR BEHAVIOR OR ACHIEVEMENTS ARE THE SAME

Treating women who ask extensive questions as trouble-makers and men as interested and bright.

Believing that women who ask for information don't know the materials, but that men who ask are smart, inquisitive and involved.

Viewing marriage and parental status differently for men and women—as disadvantages for women and advantages for men.

Attributing women's achievements to something other than their abilities, such as good luck, affirmative action, beauty, or having "slept their way to the top."

Frowning when women speak (male and female students may also do this). Men and women alike may be less reinforcing when women speak.

Judging women who speak tentatively as being less competent or knowledgeable.

GIVING WOMEN LESS ATTENTION AND INTELLECTUAL ENCOURAGEMENT

Making less eye contact with women.

Nodding and gesturing more and paying more attention in general to men than to women when they speak.

Responding more to men's comments by making additional comments, coaching, and asking questions, and responding more often to women with "uh-huh."

Calling on males more frequently in meetings and in conversations.

Calling males by name more frequently.

Coaching men but not women: "Tell me more about that."

Waiting longer for a man to respond to a question than a woman, before going on to another person.

Crediting men's comments to their owner or "author" ("As Bill said . . .") but not giving authorship or ownership to women. Sometimes a comment made by a woman is later credited to a male.

Giving men more detailed instructions for a task.

Giving women less feedback—less criticism, less help and less praise. (This is one of the critical ways in which women and men are treated differently.)

Being more concerned about men's behavior than that of women's, such as worrying about a male who doesn't participate but not being concerned about women who do not.

Giving women less encouragement to take on harder tasks.

Engaging in more informal conversation with men than with women.

DISCOURAGING WOMEN THROUGH POLITENESS

Using some forms of politeness that shift the focus from intellectual activities to social behavior: "I like to see the girls' smiling faces."

Males may perform hands-on tasks for women (as when helping them with a computer task) under the guise of being helpful, thereby depriving women of the experience and communicating lower expectations for them.

Faculty members may be excessively kind and paternalistic or maternalistic in trying to be helpful and hold women to a lower standard.

Men may tell a group that they are refraining from telling certain jokes or using certain words because there are "ladies" present.

(True courtesy and respect does not patronize, trivialize or depersonalize another person's abilities and talents, nor do they disappear when a woman acts in a way that deviates from gender stereotypes.)

SINGLING OUT WOMEN

Singling out women and other groups such as people of color: "What do you women think about this?"

Males are more likely to touch women than other men. If touch is being used to reassure or indicate friendliness, males are being excluded. Touch is often associated with power; frequently the message transmitted by a touch conveys a "power play."

DEFINING WOMEN BY THEIR SEXUALITY

Relating to women in a sexual manner—sexual comments about or toward specific women or women in general, such as discussing appearance or physical attributes or using sexual humor.

Valuing and praising women for their physical appearance, not for their intellectual ability.

Devaluing or ignoring comments made by women perceived as "unfeminine" or believed to be lesbian or bisexual.

Using the words "lesbian" and "bisexual" as pejorative terms, especially when women raise women's issues.

Engaging in sexually harassing behaviors or allowing others to do so.

OVERT HOSTILE BEHAVIOR TOWARD WOMEN

Ridiculing or making denigrating remarks about women's issues, or making light of issues such as sexual harassment and sexual assault.

Discouraging women from conducting research on women's issues.

Calling women names if they are interested in women's issues or protest sexism.

Making sexist remarks about women in general or about specific women.

USING HUMOR IN A HOSTILE MANNER

Engaging in negative body language or behavior (for example, men rolling their eyeballs) when women speak.

Hissing or ridiculing women who raise women's issues.

Denigrating or ridiculing women or engaging in other rude behaviors that express hostility to women.

Telling sexist or sexual jokes which denigrate women.

Not taking women's comments or their work seriously.

DEVALUATION

Devaluation is often used as a partial explanation or rationale for differential treatment.

Gender affects our view of someone's competence. What is viewed as male is usually seen as more important than that associated with women.

Perceptual bias is not uncommon. For instance, a woman's success, such as getting into a prestigious program, is said to result from "luck" or "affirmative action" while a man's similar success will be attributed to talent.

Women's issues may be devalued, as well as women's ways of speaking.

DEVALUATION AND POWER

It is the power difference between men and women that gives value to or devalues whatever differences exist.

Stereotypes which reinforce differences are maintained precisely because they reinforce power and privilege. Behaviors which are valued such as competitive, status-seeking behavior, are behaviors that reinforce privilege. Males may assert power and expect to be treated more favorably than females.

The Chilly Climate
Subtle Ways in Which Women Are Often Treated Differently at Work and in Classrooms

Bernice R. Sandler

1. What is a "chilly climate?" How does it impact individuals in the classroom?

2. How can stereotypes influence educational experience?

3. Look at the categories and examples provided in the essay. Are there any that seem dated today? How has the chilly climate taken new forms today?

4. What is the relationship between microinequities and systems of power?

5. Pick a behavior or attitude that contributes to a chilly climate provided in the article. Brainstorm a list of strategies that can be used to respond to this behavior.

Boygasms and Girlgasms

A Frank Discussion about Hormones and Gender Differences From *Whipping Girl: A Transsexual Woman on Sexism and the Scapegoating of Femininity*

Julia Serano

Julia Serano is a researcher in Evolutionary and Developmental Biology at UC Berkeley. She earned a PhD at Columbia University. In addition to her work as a biologist, she is a writer, spoken word performer, and trans activist. Her most recent book is Excluded: Making Feminist and Queer Movements More Inclusive *(2013).Other work has appeared in* BITCHfest: Ten Years of Cultural Criticism from the Pages of Bitch Magazine *and* Word Warriors: 35 Leaders in the Women's Spoken Word Movement. *This essay comes from* Whipping Girl: A Transsexual Woman on Sexism and the Scapegoating of Femininity *(2007).*

PRE-READING QUESTIONS

1. What effects do you think testosterone has on behavior?
2. Which do you think has more influence on our gendered behavior—biology or social construction? Why?

KEY TERMS

androgens
biology versus socialization
estrogen
hormones
nature vs. nurture debate
progesterone
pseudoscientific
sexism

socialization
socially constructed
socially exaggerated
testosterone
transgender
transsexual
transition

SEE THE THEMATIC TABLE OF CONTENTS, IF YOU WANT TO READ MORE ESSAYS ABOUT:

Bodies and Genders
LGBTQ Studies
Sexualities
Social Construction of Gender

Boygasms and Girlgasms
A Frank Discussion about Hormones and Gender Differences

Julia Serano

Though I am often reluctant to indulge people's fascination with the details of my physical transition from male to female, I will often make an exception regarding the psychological changes I experienced due to hormones. The reason for this is quite simple: Sex hormones have become horribly politicized in our culture, evident in the way that people blatantly blame testosterone for nearly all instances of male aggression and violence, or the way that women who become legitimately angry or upset often have their opinions dismissed as mere symptoms of their body chemistry. Such hormonal folklore has strongly influenced medicine, as evidenced by the countless shoddy, pseudoscientific studies claiming to verify popular assumptions about testosterone and estrogen. Of course, such overt politicization has created a significant backlash of people who now play down the role of hormones in human behavior, who argue that most of their presumed effects (making men overly aggressive and women overly emotional) are better explained by socialization—after all, young boys are encouraged to be aggressive and discouraged from showing emotions, and vice versa for girls.

Having experienced both female and male hormones firsthand, I feel it's my duty to spoil this nature-versus-nurture debate by offering the following description and interpretation of my personal experiences "transitioning" from testosterone to estrogen and progesterone. But before I begin, there are two important points that must be made prior to any discussion regarding hormones. First, contrary to popular belief, hormones do not simply act like unilateral on/off switches controlling female/feminine or male/masculine development. All people have both androgens (which include testosterone) and estrogens in their systems, although the balance is tipped more toward the former in men and the latter in women. Not only are there different types of androgens and estrogens, but these hormones require different steroid receptors to function, are metabolized by numerous enzymes that can shift the balance by converting one hormone to another, and function by regulating the levels of scores of "downstream genes," which are more directly responsible for producing specific hormonal effects. Because of all these variables, there's an extensive amount of natural variation built into the way individual people experience and process specific hormones.

The second issue to keep in mind is the difficulty in distinguishing "real" hormone effects from their perceived or presumed effects. For example, shortly after I began hormone therapy, I had a strong craving for eggs. I immediately attributed this to the hormones until other trans women told me that they never had similar cravings. So perhaps that was an effect of the hormones only I had. Or maybe I was going through an "egg phase" that just so happened to coincide with the start of my hormone therapy. Hence, the problem: Not only can hormones affect individuals differently, but we sometimes attribute coincidences to them and project our own expectations onto them.

For these reasons, I will limit my discussion here to those hormonal changes I have experienced that have been corroborated by other trans women I have spoken with. Also, rather than get into the more physical effects of hormones (i.e., muscle/fat distribution, hair growth, etc.) which are not in dispute, I will focus primarily on the "psychological" changes—in my emotions, senses, and sexuality—that I experienced early on when I began taking estrogen along with an anti-androgen, which suppresses endogenous testosterone levels, to shift my hormonal balance into the range that most adult women experience.

People often say that female hormones make women "more emotional" than men, but in my view such claims are an oversimplification. How would I describe the changes I went through, then? In retrospect, when testosterone was the predominant sex hormone in my body, it was as though a thick curtain were draped over my emotions. It deadened their intensity, made all of my feelings pale and vague as if they were ghosts that would haunt me. But on estrogen, I find that I have all of the same emotions that I did back then, only now they come in crystal clear. In other words, it is not the actual emotions, but rather their intensity that has changed—the highs are way higher and the lows are way lower. Another way of saying it is that I feel my emotions more now; they are in the foreground rather than the background of my mind.

The anecdote that perhaps best captures this change occurred about two months after I started hormone therapy. My wife, Dani, and I had an argument and at one point I started to cry—something that was not all that uncommon for me when I was hormonally male. What was different was that after about a minute or so, I began to laugh while simultaneously continuing to cry. When Dani asked me why I was laughing, I replied, "I can't turn it off." Back when I was hormonally male, I felt as though I was always capable of stopping the cry, of holding it all in, if I really wanted to. Now, I find it nearly impossible to hold back the tears once I start crying. I've learned instead to just go with it, to let myself experience the cry, and it feels a lot more cathartic as a result.

In general, even though my emotions are much more intense these days, I certainly do not feel as though they get in the way of my logic or reasoning, or that they single-handedly control my every thought or decision. I remain perfectly capable of acting on rational thought rather than following my feelings. However, what I can no longer do (at least to the extent that I used to) is completely ignore my emotions, repress them, or entirely shut them out of my mind.

The change in the intensity of my emotions is paralleled in my sense of touch as well. I cannot say for sure that my sense of touch has improved—that I am able to feel things that I couldn't before—but it surely plays a greater role in how I experience the world. Whenever I am interested in something, whether it's a book, a piece of artwork, an article of clothing, or an object or material of any kind, I feel compelled to touch it, to handle it, as though my understanding of it would be incomplete without the tactile knowledge of how it physically feels to me. In contrast, when hormonally male, I generally felt satisfied with simply seeing an object of interest.

Unlike my emotions and sense of touch, which seem to have primarily increased in *intensity*, my sense of smell has definitely increased in *sensitivity*. That is to say, I now can smell things that I was previously unable to detect. Though it sounds like a cliche, during the first spring after my transition I was blown away by how flowers smelled to me. While I'd always found them very fragrant, I suddenly smelled all of these subtle notes and perfumes that I had never been aware of before. I also had similar experiences with the aroma of certain foods. Perhaps the most interesting facet of this change for me has been sensing new smells in people. I find that men now sometimes have a really strong, somewhat sweet smell to them that I had never been privy to before. But it is not simply that I have gained the ability to pick up on male odors or "pheromones," because I also now detect new smells with women. During my transition, I noticed that when I would kiss Dani or nuzzle my nose into her neck, it felt as though fireworks were going off in my brain. I was barraged with amazingly sweet, soothing, and sensual smells that not only sexually stimulated me, but also made me feel closer to her, as if I were connected to her in a way that I hadn't been before. Indeed, the increase in my senses of smell and touch, and the way I feel more "in touch" with my emotions, has led me to feel more in tune with the world, and with other people.

Without a doubt, the most profound change that has come with my hormonal transition has been in my sexuality. In fact, the very first change that I noticed—which came during my first few weeks on estrogen/anti-androgens—was a sharp decrease in my sex drive. I noticed this for the first time at the end of a really busy week, after working many hours and being out late most nights. It suddenly occurred to me, only after the fact, that I had neither had sex nor masturbated during the entire week. While this may not seem impressive to some readers, for me, at the time, it was completely unheard-of. I could barely go a day, let alone two days, without some form of release (in fact, for much of my adult male life, masturbating was an activity that I typically indulged in one to three times a day). While my sex drive may have decreased, this surely does not mean that I have lost interest in sex entirely. I still intensely enjoy masturbation and sex, it's just that I crave it about three to four times a week rather than one to three times a day.

While the quantity of my sexual experiences has decreased significantly, the quality of those experiences has increased exponentially. Indeed, I called this chapter "Boygasms and Girlgasms" because, for me, the differences in how my body responds to sexual stimuli—how I "get off," if you will—has been the most dramatic (and in many ways most enjoyable) hormonal change that I've experienced. I began to notice these changes within the first few weeks of starting hormone therapy. Even before I lost the ability to maintain erections, I found that what used to excite me—that back-and-forth stroking action that males typically prefer—really wasn't doing the trick anymore. I just felt like I needed something more. So I started experimenting with Dani's vibrators. When I had tried them in the past, they always felt like too much stimulation, but now they suddenly felt absolutely incredible. And back when I was hormonally male, sexual stimulation would cause me to climb rather rapidly toward the peak of orgasm; if I wanted the experience to last longer, I had to keep pulling back just before I hit that precipice. But now I found that I could go way beyond what used to be the point of orgasm, writhing for fifteen minutes in a sexual state that was far more intense than I had ever experienced before. Now, my orgasms are way more in the female rather than male range: They typically take longer to achieve (but are well worth the wait), each one has a different flavor and intensity, they are less centralized and more diffuse throughout my body, and they are often multiple.

Not surprisingly, changes in my senses have also greatly influenced my sexuality. Not only am I more sexually excited by the scent of my partner, but the increase in my tactile senses make my whole body feel alive—electric—during sex. Nowhere is this more obvious than in my nipples, which seem to have a direct connection to my groin. It also has become apparent to me that I am less visual with regard to my sexuality. I don't think that I recognized this at first, probably because it is harder to notice the gradual loss of a sensation than the appearance of a new one. I only realized it about a year later, when I began taking progesterone for ten days out of the month to simulate the endogenous expression of progesterone in most women. The first thing I noticed upon taking progesterone is that my sex drive, particularly in response to visual input, sharply increased. In fact, the visual effects of progesterone very much reminded me of how I responded to visual stimuli when I was hormonally male.

Upon hearing my experience, I am sure that some people—particularly those who favor social, rather than biological, explanations of gender difference—will be somewhat disappointed at the predictable nature of my transformation. Some may even assume that I am buying into female stereotypes when I describe myself becoming a more weepy, touchy-feely, flower-adoring, less sexually aggressive person. Not only are similar experiences regularly described by other trans women, but trans men typically give reciprocal accounts: They almost universally describe an increase in their sex drives (which become more responsive to visual inputs), male-type orgasms (more centralized, quicker to achieve), a decrease in their sense of smell, and more difficulty crying and discerning their emotions.[1]

On the other hand, those who are eager to have popular presumptions about hormones confirmed will probably be just as disappointed to hear what has *not* noticeably changed during my hormonal transition: my sexual orientation; the "types" of women I am attracted to; my tastes in music, movies, or hobbies; my politics; my sense of humor; my levels of aggression, competitiveness, nurturing, creativity, intelligence; and my ability to read maps or do math. While it would be irresponsible for me to say that these human traits are entirely hormone-independent (as it is possible that fetal hormones potentially play some role in predisposing us to such traits), they clearly are not controlled by adult hormone levels to the extent that many people argue or assume.

While transsexual accounts of hormones are largely in agreement with one another, I also find it illuminating to examine the more subtle differences between our individual experiences. For example, I have heard several trans men describe how they started to consume porn voraciously upon taking testosterone. While my sexuality was definitely more visual when I was hormonally male, and I certainly enjoyed looking at porn on occasion, I still always preferred erotic stories and fantasies to pictures of naked bodies. Similarly, I have heard some trans men say that they almost never cry since taking testosterone, whereas I used to cry somewhat often (although not nearly as often as I do now) when I was hormonally male. Some trans men have also described becoming more aggressive or competitive since taking testosterone (although many others describe themselves as becoming more calm).[2] However, when I was hormonally male, I typically found myself to be the least aggressive or competitive guy in any room that I entered. This is not to say that I was passive, as I have always been motivated and eager to succeed at any task I have taken on. Rather, I have never really felt any desire to have my success come at the expense of others.

Thus, it is clear that typical male levels of testosterone, in and of itself, are insufficient to produce many of these stereotypically male behaviors, most likely because of the variability that exists from person to person in the way this hormone is processed and experienced. While a part of me is tempted to attribute my apparent imperviousness to testosterone to the fact that I am trans—that on some level, I was never fully or completely male—I also realize that many

---

[1]For trans male accounts of hormones, see Patrick Califia, *Speaking Sex to Power: The Politics of Queer Sex* (San Francisco: Cleis Press, 2002), 393–401; Jamison Green, *Becoming a Visible Man* (Nashville: Vanderbilt University Press, 2004), 98–102, 151–152; Henry Rubin, *Self-Made Men: Identity and Embodiment Among Transsexual Men* (Nashville Vanderbilt Unisversity Press, 2003), 152–163; and Max Wolf Valerio, *The Testosterone Files: My Hormonal and Social Transformation from Female to Male* (Emeryville, CA: Seal Press, 2006).

[2]Summarized in Joan Roughgarden, *Evolution's Rainbow: Diversity, Gender, and Sexuality in Nature and People* (Berkeley: University of California Press, 2004), 220–221; see also sources cited in the previous note.

cissexual people are exceptions in this regard as well. I know plenty of non-trans men who are not particularly into porn, who are not very aggressive, and/or who often cry. I have also met women who have high sex drives, who enjoy porn, and/or who are just as aggressive and competitive as the average alpha male. Thus, there seems to be more variation among women and among men than there is between the averages of these two groups.

Acknowledging this variation is absolutely crucial in order for us to finally move beyond overly simplistic (and binary) biology-versus-socialization debates regarding gender. After all, there are very real *biological* differences between hormones: Testosterone will probably make any given person cry less frequently and have a higher sex drive than estrogen will. However, if one were to argue that this biological difference represents an *essential* gender difference—one that holds true for all women and all men—they would be incorrect. After all, there are some men who cry more than certain women, and some women who have higher sex drives than certain men. Perhaps what is most telling is that, as a society, we regulate these hormonally influenced behaviors in a way that seems to exaggerate their natural effects. We actively discourage boys from crying, even though testosterone itself should reduce the chance of this happening. And we encourage men to act on their sex drives (by praising them as "studs") while discouraging women from doing the same (by dismissing them "sluts"), despite the fact that most women will end up having a lower sex drive than most men anyway.

While many gender theorists have focused their efforts on attempting to demonstrate that this sort of socialization *produces* gender differences, it seems to me more accurate to say that in many cases socialization acts to exaggerate biological gender differences that already exist. In other words, it coaxes those of us who are exceptional (e.g., men who cry often or women with high sex drives) to hide or curb those tendencies, rather than simply falling where we may on the spectrum of gender diversity. By attempting to play down or erase the existence of such exceptions, socialization distorts biological gender difference to create the impression that essential differences exist between women and men. Thus, the primary role of socialization is not to produce gender difference de novo, but to create the illusion that female and male are mutually exclusive, "opposite" sexes.

Recognizing the distinction between biological and essential gender differences has enormous ramifications for the future of gender activism. Since there is natural variation in our drives and the way we experience the world, attempts to minimize gender differences (i.e., insisting that people strive to be unisex or androgynous) are rather pointless; we should instead learn to embrace all forms of gender diversity, whether typical (feminine women and masculine men) or exceptional (masculine women and feminine men). Further, since some attributes that are considered feminine (e.g., being more in tune with one's emotions) or masculine (e.g., being preoccupied with sex) are clearly affected by our hormones, attempts by some gender theorists to frame femininity and masculinity as being entirely artificial or performative seem misplaced. Rather than focus on how femininity and masculinity are produced (an issue that has unfortunately dominated the field of gender studies of late), we should instead turn our attention to the ways these gender traits are interpreted.

The issue of interpretation becomes obvious when considering transsexuals. For example, one cannot help but notice how much more empowering trans male descriptions of hormonal transition tend to sound compared to those of trans women. Trans men experience an increase in their sex drive, become less emotional, and their bodies become harder and stronger—all of these changes having positive connotations in our society. In contrast, I have experienced a decrease in my sex drive and become more emotional, softer, and weaker—all traits that are viewed negatively. The reason for these differing connotations is obvious: In our culture, femininity and femaleness are not appreciated nor valued to the extent that masculinity and maleness are. And while embracing my own femaleness and femininity during my transition was personally empowering and rewarding, I nevertheless felt overwhelmed by all of the negative connotations and inferior meanings that other people began to project onto me. These meanings were not only projected onto my female body, but onto the hormones themselves: from the warning label on my progesterone prescription that read, "May cause drowsiness or dizziness" and "Avoid operating heavy machinery," to the men who have hinted that my female hormones were responsible for the fact that I disagreed with their opinion, and the women who sneered, "Why would you ever want to do that?" upon finding out that I have chosen to cycle my hormones.

Once we start thinking about gender as being socially exaggerated (rather than socially constructed), we can finally tackle the issue of sexism in our society without having to dismiss or undermine biological sex in the process. While biological gender differences are very real, most of the connotations, values, and assumptions we associate with female and male biology are not.

Name _____   Date _____

Course & section: _____   Instructor _____

Boygasms and Girlgasms
A Frank Discussion about Hormones and Gender Differences

Julia Serano

1. Describe the differences and similarities between Julia Serano's behavior before and after transition.

2. Explain how Serano's perspective is distinct from other perspectives on sex and gender that have been discussed in this course.

3. What is the nature argument? What is the nurture argument? Why do you think the nature versus nurture debate is so polarized? Why do you think many are invested in the nature vs. nurture debate?

4. What is Serano's position on biology and social construction as determinants of gendered behavior? Then explain *your* position.

5. Visit www.wpath.org. What are their mission, vision, and goals? Read one of the recent news stories on the WPATH website (see "News Room" tab). How does the topic relate to our discussions of biology, social construction, and/or transliberation?

The Declaration of Sentiments and Resolutions

Elizabeth Cady Stanton

Elizabeth Cady Stanton was a women's rights leader who advocated for the abolition of slavery, temperance and, most famously, for suffrage for women. In collaboration with Lucretia Mott, Martha Wright, Mary Ann M'Clintock and Jane Hunt, Stanton organized The Seneca Falls Women's Rights Convention of 1848. Stanton drafted "The Declaration of Sentiments and Resolutions," which was signed by 86 women and 32 men attending the convention. Stanton's other achievements include founding and serving as the first president of the National Woman Suffrage Association in 1869 and publishing The Woman's Bible (1895), a critique of how the Bible and religion played a role in denying women's rights.

PRE-READING QUESTIONS

1. What do you know about the declaration of independence?
2. What do you know about the women's movement? When did it start? Why?

KEY TERMS

disenfranchisement
inalienable rights
Seneca Falls Women's Rights Convention
tyranny

SEE THE THEMATIC TABLE OF CONTENTS, IF YOU WANT TO READ MORE ESSAYS ABOUT:

Feminism and Social Movements

The Declaration of Sentiments and Resolutions

Elizabeth Cady Stanton

When, in the course of human events, it becomes necessary for one portion of the family of man to assume among the people of the earth a position different from that which they have hitherto occupied, but one to which the laws of nature and of nature's God entitle them, a decent respect to the opinions of mankind requires that they should declare the causes that impel them to such a course.

We hold these truths to be self-evident: that all men and women are created equal; that they are endowed by their Creator with certain inalienable rights; that among these are life, liberty, and the pursuit of happiness; that to secure these rights governments are instituted, deriving their just powers from the consent of the governed. Whenever any form of government becomes destructive of these ends, it is the right of those who suffer from it to refuse allegiance to it, and to insist upon the institution of a new government, laying its foundation on such principles, and organizing its powers in such form, as to them shall seem most likely to effect their safety and happiness. Prudence, indeed, will dictate that governments long established should not be changed for light and transient causes; and accordingly all experience hath shown that mankind are more disposed to suffer. while evils are sufferable, than to right themselves by abolishing the forms to which they are accustomed. But when a long train of abuses and usurpations, pursuing invariably the same object, evinces a design to reduce them under absolute despotism, it is their duty to throw off such government, and to provide new guards for their future security. Such has been the patient sufferance of the women under this government, and such is now the necessity which constrains them to demand the equal station to which they are entitled.

The history of mankind is a history of repeated injuries and usurpations on the part of man toward woman, having in direct object the establishment of an absolute tyranny over her. To prove this, let facts be submitted to a candid world.

He has never permitted her to exercise her inalienable right to the elective franchise.

He has compelled her to submit to laws, in the formation of which she had no voice.

He has withheld from her rights which are given to the most ignorant and degraded men— both natives and foreigners.

Having deprived her of this first right of a citizen, the elective franchise, thereby leaving her without representation in the halls of legislation, he has oppressed her on all sides.

He has made her, if married, in the eye of the law, civilly dead.

He has taken from her all right in property, even to the wages she earns.

From Elizabeth Cady Stanton, *A History of Woman Suffrage*, vol. 1 (Rochester, N.Y.: Fowler and Wells, 1889), pages 70–71.

He has made her, morally, an irresponsible being, as she can commit many crimes with impunity, provided they be done in the presence of her husband. In the covenant of marriage, she is compelled to promise obedience to her husband, he becoming, to all intents and purposes, her master—the law giving him power to deprive her of her liberty, and to administer chastisement.

He has so framed the laws of divorce, as to what shall be the proper causes, and in case of separation, to whom the guardianship of the children shall be given, as to be wholly regardless of the happiness of women—the law, in all cases, going upon a false supposition of the supremacy of man, and giving all power into his hands.

After depriving her of all rights as a married woman, if single, and the owner of property, he has taxed her to support a government which recognizes her only when her property can be made profitable to it.

He has monopolized nearly all the profitable employments, and from those she is permitted to follow, she receives but a scanty remuneration. He closes against her all the avenues to wealth and distinction which he considers most homorable to himself. As a teacher of theology, medicine, or law, she is not known.

He has denied her the facilities for obtaining a thorough education, all colleges being closed against her.

He allows her in church, as well as state, but a subordinate position, claiming apostolic authority for her exclusion from the ministry, and, with some exceptions, from any public participation in the affairs of the church.

He has created a false public sentiment by giving to the world a different code of morals for men and women, by which moral delinquencies which exclude women from society, are not only tolerated, but deemed of little account in man.

He has usurped the prerogative of Jehovah himself, claiming it as his right to assign for her a sphere of action, when that belongs to her conscience and to her God.

He has endeavored, in every way that he could, to destroy her confidence in her own powers, to lessen her self-respect, and to make her willing to lead a dependent and abject life.

Now, in view of this entire disfranchisement of one-half the people of this country, their social and religious degradation—in view of the unjust laws above mentioned, and because women do feel themselves aggrieved, oppressed, and fraudulently deprived of their most sacred rights, we insist that they have immediate admission to all the rights and privileges which belong to them as citizens of the United States.

Name _____   Date _____

Course & section: _____   Instructor _____

The Declaration of Sentiments and Resolutions

Elizabeth Cady Stanton

1. Classify the demands made by the writers of the Declaration of Sentiments. What are the major topics of their demands? What are their specific demands?

2. Compare the Declaration of Sentiments to the document upon which it was modeled, the Declaration of Independence. How does the fight for independence from the British empire compare to women's situation as described here?

3. Why did Stanton name women's subservience as "absolute tyranny"? What social institutions have contributed to this tyranny?

4. Based on the Declaration of Sentiments and Resolutions, what advances have movements for gender equality made since 1848?

5. What about this document still seems relevant today? Based on the current social and political climate, what would you add? Write an updated version of the Declaration of Sentiments. Rename it if you would like to.

APPENDIX

Exercises

TABLE OF CONTENTS FOR EXERCISES

ANALYZE GENDERED DISCOURSES

ANALYZE DIGITAL MEDIA

ENGAGE AND TRANSFORM

OBSERVE AND PARTICIPATE

IDENTIFY THE FACTS

FOR YOUR INFORMATION

Name _____   Date _____

Course & section: _____   Instructor _____

Analyze Gendered Discourses: Clothing Stores

For this assignment, you will go to a store where clothes are sold.

CONTEMPLATE

Before going, write down some preliminary thoughts about what you expect to find:

INVESTIGATE

Name of store: Date of observation:

1. Walk through the entire store to get an overall impression. Pick five words to describe the gender messages:

2. Examine the clothing closely. Identify clothes designed for men, women, boys, girls, and unisex audience. Now describe the clothing in detail (colors, types/kinds of clothes, words on clothing, prices, sizes). List the differences in clothes aimed at men/boys and girls/women. Note the similarities.

ANALYZE AND REFLECT

3. Taken individually and collectively what messages about masculinity, femininity, and gender are promoted through the clothes and store layout?

4. Using quotes and examples from course readings and materials explain the possible consequences (both short- and long-term) of such messages.

5. Identify three changes you would propose to individuals, clothing manufacturers, and storeowners.

Analyze Gendered Discourses: Hygiene Products

For this assignment, you will go to a store where hygiene products are sold (e.g., drugstore, supermarket, grocery store, etc.).

CONTEMPLATE

Before going, write down some preliminary thoughts about what you expect to find:

INVESTIGATE

Name of store: Date of observation:

1. Walk through the hygiene section to get an overall impression. Pick five words to describe the gender messages:

2. Choose a specific type product to examine closely (shampoo, deodorant, soap, body cleansers). Identify products aimed at men, women, unisex. Now describe the products packaging in detail (colors, types/kinds of products, words on packages, prices, scents, names). List the differences in products aimed at men and women. Note the similarities.

ANALYZE AND REFLECT

3. Taken individually and collectively what messages about masculinity and femininity are promoted through the products and packaging?

4. Using quotes and examples from course readings and materials explain the possible consequences (both short- and long-term) of such messages.

5. Identify three changes you would propose to individuals, hygiene product manufacturers, and storeowners.

Name _____   Date _____

Course & section: _____   Instructor _____

Analyze Gendered Discourses: Children's Literature

For this assignment, you will go to a public library or a bookstore or with children's section to examine the construction of gender in books aimed at children.

CONTEMPLATE

Before going, write down some preliminary thoughts about what you expect to find:

INVESTIGATE

Name of store/library: Date of observation:

1. Walk through the children's section to get an overall impression. Does the store/library divide the books by gender? Pick five words to describe the overall gender messages:

2. Next select several books to examine closely. Identify books aimed at girls, boys, and unisex audience. Now describe the how gender is constructed through children's literature. Note the colors, types/kinds of stories, words on covers, images, etc. Who is included? Who is excluded? List the differences in books aimed at boys and girls. Note the similarities.

ANALYZE AND REFLECT

3. What messages about masculinity and femininity are taught through children's literature?

4. Using evidence from course texts explain the possible consequences (both short- and long-term) of such messages.

5. Identify three changes you would propose to authors, publishers, bookstores, and libraries.

Name _____   Date _____

Course & section: _____   Instructor _____

Analyze Gendered Discourses: Children's Television

For this assignment, you will examine the construction of gender in an episode of a children's television program.

CONTEMPLATE

Write down some preliminary thoughts about what you expect to find:

INVESTIGATE

Title of show/episode:

Air/Release date:

Watch mode: broadcast   on-demand

                     DVD   online   other (specify)

1. Get an overall impression. Watch the entire program. What stories are told about men, women, transgender people, boys, girls, gender? Pick five words to describe the overall gender messages:

2. Examine the program closely. What is the premise of the show? Who are the characters? What do they look like? Who is included? Who is excluded? Pay attention to the language. Describe the content (images, themes, ideology). What races are represented? Sexualities? What about socio-economic class? Ability? What roles do the characters fulfill? What skills/ attributes do they possess? Briefly outline the plot for this episode.

ANALYZE AND REFLECT

3. What messages about masculinity and femininity are taught through children's television?

4. Using quotes and examples from course texts, explain the possible consequences (both short- and long-term) of such messages.

5. Identify three changes you would propose to individuals, television networks and advertisers.

Name _____ Date _____

Course & section: _____ Instructor _____

Analyze Gendered Discourses: Children's Toys

For this assignment, you will go to a place where toys are sold to examine the construction of gender in toys aimed at children.

CONTEMPLATE

Before going, write down some preliminary thoughts about what you expect to find:

INVESTIGATE

Name of store:

Type of store: General Department   Toy store   Other (specify)

1. Walk through the toy department to get an overall impression. Pick five words to describe the overall gender messages:

2. Choose a genre (games, infant and toddler, dolls/action figures, dress up, make believe) for closer analysis. Look at several examples. Categorize the toys or games as either marketed specifically towards girls, boys, or unspecified. Describe the toys (colors, packaging, types/kinds of toys, and words on packages). List the differences in products aimed at boys and girls. Note the similarities.

ANALYZE AND REFLECT

3. What messages about masculinity and femininity are taught to children through toys?

4. Using quotes and examples from course texts explain the possible consequences (both short- and long-term) of such messages.

5. Identify three changes you would propose to individuals, toy manufacturers, and toystore owners.

Name _____   Date _____

Course & section: _____   Instructor _____

Analyze Gendered Discourses: Mainstream Magazines

For this assignment, you will examine the construction of gender in a contemporary magazine.

CONTEMPLATE

Before reading, write down some preliminary thoughts about what you expect to find:

INVESTIGATE

Name of magazine: Issue date:

Audience: Women   Men   General

Category: Fashion   Lifestyle   Health   Other

1. Flip through the magazine to get an overall impression. Pick five words to describe the overall gender messages:

Read the magazine closely. Look at the images and articles.

2. Describe the content (images, headlines, language, themes, and ideology). What does your magazine teach its readers about gender?

ANALYZE AND REFLECT

3. What messages about masculinity and femininity are taught through magazines?

4. Using quotes and examples from course texts explain the possible consequences (both short- and long-term) of such messages.

5. Identify three changes you would propose to individuals, publishers and advertisers.

Analyze Gendered Discourses: Print Advertising

For this assignment, you will examine the construction of gender in a contemporary advertisement.

CONTEMPLATE

Write down some preliminary thoughts about what you expect to find:

INVESTIGATE

Location of advertisement:

Name of product: Issue date:

Audience: Women   Men   General

1. Get an overall impression. Pick five words to describe the overall gender messages:

2. Read the advertisement closely. Look at the images and language. Describe the content (images, fonts, language, themes, and ideology). What is the ad selling? Keep in mind that in addition to the overt message to buy the product ads contain additional messages that buying the product will make the purchaser more attractive, sexually appealing, happy, successful, etc.

ANALYZE AND REFLECT

3. What messages about masculinity and femininity are taught through ads?

4. Using quotes and examples from course texts explain the possible consequences (both short- and long-term) of such messages.

5. Identify three changes you would propose to individuals, product manufacturers and advertising firms.

Name _____   Date _____

Course & section: _____   Instructor _____

Analyze Gendered Discourses: Broadcast News

For this assignment, you will examine the construction of gender in an evening broadcast news program over at least three nights. Read this entire exercise before watching your first broadcast.

CONTEMPLATE

Write down some preliminary thoughts about what you expect to find:

INVESTIGATE

Date/time of broadcast: Name of network:

1. Get an overall impression. Watch the entire program. What stories are told about men, women, transgender people, sexuality, gender? Pick five words to describe the overall gender messages:

2. Examine the newscast closely. Who are the newscasters? What do they look like? Look at the images used to accompany the stories. Pay attention to the language. Describe the content (images, themes, ideology). Keep in mind that producers make choices about what constitutes news and how to relay information to viewers.

ANALYZE AND REFLECT

3. What messages about masculinity and femininity are taught through broadcast news?

4. Using quotes and examples from course texts explain the possible consequences (both short- and long-term) of such messages.

5. Think about the way that the news is reported. Identify three changes you would propose to individuals and local, national, and international news organizations.

Name _____ Date _____

Course & section: _____ Instructor _____

Analyze Gendered Discourses: Reality TV

For this assignment, you will examine the construction of gender in an episode of a reality television program.

CONTEMPLATE

Write down some preliminary thoughts about what you expect to find:

INVESTIGATE

Title of show/episode:

Air/Release date:

Watch mode: broadcast   on-demand

                     DVD   online   other (specify)

1. Get an overall impression. Watch the entire program. What stories are told about men, women, transgender people, sexuality, gender? Pick five words to describe the overall gender messages.

2. Examine the program closely. What is the premise of the show? Who are the people? What do they look like? Pay attention to the language. Describe the content (images, themes, ideology). What races are represented? Sexualities? What about socio-economic class? Ability? Keep in mind that even in reality television producers make choices about how to relay content and storylines to viewers.

ANALYZE AND REFLECT

3. What messages about masculinity and femininity are taught through reality television?

4. Using quotes and examples from course texts, explain the possible consequences (both short- and long-term) of such messages.

5. Identify three changes you would propose to individuals, television networks and advertisers.

Analyze Gendered Discourses: Greeting Cards

For this assignment, you will go to a store where greeting cards are sold and examine gender messages in greeting cards.

CONTEMPLATE

Before going, write down some preliminary thoughts about what you expect to find:

INVESTIGATE

Name of store: Date of visit:

Type of store: General/Department   Drug store Card store

                                        other (specify)

1. Walk through the greeting card racks to get an overall impression. Are the cards separated by gender? Pick five words to describe the overall gender messages:

2. Pick several cards to examine closely (baby, wedding, Mother's/Father's Day). Pay attention to colors, images, language, themes, etc. Identify cards aimed at men, women, and unisex audience. Describe the cards in detail. What holidays do they celebrate? Who is included? Who is missing? Note specifics about the cards (colors, types/kinds of cards, words/images). List the differences in cards aimed at men and women. Note the similarities.

ANALYZE AND REFLECT

3. Taken individually and collectively what messages about masculinity and femininity are promoted through greeting cards?

4. Using quotes and examples from course readings and materials explain the possible consequences (both short- and long-term) of such messages.

5. Identify three changes you would propose to individuals, greeting card publishers, and storeowners.

Name _____   Date _____

Course & section: _____   Instructor _____

Analyze Digital Media: Gender on the Web

The purpose of this exercise is to understand how gender is represented on the internet (also known as the new media), which features a vast amount of user-generated content and data. The publishing or production model of the internet is many-to-many communication, as opposed to the one-to-many model of traditional media. Thus, this exercise will help you identify the widespread public discourse and response on the topic and treatment of gender not just on the internet but in people's day-to-day lives and interactions.

CONTEMPLATE

What do you know about gender dualism and stereotypical gendered behavior?

INVESTIGATE

1. Conduct a web analysis of gender. You can use the term "gender," the prefix "gendered . . . " or a gender-focused topic relevant to you.

   What search phrase did you choose?

   Use two different search engines (Yahoo, Google, Bing, etc.) to conduct your search and analysis. Make a note of the *top five* relevant hits from each search engine and list the urls/ weblinks below.

2. Summarize your findings and analyze them. What is the nature of content available on gender or your chosen topic related to gender? What did you learn about gender based on your data?

3. Which website did you like the most? Why?

4. Which website did you like the least? Why?

5. Did the content you analyzed reinforce or resist the stereotypes of gender? Explain.

6. How does this relate (and/or not relate) to what you learned in your coursework? Give examples.

What Do Autocomplete Algorithms Reveal About Gender?

In this exercise, modeled after the UN Women's Council Campaign that produced "The Autocomplete Truth," you will explore how people use a search engine such as Google to find out more about gender. While curiosity and subsequent search for answers is central to all learning, the campaign reveals that people often search about topics on gender with search terms that embody their personal as well as society's bias against women's agency as citizens, workers, innovators, creators, thinkers, scholars, and leaders.

Step 1

Please read more about the campaign here: http://www.unwomen.org/en/news/stories/2013/10/women-should-ads

1. What are your initial reactions to the campaign?

2. Do you think this campaign is empowering to women? How?

Step 2

In this autocomplete exercise, you will open the Google search engine and type in some phrases to see what autocomplete algorithms reveal.

For the best results, clear your previous browsing history, sign out of any google accounts (gmail, google+, etc.) and ensure that you are using a Google search bar. This will bring you the auto-complete responses drawn from local and global trends and not your own search history.

Note: Because results are based on popular trends they may change significantly over time. In addition to examining the autocomplete results, you can also search the terms and examine the results. Finally, also look at the "searches related to . . . " section at the bottom of the results page.

Examples of type-in phrases:

Women/men are . . .

Women/men can be . . .

Why do women/men . . .

Women/men should not . . .

Gender is . . .

Rape . . .

Sexual assault . . .

Minorities . . .

How to . . .

Why do gay/lesbian/straight/homosexual/queer/homophobic people . . .

Women's rights . . .

Men's rights . . .

Why do transgender people . . .

Why do (put race, ethnicity, or nationality here) women . . .

Women in the army/police . . .

Sexism/Racism/ethnocentrism in . . .

Feel free to come up with your own phrases. Not all the phrases have to be specifically on gender. Let the search engine reveal the current discourse and understanding of gender in the public psyche. Gender being a pervasive social phenomenon, there is an indefinite number of phrases you can type in. Use your imagination!

Step 3

1. What phrases did you type in? What were the autocomplete phrases?

2. What did the autocomplete algorithms reveal about gender?

3. Based on what you found out about other people's searches, list three things you learned about gender based on what people search about that surprised or confused you.

4. List three things you learned about gender based on what people search about that aligns with what you learned in your coursework on gender.

5. How is gender represented on the internet compared to how it is represented in traditional media such as magazines, films, and television? In what ways are the representations similar or different?

6. If there were one thing you would change about how gender is represented in the media, what would it be?

Analyze Digital Media: #Hashtag

For this exercise, you will conduct an online analysis of social media and gender/social justice. The purpose of this exercise is to understand how concerned people use the internet to protest injustice, promote social justice and raise social awareness. This exercise will help you identify the widespread public discourse and response on social and gender justice.

Find gender, race, class, and other identity-rights related hashtags. You can use your own Twitter or Facebook accounts, or a hashtag search site such as https://www.hashtags.org/ or http://hashtagify.me/

Examples of Hashtags:

On racialized violence: #lastwords; #BlackLivesMatter

On domestic violence: #whyistayed; #domesticviolence

On feminism: #YesAllWomen; #TwitterFeminism

Step 1: Find

List three hashtags related to identity, intersectionality, and feminism. You can choose one from each category, all three from one category or form your own categories based on the readings in this book.

1. #_____

2. #_____

3. #_____

Step 2: Observe

1. How are the hashtags being used? Are they trending?

2. Are the hashtags being misused or co-opted by some people to detract from the issue at hand?

3. Choose a favorite tweet/message. Why do you like it? Is it powerful? Insightful? Witty?

Step 3: Analyze

4. Do you think your chosen hashtags are effective social media tools for awareness-raising? Why or why not?

5. Can you identify a recent gender-justice related event or news that has generated a trending hashtag? What is the event and how are hashtag users talking about it?

6. If you were to develop a hashtag to highlight issues of gender/social justice what would it be?

Analyze Digital Media: Video Games

For this assignment, you will examine the construction of gender in a video game as well as its fan community. While some games can be played in a few minutes, others can take hundreds of hours to complete. Play the game for at least an hour to familiarize yourself with game mechanics and tone, style, and plot (if applicable).

1. Write down some preliminary thoughts about what you expect to find:

   Title of game: Publisher/Release date:

   Play mode: phone   computer   home console (specify)

                    Other (specify)

   Get an overall impression. What stories are told about men, women, transgender people, boys, girls, gender? The absence of certain types of people tells a story, too.

2. Pick five words to describe the overall gender messages:

Think about your choices as a player. Were you able to play as some characters but not others? Could you play a gender that was the same and/or different from the one you identify with in your own life?

3. Did gender have an impact on how you identified with the character you played or the abilities (fast, strong, clever, etc.) you had?

How do other aspects of identity intersect with gender representation in your game? What races are represented? Sexualities? What about socio-economic class? Ability? What roles do the characters fulfill? What skills/attributes do they possess?

4. Looking at the identities of the characters in this game, what messages are being sent?

Now, go online and research the fan community surrounding this game (using the name of the game and search word "forum" will be helpful in identifying where players are interacting with each other). Spend at least an hour looking at what people have to say about the game and how they interact with each other.

5. How do players interact with one other? Is the community civil, rowdy, etc.? Is gender an important factor in who is perceived to be playing the game and how they fit into the larger gaming community? What about issues of race ethnicity, sexuality, etc.?

Finally, how are video games, as both cultural artifact and opportunity for social interaction, reflective of the larger culture?

6. In doing your research, how did gender (or other aspects of identity) factor into the content of the game and the way in which players interacted with one another online?

7. Using quotes and examples from course texts explain the possible consequences (both short- and long-term) of what you discovered.

8. Identify possible solutions to the consequences you have identified. What changes would you propose to game designers, game manufacturers, forum moderators, gamers, members of the fan community?

Name _____   Date _____

Course & section: _____   Instructor _____

Analyze Digital Media: Feminism on the Web

For this exercise, you will conduct a web analysis of feminism. The purpose of this exercise is to understand how feminism is represented on the internet (also known as the new media) which features a vast amount of user generated content. The publishing or production model of the internet is many-to-many communication, as opposed to the one-to-many model of traditional media. Thus, this exercise will help you identify the widespread public discourse and response on feminism.

CONTEMPLATE

What stereotypes of feminism are you aware of?

INVESTIGATE

1. Choose two different search engines (Yahoo, Google, Bing, etc.). Search the word feminism. Make a note of the *top five* relevant hits from each search engine and list the urls/weblinks below.

2. Summarize your findings and analyze them. What is the nature of content available on feminism? What did you learn about feminism based on your data?

3. Which website did you like the most? Why?

4. Which website did you like the least? Why?

5. Did the content you analyzed reinforce or resist the stereotypes of feminism? Explain.

6. How does this relate (and/or not relate) to what you learned in your coursework? Give examples.

Analyze Digital Media: Feminist Organizations

CONTEMPLATE

What are the feminist organizations have you heard of? Have you visited their websites or followed them on social media? Which organizations or topics would you like to learn more about?

INVESTIGATE

Choose three of the following feminist organizations and visit their websites.

American Association of University Women (AAUW) http://www.aauw.org/

Association for Women's Rights in Development (AWID) http://www.awid.org/

The Audre Lorde Project http://alp.org/

Bitch Magazine http://bitchmagazine.org/

Code Pink: Women for Peace http://www.codepink4peace.org/

Emily's List http://www.emilyslist.org/

Feminist Majority Foundation http://www.feminist.org/

Feministing feministing.com

Frida: The Young Feminist Fund http://youngfeministfund.org/

Girl Scouts of the USA http://www.girlscouts.org/

Hollaback! http://www.ihollaback.org/#

MADRE http://www.madre.org/

Ms. Magazine http://msmagazine.com/blog/

National Organization for Men Against Sexism http://site.nomas.org/

National Organization for Women http://now.org/

OWL: Older Women's League http://www.owl-national.org/

The Sisterhood is Global Institute http://sigi.org/

The Third Wave Foundation http://thirdwavefund.org/

Women's International League for Peace and Freedom http://wilpfus.org/

The YWCA http://www.ywca.org/

Women in Black http://www.womeninblack.org/en/vigil

Which three organizations did you choose?

1. What is the mission of each of the three organizations?

2. What are their current campaigns or projects?

3. Are their analyses and strategies inclusive and intersectional? How so? If not, what or who is missing?

4. Based on these websites what are the most pressing issues of concern for feminists today?

REFLECT

In which of these organizations could you become involved? How?

Analyze Digital Media: LGBTQ Organizations

CONTEMPLATE

What LGBTQ organizations have you heard of? Have you visited their websites or followed them on social media? Which organizations or topics would you like to learn more about?

INVESTIGATE

Choose three of the following LGBT organizations and visit their websites.

Human Rights Campaign http://www.hrc.org/

International Lesbian and Gay Association http://ilga.org/

Lesbian Avengers http://www.lesbianavengers.com/

Michigan Women's Music Festival http://www.michfest.com/

National Gay and Lesbian Task Force http://www.ngltf.org/

Parents & Friends of Lesbians and Gays http://community.pflag.org/Page.aspx?pid=194& srcid=-2

Queer Rising http://queerrising.wordpress.com/

The Audre Lorde Project http://alp.org/about

The North American Man/Boy Love Association http://www.nambla.org/

Transgender Law Center http://transgenderlawcenter.org/

You may also choose to analyze a website of an anti-LGBTQ organization:

American Family Association http://www.afa.net/

Americans for Truth About Homosexuality http://americansfortruth.com/

Concerned Women for Americahttp://www.cwfa.org/main.asp

Family Research Council http://www.frc.org/

Family Research Institute http://www.familyresearchinst.org/

Focus on the Family http://www.focusonthefamily.com/

National Organization for Marriage http://www.nationformarriage.org/

Traditional Values Coalition http://www.traditionalvalues.org/

The Westboro Baptist Church http://www.godhatesfags.com/

Which organizations did you choose?

1. What is the mission of each of these organizations?

2. What are their current campaigns or projects?

3. Are their analyses and strategies inclusive and intersectional? How so? If not, what or who is missing?

4. Based on these websites what are the most pressing issues of concern for the LGBTQ movement today?

REFLECT

In which of these organizations could you become involved? How?

Engage and Transform: Politics and Representation: Who Represents You?

CONTEMPLATE

Do you know how to register to vote? How do you find out where to vote? How do you vote absentee? Do you change your address and find your new precinct?

INVESTIGATE

Federal Government

Visit http://www.house.gov/representatives/find/ to find your congressional district and representative.

What is your congressional district?

United States House of Representatives

a. Who represents you? Include name and political party of the representative.

b. Contact Information for   Contact Information for

    _____   _____

    Address   Address
    Phone   Phone
    Fax   Fax
    Email   Email

c. Go to their websites. What did you learn about them? (e.g., issues, committee assignments, record of voting, etc.)

United States Senate

a. Who represents you? Include name and political party of the representative.

b. Contact Information for   Contact Information for

_____   _____

     Address   Address

     Phone   Phone

     Fax   Fax

     Email   Email

c. Go to their websites. What did you learn about them? (e.g., issues, committee assignments, record of voting, etc.)

State Government

Visit http://openstates.org to find your state Senators and House Representatives.

What is your Senate district number?

a. Who represents you? Include name and political party of the representative.

b. Contact Information for   Contact Information for

_____   _____

     Address   Address

     Phone   Phone

     Fax   Fax

     Email   Email

c. Go to their websites. What did you learn about them? (e.g., issues, committee assignments, record of voting, etc.)

State House of Representatives

What is your House district number?

a. Who represents you? Include name and political party of the representative.

b. Contact Information for   Contact Information for

_____   _____

Address   Address

Phone   Phone

Fax   Fax

Email   Email

c. Go to their websites. What did you learn about them? (e.g., issues, committee assignments, record of voting, etc.)

Local Government

There are usually four levels of local government: county, municipal, town or township and special purpose governance (such as school boards). Types of local governing bodies will vary, but could include city councils (with a major and sometimes a city manager), municipal commission, town or township governments.

How your municipality is governed (council, commission, etc.)?

When and where are meetings held?

How do you access the agenda? What is on the agenda for the next meeting?

Identify at least two local representatives from any level (county, city, town/township, special purpose).

a. Who represents you? Include name and political party of the representative.

b. Contact Information for   Contact Information for

_____   _____

Address   Address

Phone   Phone

Fax   Fax

Email   Email

c. Go to their websites. What did you learn about them? (e.g., issues, committee assignments, record of voting, etc.)

Draft a Letter

Using the information you located above, choose a representative to contact.

Reflect on a separate sheet

- Choose a gendered topic you are passionate about and do your research.
- What is the problem? What can your elected representative do to support change related to this issue? You must have clear outcomes and requests.
- Make sure you address your letter properly (use the correct title, state that you are a constituent). State your support or opposition clearly.
- Personalize your letter. Make it clear why you are passionate about the topic.
- Be concise and make sure you proofread your letter.

Name _____   Date _____

Course & section: _____   Instructor _____

Engage and Transform: Civic Engagement on YOUR Campus

Civic engagement is a core component of all forms of democracy. Active involvement by all members leads to the positive growth and development of society. Further, it increases a community's overall potential for democratic participation and helps create close bonds within the community. While attending a university, your campus often becomes your main form of community, so it is important to become actively engaged for the betterment of the group as a whole. One way to get involved is student government. Learn more about your student government by answering the questions below!

CONTEMPLATE

What do you currently know about student government at your university? Have you interacted with members of your student government?

INVESTIGATE

Do some more research on your university's student government online or by contacting a representative to answer the questions below.

INVESTIGATE THE STRUCTURE

1. How is student government structured at your university? Are there committees? Branches? What are they?

2. How many members are there?

3. How does a student get involved in student government?

4. What is the budget allocated to student government at your university?

5. If you wanted to become a member of your student government how could you get involved? Are there elections? Appointments? What steps would you need to take?

INVESTIGATE THE ISSUES

1. What are the current issues that your student government is concerned about?

2. Choose one issue and find out the background about:
   a. Why is this issue important?
   b. What actions (if any) your student government has already taken?
   c. What will happen next? What are your opinions on this issue and how do you think it should be addressed?

REFLECT ON A SEPARATE SHEET

Brainstorm ways that your university could be improved.

If you had a concern as a student, how could you contact the members of your student government?

Do you know anyone who holds a student government position? Pass your concern on to your student government representative and have your voice heard!

Name _____   Date _____

Course & section: _____   Instructor _____

Attend an event or a meeting: Take Part in Your Community

DATE/TIME OF ACTIVITY

If you attended a meeting,
    Name of organization:

If you attended an event:
    Title of event and name of speaker (if applicable):
    Who sponsored the event?

CONTEMPLATE (BEFORE YOU ATTEND THE EVENT OR MEETING)

What is the topic of the event or meeting? What do you already know (or assume) about the topic or organization? What do you hope to learn?

PREPARE AND ENGAGE

1. Prepare two questions in advance of the event or meeting. Record them here:
   a. Question:

       Answer:

   b. Question:

       Answer:

RECORD NOTES (DURING THE EVENT OR MEETING)

Reflect on a separate sheet

What did you learn at the event? Were your questions about the topic answered?

Identify at least one topic and reading from your class that this event connects to. Explain the connection. Is there a next step with regard to this topic? Could you write to a newspaper or to a government representative about this issue? What would say? What could be done to make a difference?

Name _____   Date _____

Course & section: _____   Instructor _____

Engage and Transform: Volunteer: Take Part in Your Community

Date/time of activity:

Length of activity:

Organization:

CONTEMPLATE (BEFORE YOU VOLUNTEER)

1. What do you already know (or assume) about the organization for which you are volunteering?

2. What do you hope to learn?

3. Look up the organization on the internet. What is its mission?

4. How does it fulfill the mission? What services or programs does it offer?

5. What questions do you have about the organization?

REFLECT (AFTER YOU VOLUNTEER)

6. What happened? What did your volunteer time entail?

7. How did the work you did help the organization advance their work and their mission?

8. Any memorable encounters or exchanges? Describe them here.

REFLECT ON A SEPARATE SHEET

What did you learn about volunteering? How did the specific work you did help to further the mission of the organization?

Name _____ Date _____

Course & section: _____ Instructor _____

Engage and Transform: Attend a Public Meeting: Take Part in Your Community

For this exercise, choose a public meeting to attend. Examples include: school board meeting, city or township council meeting, town hall meeting with local politicians or other public hearing.

Date/time of activity:

Name of organization:

CONTEMPLATE (BEFORE YOU ATTEND THE EVENT OR MEETING)

Prior to attending the meeting, look online to find the agenda for the meeting.

What is on the agenda for the meeting? What do you already know (or assume) about the topics? What do you hope to learn?

PREPARE AND ENGAGE

1. Prepare two questions in advance of the event or meeting. Record them here:
   a. Question:

   Answer:

   b. Question:

   Answer:

RECORD NOTES (DURING THE EVENT OR MEETING)

Reflect on a separate sheet

What did you learn at the meeting? Were your questions about the topic answered?

Identify at least one topic and reading from your class that this event connects to. Explain the connection. Is there a next step with regard to this topic? Consider writing to your government representative about this issue. What would say in your letter?

Engage and Transform: Write a Letter to the Newspaper

CONTEMPLATE

Think of a community you belong to: local (home town, school system, campus), state, regional, or national. What community issues matter the most to you? Are they issues currently being debated or are they issues that you think are not getting enough attention?

INVESTIGATE

What is the name of your college newspaper?

How often/when is it published?

Where can you pick up a physical copy?

Is there an online edition? An app?

Read the letters the editor in the current edition.

    What are the topics of the letters?

    How long are they on average?

    Other observations to help you write your own letter:

Who are the editors?

How do you submit a letter to the editor? Include the instructions here.

What is the name of your local newspaper?

How often/when is it published?

Where can you pick up a physical copy?

Is there an online edition? An app?

Read the letters the editor in the current edition.

What are the topics of the letters?

How long are they on average?

Other observations to help you write your own letter:

Who are the editors?

How do you submit a letter to the editor? Include the instructions here.

Draft a letter to the newspaper

After reading the letters to the editor in your local paper and your campus paper, what issue matters the most to you?

Instructions:
- Find out the word limit for letters to the editor for the paper you are writing to.
- Write your letter right away, be timely. If your letter is in response to something you read about in the current issue, write in time to be considered for the next issue.
- State who you are and any relevant credentials.
- Letters will often be edited to fit space, so be sure to state the issue and your opinion early in your letter.
- Keep in mind that the letter will be short, so there is no need to elaborate on every point. (avoid name calling, hostility, etc.)

Attach a draft of a letter on a separate sheet of paper.

Engage and Transform: Acts of Resistance

CONTEMPLATE

Think of a time where someone you know either said or did something that you knew was belittling, disrespectful, or discriminatory to someone based on their race, gender, sexuality, or another identity. This can be your personal experience or an experience you watched happened with others.

What was the situation?

Did you intervene? If so, how and why? If not, why not?

What could you have done differently in the situation?

CREATE A PLAN OF ACTION

Create a plan for responding to a discriminatory comment or situation in the future (if it is applicable, you can draw upon the example discussed above). Below you will find a list of potential audiences, consider what the context is likely to be, your relationship to them, and the power differentials between you and them. What is the best approach to showing that you do not agree with this person's actions?

Friends:

Family Members:

Teachers:

Managers:

REFLECT

Which of the audiences do you think will be the most challenging to have some of these difficult conversations with? Why? What are some additional ways to show your resistance, besides direct confrontation?

Engage and Transform: Difficult Dialogue

CONTEMPLATE

Imagine a time when you engaged in a conversation about race, gender, sexuality, or a related issue and the conversation did not go as you had hoped or imagine a conversation that you would like to have on these issues. Perhaps the topic is a current event, your participation in this class or a gender or social justice issue of importance to you. Often these are difficult dialogues.

PREPARE

Rather than replaying word-by-word a conversation you have had, our goal is to create a space to imagine this dialogue and to strategize another outcome based on your participation in the conversation. Many of you will have experienced similar outcomes, thus we will imagine a general version of the dialogue.

ANSWER THESE QUESTIONS

1. What is the topic of your difficult dialogue?

2. How did this conversation end? (Often these conversations do not end well—meaning the disagreement might escalate or might create ongoing tension.)

3. How many characters does this dialogue involve?

4. Create a character sketch for each of the players in your dialogue. Clearly describe each of them. Ultimately you will be playing this script with others, so be sure to describe the characters' mannerisms, dress, actions, and words.

Character One:

Gender:

Dress:

Mannerisms/Actions:

What is this character's role in the family or in the community?

Because the dialogue will be replayed with new strategies and, hopefully, new outcomes, the actors must be very clear on the ideology of the character they are playing. The actors must act and react in character! Rate their views on social issues, particularly gender and feminist issues:

Conservative		**Moderate**		**Liberal/Progressive**
(Extremely)				(Extremely)
1	2	3	4	5

Character Two:

Gender:

Dress:

Mannerisms/Actions:

What is this character's role in the family or in the community?

Because the dialogue will be replayed with new strategies and, hopefully, new outcomes, the actors must be very clear on the ideology of the character they are playing. The actors must act and react in character! Rate their views on social issues, particularly gender and feminist issues:

Conservative		**Moderate**		**Liberal/Progressive**
(Extremely)				(Extremely)
1	2	3	4	5

Script:

How does the dialogue begin?

How do you expect the different characters to respond?

Anticipated ending: How do you anticipate the dialogue to end?

Hoped for ending: How would you like this conflict to resolve?

What could you have done differently in the situation?

REHEARSE THE SCRIPT

Choose class members to play out the script with you. You should play yourself. Give each player a sketch of the character they are playing and give them a script. Play the script one time as you anticipate it would go, without changes.

As a group (or with an audience), brainstorm ways that *you* can respond differently in conversation. What are some strategies and alternate reactions that you might use when you have this conversation again?

Reenact the dialogue with the changes. Then discuss the effectiveness of various strategies. Reenact the scene with new strategies until a resolution is reached.

PARTICIPATION GUIDELINES

1. Change is the goal, but it must be real not magical. No magical transformations!

2. After the scene has been enacted once all the way through, participants can stop the action to: announce that the scene has lost reality or to ask a character or characters questions and to take the part of the feminist to act out new strategies.

3. Our focus will be on what you can do. The change in the other actors in the scene *must be* in response to your efforts. We can take the role of the other actors in the scene in order to try to understand them and to present problems (especially to make the scene more realistic).

4. Take risks! Take this experience as the opportunity to practice, to share what we know and to test possibilities!

REFLECT

What happened?

What new strategies did you gain from your collaboration with your peers?

What advice do you have for others who engage in difficult dialogues?

Observe and Participate: Feminist Dinner Party

CONTEMPLATE

Have you ever spoken with your friends about gender issues, sexism, feminism or social justice issues? If so, what topics came up? If not, what gender and feminist issues would you like to talk about with your friends?

INVESTIGATE

Host a "feminist dinner party" or coffee or something similar. This does not have to be a real dinner party; you may meet friends on campus or have them over for coffee. No cooking is required. Choose three to five guests and bring them together to discuss feminism.

Who are your guests? Why did you invite them?

In advance of the dinner party, prepare at least five questions to ask your guests about feminism, gender, things you have learned in class, etc. Let your readings for class be your inspiration.

   1.

   2.

   3.

   4.

   5.

RECORD

Describe what happened at the "feminist dinner party"? How did your friends answer your questions?

REFLECT ON A SEPARATE SHEET

Think about what happened. What did you learn about your friends? How does what happened relate to issues raised by feminism and by your course readings and discussions?

Observe and Participate: Elevator speech

CONTEMPLATE

In previous conversations you have had about feminism, what was the conversation like? What topics were discussed? What were the participants' perspectives?

INVESTIGATE

For this exercise you need to create a short, engaging speech where you explain feminist ideas and concepts in a format that is appropriate for a general audience. The term elevator speech comes from the idea that you could give your speech in the amount of time you have during an elevator ride (1–2 minutes).

What does feminism offer? Identify four concepts from class discussions and readings that are appropriate for a general audience. Write them in your own words.

1.

2.

3.

4.

What are the benefits? Explain how your listener may benefit from feminism.

1.

2.

3.

4.

Now you need to practice your speech out loud. Make sure you are using direct and clear language. Define any terms. Become familiar with your key points. Time yourself.

1st attempt _____

2nd attempt_____

3rd attempt_____

Finally, go out and give your speech to someone (friend, roommate, family member etc.).

REFLECT

How did they react? What feedback did you get? What would you change about your speech now?

Name _____   Date _____

Course & section: _____   Instructor _____

Observe and Participate: Participant Observation: "Fly on the Wall"

For this exercise, you will choose a setting to analyze and explore the idea that institutions produce gender differences. You will observe interactions and events going on in a public space, for example, in the grounds and buildings on campus, a shopping mall, park, street fair, concert, church or some other organization. While you will be a part of your chosen setting's human environment, you will act as a non-participant observer.

INVESTIGATE

Describe the space you observed and explain why did you choose that particular setting?

How does this setting usually "create" and reproduce gender norms? What expectations or preconceived notions did you have before you began your observation?

How is this space gendered?

List the three most significant observations.

Briefly analyze your findings. What did you learn about gender difference and gender norms? How do your findings and observations relate to theoretical perspectives on gender that you learned about in your coursework, for example, androcentrism, gender polarization, biological determinism, etc.?

Observe and Participate: Feminism Survey

Step 1

Administer this informal survey about people's ideas and attitudes about feminism to five respondents. Inform participants that this research will be used for class purposes only and will not be used outside the classroom. Record answers below.

Question 1: I would use the following terms to describe a person with a strong opinion about women's rights issues.

Respondent	Answers
1.	
2.	
3.	
4.	
5.	

Question 2: Fill in the blank. A feminist is _____.

Respondent	Answers
1.	
2.	
3.	
4.	
5.	

Question 3: Is feminism today relevant to most women?

Respondent	Answers
1.	
2.	
3.	
4.	
5.	

Question 4: Is feminism relevant to you personally?

Respondent	Answers
1.	
2.	
3.	
4.	
5.	

Step 2: Reflect on your gathered data

Based on your gathered data, what are the three most positive and negative responses to feminism?

Does your data support stereotypes that circulate about feminism? Why or why not?

Based on your gathered data, is there a relationship between people's favorable or unfavorable response to feminism and their beliefs about its relevance?

Did your findings surprise you? Why or why not?

If you were to create in-depth interview questions based on this exploratory survey on people's responses to and attitudes about feminism what would your questions be?

Observe and Participate: Oral History Exercise

The purpose of this assignment is for you to understand changing processes of gender socialization. You will conduct interviews of three people of different generations—ideally from the age brackets 20–40; 41–60 and 61+ years—about how each was socialized by family and school. When you have completed the interviews, write up a report on your findings.

Before conducting each interview, ask for permission to share your interview write-up with your classmates and instructor. Clearly explain that this exercise is for a class and will not be used in any way outside of the class.

Step 1: The Interviews

Through semi-structured interviews, you will attempt to find out how the people you interview learned about and experienced gender in their childhood, youth, and early adulthood. Make sure to explore the questions presented here, and any others you think would provide information. Just be sure to ask the same questions of each person. Do not interview the people together because they might contradict one another!

1. What chores did girls and women do at your house when you were growing up? How did you feel about that *then*?

2. What chores did boys and men do at your house when you were growing up? How did you feel about that *then*?

3. Were the punishments administered to boys and girls different? If so, how?

4. Were the presents given to boys and girls different? If so, how?

5. What subjects and activities did you enjoy most at school? Why?

6. What were the expectations for boys about dating? For girls?

7. Were there subjects or activities you were interested in, but could not or did not pursue? Why not? How did you feel about that *then*?

8. Did one or both of your parents work outside the home while you were growing up? What work did they do? Do you think those work patterns influenced the kind of work you have done in your own life? How?

9. Over your lifetime, what did you see as the main changes in how gender affects people's lives. Overall, would you say these changes are positive or negative?

Step 2: The Report

Write down the names (you can use pseudonyms to protect privacy) and ages of your respondents. What is their gender? What is your relationship to them?

Write a report describing the findings from your interviews in a concise, logical, and respectful paper. In your conclusion, address one aspect of your own gender socialization that you are thinking about in new ways as a result of doing this oral history exercise. Brainstorm your conclusions here. Attach your report to this exercise.

Identify the Facts: Composition of Our Communities

CONTEMPLATE

Think about the state where you grew up and/or currently live. What do you estimate is the racial/ethnic composition of your state? How many people have a Bachelor's degree or higher? How many people live below the poverty level? What percent of businesses are owned by women?

INVESTIGATE

Visit the United States Census Bureau [http://www.census.gov/] and enter the term "State and County QuickFacts" in the search box and then click on the top result to access the State & County QuickFacts page.

Select the *state* you chose above and find the answers to these questions:

1. Race/ethnicity make-up of your state:

2. Percent having a Bachelor's degree or higher:

3. Average persons per household:

4. Median household income:

5. Percent of persons below the poverty level:

6. Percent of black-owned firms:

7. Percent of Hispanic-owned firms:

8. Percent of American Indian, Alaska Native-owned firms:

9. Percent of Asian-owned firms:

10. Percent of women-owned firms:

REFLECT ON A SEPARATE SHEET

Look back at the answers to your contemplation questions; what information do you find surprising? What met your expectations? Think about your daily experience in this state. Based on the demographic data you found, do you regularly see evidence of this (i.e., persons below the poverty level or women-owned firms)? Why or why not? Why so you think some of these are more visible than others?

Part Two

INVESTIGATE

Select the *city* where your university is located and/or another city in your state and answer the following:

1. Race/ethnicity make-up:

2. Percent having a Bachelor's degree or higher:

3. Average (mean) travel time to work, in minutes, for workers over the age of 16:

4. Average persons per household:

5. Median household income:

6. Percent of persons below the poverty level:

7. Percent of black-owned firms:

8. Percent of Hispanic-owned firms:

9. Percent of American Indian, Alaska Native-owned firms:

10. Percent of Asian-owned firms

11. Percent of women-owned firms:

REFLECT ON A SEPARATE SHEET

How do these numbers compare to the state data? What information do you find surprising? What met your expectations? Which pieces of this information are regularly visible? Which pieces of information are invisible or harder to see? Why is this?

Identify the Facts: Gender and Race Based Health Disparities

CONTEMPLATE

What are health disparities? Define in your own words and list examples.

INVESTIGATE

Go to Healthypeople.gov/2020 and look at the list of subjects and topics addressed by this program.

What are some of the topics listed on the website that you did not list above?

Now pay particular attention to those topics that may have a gender or race based disparity. What are those topics?

Look at the data for sexually transmitted infections. What are some of the disparities listed? List at least three.

Look at the data for Lesbian, Gay, Bisexual, and Transgender Health. What are some of the topics and disparities listed? List at least three.

Choose one additional health subject. What are some of the topics and disparities listed?

REFLECT ON A SEPARATE SHEET OF PAPER

Write a reflection on your investigation. Why are health disparities an important gender issue? Why are health disparities an important race issue? Provide examples and support from your investigation.

Name _____   Date _____

Course & section: _____   Instructor _____

Identify the Facts: HIV/AIDS History, Activism, and Resources

CONTEMPLATE

What do you know about the history of HIV/AIDS? What resources are available to learn about HIV/AIDS activism?

Consider this context: the HIV/AIDS epidemic has been an important site for examining social inequalities and injustices related to sexuality and homophobia, race and racism, gender and sexism. Importantly, the epidemic has also galvanized activism and organizing to address these issues, all of which continues today.

The beginning of the epidemic is infamous because of the visible signs of disease on the bodies of those who were HIV positive and because of the widespread social panic and overt discriminatory practices that resulted. Yet today, after more than 30 years, the epidemic has not ended nor have the social injustices surrounding HIV been resolved. The history is well known, but younger people are less aware of what the epidemic meant, the ways in which our government neglected HIV, or the successful activism that resulted in access to more affordable medications.

There are many resources that can help you in learning more about the history of AIDS activism.

Websites

www.actuporalhistory.org: a collection of over 100 interviews with AIDS activists.

www.actupny.com: the work of ACT/Up today, including current campaigns and news issues

www.actupny.org: includes many original documents, capsule histories, and timelines

Films

United in Anger: A History of ACT/UP, 2012, Dir. Jim Hubbard

How to Survive a Plague, 2012, Dir. David France

There are several previews of the films, interviews with the directors, etc. available online.

INVESTIGATE

Use the resources available to you online to learn more about ACT/UP and AIDS activists and answer the following questions.

1. When was ACT/UP formed and why? (See the 1987 Capsule History on actupny.org)

2. Describe some of ACT/UP's most influential actions.

3. Look up Larry Kramer, Sarah Schulman, Jim Hubbard, and Peter Staley. Who are they? What are they known for? Provide a 2–3 sentence biography for each. Use a separate sheet if necessary.

REFLECT ON A SEPARATE SHEET

Write up an introductory history of ACT/UP and AIDS activism based on your research. Include a list of five questions you still have at the end of the report. What would you like to know more about? What questions do you still have? What new questions were raised during your research?

Name _____   Date _____

Course & section: _____   Instructor _____

Identify the Facts: Employment and Earnings

CONTEMPLATE

In order to have the best chances for a successful career it is necessary to be informed and prepared for entry into that occupation. For women, this is even more important because of the persistent wage gap that has been documented across many industries. What occupation are you preparing yourself for? How many people are employed in this industry? Geographically, where are the most jobs for that particular occupation? Is there a wage gap by sex and/or race for this industry?

INVESTIGATE

Go to the Department of Labor Women's Bureau, found at www.dol.gov/wb. Click on the "Data and Statistics" link found on this page.

1. List five of the most common occupations for women workers.

2. List five of the highest paying occupations for women workers.

3. List five non-traditional occupations for women workers.

4. Using the "Earnings Ratio" link, find the gender wage gap for the most current year available. (In other words, what was the average ratio of women's earnings to men's?) *Note*: Click on the graphs found at the Department of Labor website for the dataset.

Go to http://www.bls.gov/cps/earnings.htm . Find information (including charts) on weekly earnings.

1. What is the weekly median earnings for
   a. White women
   b. White men
   c. Black women
   d. Black men
   e. Asian women
   f. Asian men
   g. Hispanic women
   h. Hispanic women

Go to www.bls.gov/ooh and search the Occupational Outlook Handbook for an occupation that interests you.

1. For your chosen occupation, what educational background do you need? What skills are required?

2. What would your average day look like in this occupation?

REFLECT ON A SEPARATE SHEET

Write a two-page report discussing your findings. Discuss what the data and trends you found will mean for you and other individuals in the workforce.

Identify the Facts: What is Women and Gender Studies?

CONTEMPLATE

What comes to mind when you hear "women and gender studies"? What do you expect to study/learn in this course?

INVESTIGATE

Search "What is Women and Gender Studies?" on YouTube. Choose several videos to watch. *Suggestion*: UT Women's and Gender Studies (University of Texas)

1. What are the core ideas presented? What are some of the shared definitions/qualities of Women and Gender Studies?

2. Visit the National Women's Studies Association website: www.nwsa.org. Read the "About NWSA" tab and the "What is Women's Studies" tab. What do the NWSA definitions add to your knowledge of WGS? How do NWSA's definitions compare to other sources (including what you have read in the course textbooks)?

REFLECT

Imagine a friend or family member from home asks you what you are enrolled in this semester. After you share your course schedule, they ask, "What is Introduction to Gender Studies or Women and Gender Studies?"

Write an imagined response to this question. This should be a thorough response encompassing the various perspectives you have encountered, the similarities and differences among these, and can also include a discussion of how this aligned or did not align with your expectations.

Name _____   Date _____

Course & section: _____   Instructor _____

Identify the Facts: Composition of Your School

CONTEMPLATE

Think about the college or university you attend. What do you estimate is the gender and racial/ethnic composition of your school? How diverse do you think your school is? What makes you think so?

INVESTIGATE

Visit the webpage of your university. Some of this information may be found on the website for your school's Office of Admissions or on another page that provides an overview of your school, but you may have to dig a little deeper. Consider the institutional research office or a diversity office for more information.

Find the answers to these questions:

1. Total student body
   a. Undergraduate students:
   b. Graduate students:
   c. International students:

2. First time in any university (FTIAC):

3. Transfer Students:

4. Gender make-up of your school's student body
   a. Female:
   b. Male:
   c. Transgender:
   d. Gender not reported:

5. Veterans:

6. First Generation College Students:

7. Low income students:

8. Race/ethnicity make-up of your school's student body:
   a. American Indian or Alaskan Native
   b. Asian or Pacific Islander
   c. Black or African American
   d. Hispanic or Latino
   e. White
   f. More than one ethnicity
   g. Unduplicated minority
   h. Not reported

9. Now that you have compiled data on your school's student body, compare it to a previous year. What trends do you notice? How is the student body changing at your school?

REFLECT

Look back at the answers to your contemplation questions; what information do you find surprising? What met your expectations? Think about your daily experience at your school. Based on the demographic data you found, do you regularly see evidence of diversity on your campus? Why or why not? Why so you think some of these are more visible than others?

Part Two:

CONTEMPLATE

Think about the classes you have enrolled in. What do you estimate is the gender and racial/ethnic composition of your faculty? How diverse do you think the faculty at your school is? What makes you think so?

INVESTIGATE

Find out more information about the faculty at your school. Some of this information may be found on the website for your school's Office of Admissions or on another page that provides an overview of your school. You may have to dig a little deeper; consider the institutional research office or a diversity office for more information.

Find the answers to these questions:

1. Faculty by rank:
   a. Instructors:
   b. Visiting Assistant Professors:
   c. Assistant Professors:
   d. Associate Professors:
   e. Full Professors:
   f. Distinguished Professors:

2. Gender make-up of the faculty:
   a. Female:
   b. Male:
   c. Transgender:
   d. Not reported:

3. Race/ethnicity make-up of the faculty:
   a. American Indian or Alaskan Native
   b. Asian or Pacific Islander
   c. Black or African American
   d. Hispanic or Latino
   e. White
   f. More than one ethnicity
   g. Unduplicated minority
   h. Not reported

4. What is the gender breakdown of faculty by rank? What is breakdown of faculty by rank and race/ethnicity?

   a. *Faculty by rank*   *Gender*   *Race/Ethnicity*

   Instructors

   Visiting Assistant Professors

   Assistant Professors

   Associate Professors

   Full Professors

   Distinguished Professors

   b. What patterns did you notice?

REFLECT

Look back at the answers to your contemplation questions; what information do you find surprising? What met your expectations? Think about your daily experience at your school. Based on the demographic data you found, do you regularly see evidence of diversity on your campus? Why or why not? Why so you think some of these patterns exist?

REFLECT ON A SEPARATE SHEET

How do these numbers compare to the state data? What information do you find surprising? What met your expectations? Which pieces of this information are regularly visible? Which pieces of information are invisible or harder to see? Why is this?

Name _____   Date _____

Course & section: _____   Instructor _____

Identify the Facts: Gender, Race, Sexuality and Incarceration: Understanding Correctional System Populations

CONTEMPLATE

What do you know about mass incarceration in the United States? Are certain people imprisoned more than others? How do gender, race, and sexuality impact this? How is this information conveyed?

INVESTIGATE

Visit the *Bureau of Justice Statistics* [www.bjs.gov] and enter the term "corrections" in the search box. Look for the "Publications & Products" heading and access the most recent reports.

1. How many U.S. adults are under the supervision of adult correctional systems?

2. What percent of the population is this?

3. Is there information pertaining to gender and race? If so, what does this information highlight?

Using the menu, click on the "Prison Rape Elimination Act" section or enter this term in the search box.

1. What is the Prison Rape Elimination Act? How is the Bureau of Justice Statistics involved?

2. Access one of the Bureau's most recent reports or press releases; what information does the report highlight?

Visit *The Sentencing Project* website [www.sentencingproject.org] and click on the link to the interactive map.

1. What information is provided about the corrections population?

2. What is the racial breakdown of incarcerated individuals?

3. Click on the "Women" heading or enter this term in the search box to access information pertaining to gender. What information is provided?

4. What is the purpose of "The Sentencing Project"?

5. How are they using the data and statistics provided to convey their message?

Visit the *Prison Policy Initiative* website [www.prisonpolicy.org]. Using the menu headings or the search box, find their more recent publications.

1. What information is provided?

2. Does the information highlight certain groups (i.e., race, gender)? Why or why not?

3. What is the purpose of the Prison Policy Initiative?

4. How are they using the data and statistics provided to convey their message?

REFLECT ON SEPARATE SHEET

Compare how information is presented by the Bureau of Justice Statistics to The Sentencing Project and Prison Policy Initiative. What are the similarities? Differences? Consider how the information is presented—is one format more effective than another? How does this relate to the purpose of each entity?

Identify the Facts: Sex Ed Scavenger Hunt!

CONTEMPLATE

Since coming to your campus what sexual healthcare resources have you been made aware of? Do you know what sexual health resources are available on your campus on in your community? If you needed sexual healthcare where would you go first in your community?

Instructions: Collect the facts about your local resources.

1. Identify the organizations on your campus that work on sexual healthcare and education related topics.
   - What programs or events are they responsible for?
   - Find the groups meeting times and locations. List them here.

2. Investigate at least two resources on campus or in the community that provide sexual education and/or reproductive and sexual healthcare. You can visit their website, call, or, if possible, visit the location.
   - What services do they provide?
   - Do they require appointments?
   - What are the fees, if any, for the services?
   - Do they identify any current changes in rates of sexually transmitted infections, changes in local or state laws or policies? Any breaking news concerning sexual health?

REFLECT

If a friend needed access to additional information on sexual healthcare, where would you refer them in your community? Why?

What resources are missing or not easily accessible in your community? What could be done to make these resources more available?

Next Steps

Share your ideas with the campus and community organizations identified or start your own organization to address these issues!

Identify the Facts: Women and Politics

Visit the Center for American Women and Politics website (http://www.cawp.rutgers.edu). Click on the "Facts" tab. Explore the links listed to find current information on the rate of participation of women in politics, including running for office and voting patterns.

CONTEMPLATE

What do you know about women in politics? Can you name women politicians or elected officials at the local, state, or federal level? What kinds of issues do you think women voters tend to support?

INVESTIGATE

1. In the section labeled Facts on Women Officeholders, Candidates, and Voters, click on "Current Numbers."

   How many women are in office?

   Federal Executive Branch:

   U.S. Supreme Court:

   Congress

       U.S. Senate:

       U.S. House:

   Statewide Executive:

   State Legislatures (total):

       Senate:

       House/Assembly:

   Mayors:

2. Under the Voters Tab, find Voter Turnout and look for information on voting trends of women and men. Report your findings below.

3. Under Gender Gap, find links to information about voters' attitudes and/or policy preferences. Report your findings below.

REFLECT

What did you learn about differences in voting habits for women and men? Differences in attitudes about government between women and men? Did this challenge your beliefs about politics and political representation? What do you think could be done to begin changing these gender gaps in politics?

Identify the Facts: Sexual Assault Reporting on Campus

CONTEMPLATE

What do you know about sexual assault on your campus? What resources are available to you? What do you know about your campus' sexual offense policy?

INVESTIGATE

1. Choose any search engine, and search for "The Jeanne Clery Disclosure of Campus Security Policy and Campus Crime Statistics Act." More information is available at the website of the U.S. Department of Education or the Clery Center for Security on Campus (http://clerycenter.org/)
   a. What is the Clery Act?
   b. Which schools are required to participate?
   c. What is required of participating schools?

2. Is your school required to participate? If so, search your campus' website for "Clery Act" to find reporting statistics for your school. What did you learn about:
   a. Sexual assault procedures and protocols on your campus
   b. Sexual assault statistics on your campus

3. What is a timely warning? When are they issued? What information is required of them? Have you received one at your university? What information did it contain?

4. Now search your campus' website for "sexual assault." What resources are available to you? Are there student organizations that address sexual assault on your campus? List them.

5. How does your school define sexual assault? Sexual consent? What are the procedures for reporting a violation of these policies on your campus?

6. When a concern is raised about a campus' compliance with Clery reporting, the U.S. Department of Education launches an investigation. Visit the website of Federal Student Aid, an office of the U.S. Department of Education: (https://studentaid.ed.gov/about/data-center/school/clery-act)

    Under what circumstances is an investigation launched?

7. Review one report. You can search Clery Act Reports by school and by year. Look first to see if there is a report for your university, then look by report year and choose a report to review.

    What were the findings of the report?

    What actions was the school required take?

REFLECT

Was your school's policies and data reporting easy to find? What the information clear and accessible? What changes would you suggest for disseminating this information to the campus community? What changes to your campus policies would you suggest after doing this research?

Name _____   Date _____

Course & section: _____   Instructor _____

For Your Information: How to Read a Scholarly Article

JOURNAL AND AUTHOR

- Is the journal refereed or peer-reviewed? Use Ulrichs Web database to find out whether the journal is refereed, how often it is published, who publishes it, etc. If Ulrichs is unavailable, go the journal's homepage to find this information.

- What are the authors' credentials? Are they affiliated with a university? A research organization? A government agency? (see the authors' biography included in the article or see their web page)

PRE-READING

- Skim these first:
  - Abstract
  - Introduction
  - Discussion/Conclusions
- Based on that first review, answer these two questions:
  - What is the article about?
  - What point are the authors trying to make? What is their argument?

TAKE NOTES

- After pre-reading, read through the whole article.

- In the margin, summarize each paragraph using only a couple of words or a short phrase.

- Question what you read. What was the subject of the article? How did they analyze it? What were their conclusions?

- List three or four of the most important points in the article; this will help you find those main points later and will help you organize your own thoughts.

- Circle jargon, unusual phrases, technical terms, etc. You can look for definitions/examples or you can use them as keywords to search for more articles later.

- Highlight only quotations that you just cannot word better (or paraphrase) yourself. Those will be the cited quotations you use in your own writing. Be *very* selective about what you highlight.

- *Underline* references (in the bibliography or reference section) that relate to your project; you can look those up later.

- At the top of each article, jot down two points: What is useful or important about this article? And what are the article's biases, limitations, weaknesses, or omissions?

REFLECT

Taking thorough notes and writing briefs summaries are some of the best ways to retain what you read and learn.

Based on your notes, write an evaluative annotation of the article. An evaluative annotation has two components. First, it provides a short summary of the content of the article. Second, it provides a critique of the content. What was most useful about the article? What was unclear or missing in the article? Who would you recommend this article to?

Name _____   Date _____

Course & section: _____   Instructor _____

For Your Information: Scholarly Journals, Popular Journals, Trade Journals

	Scholarly Journals	Popular Journals	Trade Journals
Purpose	Informs/reports on original research done by scholars and experts in the field.	Entertains and informs a general audience without providing in-depth analysis.	Reports on industry trends, new products or techniques useful to people in a trade or business.
Authors	Articles are written by subject specialists and experts in the field.	Articles are written by journalists, freelance writers, or an editorial staff.	Articles are written by specialists in a certain field or industry.
Audience	Intended for a limited audience —mainly researchers, scholars, and experts.	Appeals to a broad segment of the population.	Intended for people in a particular profession, business, or industry.
Appearance	Simple cover design, few images or ads. May include charts, graphs, data.	Glossy, colorful, many images and lots of advertising.	Often glossy paper; images/advertisements relate to specific field or profession.
Article length	Tend to be lengthy, may include original research, in-depth analysis, very specific focus.	Typically brief, from less than one page to several pages.	Short to medium length articles.
Content	Original research, literary criticism and theory, literature review, in-depth analysis of topic.	Short, feature-length articles, news and general interest topics.	Articles about professional trends, new products or techniques, industry-related news.
Writing style	Use terminology, language and jargon relevant to the discipline.	Simple language used, written for general public.	Technical, field-specific language used, assumes reader familiar with industry.

	Scholarly Journals	**Popular Journals**	**Trade Journals**
References	Articles typically include references, notes, works cited.	Articles typically do not have references.	Articles sometimes have references.
Examples	*Shakespeare Quarterly* *Journal of the American Medical Association*	*Newsweek* *Rolling Stone* *Sports Illustrated*	*Automotive News* *Strategy & Business* *Advertising Age*

INDEX